Pál Teleki

20TH-CENTURY HUNGARIAN STATESMEN

Volume II

Pál Teleki
(1879–1941)
The Life of a Controversial Hungarian Politician

BALÁZS ABLONCZY

Translated from the Hungarian by
Thomas J. and Helen D. DeKornfeld

Helena History Press

Second English edition ©2024 Balázs Ablonczy
Originally published as *Teleki Pál* © 2005 by Osiris Kiadó

English edition translated from the original Hungarian
by Helen D. Kornfeld and Thomas J. Kornfeld

First English edition originally published jointly by the Center for Hungarian Studies and Publications, Inc., Wayne, NJ and the Institute of Habsburg History, Budapest in 2006.

All rights reserved

Published in the United States by:
Helena History Press LLC

H P

A division of KKL Publications LLC, Reno, NV USA
www.helenahistorypress.com

Publishing scholarship about and from Central and East Europe

ISBN: 978-1-943596-32-4 (hardback)
ISBN: 978-1-943596-39-3 (ebook)

Copy Editor: Krisztina Kós
Graphic Designer: Sebastian Stachowski

Contents

Preface 1
Family, Descent, and Youth 5
The Years of Learning (1897–1918) 13
    Schools and Schoolmasters 13
    First Steps in Politics 19
    Geography and Turanism 24
    Soldier and Politician during World War I 38
In the Revolution, the Counterrevolution,
and in the Government (1918–1921) 53
    The Counterrevolutionary 55
    For the First Time at the Head of the Country 77
"Educating the Nation": Revision and Conservatism (1921–1938) ... 99
    The Occasional Diplomat 102
    Organizer and Ideologue of the Revision 112
    Mosul Episode 124
    Political Tempests 132
    Workshops of the Elite: Eötvös College, Boy Scouts and Youth Movements 140
    Political Views 157
    Geography, Homeland Studies, and the Study of Village Life 165
    The Everyman 169
Back into Politics (1938–1941) 179
    Imrédy's Minister of Education 179
    At the Head of the Government. First Steps in Foreign
        and Domestic Policies 188
    Subcarpathian Ruthenia 193

The Second Anti-Jewish Law 196
The 1939 Elections 202
Political Undertow 206
In the Shadow of the War 208
Social Reform Policies 212
Neutrality or Revision? 216
Transylvania 225
Additional Reforms 237
The Yugoslav Crisis 243
Suicide 247

Afterword 253

Bibliography 263

Preface

The life and work of Pál Teleki are among the hot topics in contemporary Hungary. The 2004 plans for erecting a Teleki statue triggered astonishing passions and public debates.¹ The controversy swirling around the proposed monument was not limited to historic issues but reflected the current divisions in Hungarian public opinion, the inability to reach consensus and the problem of coming to terms with the past.

I learned only after the completion of the Hungarian version of this book, that, indirectly, I also had a personal link with the late scholar and prime minister. For some of the school reforms he introduced were still in place at the school I attended as a youngster.

I also had a link with him through my grandfather. He was a student at the famous Sárospatak Protestant Boarding School in 1933, when, as a member of the school's Boy Scout troop he attended the World Boy Scout Jamboree in Gödöllő. My grandfather died more then twenty-five years before I was born and leafing through family archives, I found a postcard he had written to his parents from the jamboree. There is nothing particularly interesting on it. A seventeen-year-old boy advises his parents that he is well, is busy exchanging memorabilia with other scouts, is amazed by the Japanese and Armenian scouts, and asks that the stamps on the postcard be saved for his stamp collection.

The more then seventy-year-old card suddenly and personally brought to light the presence of a twentieth century Hungarian politician and I found out that I

---

1 Balázs Ablonczy, "Un débat historique manqué. Le cas Teleki en Hongrie," *La Nouvelle Alternative* (Paris) 21, nos. 69–70 (June–September, 2006): 135–146.

had a personal link to Teleki, the organizer and head of the jamboree. This should not have affected what I had to say in this book or, at least, I hope that it had not.

Studying Teleki is made very difficult by the fact that there is no single collection of personal papers. According to some, it was the prime minister himself who destroyed the papers in 1938, while according to others, the papers kept at the monastery in Pannonhalma were burned by the abbot in the spring of 1945 when the Soviet authorities were asking for them. Thus, in the absence of internal documents, I had to study his life from the outside. I had to identify and find the individuals, organizations and establishments with whom Teleki had a relationship and had to use the documents thus examined to reconstruct Teleki's life and career. The research was just like the writing of a mystery novel. I wandered down a number of cul-de-sacs but the excitement of a number of unexpected discoveries was ample compensation. By using the widest possible base for sources and information, it was my goal to present a picture of Pál Teleki that was not a hagiography, a genre commonly used in works about him, yet did not show only the darker sides of his political life, a genre which has recently gained in popularity.

Biographies or biographical studies are, according to traditional historiographic theory, never of interest in and of themselves. A biography must raise questions and must list a series of "whys" and "hows" in order for the author to be able to answer his or her own questions. A biography of Pál Teleki makes this particularly difficult because his life cannot be confined within the boundaries of a narrow historical analysis. He was a politician but his life must be approached from a geographical, intellectual, educational, and even psychohistorical perspective. His biography is made much more interesting by demonstrating the influences and choices which guided his ascent in public life, what forces impacted him, how he networked and also, how he lived, how much he earned, and how he answered the telephone. I endeavored to satisfy many of these requirements but am aware of the fact that the results could fall far short of the expectations.

Writing about somebody's life is tempting providence. Many people assisted me in my work but there are some who must be thanked quite particularly. It was my professor, Ignác Romsics, who drew my attention to Teleki and who assisted my work for a number of years with much encouragement and careful pruning. He honored me by a careful and thoughtful reading of the text and by giving me valuable advice. The remaining errors are all mine. Another professor to whom I am very grateful is László Kósa who, from the beginning of my studies, observed and generously supported my researches. Without the help of my family all of this would have come to nothing and this book would never have seen the light of day without the assistance and support of my parents, my wife Zsófia and her parents. Professor András Gerő, the director of the Habsburg Institute in Budapest, most kindly encouraged the preparation of a version that would be translated into English. I am grateful for his help.

Family, Descent, and Youth

Opinions about the origins of Pál Teleki's family and about the beginnings of his soaring career are divided. According to one version, the family fled the Ottoman armies advancing across the Balkans in the fourteenth and fifteenth centuries and were given property in the fifteenth century in south-east Hungary, in counties Bihar (Bihor), Arad (Arad), Békés and Zaránd (Zărand). (All of these areas are presently in Romania.) The property included the farmstead of Telek (Teleac) in Békés County as well as property in Zágorhíd (Zagăr) and Szék (Sic). It was this last settlement that provided the predicate for the family that was known as Teleki of Szék.

According to others our first information about the family dates back to the second half of the sixteenth century. The Garázda and Teleki families lived and were active in Transylvania, which was half-independent principalty between 1541 and 1690. This was on the overlapping edges of the Ottoman and Habsburg Empires. The best known figure of the family was Mihály II Teleki, who was born in the early 1630s and who at an early age became the court postmaster to György II Rákóczi, the prince of Transylvania. His career advanced under Mihály Apafi. He could look back on a meteoric career and at the end of the 1680s he was the lord lieutenant of Fehér (Alba), Torda (Turda) and Máramaros (Maramureş) Counties, captain-general of Csík-Gyergyó-Kászonszék, commander of the two most important fortresses of Transylvania, Chust (presently in Ukraine) and Kővár (Cetatea Chioarului), the tax farmer of the prince's title, the commander in chief of Transylvania, a councilor and the most important Transylvanian negotiator with the Habsburg empire. He skillfully escaped from the Turkish entanglements, became oriented toward Poland and participated in the return of Transylvania to the Habsburg empire. A ruthless but imposingly stylish magnate, he was the last major Transylvanian politician of the seventeenth century who could come to terms with Transylvania's independence but also with an overall European and south-east European constellation. His task was largely complete when he fell in the battle of Zernyest (Zărnești) on August 21, 1690, fighting on the side of the Habsburg emperor.

In recognition for his services Mihály Teleki was awarded the title of count of Hungary by the Emperor Leopold I, in 1685. In 1697 the title of count of the Holy Roman Empire was added, posthumously, by the emperor.[1] This patent also formally established the family coat of arms. Mihály Teleki had thirteen children. Two of these, Mihály III and Sándor, had numerous descendants and during the eighteenth and nineteenth centuries the Telekis constituted an ever increasing, frequently intermarrying family both in Transylvania and also in Hungary. The Protestant branch acquired large estates in Pest, Pilis, Solt, Kiskun and Nógrád Counties. They endowed libraries, gathered collections of art, became generous contributors to Hungarian culture and many of them entered the learned professions. One historical work lists twenty-five Telekis, who by virtue of their literary activities and other contributions, deserved the attention of posterity.[2]

We know little about Ede Teleki (1813–1875) Pál Teleki's grandfather. He attended the Kolozsvár (Cluj) Lyceum from 1828 to 1832 and then lived on his estate at Paszmos (Pasmuș). He was married to Countess Matilda Haller in 1837 in Váradolaszi (Oradea) and they had six children. The fourth of these, Géza was Pál Teleki's father, born in Dés (Dej) on September 28, 1843.[3] Although Ede Teleki was a member of the Upper House of the first revolutionary parliament in 1848–49 he did not attend the sessions. The Transylvanian events of the anti-Habsburg Hungarian War for Independence left its marks on the family. The largely Romanian and German inhabitants of Paszmos stormed the chateau during the civil war in Transylvania, looted, burned and partially demolished it. The Teleki family was forced to flee from Paszmos and eventually chose their estate in Kővárvidék (Chiorana) as their new residence. Their new chateau was located in Pribékfalva (Pribilești) with estates in the villages nearby.

---

1 "A gróf Teleki család németbirodalmi grófságáról" [About the Teleki family's German imperial count title], manuscript, Teleki-Degenfeld Papers, cs. 1, t. 1, P 2026, Magyar Nemzeti Levéltár Országos Levéltára [Hungarian National Archives] (hereafter cited as MNL OL).
2 József Szinnyei, *A Széki gróf Teleki család írói* [The Authors among the Count Teleki Family of Szék] (Budapest: Viktor Homyanszky, 1910).
3 János Gudenus, *A XX. századi magyar főnemesség genealógiája. SZ-ZS.* [Genealogy of the Twentieth Century Hungarian Aristocracy] (Budapest: Heraldika, 1998); and Béla Pámány, ed., *Az 1848–49-es magyar népképviseleti országgyűlés történeti almanachja* [The Historical Almanac of the 1848–49 Hungarian Representative Assembly] (Budapest: Magyar Országgyűlés, 2002), p. 1121.

Géza Teleki was six years old when the family had to flee from the Romanian villagers attacking the ancestral chateau. The youngster was deeply affected by the sudden move and by all the excitement surrounding it. He was never in doubt whom to blame and in his letters written many years later the only political or social comments were critical of Romanian national movements.[4]

Géza Teleki studied in several religious schools and finally graduated from Marosvásárhely (Tîrgu Mureş). Even as a young man he enjoyed writing and, as an adult, published a number of articles in various papers. For one year in 1863–64 he attended the Academy of Agriculture and Forestry in Hohenheim, Württemberg. Returning home he became honorary sheriff in Kővárvidék County, studied law and was elected in 1866 as county recorder, the third highest elective position in the local administration.[5]

Géza Teleki entered national politics and after 1875 represented Nagynyíres (Mireşu Mare) in parliament on a liberal ticket.[6] He made no waves in the House and his maiden speech was not delivered until fourteen years later. One of the great representatives of Hungarian liberalism, Kálmán Tisza formed a government during the summer of 1889 and invited the largely unknown Teleki to become his minister of the interior. Teleki's ministerial career was cut short in March 1890 when Kálmán Tisza resigned. In recognition of Teleki's contributions, the monarch appointed the forty-six-year-old count as a privy councilor. Subsequently, Teleki was engaged in social activities and in the management of his estates. According to 1893 data he owned 2,527 acres of land which was considered a small estate even by Transylvanian aristocratic standards.[7] On August 28, 1871, Géza Teleki married the nineteen-year-old Irén Muráti (or Muráthy) the daughter of the merchant of Greek origin Konstantin Muráti. Muráti was described in the city register as a 'householder'.

It is practically impossible to define "Greek" nationality in the Hungarian context of the period. The Hungarian language of the eighteenth century used the term "Greek" to define somebody who was a Greek national, who was of the Greek

---

4 Letter from Géza Teleki to Sándor Szilágyi, Pribékfalva, October 20, 1894, and August 25, 1895, Levelestár [Correspondence Section], Országos Széchényi Könyvtár [National Széchényi Library] (hereaftercited as OSZKK).
5 L. M., "Gróf Teleki Géza" [Count Géza Teleki], *Vasárnapi Újság*, June 23, 1889, pp. 393–394.
6 The electoral district was later renamed and thus Géza Teleki represented the Nagysomkút (Şomcuta Mare) district until 1905.
7 Károly Baross, *Magyarország földbirtokosai* [Hungarian Landowners] (Budapest: Hungária Könyvnyomda, 1893), pp. 358–359, 424–426, 626–627, and 680–681. See also István Lörintei, *Magyarország nagybirtokosai* [Large Estate Owners in Hungary] (Szatmár: n.p., 1893), p. 21.

Orthodox religion, who was a Greek-speaking Balkan resident or simply a merchant coming from the Balkans.[8] The general term "Greek" was used to refer to the true Greeks from the southern part of the Balkans, but also to Bulgarians, Serbs, Macedonians, Albanians and those Aromanians who came from Macedonia. In the eighteenth century Greeks settled in the larger cities, bought real estate and engaged in a variety of commercial activities. Members of the Greek community in Pest could rise to almost any level. A number of them were given a patent of nobility by the emperor and families like the Haris, Lyka, Manno, Sima and Nákó rose to great heights and became the very symbols of wealth.[9]

The fact that Count Géza Teleki married the daughter of a Pest Greek bourgeois was unusual not only in his social group but in the endogamous Greek society as well. The Muráti family, whose name originally was Muratis, came from the north of Greece and it is not entirely certain that they were of Greek ethnicity. For a payment of fifty forints, Panajot Muráti became a citizen of Pest. In 1827 he was already the owner of the one-story house which was later torn down and on the site of which the handsome palace, in classical style, was built in 1831. It still stands at the corner of József Nádor Square and Harmincad Street. Later it was known as the Teleki Palace.[10] His heir was his nephew, Konstantin Muráti, known as Szilárd Muráti, who was born around 1813 and whom he brought from his native Greece at age seven, took into his house and had educated. Szilárd (the Hungarian version of Konstantin) Muráti became a Pest citizen in 1844. He was already married and his wife, nee Mária Sacelláry, was also the offspring of a Greek family. Szilárd put his money into real estate and made a large fortune. In the 1880s, in addition to the house on József Nádor Square, he had six other properties in the fifth, sixth and seventh districts of the city.[11] Starting in the 1850s Szilárd Muráti's social standing kept rising. In 1857 he became a city councilor. Of his four daughters three were married to Greek families and thus Muráti became related to the Vrányi, the Curty and the Baron Economo families. The Muráti descendants always clung to their

---

8   Ödön Füves, "Görögök Pesten (1686–1931)" [The Greeks in Budapest (1686–1931)] (PhD diss., Magyar Tudományos Akadémia, 1972), vol 1, p. 12.
9   Mihály Pásztor, "A százötven éves Lipótváros" [The 150 year-old Borough of Lipótváros] *Statisztikai Szemle* [Statistical Reports] 93, no. 4 (1940): 66–67.
10 Jenő Pallós and Lajos Illyefalvi, *Pest és Buda polgárjogot nyert lakosai 1687–1848* [The Residents of Buda and Pest Who Received Citizenship 1687–1848], p. 213; Ödön Füves, "Pesti görög háztulajdonosok" [Greek house owners in Pest], *Antik Tanulmányok* 17, no. 1 (1970): 50; and László Lugó Lugosi, Olivier Joyeux, and Cecile Vrain, eds., *Megújulás-Renouveaux* (Budapest: Credit Lyonnais, 2003), 35–35. The nicely renovated building is today the headquarters for the Bank of China Budapest branch.
11 *Budapest Cím es Lakásjegyzék 1882* [Register of Addresses and Homes in Budapest, 1882] (Budapest: Franklin Nyomda, 1882), pp. 39–40, 42, 47, 48, and 51.

Greek identity but scattered during the first few decades of the twentieth century and settled in a number of European cities including Trieste, Vienna, Athens, Marseilles and Paris.

Soon after the wedding Géza Teleki moved into the house on József Nádor Square. According to friends of the family, the marriage was a very harmonious one with the young husband deeply in love with his bride, who is said to have ruled the household with a fist of iron. The only shadow cast on the marriage was the fact that the couple initially had no children. The first several, hopefully awaited, children all were born dead.[12] There was great joy in the house when on November 1, 1879, after eight years of marriage, a healthy and hale heir was born, Pál János Ede Teleki from Szék.[13]

The small newborn brought such joy to the parents, that for gratitude to the Holy Virgin, they dressed him in her color of blue for the first six years of his life. The little Pál Teleki learned German before he went to school and even knew some Greek.[14] In a later comment it appears that the early knowledge of these two languages was no accident because in the Muráti house the principal languages were Greek and German with Hungarian a poor third.[15] Presumably only the servants spoke Hungarian. It was in this patriarchal house, noisy with aunts, uncles and cousins, that the little Pál Teleki spent his first years, primarily under the supervision of his mother. His father was frequently away on his official duties. The management of far-flung estates and the required social contacts, e.g. hunting, frequently called him away from the home on József Nádor Square. It was during these years that the strong and intimate relationship between mother and son developed, which was, however, always based on an evident authoritarian base. Irén Muráti did not tolerate any contradictions. Her teenage son respected and feared

---

12 Ferenc Fodor, *Teleki Pál* (Budapest: Mike es Társa Antikvárium, 2001) 19.
13 Copy of Pál Teleki's baptismal certificate. Register of birth in the Basilica of St. Stephen in Budapest, Vol. F., fol. 600, no. 492. He was baptized on December 7, 1879. The Godparents were Count Pál Degenfeld and Mrs. János Economo, née Ilona Muráti. Magyar Földrajzi Múzeum Archívuma [Archives of the Hungarian Geographical Museum] (hereafter cited as MFMA).
14 Fodor, *Teleki Pál*, p. 20; and Kálmán Mikszáth, "A T. Házból vagy a 3-dik paragrafus viszontagságai vagyis görögök es szkíták" [From the Honored House, or the adventures of the third paragraph, namely the Greeks and the Scythians], in *Cikkek és karcolatok* [Articles and Sketches], vol. 16, *1883. április–1883. augusztus*, in *Mikszáth Kálmán összes művei* [The Collected Works of Kálmán Mikszáth], ed. István Rejtő (Budapest: Akadémiai Kiadó, 1972), vol. 66, p. 15.
15 Letter from Pál Teleki to Sándor Dobrovits, Budapest, May 17, 1940, Kéziratok [Manuscripts], V.B. 0805, Központi Statisztikai Hivatal Könyvtára [Library of the Central Statistics Office] (hereafter cited as KSHK).

her from afar and was convinced that she would always discover every minor distortion of the truth.[16]

The family usually spent the summers in Pribékfalva (Pribileşti) and the winters in Budapest. While in the country, the young Pál and the children from the neighboring estates were instructed by a teacher from Nagysomkút (Şomcuta Mare) at Kővárvidék (Chiorana) and also had some instruction from their nannies. His annual final exams were taken at the Lutheran elementary school on the Deák Square. There is a photograph which shows the father looking with paternal pride on his six-year-old son. In this period of his life the playmates of the little Pál were his cousins Edina and Jenő, the children of Sándor Teleki of Nagysomkút and Zoltán Takáts Felvinczi, the future renowned art historian and orientalist. The nearby Szamos [Someş] River and the eight acre park of the chateau provided an ideal playground for the children. In his teens Pál could use the library of the chateau which was celebrated for its huge collection of books and pictures and included every book that was ever written by a member of the Teleki family. It was Pál himself who eventually arranged the 3,200 volume collection, cataloged it and used it diligently. His love of books stayed with him until his death. In his younger days, the boy also liked to play with lead soldiers, was crazy about the Karl May stories and challenged his friends to tricycle races. About this time he decided that he wished to become a navy officer.[17] He was thrilled with the equipage that his parents gave him on his fourteenth birthday and he proudly drove the poneys on the streets of Pribékfalva and in the park of the chateau.[18] Even though he was small, lightly built and frequently ill, he loved horses and enjoyed riding even in much later years. The local friends and playmates were soon joined by the young members of the Transylvanian and Hungarian aristocratic families. They included the sons of Count Frigyes Wenckheim, Marquis György and Marquess Edina Pallavicini and the young Counts Esterházy from Csákvár, including Móric the future prime minister. Pál Teleki was known to his friends as "Bóli" and soon became a favorite of the social group. He was a very clever artist and could draw excellent caricatures in a few minutes. A good dancer, he loved to participate in all sorts of fun. It was at this time that he started collecting stamps which continued until the end of his life.

The usual aristocratic education naturally had to include hunting. At his first participation in a hunt, while in the company of his father and his cousins, the

---

16 Gräfin Margarethe Bethlen, "Bóli," *Pester Lloyd-Abendblatt*, April 5, 1941, p. 3.
17 Fodor, *Teleki Pál*, p. 21; and Kálmán Nyikos, "Teleki Pál a tanár" [Pál Teleki the teacher], *Magyar Nemzet* [Hungarian Nation], April 5, 1941, p. 6.
18 Letter from Géza Teleki to Gyula Schönherr, Pribékfalva, July 18, 1894, Fol. Hung. 1811, OSZKK.

eleven-year-old Pál shot a few rabbits. It was here that his passion for hunting began and his recollection of these early days with all their details remained the subject of many future conversations. Géza Teleki, who was present on this famous occasion wrote, "My Pál wanted to shoot a rabbit. I did not wish him to do this with others, without my being present and thus, even though unwell, went out with him....You may imagine Pál's delight when he has shot a rabbit."[19] He also became very interested in ornithology, shot a large number of birds and sent them to the taxidermists at the National Museum in Budapest.

After completing the elementary school, Pál Teleki became a private pupil at the Piarist Gymnasium [High School] in Budapest. He spent practically no time at the school and just took the final exams, as authorized by the Ministry of Education.[20] The exams were taken every May between 1889 and 1897. His perfect record had only two minor lapses. In year seven he received only a "satisfactory" in drawing and in the eighth year he had the same grade in mathematics.[21] The poor grade in drawing is surprising because the testimony of contemporaries and a number of surviving sketches indicate that Pál Teleki had considerable talent. The educators attended to both religious and secular studies. The young Teleki did not need the instruction in languages offered by the gymnasium because already in childhood he learned four languages in addition to Hungarian. He spoke and wrote French extremely well, even though in later years he occasionally misspelled words. He learned some Greek from the relatives of his mother. He spoke German fluently and even as an adult he communicated with his mother in German. His command of written German was less than perfect and he occasionally composed a text in a "sloppy, Hungarian-Austrian style."[22] He learned some Romanian in Pribékfalva in order to communicate with the local inhabitants and with the servants at the chateau. He learned English from a private tutor, knew a few words of Dutch and could offer a toast and conduct a conversation in Italian.

---

19 Letter from Géza Teleki to Gyula Schönherr Pribékfalva, n.d., Fol. Hung. 1811, OSZKK.
20 The first exam is found in the Budapesti Piarista Gimnázium Iratai [Papers of the Budapest Piarist High School], 1591-1889/1890, Nándor Lutter District Superintendent to the High School, May 15, 1890, the last one, ibid., 1997-1895/96, Béla Erdődi District Superintendent to the High School, May 4, 1896, Magyarországi Piarista Rendtartomány Központi Levéltára [Central Archives of the Piarist Province in Hungary] (hereafter cited as MPRKL).
21 Roster of students for the year 1895/96, no. 59; and roster for 1896/97, no. 53, Papers of the Budapest Piarist High School, MPRKL.
22 Aladár Szegedy-Maszák, *Ősszel az ember visszanéz* [In the Autumn One Looks Back] (Budapest: Európa-História, 1996), vol. 1, p. 249.

He completed his baccalaureate exam in June 1897. The examining board listed Teleki and seven others as „outstanding" from a class of forty-three.[23] The exam indicated that the young man, educated in almost complete isolation, had acquired sufficient knowledge and information, not only to compete with his contemporaries but to be of a standing with the best of them.

---

23 Baccalaureate records, June 14-18, 1897, and baccalaureate rosters 1892-1905. The data for the baccalaureate exam in May-June 1897 show under no. 59/586 that Teleki received top grades in religion, geography, philosophy, propedcutics, natural history, and drawing, Papers of the Budapest Piarist Gymnasium, MPRKL.

The Years of Learning (1897–1918)

Schools and Schoolmasters

In the autumn of 1897 he entered the Law and Political Science faculties of the University. At the turn of the nineteenth and twentieth centuries the study of law was not yet as demanding as later and the students had ample time for hunting, carousing, cards and balls. The young Teleki also traveled and we know that in May 1899 he went to Fiume [Rijeka], Abbázia [Opatija], and Venice. It was a part of his regular schedule to attend the three-day Race Ball every autumn in Szatmárnémeti [Satu Mare]. It was at this time that the "not very handsome but very engaging" Teleki became well known. He danced with great enthusiasm and even in later years he was proud of his dancing ability, particularly of the *csárdás*.[1] It was probably during his university years that he traveled abroad alone for the first time. During the summer of 1887 or 1888 he went to London, Ostend, and the Rhineland, giving enthusiastic reports about his experiences. He was also involved in more serious matters. It was during these years that his interests focused increasingly on geography. We do not know who the major influences were. It could have been his geography teacher, József Bartos or, perhaps, his distant relative Sámuel Teleki, the Africa explorer. Contrary to frequent allegations in the popular literature, Sámuel Teleki was not Pál Teleki's uncle or Géza Teleki's cousin. Pál Teleki wrote a study on the history of early Asian travel and presented it at the December 1898 meeting

---

1 András Hóry, "A Belmagyar utcától a Dísz térig" (From the Belmagyar Street to the Dísz Square), nts. 10864/2, 136, Kézirattár [Manuscript Division], Magyar Tudományos Akadémia Könyvtára [The Library of the Hungarian Academy of Science (hereafter cited as MTAKK); and Klára Tüdős, "Rongyok" [Rags], vol. 2, ms. 10907/11, fol. 206, MTAKK.

of the Hungarian Geographical Society.² The report about the presentation noted with approval that Count Teleki proved that, "He had arrived along the rough path of scientific endeavors to the point where everybody has to stand on his own regardless of age and social position." Even though the writer of the review had some reservations he did say that the young count withstood the scientific test with "talent and knowledge."³ For the next two decades Teleki had a commanding presence in Hungarian science in the fields of the history of travel and the history of cartography. He was preparing to write a monograph on the history of maps. At the beginning of his university studies he became acquainted with Lajos Lóczy (1848–1920), who was a professor at the University in Budapest and also the chairman of the Department of Geography. Lóczy was one of the leaders of Hungarian Geographical Sciences. His training was not in geography, he was a graduate of the Swiss Federal Institute of Technology (ETHZ) in Zurich. His geographical approach was strongly affected by geology and he was heavily indebted to Ferdinand Richthofen's morphologic geography. Yet, he was receptive to all the various new directions.

Geography in Hungary at that time had two university settings, Budapest and Kolozsvár [Cluj]. Formal training also took place in the teachers' colleges, in the Institute of Geology and in the Institute of Meteorology. The only geographical periodical, the *Földrajzi Közlemények* [Geographic Reports] was published by the highly reputable Hungarian Geographical Society. At the turn of the century the study of Hungarian geography started to move in a new direction. The natural geograpy school, associated with the name of Carl von Ritter and that was supported by János Hunfalvy (1820–1888), Lóczy's predecessor as a chair of the Department of Geography, began to lose its appeal. The new direction was introduced by Friedrich Ratzel (1844–1904) and focused on exploring anthropological and political geography. The work of the Leipzig scholar very soon appeared in the Hungarian literature. His fundamental work *Anthropogeographie* was published in Hungarian translation in 1887 and Ratzel had a very strong influence on Hungarian geography without ever achieving complete domination.⁴ His ideas, however, caused considerable controversy in future years. His detractors pointed out that some of his conclusions, and the general trend of his approach, tended toward geographi-

---

2   Pál Teleki, "Korszakok az ázsiai felfedező utazások történetében" [Periods in the history of Asian exploratory travels], *Földrajzi Közlemények* [Geographic Reports], (1899): 15–20.
3   -én [Gyula Sebestyén], "Gróf Teleki Pál: 'Korszakok az ázsiai felfedező utazások történetében'" [Count Pál Teleki: "Periods in the history of Asian exploratory travel"], *Ethnographia*, (1899): 129–130.
4   Zoltán Hajdú, "Friedrich Ratzel hatása a magyar földrajztudományban" [The Influence of Friedrich Ratzel on Hungarian geographical science], *Tér és társadalom* [Space and Society], no. 3 (1998): 96–99.

cal determinism. It was he who first worked out the concept of "Lebensraum" as a geographical hypothesis and there is no doubt that his ideas were fruitful stimulants in the geography of the turn of the century. Instead of just amassing data and describing and analyzing the natural environment, Ratzel viewed geography as the broadest possible science the purpose of which was the study and description of the world's surface and which was divided into two major approaches; the natural/physical one and the human and cultural one. He was principally interested in working out the latter part. His influence can be seen clearly in Teleki's doctoral thesis in political science, written in 1904.[5] Teleki joined the Lóczy circle not only for instruction but he also found a master and friend in Lóczy's associate, Jenő Cholnoky, who became a life-long friend.

Teleki was interested in other things as well. In the spring of 1898 he matriculated for one semester at the College of Fine Arts [Mintarajziskola, today Képzőművészeti Egyetem], but it became rapidly evident that he would never become a professional artist. He dropped out after one semester, but it was here that he became acquainted with István Zichy, the future director of the Museum of Fine Arts and with the painter Ferenc Szablya-Frischauf.[6]

The young man flirting with geography was clearly not very interested in law and entered law school only because his parents wanted him to. A law degree was an absolute requirement for a future in an administrative and public career. The obedient son did finish his legal studies. He completed his first set of exams (Hungarian civil law, politics, ecclesiastic law, legal theory and international law) in June 1901 and immediately indicated to Lóczy that he would like to apply for the vacant position of assistant in Lóczy's department. His parents, however, wanted him to have some agricultural training and therefore he matriculated on October 1, 1901, in Magyaróvár at the Agricultural School. It was almost certainly his father who insisted on this step because Géza Teleki's health was deteriorating and he felt that somebody had to relieve him from the management of the estates. The student body in Magyaróvár included many scions of the large estateowning families. Since Pál Teleki was not a regular student, he could get only a certificate of attendance. His achievements were modest but sufficient for him to manage his estates. This year remained an unpleasant memory for another reason. At the second major law exam, in economics, administrative and financial law, and statistics in April 1902,

---

5 Ibid., 98.
6 Gusztáv Keleti, ed., *Az Országos Magyar Királyi Mintarajz-iskolának és Rajztanárképzőnek Értesítője az 1897–98 tanévről* [Bulletin of the National Royal Hungarian Pattern Design School and Drawing Master Training School for the Academic Year 1897–98] (Budapest: Franklin Nyomda, 1898), p. 82.

the examining committee rejected his work. One year later, in March 1903 Teleki flunked again and was made to take a make-up exam in administrative law.[7] This did not affect him very much and a month later he successfully passed the exam. During the entire 1902–03 academic year he could work with Lóczy as an intern. It was at this time that his professor told him to focus on studying for four years and not to publish anything.[8] Prior to this, however, he had to complete his doctoral dissertation in political science.

He started this project during the summer of 1903 and it became a work that explored German and British specialized literature and with its depth and precision far surpassed the contributions of his contemporaries. He endeavored to show on eighty-four single-spaced pages, and with the backing of contemporary anthropological literature, how communities and the elements of statehood developed among primitive people.[9] He wished to prove with his dissertation that the achievements of the natural sciences during the past fifty years had created an "entirely new worldview." According to him the political scientists had not benefited from this and that many points of view could be encountered in this area that were diametrically opposed to the clearly demonstrated facts presented by natural science.[10] He postulated that the human being creating a state was the highest form of the natural evolutionary chain and thus he approached the entire matter from a biologic and anthropologic perspective. He did not abstain from analyzing the role of sex, of promiscuity and of the sexual impulses and he concluded that in addition to the family, the most important factor in the appearance of the state or its more primitive form, the community, were religion, property and moral and spiritual attributes.[11] It should be noted that he was very reserved in the assessment of the importance of religion. In this way, he took a very strong position claiming that the state was the result of a natural development and sharply criticized those who emphasized the importance of the contractual and patriarchal forms in contemporary Hungarian legal and political science.

---

7   "Államtudományi szigorlati jegyzőkönyvek" [Register of examinations in political science], vol. 2, 1897–1903, fol. 452, Eötvös Loránd Tudományegyetem Levéltára (Archives of Loránd Eötvös University)] (hereafter cited as ELTE Lt).

8   Lóczy Papers, 222/8065/22. Pál Teleki's letter to Lajos Lóczy, illegible address, April 26, [no year], Tudománytörténeti Gyűjtemény [History of Science Collection], Magyar Természettudományi Múzeum [Hungarian Museum of Natural History] (hereafter cited as MTM TtGy).

9   Count Pál Teleki, *Az elsődleges államkeletkezés kérdéséhez. Államtudori értekezés* [The Primary Emergence of Statehood. Political Science Dissertation] (Budapest: Kilián Frigyes utóda, 1904).

10 Ibid., p. 3.

11 Ibid., p. 45.

He presented Ratzel's theory in a strongly deterministic light in his dissertation. "States develop from nationalities in most places by the effects of the territorial conditions. The development is promoted principally by great plains and by the nomadic type of life that they promote. In Africa it was nomadism that led to the evolution of states. It is nomadism that nourishes the most powerful spring of historic evolution, namely, the drive for expansion and the desire for control."[12] The steppe as a laboratory for political geography is an idea that keeps recurring throughout his entire career and becomes particularly prominent during the 1910s when the study of the formation of states in the plains became one of the most distinguished areas for investigation related to the Turanian movement. For Teleki "community life" as a "mighty weapon in the struggle for existence" was a goal and not a means in the fight for survival. It is for this reason that it is impossible to state that the tendency of primitive peoples to form a state is characterized by rational goal-orientation, because this would assume the basis for serious abstractive ability. As Teleki would phrase it, it would require a serious, goal-oriented thought process. In fact, on this issue he departed from the presentation of largely Asiatic, Oceanic or South American examples and the Kővárvidék County estate owner emerged from behind the scientist, "We don't even have to go so far a field. The Moldavian Romanian or the Máramaros Ruthenian would be equally incapable of such abstract reasoning."[13]

The evolution of the state community and of the family as a seminal component inevitably led to the consideration of the ruling powers. Who will lead the newly formed community and how will it be done? There was no doubt in his mind that the basis of the leadership was crude physical power that could be put to work in war and in domestic fights. This crude power, however, sufficed for the leadership for only a limited period of time. In time it had to be replaced by courage and skill and in an expanded area and with time, by wisdom.[14] According to Teleki, this initially spontaneous development of the state had changed, very slowly, to a goal oriented plan and the state evolved under the guidance of a strong personality from the clan and tribe and their blood relationships. This state was in no way identical with the family concept of the modern state. The political science doctoral dissertation with its didactic statements and repetitions gives the impression of a carefully considered, logically constructed work. It does have doctrinaire overtones in

---

12 Ibid., pp. 58–59.
13 Ibid. pp. 59–61.
14 Ibid., pp. 79–81.

trying to impose its themes on political science, but his references are very far reaching from Friedrich Engels, through Ratzel and Lewis H. Morgan, to the two great left-wing thinkers in Hungary of the day, Gyula Pikler, and Bódog Somló.

The political science dissertation was accepted and Pál Teleki was awarded the doctorate on December 19, 1903, by Jenő Balogh, the dean of the faculty. The young man continued to be fascinated by biological problems. Having read Herbert Spencer's *Principles of Sociology* in 1900 and having dedicated his political science dissertation to the radical Gyula Pikler, it seemed natural that he published his articles on the pages of the new and very influential liberal journal, the *Huszadik Század* (Twentieth Century], During 1904 Teleki had several publications. In a long and enthusiastic article he welcomed and described the first issue of the German *Archiv für Rassen- und Gesellschaftsbiologie*,[15] The series was the most important organ of the eugenic movement and its review gave Teleki the opportunity to expound his own perspectives on the biological foundations of society. The description of the publication closes with a categorical statement, "The single realistic basis of the social sciences is biology."[16] Four lesser papers were also published in *Huszadik Század* during 1904. In these he again concluded that he viewed society as a biological organism,[17] that he enthused about the views that placed science over religion and that he envisioned a society based on the rule of the elect with less individual freedom and greater solidarity.[18] He proudly argued for the evolutionary connection between ape and man.[19] In discussing a German paper he argued that evolution was not in opposition to the recognition of a "higher power or divinity" and should not shake anybody's faith in God. The editors of the periodical found it necessary to comment on the above and state that this was valid only for those who had already broken with all types of "religious dogmatism" because the "Biblical Creator God was incompatible with Darwinism."[20] In contrast, Teleki believed that Darwinism was not only not opposed to religion but that, "it gave our morals a more secure base, supports and promotes our endeavors to improve the race,

---

15 Count Pál Teleki, "Társadalomtudomány biológiai alapon" [Social science on a biological basis], *Huszadik Század* (Twentieth Century] 1, no. 4 (1904): 318–322.
16 Ibid., p. 321.
17 Pál Teleki, "Politikai embertan" [Political anthropology], *Huszadik Század* 2, (1904): 73–75.
18 Pál Teleki, "Az emberi termeszetről" [Of human nature], *Huszadik Század* 2, (1904): 241–243.
19 Pál Teleki, "Az ember származásának egy újabb bizonyítéka" [New evidence for the origin of man], *Huszadik Század* 2, (1904): 599–601.
20 Count Pál Teleki, "Leszármazástan az iskolában" [Evolution theory in the schools], *Huszadik Század* 1, no. 5 (May 1904): 410–11.

strengthens the feeling of racial coherence and thus serves patriotic goals."[21] His association with the periodical soon came to an end but not for intellectual reasons. Teleki returned home to Kővárvidék and took on his administrative responsibilities. He was appointed as an honorary district administrator.

First Steps in Politics

The Nagysomkút district is in the southeast corner of Szatmár County and was considered a poor district. Of the 2,315 inhabitants Nagysomkút, the district seat itself 942 were Hungarians, 1,278 Romanians and 51 Germans. More than half of the Hungarian residents were Jewish. They were largely in charge of the commercial and financial affairs of the district. The local Romanian population lived apart from the Hungarians.

It was here that the young Pál Teleki arrived, on his family's insistence, to start his administrative career. To be an honorary administrator meant that the individual was an unpaid intern. He was appointed by the lord lieutenant [főispán]. The honorary official could get a salary only if the deputy lord lieutenant started proceedings against an official, suspended him and gave the job to the honorary official. The honorary officials were important because eventually most of the regular county administrative officials came from their ranks.[22]

Teleki followed his superiors and enjoyed the wide ranging activities in the familiar surroundings. He was proud of the fact that he could communicate with all the people in the district in their own language. This "administrative polymathy" was characteristic of his later activities as well. He wanted to engage in science but the events in domestic politics determined a different career for him.

On October 7, 1904, Prime Minister István Tisza announced that by amending the rules of the Lower House, he wished to make the activities of parliament more effective and wished to eliminate the technical obstructions with which the opposition could paralyze the House. The revision of the House rules, in violation of the House rules themselves, infuriated not just the opposition. Nineteen representatives, mostly aristocrats, resigned from the government party and joined the oppo-

---

21 Ibid., p. 410.
22 Béla Sarlós, *Közigazgatás és hatalompolitika a dualizmus rendszerében* [Administration and Power Politics under the Dualist System] (Budapest: Akadémiai Kiadó, 1976), pp. 52–58.

sition. They included Count Géza Teleki. On January 3, 1905, the King and Emperor Francis Joseph prorogued parliament and new elections were scheduled.[23]

The Nagysomkút electoral district had been considered for many years to be the private property of Géza Teleki. When a "dissident party" consisting of the "moderate opposition," followers of Gyula Andrássy, Jr., who had left the government party, appeared in the district in December 1904, its leaders decided to nominate Pál Teleki as their candidate. The young politician accepted and ran unopposed in the district. Teleki spent a considerable sum in order to gain the goodwill of the electorate. He paid for the dinners of the two hundred and ten soldiers and twelve officers who were assigned to the district for the elections for three days.[24] He donated six hundred crowns to have the synagogue in Nagysomkút repainted.[25] He had himself elected to the Kővárvidék Civic Association and became a member of the Board of Directors of the Kővárvidék Savings Bank. The financial and social sacrifices of the family were crowned with success. On January 20, 1905, Pál Teleki was elected unanimously as a representative of the Andrássy opposition party. Countrywide the Independence Party gained more votes than the Liberal Party and, jointly with their allies, they could count on a majority in the Lower House.

This represented a turning point in the history of the Dualist system in Hungary and it was for the first time that the opposition gained the majority. This group opposed the Compromise and voiced the demands of the country in a way unacceptable to the monarch. The opposition proved to be completely unyielding in its demands and the Austrian General Staff, in complete secrecy, worked out "Plan U," the plan for the occupation of Hungary if no political solution could be found for the impasse. The Lower House met a few times but accomplished nothing meritorious. King Francis Joseph finally resolved the crisis temporarily by appointing Baron Géza Fejérváry, the former minister of defense, to lead a government of officials without the backing of parliament. For Szatmár County the new government became even more significant because its former lord lieutenant, József Kristóffy, became the new minister of the interior. After the government introduced itself to parliament, Pál Teleki joined his father in participating in the county-wide opposition to the new government. We find the Telekis in the first rank of those who voted against the Budapest government which they considered

---

23   The events are summarized by Gusztáv Grátz, *A dualizmus kora* [The Age of the Dualism] (Budapest: Akadémiai Kiadó, 1993), 52–58; and Gábor Vermes, *István Tisza. The Liberal Vision and Conservative Statecraft of a Magyar Nationalist* (Boulder, CO: East European Monographs, 1985), pp. 107–123.
24   "Katonákat kérünk" [We request soldiers], *Kővárvidék*, February 5, 1905, p. 1.
25   *Kővárvidék*, February 12, 1905, p. 3.

to be illegitimate. They not only protested but financially assisted the officials who had been dismissed.

In November 1905 the Andrássy opposition assumed the name of Constitution Party [Alkotmánypárt] and Pál Teleki joined it. Initially no one obeyed the new government, taxes could not be collected, there was no budget and gradually the funds collected for county resistance were exhausted. Most of the counties began to bow to the government but the Fejérváry administration had no political support at all. While the national resistance appeared to be crumbling, the monarch consistently refused to comply with any request from the coalition relative to the strengthening of the Hungarian aspects of the common army. In February 1906 the monarch prorogued the parliament. It appeared that the crisis had come to full bloom. Yet, at the time there were already considerable behind-the-scenes discussions that resulted in the monarch accepting the resignation of the Fejérváry government and in the appointment of Sándor Wekerle, a moderate politician of the opposition as prime minister in April 1906. In the "April Agreement" the coalition gave up its military demands, such as the use of the Hungarian language for commands, the requirement that all officers spoke Hungarian and that Hungarian emblems be used in the common army. The coalition also agreed to vote for an increased recruitment and for a new budget, the extension of the customs union, the release of the Fejérváry and Tisza governments from personal and fiscal responsibility and for the enactment of the commercial agreements. The coalition promised to enact a broad extension of the franchise and to hold elections.[26]

This development came as a surprise to Pál Teleki. He hunted during the winter, was frequently invited to house-parties and was also preparing an illustrated lecture on the discovery of Japan for the Geographical Society.[27] He left for a two month research trip and went to visit relatives in Triest (Trieste), via Vienna, and then to Paris. During the day he worked in the Bibliothèque Nationale and in the Navy Map Collection looking for ancient maps. He copied them on tracing paper and made photocopies of the rare pieces. He bought maps and old books and in the evening went to the theater or met old friends.[28] He wrote two smaller scientific papers and became friendly with a number of French geographers including Henri

---

26 Grátz, *A dualizmus kora*, pp. 103–107.
27 Letter from Pál Teleki to Lajos Lóczy, Pribékfalva-Fehérszék, December 1, 1905, Lóczy Papers 806/5, MTM TtGy; and Letter from Pál Teleki to Lajos Lóczy, Pribékfalva-Fehérszék, December 4, 1905, Lóczy Papers, 806/6, MTM TtGy. In published form, see Pál Teleki, "Japáén szerepe Amerika felfedezésében" [The role of Japan in the discovery of America], *Földrajzi Közlemények*, no. 1 (1906): 1–13.
28 Letter from Pál Teleki to Lajos Lóczy, March 22, 1906, Lóczy Papers, 806/7, MTM TtGy.

Cordier and Marcel Gabriel, the head of the Map Collection at the Bibliothèque Nationale.[29] It was in Paris that he learned that with the effective cooperation of Lajos Lóczy the Geographical Society had elected him to its board of directors.

The scheduled elections induced him to return earlier than planned from his trip. On April 16, 1906, he was already in Nagysomkút where he started his campaign. The large group of people assembled in the courtyard of the local inn was addressed by the parish priest who reminded them of Teleki's outstanding personality and political achievements. The compliments caused enthusiasm and the candidate was carried around the yard on the shoulders of the electors. He gave his speech in both Hungarian and Romanian. He recalled the accusations against Fejérváry and Tisza and considered the agreement between the monarch and the coalition to be a major victory over the enemies of the country and of the constitution. In response to a prearranged question he indicated that it was a base calumny that the franchise would be linked to the ability of reading and writing Hungarian. No decent Hungarian could ever endorse such a step, "least of all the son of Lajos Kossuth [Ferenc Kossuth, one of the leaders of the coalition] whose father freed the serfs and thus took the first step toward making all nationalities equal." He could not deny, however, that the coalition had to give up its military demands, but he suggested that this retreat would be only temporary. The most important matter, as far as he was concerned, was that the good relations between the monarch and the country had been reestablished and that henceforth appeals could be made "to a well informed monarch and not to a misled one." For this reason he invited everybody to support the government. The themes in his speech came largely from the ideas of the conservatives and could also be seen in the program of the Austrian Christian-Socialists.

The elections were not as uneventful as the ones the preceding year. Teleki had an opponent as the Romanian National Party ran Alexandru Vaida-Voevod, the future Romanian prime minister (1919- 1920, 1932, 1933), against him. Because of the tensions in the country and because of the nationality issue in this district a large number of troops were sent in to maintain order. The day of the elections, May 3, was more reminiscent of a military manoeuver than of a political process and 825 soldiers were stationed in and around the village.[30] The voters of the two

---

29 For his articles, see "Értesítés a roueni rézföldgömb és az 1554. évi Gastaldinak tulajdonított térkép között felfedezett hasonlóságról" [Report on the similarities discovered between the Rouen copper globe and the map of 1554, attributed to Gastaldi], *Földrajzi Közlemények*, no. 4, (1906): 107–109; and "Descaliers Mappemonde-ja" [Mappemonde of Descaliers], *Földrajzi Közlemények*, no. 5 (1906): 185–186.
30 "A választás előtti nap" [The day before the election], *Kővárvidék*, May 6, 1906, p. 1.

The Years of Learning (1897–1918)

parties were carefully segregated. The voting began at nine in the morning on May 3 and lasted until four, the next morning. Of the almost 4,000 electors in the district 3,048 cast their ballot. Seventeen hundred and six voted for Teleki and 1,342 voted for Vaida-Voevod.[31]

In spite of the large number of soldiers, the voting did not proceed without trouble. At the little village of Karulya [Coruia] gendarmes fired into a group that protested against some police regulations and got into a melee. Two men were killed, and four were wounded some from bullets and some from bayonets. It is a fact that both dead and all of the wounded were Romanians but both groups (the pro-Telekis and those protesting against him) fighting were Romanians because in this village almost the entire population was Romanian.[32]

Vaida-Voevod was elected in another district and thus, at one of the first sessions of the new parliament he held Teleki accountable for the shooting and demanded that he give up his mandate since it was stained with human blood. In a brief comment, Teleki denied having had anything to do with the incident.[33] This minor exchange was Teleki's sole uttering in the Lower House between 1906 and 1910 and in 1910 he asked not to be renominated. Although he was a member of the leadership of the Constitution Party for a while, and a member of some minor committees, his political activities were limited to representing Szatmár County delegation at the reinterment of the ashes of Prince Ferenc II Rákóczi, the Hungarian revolutionary leader, who died in 1735 in his Turkish exile. The ceremony took place in October 1906 and Teleki was present both in Budapest and Kassa (Košice).[34] He was not active politically within his district either. He rapidly became bored with the minor problems of the electorate, was absent from most social gatherings and even his parliamentary reports diminished. After the major political excitement had abated, Teleki no longer felt that participation in public affairs was absolutely essential. He turned increasingly toward geography and science. "That damned representative activity takes too much time," he wrote to his colleague Jenő Cholnoky.[35] The Independence Party opposition did not stay in power for very long. Their government fell ignominiously in 1910 because practically none of its promises had been

---

31 Ibid.
32 "Választási tragédia" [Election tragedy], *Kővárvidék*, May 13, 1906, pp. 1–2.
33 Képviselőházi napló [Journal of the House of Representatives], 1906–1910, May 30, 1906, vol. 1, pp. 54–0.
34 *Kővárvidék*, October 28, 1906, p. 3.
35 Letter from Pál Teleki to Jenő Cholnoky, Pribékfalva, August 2, 1906, Letters, 1906, Cholnoky Papers, box 1, MFMA.

fulfilled. At the 1910 elections, the National Labor Party, the reorganized conservative-liberal government party, was triumphantly returned to power.

Geography and Turanism

Starting in the summer of 1906 he again became involved in geography. He traveled throughout Europe searching for old maps. After Christmas 1906 he fulfilled an old dream that originally oriented him toward geography. During the first days of 1907 he started off to Africa. In Egypt he visited Cairo and stayed for two weeks. He went to Memphis and climbed the pyramids. He took the train to Aswan and then took a boat and sailed down the Nile. There was no opportunity for geographical discoveries because this area was well known. Teleki did make geographical observations, made minor corrections on the maps and went hunting.[36] It was on this trip that he collected the trophies, antelope heads, weapons and shields, that a decade and a half later decorated his office. It was along the Nile that he shot the hippopotamus whose mounted snarling muzzle caused palpitations to the visitors to the Pribékfalva chateau who encountered the monster for the first time.[37]

Returning home he immersed himself in geography. His topic had been alive in his mind ever since 1905 and involved the historical cartography of the discovery of Japan. He visited all the great map and chart collections, in Europe. He was a frequent visitor to the Rijksarhief in The Hague, The British Museum, The Royal Geographical Society and the Bibliothèque Nationale. He usually stayed in the same hotels. His favorites were the Hotel des Indes in The Hague, the Hôtel Mirabeau in Paris and the elegant Claridge's in London. He sent the individual chapters of his manuscript on the discovery of Japan from Pribékfalva to Jenő Cholnoky in Kolozsvár who then read and corrected the finished parts of the work.[38] In Geneva in 1908 he presented his findings at an International Congress. The manuscript on which he had worked so hard was published in 1909.[39]

---

36 Letter from Pál Teleki to Lajos Lóczy, Khartoum January 27, 1907, Lóczy Papers, 806/9, MTM TtGy; Postcard from Pál Teleki to Lajos Lóczy, Ed-Duem, January 30, 1907, and n.p., February 17, 1907, Lóczy Papers, 222/ 806, MTM TtGy.
37 Information from Ioan Botez, retired veterinarian in Pribileşti [Pribékfalva], Judetul Maramureş, Romania in September 2001.
38 For his autobiography, see Jenő Cholnoky, *Vár ucca tizenhét* [17 Var Street] (Veszprém: Veszprém Önkormányzata, 1998), p. 300.
39 Count Pál Teleki, *Atlasz a japáni szigetek cartographiájának történetéhez* [Atlas for the Cartographic History of the Japanese Islands] (Budapest: Kilián Frigyes utóda, 1909).

The Years of Learning (1897–1918)

The huge volume, covering a sizeable desktop when opened, is basically the cartographic history of the discovery of Japan. In the second part of the work, Teleki published Matthijs Quast and Abel Tasman's 1639 travel diary in Dutch with a Hungarian translation. In the 168 pages of the work he reviewed the entire history of the discovery of Japan, with twenty maps and copious references.[40] The reception of the book in Hungary was favorable and so was the international reception of the German version.[41] Teleki was elected to the Old Map and Chart Committee of the Geneva International Geographical Society and the Paris Geographical Society awarded him the Jomard Prize for 1911 in recognition of his book[42] The Jomard Prize consisted of the collected works of Edme-François Jomard, known as the *Monuments de Géographie,* and was awarded to thirty-six scholars. The sponsor of the award was the same Henri Cordier, to whom Teleki expressed his thanks in the introduction of his work. In his report Cordier compared the Hungarian work to the work of Otto Nordenskjöld, the Swedish scholar, who wrote a history of the map and chart making of the fifteenth and sixteenth centuries. Cordier also said that the prize was a suitable recognition of a mighty work.[43] Teleki wished to introduce the models he saw in Paris into Hungarian scientific life. He funded a prize in Budapest and asked the Board of Directors of the Hungarian Geographical Society that a copy of his *Atlas* be awarded every three years to the author of the best paper published in the *Földrajzi Közlemények.*[44]

Teleki had great plans for Hungarian cartography. He made a public announcement in which he invited the general public to advise the Hungarian Geographical Society about any old, manuscript map or chart and also proposed the establishment of a Geographical museum, modeled after the Museum fur Vergleichende Landeskunde in Leipzig.[45] These were the years when he became immersed in the Hungarian geographical sciences. On Lajos Lóczy's invitation, he was nominated for secretary general of the Hungarian Geographical Society. Just before this nomination he had developed doubts and concerns about his own suitability for scien-

---

40 Pál Teleki, *Catalogue of Books, Atlases and Maps Relating Especially to the History of Cartography and Discovery of Asia from the Library of Count Paul Teleki* (Budapest: Pál Teleki, 1935).
41 E. L. Stevenson, "Atlas zur Geschichte der Kartographie der japanischen Inseln," *Bulletin of the American Geographical Society* 64, no. 6 (1911): 480.
42 Fodor, *Teleki Pál,* p. 30.
43 "Assemblée Générale du 28 Avril 1911," *Actes de la Société de Géographie* 23, no. 6(1911): 480.
44 Földrajzi Közlemények 39, no. 4 (1911): 189–190.
45 Count Pál Teleki, "Felhívás Magyarország kartográfiájának ügyében" [Appeal in the matter of Hungarian cartography], *Földrajzi Közlemények* 39, no. 2 (1911): 47–50; and Count Pál Teleki, "Földrajzi museum" [Museum of Geography], *Földrajzi Közlemények* 39, no. 3 (1911): 152.

tific endeavors. At the beginning of 1911 he called the history of cartography "incomprehensible, strange and boring," called his presentation "my folly" and predicted that he would be a complete failure. "The presentation will be such a stupidity that it is not worth the photographic plate."[46] Two months later his concerns about his own suitability became more accentuated, "From a scientific perspective the results of my work to date are that I see that my knowledge and my work are inadequate and amateurish and that I truly do not belong among the serious geographers." He considered himself to be inadequate for the general secretaryship of the society and even resigned from the board of directors and from his position as a "corresponding member."[47] Lóczy insisted, however, and even made the acceptance of his own presidency contingent upon Teleki being the secretary general. Lóczy also indicated that after his term of office, his pupil could assume the presidency of the society. Teleki agreed to be nominated but still voiced his doubts,

> I do not consider myself suitable for this position and even less for the presidency. I am not an expert in geography and know only about the area that I have worked in. I know little about natural science, physical and geological geography. I have completely lost interest in history, have lost my self-confidence, my nerves are so bad that I don't know if I will be suitable for any serious activity.[48]

These doubts and self-flagellations, occasionally combined with a desire to escape, remained a constant feature of Teleki's geographical and scientific career and later even grew into a definite death wish. Lóczy, however, had some potent arguments and the Hungarian Geographical Society elected Teleki as its secretary general, at the March 11, 1911, meeting with fifty-four votes. He thus became Cholnoky's successor.[49]

The honor was without a doubt beneficial for his depression. In the subsequent months Teleki was effervescent and generated multiple plans for the renewal of the society's activities and publications. He recommended the establishment of lectu-

---

46 Letter from Pál Teleki to Jenő Cholnoky, Budapest, January 11, 1911, Letters, January to July 1911, Cholnoky Papers, box 4, MFMA.
47 Letter from Pál Teleki to Lajos Lóczy, London, March 13, 1911, Lóczy Papers, 806/15, MTM TtGy.
48 Letter from Pál Teleki to Lajos Lóczy, March 25, 1911, ibid.
49 Minutes of the March 30, 1911, meeting, dossier 2 (1911), no. 30 (1911), no. 15 on the agenda, and the detailed results of the voting, no. 30 (1911), and no. 15, Magyar Földrajzi Társaság Irat- és Levéltára [Archives of the Hungarian Geographical Society] (hereafter cited as MFT IL).

res, courses of study and debate sessions. He wanted to find new writers to prepare minor articles for the *Földrajzi Közlemények,* wished to reorganize the book review section and to establish a department of economic geography. These would have oriented the work in a "practical and manifestly economically useful" direction. He wished to publish the best geography papers in foreign languages, wished to establish local chapters nationally and was considering the establishment of another periodical for the general public.[50] He also wished to upgrade the library and have foreign periodicals bound but there was no money in the treasury. "We ought to kill some Jew for this" he wrote in a letter to Cholnoky.[51] This is the only instance in Teleki's pre-1919 private or public papers in which a comment reflects a prejudice against the Jews. It seems that he shared the prejudice with many others who equated "Jew" with "rich person."

Not all of Teleki's plans materialized and some only partially. The position of secretary general proved to be much more onerous than Teleki had ever foreseen. He was constantly engaged in mediating between the warring factions within the society. He took over the majority of the shares of the Hungarian Geographical Institute, Inc. [Magyar Földrajzi Intézet, Rt.] which, was not a scholarly organization but the publishing arm of the society engaged principally in printing maps. It was Lóczy who talked him into it and it was a real financial burden even on a count. It was probably this matter that made him sell two houses in Nagysomkút for fifty-six thousand crowns.[52] He had no luck with the company. It swallowed up increasing sums of money and also resulted in serious disagreements among a number of Hungarian geographers, ultimately even with Lóczy himself. The situation was further aggravated by Teleki getting involved in a conflict with Géza Czirbusz, the Piarist priest professor who was Lóczy's successor in the Chair of Geography at the University of Budapest. This conflict lasted for years and was characterized by numerous unedifying episodes.

The enthusiastic and outspoken priest translated Adriano Balbi's *Universal Geography* into Hungarian with major emendations and in his works *Nemzeti*

---

50 Minutes of the June 2, 1911, board of directors meeting, dossier 2 (1911), no. 34 (1911), no. 7 on the agenda, MPT IL; Details of proposal, dossier 2 (1911), no. 34 (1911), no. ad 7, p. 7, MFT IL; Minutes of the November 23, 1911, board of directors meeting, dossier 2 (1911), nos. 3-5 on the agenda, MFT IL; Letter from Pál Teleki to Jenő Cholnoky, Budapest May 9, 1911, Letters, January-June 1911, Cholnoky Papers, box 4, MFMA; and Letter from Pál Teleki to Jenő Cholnoky June 3, 1911, Letters, January-June 1911, Cholnoky Papers, box 4, MFMA.
51 Letter from Pál Teleki to Jenő Cholnoky, Budapest April 19, 1911, Letters, January-June 1911, Cholnoky Papers, box 4, MFMA.
52 *Kővárvidék*, August 27, 1911, p. 2.

művelődés geográfiája [Geography of National Culture] and *Anthropogeográfia* [Anthropogeography] he radically reoriented Hungarian geographical thinking. In his approach he was close to the French anthropogeographers, Vidal de la Blache and Jean de Brunhes. Czirbusz recognized the importance of evolving regional scholarship and of the concept of space. He was very critical of the general conditions in Hungary and did not share the end-of-century enthusiasm that became increasingly strong in the geographical disciplines and that was so optimistic about Hungary's mission and forthcoming great power position. In a number of areas he was well ahead of his times, of his Hungarian colleagues and in some areas even of international scholarship.[53]

Czirbusz's victory at the University caused a major uproar in geographical scholarly circles. In the press, the university and scientific circles a merciless persecution developed against the scholar. One of the leaders of this "hunt" was Teleki and he was not particularly squeamish. He attacked Czirbusz in every type of paper, liberal, freemason, opposition and government party.[54] The attack was not limited to the pages of the newspapers. The votes taken by the Hungarian Geographical Society in the 1910s consistently show a major endeavor to expel him from the scientific arena. In the *Földrajzi Közlemények* his works were not even mentioned. Pamphlets were written against him and there were even anonymous postcards attacking Czirbusz. Teleki was inflamed:

It is in the interest of the issue that this article [in the liberal government party Magyar Figyelő*] be very good. For this reason I must ask you to help. In the* Nyugat *I will also write. I believe that in the* XX. Század *I will as well....Please help because he [Czirbusz] is very active and we must knock him dead. Otherwise there will be trouble. I am willing to go to the limit.*[55]

---

53 Zoltán Hajdú, "Czirbusz Géza: a magyar társadalomföldrajz 'temetetlen' megalapítója" [Géza Czirbusz, the "unburied" founder of Hungarian social geography], in *A magyar társadalomföldrajzi kutatás gondolatvilága. (Tanulmányok a hatvanéves Mészáros Rezső köszöntésére)* [The World of Ideas of Hungarian Social Geography Research. Essays in Honor of the Sixtieth Birthday of Rezső Mészáros], ed. Jolán Palotás Abonyi, József Becsei, and Csaba Kovács (Szeged: SZTE Gazdaság és társadalomföldrajzi Tanszék, 2002).

54 Pál Teleki, "A kétféle földrajzról ami nincs" [About the two types of geography that do not exist], *Világ* [World], December 17, 1912; Pál Teleki, "Megjegyzések egy könyvről. Dr. Czirbusz: Geográfia" (Comments on a book. Dr. Czirbusz, Geography), *Az Újság* [The News], December 8, 1912; Pál Teleki, "Czirbusz G. könyvének bírálata" [Critique of G. Czirbusz's book], *Pesti Napló* [Pest Daily], December 3, 1912.

55 Letter from Pál Teleki to Jenő Cholnoky, Budapest, December 20, 1912, Cholnoky-Teleki dossier, Cholnoky Papers, MFMA.

The Years of Learning (1897–1918)

Teleki sent word to the professor through one of his assistants, that, "he had two days to resign his chair" in which case he would get his pension. If he did not, his opponents would create a "national scandal" and thus force him to resign. In that case he would get no pension and would never work at the university again. Initially Czirbusz stood his ground against his attackers and responded vigorously, but he was a sick man. He had cardiac problems and soon developed hallucinations. He was convinced that Teleki was trying to kill him. In the last stages of the disease he made peace with Lóczy and died in 1920.[56]

The tempests of social life had a detrimental effect on Teleki. The increasing responsibilities, the financial risks and the ongoing intrigues finally produced such an emotional crisis in him that he once again started to doubt his abilities. "The problem is that we cannot even defend ourselves. You are far away and I am a poor amateur. Nobody guided me, I did not learn and I can do nothing for geography," he wrote to Cholnoky. He spoke of "little knowledge," "bad style," and called one of his articles "idiotic nonsense."[57] He spoke of his "nervousness" that should be treated and he also mentioned that he was discouraged and did not consider himself suitable to be the secretary general.[58] These mood swings returned later in his life as well. He complained much about his nerves and about his uselessness but these periods were followed by electrified, productive and cheerful periods.

It would be a mistake to assume that the life of the Geographical Society consisted of nothing but continuous intrigue, warfare and sterile disputes. One of the earliest Hungarian scientific bodies, the Geographical Society, was a recognized component of international scholarly activities. The society made major contributions to the updating of geographical studies in Hungary. Its leaders bombarded the Ministry of Culture and Education with memoranda asking that geography be recognized its proper position as a subject of national education.[59]

---

56 Letter from Géza Czirbusz to Lajos Lóczy, Budapest, June [January?] 9, 1916, the Cholnoky-Horusitzky Dispute dossier, Lajos Lóczy, Sr. Papers, Magyar Bányászati és Földtani Szolgálat Tudománytörténeti Gyűjtemény [Hungarian Mining and Geological Service, History of Science Collection] (hereafter cited as MBFSZ TtGy).
57 Letter from Pál Teleki to Jenő Cholnoky, Budapest, April 10, 1912, Letters, January-June 1912, Cholnoky Papers, box 4, MFMA; and Letter from Pál Teleki to Jenő Cholnoly, Budapest, December 28, 1912, Letters, July-December 1912, Cholnoky Papers, box 4, MFMA.
58 Letter from Pál Teleki to Jenő Cholnoky, Budapest, February 11, 1913, Letters, January-June 1913, Cholnoky Papers, box 4, MFMA; and Letter from Pál Teleki to Jenő Cholnoky, Budapest, March 25, 1912, Letters, January-June 1912, Cholnoky Papers, box 4, MFMA.
59 Memorandum from Pál Teleki and Jenő Cholnoky to Minister of Culture and Education Béla Jankovich, Budapest, December 11, 1913, dossier 2 (1913), no. 40(1913), MFT IL.

The Geographical Society participated in a large number of international activities and the leadership of the society participated in the 1913 Congress in Rome where Teleki presented a paper, "Magyarország kartográfiájának története az Alföldi Bizottság tükrében" [The history of Hungarian cartography in the mirror of the Great Plain Committee].[60] The international importance of the society is shown by the fact that when the American Geographical Society was celebrating its sixtieth birthday an invitation was sent to the Hungarian Geographical Society. A transcontinental trip across the United States was planned in honor of the occasion and the Hungarian scholars would be welcome in that exclusive international company.[61] In Budapest Teleki and Cholnoky were elected to represent Hungarian geography on this trip and at the festivities accompanying the opening of the new headquarters of the American society in New York. The trip was quite expensive but meant much for Teleki's career.[62]

The friends left Budapest on August 12, 1912, and started on August 22 from New York on an almost two month long tour of the United States. The first stop was Albany and then Buffalo, Detroit, and Chicago. From there they proceeded to Duluth, and then via the Yellowstone National Park to Seattle. Thence to San Francisco and then across the Rockies to Salt Lake City and Denver. After a small detour to Santa Fe and Phoenix, they visited Kansas City, Memphis, and Birmingham. After a stay in Washington, D.C., the two tired scholars arrived back in New York.[63] Teleki was fascinated by the varieties of scenery and wrote home that, "Everything here in America is of glorious proportions and in a natural, uncovered simplicity."[64] He liked Seattle, Tacoma, Portland and San Francisco, rebuilt magnificently after the Great Earthquake. He also liked Denver and Santa Fe. He was enchanted with the Grand Canyon. "I was speechless when I first saw it...even the Americans cannot exaggerate its beauty."[65]

---

60   X. Congresso Geografico Internazionale, Diario, no. 3. p. 7.
61   For the invitation, see minutes of the board of directors, October 13, 1911, dossier 2 (1911), no. 34 (1911), no. 5 on the agenda, MFT IL.
62   For the trip see a somewhat egocentric but readable description by Jenő Cholnoky, *Utazásom Amerikába Teleki Pál gróffal* [My Trip to America with Count Pál Teleki] (Budapest; Vajda-Wichmann, [194?]). See: Steven Seegel: *Map men. Transnational Lives and Deaths of Geographers in the Making of East Central Europe*. Chicago, 2018, Chicago UP. 34-40.
63   "The Society's Transcontinental Excursion of 1912," *Bulletin of the American Geographical Society* 44, no. 9 (1912): 667; and ibid., no. 11 (1912); 848–849.
64   Letter from Pál Teleki to Lajos Lóczy, Salt Lake City, September 24, 1912, Lóczy Papers, 806/17, MTM TtGy.
65   Letter from Pál Teleki to Lajos Lóczy. Hotel El Tovar at the Grand Canyon (Arizona), October 3, 1912, Lóczy Papers, 806/18, MTM TtGy.

There were inconveniences as well. The two travelers were constantly battling dirt because the facilities for bathing were very limited. They were unhappy with their accommodations on the trains and with the American menu based largely on canned food. When the two Hungarians had to sleep in one bed in a tent, it was pure hell according to them. Cholnoky snored and Teleki pushed him out of bed. These inconveniences were insignificant compared to the enormous benefits of the trip.

It was not only the trip itself that was a memorable experience for Teleki, but so were the personalities of the fellow travelers. The participants represented the very best of European and American geography and most of their names appear in Teleki's correspondence and later scholarly contacts. W. M. Davis was considered the outstanding representative of physical geography and Teleki also established excellent relationship with Isaiah Bowman. The companions included Carl Uhlig from Tübingen, the expert on anthropogeography, Emile Chaix from Switzerland, Emmanuel de Margerie from Paris, and Emmanuel de Martonne, the professor at the University of Lyon, who was an old acquaintance of the two Hungarian scholars. The forty-three non-American travelers included British, Italian, Austrian, and Russian scholars. The discussions and debates with these scholars frequently played an important role in Teleki's subsequent international scientific liaisons.[66]

His first impressions were about the American way of life and its rhythm which made an impression of impermanence on him. "The tempo of your life and your use of natural forces is faster than ours but not as profound." By "ours," he meant European. He emphasized that in individual liberties, in the comforts and conveniences of every-day life and practicality-using the railroads as his principal example— America was left behind the Old World. "Compared to us Hungarians, they are slaves to a standard way of life and to practices that are not individually limiting. It is evident that this systematic uniformity of treatment promotes the meaningful feeling that all men are of equal value and of overall equality."[67]

It occurred to him early on the trip that the United States was the country of the businessman and of the businesspeople. In Hungarian economic geography Teleki's importance cannot be overestimated and it was the American trip that broadened his perspective. He summarized the experiences of the trip in a book

---

66 For a list of the participants see "The Society's Transcontinental Exursion," pp. 664–665.
67 Count Pál Teleki, "Amerikán keresztül" [Across America], *Amerikai Magyar Népszava* [American Hungarian People's Voice], October 3, 1912, p. 2.

written at the university ten years later.⁶⁸ The work is characterized by a strong historical approach. He touched on the Monroe Doctrine, Native American culture, American constitutionalism and innumerable other items which are not directly linked to geography, but to which he could cleverly and wittily assign both economic and geographical roots. Yet this did not make his approach deterministic. Teleki used the example of the United States to demonstrate his conviction that life on the surface of the globe was a homogenous whole. In its study numerous branches of science can and must be involved and the elucidation of the relationships and understanding the system was the principal responsibility of the geographer.

In his thinking the region emerged as a gigantic interrelated system. In the life of the region man was a shaper and potentially a dominant force for change. Man can raise dormant natural energies, change the vegetation covering the area, change the animal life of the region, and utilize the liberated energies for economic productivity.

Using the words of Henri Bergson, Teleki calls the summary of natural forces a "creative synthesis." Consequently, the political community and the state are simply, "the summation of the forces of nature in a specified area." The more regions that are contained in one state and the more varied the regions, the stronger and more powerful the state and the more able to maintain an economic existence within its own borders by an exchange of products between its various component regions. Teleki saw the United States as a perfect example of this concept. He believed that by virtue of its wealth the American economic orientation had two goals: world commerce and world power. These goals suggested that America was striving for the control of the world.⁶⁹

Because of his work in economic geography and the international success, Teleki received the recognition in Hungary that encouraged his further activities. In 1913 the Hungarian Academy of Science elected him as a corresponding member and starting that year he lectured, on economic geography, on an experimental basis, at the Teachers of College of Commerce. Perhaps the academy membership and teaching made him forget the sense of failure for not being appointed lecturer at the university. The university continuously delayed the appointment process.

When Lóczy retired from the presidency of the Geographical Society in 1914, Jenő Cholnoky assumed that position and retained Teleki as the secretary general.

---

68   Count Pál Teleki, *Amerika gazdasági földrajza különös tekintettel az Észak-amerikai Egyesült Államokra* [American Economic Geography with Particular Reference to the United States of America] (Budapest: Centrum Kiadovallalat, 1922).
69   Ibid., pp. 70–72.

The voting indicated that not all members were pleased with his work, but Cholnoky insisted of retaining him, presumably to some extent because Teleki tactfully smoothed out the recurrent scandals caused by Cholnoky's sanguine temperament.[70]

The Geographical Society was not the sole venue for the activities of the Hungarian geographers in the 1910s. Many of them were not satisfied with the activities of the society which were largely limited to highly technical matters. They wished to voice their own views, derived from geography, and arrived at by accepting social and political responsibilities. The rise of the geographical societies of the era was tightly linked to the surge of imperialism and colonialism that characterized the second half of the nineteenth century.[71] In the Hungarian society there was some early evidence of activity in this far-flung political enterprise but it soon disappeared. In the spiritual structure of the society, at this time, the Hungarian economic and political advances into the Balkans took a prominent position. At the beginning of the century many felt that the time had come to indicate strategic goals for Hungarian policies emerging from the crisis years of 1905-1910. Many viewed foreign policy expansion as their primary goal. These endeavors coincided with the intents of the domestic followers of the dominant literary and artistic Orientalism that ruled Western Europe prior to the turn of the century. The endeavors also resonated with the battles about echoes of the "Ugro-Turkic War" raising the question of the relatives of the Hungarians, raging in the Hungarian scientific arena of the 1870s and 1880s. These ideas were the background from which the so-called Turanism of the 1910s emerged.[72]

The term "Turanian" was originally coined by the British linguist of German extraction, Max Muller, who listed the languages spoken by the European and Asiatic nomads, which were non-Indo-European and non-Semitic, as Turanian.[73] His classification was rapidly surpassed by comparative linguistics and today even the geographic determination of the so-called Uralo-Altaic has been rejected, even though the popularity of the term still lingers. The first who drew attention

---

70 General meeting minutes. March 19, 1914, no. 15 on the agenda, dossier 194, no. 1 (1914), MFT IL.
71 Alfred Fierro, *La Société de Geographie 1821–1946* (Paris: Honore Champion, 1983). See also the strongly Marxist synthesis of the German Geographical Societies by Franz-Joseph Schulte-Althoff, *Studien zur politischen Wissenschaftsgeschichte der deutschen Geographie im Zeitalter des Imperialismus* (Paderborn: Schoninghausen, 1971), pp. 18–21, 43–45, and 192–195.
72 About the whole ideology, see: Ablonczy Balázs, *Go East! A History of Hungarian Turanism*. Bloomington, 2022, Indiana University Press.
73 Ildiko Farkas, "A turanizmus" [The Turanism] (PhD diss., ELTE BTK, 2001), p. 9. The author wishes to thank Dr. Farkas for the courtesy with which she made the manuscript available.

to the Eastern and Turanian roots of the Hungarians was Ármin Vámbéry the Turkologist and explorer of Asia. His study entitled A *magyarok eredete* [The Origin of the Hungarians], published in 1882, generated the above mentioned "Ugrian-Turkic War" in the Hungarian scientific community. Vámbéry was the first one to talk about the Turanian people and also sketched the extent of an ancient pan-Turkish empire that dominated Asia from China to the Mediterranean.[74] Even though Vámbéry later made sure that he not be regarded as the proponent of some pan-Turanian plan, his writings are interpretative and there was an increasing number of students who gained inspiration from them. A number of expeditions to the East also furthered the popularity of the Turanian concept.[75] Many of the leaders of Hungarian literature were also affected by the idea of Eastern relations and the concept of mission. It could be noted during the Russo-Japanese War that in Hungary there was considerable sympathy toward Japan, that "distant Turanian relative."

The concept was supported by intellectuals, artists, and politicians at various levels and with various motivations. The goals were different. For some the East represented only an area of Hungarian political and economic dominance in the competition between Hungary and the Germans and Austrians in the Balkans. For others it meant a closer economic cooperation with the Near East and with certain regions of the Ottoman Empire with Budapest becoming a cultural center for the East, the Turks, the Bosnians and the Bulgarians. The more daring envisaged Hungary as the westernmost bastion of the 150 or even 600 million people of Turanian ethnicity. The Hungarians were viewed as the tip of a lance, as the leaders of the triumphant Turanians against the two threatening Pan-movements, Pan-Germanism and Pan-Slavism, bringing a new center of power to Eurasia.

The Turanian Society, established on December 3, 1910, tried to combine very different interests and differing motives. The participants could be divided into three general groups. The first and most important group consisted of the scholars and travelers through whom the concept was first raised in Hungarian public opinion. This group included the geographers, Lajos Lóczy, Jenő Cholnoky, Pál Teleki, and a number of Orientalists, Turkologists and ethnologists who together provided the new organization with a fund of legitimate intellectual capital.

---

74 Ibid., pp. 24–28.
75 Joseph A. Kessler, "*Turanism and Pan-Turanism in Hungary: 1890–1945*" (PhD diss., University of California, Berkeley, 1967), pp. 77–78.

The second group included the aristocrats, politicians and financial people who were interested in the Turanian concept. They included the writer and future minister of foreign affairs, Miklós Bánffy, Ignác Darányi, the former minister of agriculture and István Tisza, the president of the Lower House and both former and future prime minister, Albert Berzeviczy, the minister of culture, Ferenc Chorin, and József Deutsch Hatvany, capitalists, István Bárczy, mayor of Budapest, Géza Teleki, and Mihály Károlyi, the future president of the republic.

The third group consisted of the intellectuals calling themselves Turanians, scientists who consciously embraced the Turanian ideology. It was from this latter group that the right-wing extremists, who represented the most radical and exaggerated form of Turanism, emerged after the war.[76] One of the prime movers of the organization was Alajos Paikert, economist, agriculturalist, fighter for world peace, poet and designer of a machine that would dig trenches for soldiers. At the beginning of the century he served in Washington as an expert representing the Ministry of Agriculture. It was here that he became acquainted with the Pan-American movement and became convinced that the future belonged to the Pan-movements.[77] Returning to Hungary he worked in the Agricultural Museum and it was here that the Turanian Society had its first administrative center.

The goals prominently featured the establishment and/or strengthening of economic contacts in the Balkans and in the Near East. In order to get the area better known, and to raise the level of interest in the region, a series of lectures was planned in Budapest, a Turanian boarding school was planned and contacts were to be made with the "Turanian leaders." The society first elected Teleki as vice president and then as president. He was also the editor in chief of the society's periodical, *Turán*. It was on the pages of this publication that he expounded his ideas about the mission of the society.[78] In his article he mentioned the German commercial intrusion as an example and a challenge for the Turanian Society. He used geographical arguments why exploration of the East improved the understanding of Hungary and of Hungary's past and drew a parallel between the Central Asian steppes and the Hungarian Great Plain. His primary goal was "the study of the related Turanian peoples and the establishment of contacts with them" and "a leadership role for Hungary, economically and scientifically, in the Turanian family of peop-

---

76 Farkas, "A turanizmus," pp. 62–64.
77 Kessler, "Turanism and Pan-Turanism," pp. 91–95.
78 See Pál Teleki, "Bevezető a Turán című folyóirathoz" [Introduction to the periodical called Turan], in Pál Teleki, *Válogatott politikai írások és beszédek* [Selected Writings and Speeches], ed., Balázs Ablonczy (Budapest: Osiris, 2000), pp. 9–13.

le."⁷⁹ The goals of the society were appreciated by the Hungarian government, but not to the degree expected by the founders. They received only two thousand crowns annually until 1914.

In spite of the distinguished membership and the great goals things did not progress in an orderly manner. There was never enough money. Among the bills presented to the society a number carry the marginal note scribbled by Paikert: "Paid from my pocket."⁸⁰ Personal antagonisms also appeared promptly. Teleki was initially on good terms with Paikert but soon the clouds appeared. On November 7, 1911, Paikert wrote, "To the apartment of Count Pál Teleki for a lengthy and detailed discussion. I told how I felt about his endless delays. The Turanian Society has to succeed with or without Teleki. If he is the president he must be with us all the way."⁸¹ In his recollections Paikert admitted that their relationship deteriorated, "I have always regretted that we could not stay together in public life, working together on the great problems of the day."⁸² Paikert resigned at the beginning of 1912 and the formerly enthusiastic comments in his diary stopped. Both stayed in the society but their relationship never again was as friendly and open as during the first few weeks and months. During one of his depressions Teleki wanted to resign from the presidency, but did not do so.⁸³ The affairs of the society did not progress well. According to the attendance lists, the series of lectures organized by the society in November 1911 and held in the building of the academy, rarely had more than twenty listeners. The outbreak of the war closed the first phase of the activities of the Turanian Society. The organization ceased to function and the periodical ceased to appear after the first few issues.

Teleki at that time was in his mid-thirties. His appearance had not changed much when compared to the picture of the young man who in 1904 went to fight for the Nagysomkút seat in parliament. The things that strike the person viewing the old picture are the foppish dress, the ears sticking out, the heavy eyebrows and the piercing grey eyes. When he laughed or frowned, his swarthy face became wrinkled and after the years these wrinkles remained. In contrast with his father who had a full head of hair until his old age, Pál Teleki was becoming bald at the end of

---

79 Ibid., p. 11.
80 Elnöki iratok [Presidential Documents], A Turáni Társaság iratai [Papers of the Turanian Society], cs. 1., t. 1, passim, P 1384, MNL OL.
81 Paikert Alajos évről évre szóló kis naplója (Day by day diary of Alajos Paikert], November 7, 1911, Oct. Hung., 1445/1, OSZKK.
82 Alajos Paikert, Chapter Ten, "The Turanian Society," in "Életem" [My Life], Alajos Paikert Papers, 1/13338, Magyar Mezőgazdasági Múzeum, Adattár [Archives, Hungarian Agricultural Museum].
83 Letter from Pál Teleki to Lajos Lóczy, London, March 3, 1911, Lóczy Papers, 806/15, MTM TtGy.

his twenties. He was short and had small bones. Although he was healthier than in his childhood it still happened that he was hospitalized. Because of his poor health he was exempt from military service.

In 1908 Teleki met Countess Johanna Bissingen-Nippenburg, the daughter of Count Rudolf Bissingen-Nippenburg, a retired lieutenant in the common army, and of Georgine Mocsonyi. The Bissingen family was an Austrian family of military nobility that had settled in Hungary. It had estates in the southern part of Hungary that are presently in Serbia and Romania. The estates were located in counties of Temes and Krassó- Szöreny and amounted to almost 2,900 acres.[84] The father died at age forty-eight and thus the widow had to raise and marry off their four daughters.[85] The oldest one, Countess Hanna was born 1889 and was ten years younger than Teleki. At the beginning of September 1908 Teleki modestly informed his master and his friends that "a few days ago I became engaged to Countess Hanna Bissingen."[86] The betrothal was held in Budapest in November 1908 in St. Stephen's Basilica. Teleki's witnesses were János Economo and Gyula Teleki. The marriage of Teleki and his nineteen-year-old bride was blessed by Tibor Boromissza, the bishop of Szatmár.[87] Numerous members of the Hungarian and Transylvanian aristocracy attended the wedding. They included Margit Bethlen, István Bethlen's wife whose mother, Lívia Mocsonyi, was Georgine Mocsonyi's sister.[88] Thus Pál Teleki and István Bethlen, whose mother, was a Teleki, also became related through marriage.

According to friends, the marriage was free of major storms. Countess Teleki did not manage money well and there were always shortages in the sums required to run the household. It was perhaps for this reason that there were tensions between Teleki's mother and his bride. The young woman participated in her mother-in-law's benevolences on the family estates and during the winters she also frequently assisted the needy of the area.[89] According to pictures taken at the time, Countess Teleki was attractive and appealing, albeit inclined towards corpulence. She was a faithful partner of her husband throughout their life together even

---

84 Lőrintei, ed, *Magyarország nagybirtokosai*, p. 20; Baross, *Magyarország földbirtokosai*, p. 382.
85 For the death, see *Szalon Újság* [News of the Salon], January 15, 1905, p. 5.
86 Letter from Pál Teleki to Jenő Cholnoky, Pribékfalva, September 12, 1908, Cholnoky-Teleki correspondence dossier, Cholnoky Papers, MFMA.
87 Marriage register extract for Pál János Ede Teleki and Johanna Maria Bissingen, in the register of St. Stephen Basilica, vol. H, page 74, no. 296, copy, November 25, 1908.
88 *Szalon Újság*, November 30, 1908, p. 3.
89 *Kővárvidék*, November 1, 1914, p. 3.

though she participated in her husband's public appearances as rarely as possible and instead engaged in following her own interests.

The marriage was blessed with two children. Mária, known in the family as Majcsi, was born in March 1910 and Géza on November 27, 1911. During the 1910s Teleki was frequently away from his children because of his travels and social obligations. Every summer, however, they were together at Pribékfalva. The grandfather was delighted to have a grandson with the same name. He had not known his own grandfather, nor did Pál Teleki know Ede Teleki. His pleasure was shortlived, however. Ever since the 1890s, Géza Teleki suffered from arthritic pains. He was over sixty, had increasing difficulties with walking and was frequently unwell. He was a regular visitor at various Hungarian and European watering places.[90] A few days before his seventieth birthday Géza Teleki was admitted to a clinic in Budapest for a minor surgical procedure. His heart could not tolerate the strain and on September 27, 1913, he died. Thus all the family estates and all the financial matters became Pál Teleki's responsibility.

Soldier and Politician during World War I

On June 28, 1914, Gavrilo Princip shot and killed Archduke Francis Ferdinand and his wife Countess Sophie Chotek in Sarajevo and one month later the Dual Monarchy declared war on Serbia. The mobilization orders pulled Pál Teleki away from his wife and two small children but also freed him from a very large number of domestic responsibilities.

He became a soldier in a very odd organization. The Royal Hungarian Volunteer Automobile Corps was established in 1909 in order to ease the severe transportation shortages of the Royal Hungarian Army (honvédség). Its members agreed to participate in manoeuvers during peacetimes on two or three occasions and to report immediately for duty with their own vehicle in case of a general mobilization. Teleki entered the organization as a volunteer lieutenant. The use of automobiles was one of the innovations of the new century that Teleki not only tolerated but liked. On boat trips he was usually sick and was sick later on airplanes as well. The first time we know of him having an automobile was in 1908. By purchasing an auto Teleki assumed a role in a peculiar organization of prewar Hungarian society, the association of automobile owners. The Royal Hungarian Automobile Club

---

90 Letter from Countess Géza Teleki to Gyula Wlassics, August 18, 1896, Gyula Wlassics Papers, box 8, t. 26, P 1445, MNL OL.

(MKAC) played a major role in automobile use in Hungary, in mechanical improvements and in the creation of an automobile subculture. In this Teleki assumed a significant role.

Teleki was one of the founders of the Royal Hungarian Volunteer Automobile Corps, composed of members of the Royal Hungarian Automobile Club, and he participated in the first parade of the association on the field of Rákos, near Budapest. From time to time the young count went on military exercises as well. He did this during the month when his father died and he was in Bohemia. He took part in another military exercise early in 1914. Until March 1912 he owned a Laurin-Klement automobile and next he bought a Fiat with which he entered the MKAC race to Constantinople. It was because of his love for the automobile that he accepted a position on the Board of Directors of the Arad Westinghouse Company, Inc., in 1908 and early in the 1910s he did the same for the Arad Hungarian Automobile Company (MARTA).[91] It was in his role as a director that he participated in one of the first taxi trips in Budapest. The first Budapest "green taxi" ride occurred on June 1, 1913. The driver was János Rossmann and the passenger was Count Pál Teleki.

He received his call-up notice in Pribékfalva on July 28, 1914, and immediately departed for Budapest. He said good-by to his friend, "We have an invitation for November by the Danish Geographical Society for a conference of general secretaries. Now, of course, who knows what will happen. God be with you."[92] On July 31 he left Budapest for Sarajevo where he was ordered to report.[93] He drove all the way through Croatia and Bosnia and arrived on August 2. The volunteers were assigned directly to the military command. Their duties were far removed from the dangers facing the regular infantrymen. They transported staff officers, carried food and packages and very occasionally picked up a wounded soldier. The lucky ones could drive General Oskar Potiorek, the commander of the army against Serbia. On August 30 the group was transferred to Doboj to be closer to the line of advance of the Sixth Austro-Hungarian Army. The jolly volunteers ate at the table of the county chief, had little to do and reviled the leadership of the army, including their Commander, Potiorek.[94] One eyewitness noted that the activities of the group

---

91 *Magyar Automobil Újság* [Hungarian Automobile News], December 12, 1908, p. 4; and *Magyarország tiszti cím és névtára* [The Register of the Name and Title of the Hungarian Officers] 32, (1913): 692.
92 Letter from Pál Teleki to Jenő Cholnoky, Pribékfalva, July 28, 1914, Cholnoky-Teleki separate dossier, Cholnoky Papers, MFMA.
93 Szüllő Géza naplójegyzetei a szerbiai hadjáratról (1914) [Géza Szüllő's diary entries for the Serbian campaign (1914)], fol. 24, Quart. Hung. 2596, OSZSZK.
94 Néhai dr. Thallóczy Lajos osztályfőnök hátrahagyott irata stenografált részének átírása [Transcript of the papers of the late Head of Division, Dr. Lajos Thallóczy], September 5, 1914, fols. 2185-2187, Fol.

were like a "churchyard party" and that, "these automobilists have a damned good time."⁹⁵ Teleki experienced the apathy that followed the initial enthusiasm when, at the end of September, they had to move again. He undoubtedly was much relieved when he was ordered to join the General Staff in order to prepare maps. At least he had something useful to do.

Initially the Austro-Hungarian Army was unable to overcome the valiant resistance of the Serbs. In the battle along the Drina and in the fight around Sabac, the Austro-Hungarian forces piled failure upon failure because of poor preparation and a bad war plan. When during the fall it became possible to move the battles onto Serb territory, the forces of the Monarchy were unable to make their successes permanent. The recently captured Belgrade had to be evacuated and in December they had to withdraw beyond the Drina. The Fifth and Sixth Army lost 200,000 dead and wounded.⁹⁶ All this did not seem to affect the automobilists to any great degree. For example, Teleki's wife could visit him at the front. It was typical of the special situation of that formation that the first time Teleki heard artillery Fire was three months after he was called up and only because he was visiting the front. In November 1914 the army command and Teleki moved to a place in occupied Serbia. "We are in a foggy, miserable place," he wrote home, "It ruins everything, equipment, people and spirit."⁹⁷ In December 1914 Teleki was promoted and became a first lieutenant in the Irregular Volunteer Service.⁹⁸ During these months he was mostly bored but read a great deal, mostly political and literary works. He corresponded with foreign geographers, including Americans. He made a variety of prognostications about when and how the killing would come to an end.

In March 1915 he assumed that that the end would come in a year and a half, but a few months later he predicted that the end would come in six months.⁹⁹ In September 1915 he was even more optimistic and saw the beginning of the negoti-

---

Hung. 1677/3, no. 2321, OSZSZK. It was Iván Bertenyi, Jr. who drew my attention to this document, I am grateful for his help.
95 Lajos Thallóczy, Tagesrelazion wahrend einer Dienstreise, fol. 117, Fol. Hung. 1678, OSZSZK.
96 Ferenc Julier, *1914–1918 A világháború magyar szemmel* [1914–1918, The World War through Hungarian Eyes] (Budapest: Magyar Szemle Társaság, 1933), pp. 29–34, and 76–80.
97 Army post card from Pál Teleki to Jenő Cholnoky, n.p., November 28, 1914, Cholnoky-Teleki separate dossier, Cholnoky Papers, MFMA; and Letter from Pál Teleki to Jenő Cholnoky, s.l., October 22, 1914, Scientific and Official Correspondence, box 4, Cholnoky Papers, MFMA.
98 Budapesti Közlöny, December 15, 1914, p. 1.
99 Army post card from Pál Teleki to Jenő Cholnoky, n.p., March 18, 1915, Teleki-Cholnoky separate dossier, Cholnoky Papers, MFMA; and Letter from Pál Teleki to Jenő Cholnoky, n.p., May 14, 11915], Scientific and Official Correspondence, Cholnoky Papers, box 4, MFMA.

ations occurring by Christmas.¹⁰⁰ When this prophecy also proved wrong, he still deluded himself at the beginning of 1916 and wrote, "It is my impression that it will be over by winter."¹⁰¹ It took a long time before he realized that this war was very different from any preceding ones. He had many more furloughs than the average soldier and, later on could be absent from the front for three to four months. He found military service increasingly destructive to the spirit and turned his attention more and more to the political consequences of the hopefully victorious conclusion of the war. Yet, for the time being he could not leave the service.

When Italy entered the war in May 1915, Teleki was transferred to the southwestern front as a command officer. He was pleased to finally receive a responsible task and he was placed in charge of a railway station. The station of Stanjel was an important junction in assuring the movement of supplies to the southwestern front and thus became the target of an Italian air raid. Teleki was instrumental in controlling the situation and in averting a panic. In recognition of the, "bravery demonstrated in the face of the enemy" the monarch was pleased to express "the highest complimentary recognition."¹⁰² The recognition did not help the apathy that seemed to have become permanent and he could not even joke about how long his hair had become. The inactivity drove him to despair. "I must say that I have enough of the war, this inactive, senseless life is for animals only."¹⁰³

Starting with the autumn of 1915 he spent increasingly more time at home and even though he had to go back to the front, he found a way to create a home-like environment for himself. He celebrated Christmas 1915 in Marburg [Maribor] with his family and children. In 1916 he returned to his old formation but after a six-week furlough in March he was permanently assigned to the rear areas. The Automobile Corps was formally disbanded during the spring of 1916. The officers were assigned to regular units and those older than forty-four years and the volunteers were assigned command posts. This would have been Teleki's assignment but by this time he had received an important government task. He was relieved from

---

100 Army post card from Pál Teleki to Jenő Cholnoky, n.p., September 1, 1915, Teleki-Cholnoky separate dossier, Cholnoky Papers, MFMA.
101 Army post card from Pál Teleki to Zoltán Felvinczi Takáts, n.p., January 28, 1916, Felvinczi Takáts Papers, A 2669, Hopp Ferenc Kelet-Ázsiai Művészeti Múzeum Adattára [Archives of the Ferenc Hopp East-Asian Art Museum].
102 Fodor, *Teleki Pál*, p. 35; *Kővárvidék*, September 19, 1915, p. 2.
103 Postcard from Pál Teleki to Jenő Cholnoky. n.p. (Südwestfront), September 1, 1915, Teleki-Cholnoky separate dossier, Cholnoky Papers, MFMA.

front duty for an extended period of time and was formally discharged in the spring of 1917.[104]

Already during his long furlough in 1915 the idea came increasingly to his mind that his experiences at the front and in the Balkans could be used to serve the ideas that were his guiding lights prior to the war. He continued to be preoccupied with the Hungarian advances into the Balkans. He believed that the role assumed by Hungary in the war increased the weight of the Hungarians within the Monarchy. In his opinion the Germans considered the Hungarians to be the better soldiers and therefore better associates. According to Teleki, the nationalities hated Austria because its impotence had become manifest.[105]

Personal antagonisms and lack of funds kept the Geographical Society from creating an administrative framework for the Hungarian advances into the Balkans. The government of István Tisza did believe, however, that a revived Turanian Society might have a role here. Support of the organization, revived under the name of Hungarian Eastern Cultural Center, was also viewed as a foreign policy gesture toward the allied Bulgaria and Turkey. The Ministry of Religion and Public Instruction provided substantial sums to the organization and charged it with broad responsibilities.[106] The Prime Minster's Office arranged for space for them in the Parliament building. On May 2, 1916, in the great hall of the academy, the Turanian Society—Hungarian Eastern Cultural Center was formally inaugurated. Béla Széchenyi, the traveler and son of the great nineteenth century reformer István Széchenyi, became the president. Seven associated presidents and a large number of vice presidents were also chosen. Expert groups were established within the organization including periodical and book publishing, land and natural sciences, education and instruction, linguistics and ethnography, history, arts, propaganda, and popular education. A working committee of three members was entrusted with the coordination of this huge organization and its members were Miklós Bánffy, Pál Teleki and the writer Gyula Pekár. Nominally, Teleki was just one of the vice presidents but by virtue of his experience and involvement he exerted considerably greater influence than the others.

---

104 llosvay Lajos VKM-államtitkár átirata a Magyar Keleti Kultúrközpontnak [Memo from secretary of state in the Ministry of Culture and Education, Lajos llosvay, to the Hungarian Eastern Cultural Center], Budapest, April 18, 1917, Papers of the Turanian Society, 1 cs., 1. t., 1917-1-637, P 1384, MNL OL.
105 Army post card from Pál Teleki to Jenő Cholnoky, Sudwestfront, September 1, 1915, Cholnoky-Teleki separate dossier, Cholnoky Papers, MFMA.
106 Farkas, "A turanizmus," pp. 69–74.

Subsequent to its revival during the war, the cultural center developed a number of additional goals for itself. These included the nurturing of the Bulgarian and Turkish relations, the reception and education of Bosnian, Bulgarian and Turkish students in Hungary, propaganda among the Muslim- or Turanian-speaking prisoners of war, preparation for economic expansion and establishing contact with "Turanian" political leaders who had escaped from Russia.[107] Teleki, as usual, was enthusiastic at the beginning of the enterprise. He wrote, "Freed from the shackles of penury and excessive idealism, things are progressing very nicely."[108] At the beginning of his involvement, Teleki became interested in the possibility of organizing an expedition to the Serb-Albanian area. He strongly supported the idea and did everything in his future positions to obtain money and permission for such expeditions. Very soon Bosnian, Bulgarian and Turkish students arrived to enroll in Hungarian schools and 100–150 Turkish, 30–40 Bosnian and about 25 Albanian students were accepted in various Hungarian schools of higher education. At the beginning of 1918 students came even from the newly established Crimean Tatar Republic.[109] Teleki visited all the schools designated for these students and organized their reception and placement.

The results proved disappointing to the originators of the plan. The students could not adapt to the Hungarian way of life, considered the discipline to be excessive, e.g. a prohibition to enter a cafe, and felt the pocket money they received to be insufficient.[110] Teleki made several trips to the Balkans and to Istanbul [Constantinople] in connection with students and with other, no longer clear "Turanian cooperation" matters.

In addition to the practical and educational issues, Teleki's primary goal was the creation of a scientific basis for Hungarian research and exploration in the East and in the Balkans. Hungarian botanists, ornithologists and geographers studied the Balkans. Some of these endeavors were published by the Hungarian Academy of Science after the war in a stout volume for the scientific community.[111] The first Hungarian cultural institute established abroad was in Constantinople. It was

---

107 Kessler, "Turanism and Pan-Turanism," p. 145.
108 Letter from Pál Teleki to Lajos Lóczy, Budapest, May 8, 1916, Cholnoky-Horusitzky debate dossier, Lóczy, Sr. Papers, MBFSZ, TtGy.
109 Farkas, "A turanizmus," pp. 71-74; and Kessler, "Turanism and Pan-Turanism," p. 147.
110 Letter from University Professor Vilmos Pröhle to the Hungarian Eastern Cultural Center, January 11, 1917, Turanian Association, cs. 1, P. 1384, MNL OL.
111 Ernő Csiki and Pál Teleki, eds., *A Magyar Tudományos Akadémia Balkán-kutatásának tudományos eredményei* [The Scientific Results of the Balkan Studies and Research of the Hungarian Academy of Science] (Budapest: MTA, 1926–1940), 3 vols.

independent of the Turanian Society but Teleki and his associates soon realized the importance of the institute and took it under their wings. "In Teleki we have a certain and strong supporter" wrote Antal Hekler in the spring of 1918. Hekler was an art historian who was the director of the institute.[112] In Budapest Teleki was very busily engaged in centralizing the efforts of the various organizations collecting books and periodicals dealing with Eastern subjects. These organizations were the Budapest Municipal Library, the Library of the Eastern Commercial Academy, and the Hungarian Academy of Science and Teleki wished to use their materials to establish a large, united Eastern collection.

In the creation of a scientific basis a major role was certainly played by the revived *Turán* that was republished early in 1917 under Teleki's editorship. The periodical was set carefully on good paper and, occasionally, illustrated with pictures and drawings. In ten issues per year it popularized the concepts of the Hungarian Eastern Cultural Center. The periodical carefully surveyed the results of Eastern exploration and of Turanism studies published in the international scientific press and it did not limit its attentions to the Central Powers. The works of British, French and American authors were frequently reported at great length and with very favorable comments. The ongoing war intruded into the articles only to the extent that in the 1918 issues border problems and the geographical determination of certain areas suggested the direction of the Hungarian preparations for peace. Teleki wrote a number of reviews and two major articles for the *Turán*.

In his article entitled "Táj es faj" [Region and race] Teleki presented to the public his thoughts that he had summarized at the May 1916 general meeting of the Turanian Society. It was supplied with copious footnotes which embraced the results of sociology, biology, historical studies, esthetics and ethnography.[113] He defended Turanism against the critical comments of the Turkologist, Gyula Germanus which were published in 1916. Teleki claimed that for him Turanism did not have a racial message but a message of geographical coherence. In his thesis he distanced himself from anthropographic geographical determinism, the milieu theory of Hippolyte Taine, Arthur de Gobineau, and from some of Ratzel's followers. It was obvious for him that race, including the Turanian, was the "determinant factor in creating a region." In this way Turan was a regional concept and not

---

112 Letter of Antal Hekler to an unknown recipient, Constantinople, May 12, 1918, Hekler Antal, "Személyes emlékek" [Personal recollections], MDK-C-I-76/40, ELKH BTK Művészettörténeti Kutatóintézet, Adattár [Center for Humanities, Art History Research Institute, Archives].

113 Count Pál Teleki, "Táj es faj" [Region and Race], *Turán*, no.l (1917). Republished in Teleki, *Válogatott politikai írások*, ed. Ablonczy, pp. 14–26.

linguistic, anthropologic, or ethnographic. The interrelated steppes of central Asia produced a determinant pressure on the people who lived there. These nomads entering the furnace of the steppe became "strengthened and amalgamated" and then "widely distributed what they had learned."[114]

Gyula Germanus and the essayists belonging to the *Nyugat* [West] circle, particularly Zoltán Szász, were not convinced by these arguments. Szász considered Turanism an "anticuitural racial seclusion" while Germanus considered the entire ideology completely ahistorical.[115] These criticisms induced Teleki to produce a forty page paper with more than two hundred footnotes to refute the critics of Turanism. In the essay entitled "A Turán földrajzi fogalom" [Turan is a geographic concept] argued against the dilettantism that has overtaken Hungarian protohistory research and used many arguments to prove that Turanism was an old and established geographical concept.[116] It was the region that forced its inhabitants to move from time to time to lead their animals to new pastures from land that had become a desert and sometimes just to wage war against their neighbors. In his definition of a geographic area he was much more careful and viewed the Turan as a "wandering" region, open from many sides and extending from the Amu Darya northward and to the east of the Caspian and Black Seas.[117] His views, while not free of some exaggerations and reminiscent of a personal diary, were generally of a moderate tone and tried to offer some compromises. He tried to maintain the scientific legitimacy of the concept and to trim off the historical excesses while at the same time repudiating Germanus's attack that he considered dangerous from a scientific point of view, particularly since its first part appeared on the pages of the Tisza party's *Magyar Figyelő*.

These reasonable views were not universally accepted by the Society. On the pages of *Turán* and in other publications articles appeared from the pen of authors belonging to the Turanian group that predicted a Hungarian great power position. They were unrealistic and scientifically insupportable.

Romania's entry into World War I and the invasion of Transylvania by Romanian troops in August 1916 moved Teleki to revise his plans for public service. The

---

114 Teleki, *Válogatott politikai írások*, ed. Ablonczy, pp. 21, and 25–26.
115 Szász wrote several newspaper articles on this subject but for the most important one see Zoltán Szász, "Turanizmus," *Nyugat*, no. 16 (1916): 267–275; and Gyula Germanus, "Turanizmus és történelem [Turanism and history], *Történeti Szemle* (1917): 380–384; and Germanus, "Turán I–II," *Magyar Figyelő* [Hungarian Observer], March 1916, pp. 405–420, and April 1916, pp. 223–37.
116 Pál Teleki, "A Turán földrajzi fogalom" [The Turanian geographical concept], *Turán*, nos. 1-2 (1918): 46, and 49–51.
117 Ibid., pp. 55–74, passim.

appearance of Romanian troops in Southern Transylvania and their initial military successes there made him report for immediate service. He was assigned to a military command in Nagyszeben [Sibiu] in September.[118] He was no longer satisfied with such an assignment and believed that the time had come for him to return to the political life of the country and again become a Member of Parliament. It happened very conveniently that the representative of Keszthely died and the thirty-seven-year-old Teleki decided to run for the vacant mandate/seat. The parties had voluntarily agreed to a "Treuga Dei" [truce] during the war and the intent of preserving the distribution of mandates, added to a reluctance to engage in electoral battles, meant that once again Teleki ran without any opposition. In his speech outlining his program, in October, he spoke about local problems, gently criticizing the government and being somewhat harsher in his criticism of the military leadership for wasting Hungarian blood. Of the major domestic political issues the only one he addressed was the nationality problem. He demanded a strong and purposeful national policy because, "Our enemies view permissiveness as weakness and therefore we must demonstrate strength in all areas."[119] Without an opponent and without any incident he was elected to represent the Keszthely district.[120] After an interval of six years he was back in national politics.

He immediately found a niche for himself that drew attention to him. It was related to the conduct of the war and he had no competition on this subject. He returned to parliament as an expert in social, health and welfare matters and as an expert politician in matters of racial hygiene. His attraction to the biologic approach to social problems was not new and articles written for the *Huszadik Század* clearly show his youthful orientation in this direction.

During the second half of the nineteenth century a number of thinkers were pondering the relationships between a firm conviction in technical progress and in the advancement of society and the decline in religious life. Many of them concluded that the Darwinian theory of the origin of the species and of natural selection could be used for the improvement of society. The hitherto omnipotent theory of liberalism could be bypassed and had to be bypassed in the interest of higher social goals. It would be possible to select individuals who were valuable for promoting the progress of society and to endeavor to increase their numbers while at the same

---

118 Letter from Pál Teleki to Jenő Cholnoky, Budapest, September 9, 1916, Letters 1916, Cholnoky Papers, box 1, MFMA; Letter from Pál Teleki to Lajos Thallóczy, Budapest, October 6, 1916, fond XI/983, OSZKK.
119 *Keszthelyi Hírlap* [Keszthely News], October 22, 1916, pp. 1–2.
120 Ibid., October 29, 1916, p. 1.

time repressing the proliferation of individuals worthless for society, such as those with criminal tendencies, alcoholics or the mentally and/or physically disabled.[121] In the Anglo-Saxon area the eugenic endeavors were linked to the name of Francis Galton, the British anthropologist who was committed to breeding a healthier human race. In the Germanic area the term "racial hygiene" became synonymous with eugenics and became the ideology of a number of groups. Utopians, neoconservatives, socialists, physicians and public health experts were committed to the concept of preventing society's "degeneration," maintaining its effective functioning and making its activities rationally predictable. Racial hygiene does not necessarily lead to national socialism although some of its supporters voiced anti-Semitic views. The movement cannot be regarded as the immediate precursor of national socialism even though many of its followers ultimately landed there.[122]

The father of the German racial hygiene movement and its most creative figure was Alfred Ploetz (1860–1940) who was initially a socialist and who tried to combine the principles of socialism and Darwinism. Between the two wars he came very close to the Nazis. His ideas were colored by utopianism and he participated in the United States in the establishment of a settlement, "Ikaria," based on racial hygienic principles. After the failure of the enterprise, he attempted a similar development in one of the suburbs of Berlin. It was his book *Die Tüchtigkeit der Rasse und der Schutz der Schwachen* published in 1895, that made "racial hygiene" a household word. Ploetz fought against the spread of alcoholism and sexually transmitted diseases and urged the development of governmental population policies. Together with his followers, he established the periodical *Archiv für Rassen- und Gesellschaftsbiologie* in 1904, the first few issues of which were welcomed enthusiastically by Teleki. It was Ploetz who was the force behind the establishment of the German Racial Hygiene Association, in 1905.[123]

Teleki met Ploetz and, in spite of the twenty year difference in their age, a friendship, or at least a good scientific relationship, developed between the two men.[124] As early as 1911, Teleki attended a racial hygiene meeting in Dresden.[125] He saw it

---

121 Peter Weingart, Jurgen Kroll, and Kurt Bayertz, *Rasse, Blut und Gene—Geschichte der Eugenik und Rassenhygiene in Deutschland* (Frankfurt am Main: Suhrkamp, 1988), pp. 121–125.
122 Paul Weindling, *Health, Race and German Politics between National Unification and Nazism, 1870–1945* (Cambridge: Cambridge University Press, 1989), pp. 6–7.
123 About Ploetz, see ibid., pp. 64–67, and Weingart, Kroll, and Bayertz, Rasse, Blut und Gene, pp. 189–205.
124 Weindling, *Health and Race*, p. 150.
125 Postcard from Pál Teleki to Jenő Cholnoky, Pribékfalva, August 16, 1911, Letters, July-December 1911, Cholnoky Papers, box 4, MFMA.

as a reward for his early activities when István Apáthy, professor at the University of Kolozsvár, offered him the presidency of a new organization, the Egyesületközi Magyar Fajegészségügyi Bizottság [Joint Hungarian Racial Hygiene Committee) that was being established at the beginning of 1914. He was delighted and wrote, "I have been interested in eugenics for many years, of course as a modest amateur" and "my active endeavors were largely limited to geography, I have remained an enthusiastic supporter of these endeavors."[126] Teleki participated in the first meeting of the committee at the end of January 1914. At this meeting the Hungarian Social Science Association, the Medical Society, and the National Public Health Association were also represented. All these activities, however, were brought to a halt by the war. The organization languished during the first year of the war but the matter was kept alive by Teleki. He wished to have some printed propaganda material to convince the population and to ward off the dangers, thinking primarily about the fight against syphilis.[127] During his brief furloughs he endeavored to keep the activities of the committee alive.

When Teleki finally returned from the front he became increasingly interested in the activities of the committee. His guide in these activities was Géza Hoffmann who had been the Monarchy's consul in Chicago around 1910 and then was moved to Berlin where he came in contact with the German racial hygiene movement. He published articles in the *Archiv* and published a book in Munich about the eugenic movement in the United States in which he described "negative" eugenic proposals such as sterilization, etc. These were rejected by the majority in the German movement and were called a return to barbarism.[128] Hoffmann took a leading role in the Hungarian movement as well. It was with his participation that in November 1917, the committee was expanded to become the Population Policy and Racial Hygiene Association with István Apáthy as vice president and Pál Teleki as president. The association published a periodical with the title of *Nemzetvédelem* [National Defense] that had as its primary purpose the fight against sexually transmitted diseases. The *Nemzetvédelem* and the early forum of the Hungarian radical and anti-Semitic right wing, *A Cél* [The Target] overlapped in some areas both as far as

---

126 Letter from István Apáthy to Pál Teleki, Kolozsvár, January 14, 1914, and Pál Teleki's answer to Apáthy, Budapest, January 16, 1914, Apáthy István Levelezése [Correspondence of István Apáthy], A Magyar Társadalomtudományi Egyesület iratai [Papers of the Hungarian Social Science Association], Quart. Hung. 2454/11, OSZKK.
127 Letter from Pál Teleki to István Apáthy, n.p. (Military Post Office no. 149), August 30, 1915, Papers of István Apáthy, fols. 71-72, *Quart. Hung.* 2453, OSZKK.
128 Géza von Hoffmann, *Die Rassenhygiene in den Vereinigten Staaten von* Nordamerika (Munich: J. FOL. Lehmann, 1913); and Weingart, Kroll, and Bayertz, *Rasse, Blut und Gene*, pp. 286–288.

authors and subjects were concerned. The Stefania Society was founded by József Madzsar for the protection of pregnant women. He was a belligerent atheist, free mason, later communist and one of the leaders of the eugenics movement in Hungary. A number of the young physicians and experts who took part in the movement later surfaced in the health organization of the short-lived Hungarian Soviet Republic of 1919.[129]

In his first major parliamentary speech, Teleki embraced the goals of the association. Without mentioning the name of the recently formed group he described its program and drew attention to the issues considered to be important by the association, decrease of the birthrate, tuberculosis, sexually transmitted diseases and alcoholism. He indicated that an extremely important matter was the family assistance for those where the breadwinner was in the military. In the matter of government grants of land to those who were discharged he emphasized the importance of assessing the health of the family receiving the land and determining the number of children. He considered the regulation of emigration and immigration to be important and insisted that only "racially important people" could be or should be allowed to be repatriated to Hungary from the United States. In the conclusion he mentioned the activities of the "population policy center," namely the association, and the parliament's and the government's attention to the problems he listed. He stated that these groups had to find answers to these problems promptly because in case of a peace treaty and the ensuing demobilization catastrophic public health problems might arise, particularly in the area of sexually transmitted diseases.

It was perhaps due to this speech or to his involvement with the Population Policy Association that, when Prime Minister István Tisza resigned on May 24, 1917, the new head of government, Móric Esterházy, who was even younger than Teleki, asked him to assume an important position. Their acquaintance and friendship dated back to the 1890s and Esterházy also demonstrated a strong interest in social policies. It is therefore not surprising that in June 1917 he appointed Pál Teleki to the presidency of the Országos Hadigondozó Hivatal [National Office for Veteran Affairs].[130]

Teleki's interests in social policies were based on the activities of his father. He was acutely aware of the immense suffering caused by the war and tried to do whatever he could by his own efforts. In October 1914 he opened a fifty bed hospi-

---

129 Mária M. Kovács, *Liberalizmus, radikalizmus, antiszemitiztnus* [Liberalism, Radicalism, and Anti-Semitism] (Budapest: Helikon, 2001), pp. 60–66.
130 Minisztertanácsi jegyzőkönyvek [Minutes of the Council of Ministers], June 20, 1917, no. 6 on the agenda, box 108, K 27, MNL OL.

tal in the Pribékfalva chateau at his own expense and enlarged it with twenty-five additional beds in December. In Fehérszék he set up another auxiliary hospital with eighteen beds. He gave thousand crowns to to families where the head of the family was called to military service, and at Christmas distributed firewood and potatoes to the needy in addition to the usual clothing and shoes.[131] As time went on he realized that individual efforts were insufficient and that significant governmental involvement was required.

The Országos Hadigondozó was established in March 1917.[132] Teleki considered the implementation of the principles of the Racial Health Issues Association in the management of the disabled. In his first letter addressed to the organizations caring for the disabled, to the employment agencies, and to other organizations, he admonished the recipients that racial health should take precedence in their involvement with the disabled. They should try to convince the disabled to move away from the cities and not flood the advanced training programs. They should extol the advantages of rural life and should emphasize that agriculture provided a better livelihood than industry. The president directed that the multi-children families should be given high praise, that the "intimacy of family life" should be increased, and that the disabled should be encouraged to overcome their disabilities in establishing families. In contrast to popular belief battlefield injuries were not hereditary and marriage should be opposed only if there were illnesses that would endanger children, such as tuberculosis and mental illness. Consequently emphasis had to be placed on enlightenment and education.[133]

The office could limit its activities to matters of racial hygiene. Offices were opened throughout the country, cooperating with chambers of commerce and industry. In twenty different locations employment agencies for the disabled were established, schools for the disabled were set up and workshops for prostheses were opened. He created a factory organization and established a green living area around it. He also opened sanatoria for pulmonary diseases. The office became engaged in the problems of war widows and war orphans and was in charge of assistance to the families of the men on active duty.[134] Teleki did not have an easy task in managing

---

131 *Kővárvidék*, October 11, 1914, p. 2; *Kővárvidék*, December 13, 1914, p. 1; and *Kővárvidék*, October 31, 1915, pp. 1–2.
132 Pál Petri, *A magyar hadigondozás történetének vázlata* [Sketch of the History of the Hungarian Veteran Affairs] (Budapest: Országos Hadigondozó Hivatal, 1917), p. 7.
133 "Körlevél az eugenikáról" [Circular letter on eugenics], *Szociálpolitikai Szemle* [Social Policy Review], no. 6 (1917): 169–171.
134 Petri, *A magyar hadigondozás*, pp. 26–40; Count Pál Teleki, *Szociálpolitika és hadigondozás* [Social Policies and Veteran Affairs] (Budapest: Országos Hadigondozó Hivatal, 1918), pp. 10–21; and Antal

the organization. His practices, that he referred to as "individual handling," consisted of tailoring the care to the needs of the individual disabled. This approach had to be defended on the floor of the Lower House. In general, however, the important representatives of political life were satisfied with Teleki's performance. When there was a government crisis in the spring of 1918 and Esterházy resigned, József Szterényi was trying to form a government and had destined the Ministry of the Interior for Teleki.[135] Finally, Sándor Wekerle's government remained and Teleki continued his work as head of the Office for Veteran Affairs.

He had to continue his work in the Geographical Society as well and, much against his wishes, he was again elected secretary general.[136] His relationship with Lóczy improved and 1917 Teleki could give his acceptance speech at the academy and take his seat with the learned members of that body. The acceptance speech, much enlarged, was published during the same year in book form.[137] In a letter written to his friend at the beginning of 1916 he indicated the direction his interest was turning to, "Studying the history of the development of geographical feelings, I see that it is closely associated with the history of the concept of region."[138]

He began his work sometimes during the second half of 1915, while still periodically at the front. In his great essay on the history of science he endeavored to show how the perception of region in geographical science and the realization of the true subject of geography changed from ancient times to the twentieth century. The logical review of his subject and amount of material used for the essay are impressive and the impression is lessened only by the occasional clumsiness of expression. Subjecting all significant geographical trends to criticism, he formulated the foundations of his own concept of the region. According to him, man becomes "a factor in the [geographical] genesis of the region" through socialization and his activity can only be understood and appreciated by accepting this theory. In order to be able to analyze the complex relationship between man and space, geography

---

Papp, *Gróf Teleki Pál országgyűlési beszédei* [The Parliamentary Speeches of Count Pál Teleki] (Budapest: Studium, 1944), vol. 1, pp. 25–41.
135 József Szterényi, *Régmúlt idők emlékei* [Memories of Times Long past] (Budapest: Pesti Könyvnyomda, 1925), p. 95.
136 Minutes of the general meeting of April 26, 1917, no. 26, 1917, MFT IL.
137 Pál Teleki, *A földrajzi gondolat története* [The History of Geographical Thought] (Budapest: Kossuth, 1996).
138 Letter from Pál Teleki to Zoltán Felvinczi Takáts, n.p. (Military Post Office no. 149, Südwestfront), January 10, 1916, Felvinczi Takáts Papers, A 22662, Archives of the Ferenc Hopp East-Asian Art Museum.

had to change and become multi-layered. Simple physical geography was no longer sufficient and geography had to focus on the region as an organic unit of life.[139]

In his analysis the historical elements were given a large role but the bases of geography assumed a quasi-philosophical character in his thinking. The position he assigned to geography was located at the juncture of history, the social sciences, (e.g. psychology and sociology) and the natural sciences.[140] The all encompassing definition of his activities was the "synthetic geography" and that "this science had an epistemologically independent subject, having an organic unity of existence and a role in the various areas of the Earth's surface." This subject was complex and hence could not be studied with the tools used in the other natural sciences. If somebody wished to approach geography in that way it was no longer the study of an entire area, but, at best, the determination of a detail that could no longer claim to represent all of geography.[141]

A later reviewer considered Teleki's work to be of seminal importance in Hungarian geography where theoretical works were rare. According to the eminent geographer Tibor Mendöl, Teleki was at that time and for a long time thereafter, "the most literate Hungarian geographer and most eminent in international science as well." Speaking of his book he stated that its appearance was, "a great event. It set the direction for the future formation of Hungarian geographical perspectives. Its importance and necessity can be appreciated only if we understand the intellectual chaos that was predominant in Hungarian geography at the time, as far as basic problems were concerned."[142]

The historic upheavals, however, resulted in Teleki having very little opportunity in the forthcoming period to think about his geographical theories. Hungary had lost the war.

---

139 Zoltán Hajdú, "Teleki Pál tájelméleti munkássága" [The work of Pál Teleki on landscape theory], *Földrajzi Közlemények*, nos. 1–2 (2001): 56.
140 Teleki, *A földrajzi gondolat története*, pp. 153–154.
141 Ibid., pp. 146–147.
142 For material for the proposed book on the Eötvös College, see Tibor Mendöl, "Teleki Pál, a földrajztudós" [Pál Teleki, the geographer-scholar], fol. 4, Ms. 5982/118, MTAKK.

In The Revolution, The Counterrevolution, And In The Government (1918–1921)

The four years of war took their toll on the Monarchy but the empire, considered by many to be dilapidated, withstood the blows for a surprisingly long time. It survived the death of Francis Joseph, it survived the tsarist empire and it successfully repulsed the attacks of its former allies, Romania and Italy. The end result, however, could not be delayed for long.

Seeing a defeat and the collapse of the Central Powers on the horizon, King Charles IV entrusted Count Mihály Károlyi on October 31, 1918, with the formation of a new government. It was on the same day that István Tisza, the former prime minister, a conservative statesman and the emblematic figure of the regime was murdered in his home by armed men. At this time Budapest was permeated by a revolutionary spirit. The Károlyi government declared itself to be a "government of the people," and asked that Károlyi be relieved from the oath he took to the Monarch and took a new oath to the National Council, the ad hoc central organ of the revolution. The Social Democrats, Bourgeois Radicals and the Károlyi Party Independentists, had as their goal the realization of a democratic Hungary. The nationalities, their emigre leaders and the heads of the surrounding small countries were not satisfied with this solution. In Budapest on November 16 the republic was declared and on January 11, 1919, Mihály Károlyi became its president. Even though Károlyi negotiated a military convention in Belgrade with the commander of the French Balkan forces, on November 13, 1918, Romanian, Czech, and Serb troops invaded Hungary with covert French assistance. Romanian troops occupied Kolozsvár [Cluj in Romanian] on December 24 and Czech legionnaires occupied Pozsony on January 1, 1919. There was a flood of refugees from the occupied territories entering the areas still under Hungarian control. The government tried to salvage the tragic domestic and foreign policy situation. It gave autonomy to the Ruthenians, the Slovaks and the Germans. The minister of nationalities without portfolio, Oszkár Jászi, tried unsuccessfully to convince the Romanians to remain within their country. The new leadership announced land reform and Károlyi started the process on his own estate. A new election law was promulgated that guaranteed all residents the secret ballot and extended the franchise to women as well. Elections were planned for April 1919. These measures were accompanied by social policy reforms which, however, were hampered by the rapidly increasing inflation.

In foreign policies the new system relied entirely on the goodwill of the Entente and made numerous attempts, through semi-official channels, to make contact with French, Italian and British decision-makers and with the leaders of the surrounding countries. In these endeavors the Károlyi government initially enjoyed the support of the entire Hungarian political elite. As the months went by, it became increasingly apparent that the Wilsonian principles were violated by the occupation of Hungarian territories and by the harsh treatment of the Hungarian population in those areas. More and more eminent politicians, like Gyula Andrássy, István Bethlen and the right wing of the Independentist, turned against the government. Similar moves were made by some officers who were now becoming acquainted with public life, e.g. Miklós Kozma and Gyula Gömbös. The defensive activities of the democratic government were largely negated by its general antiwar sentiments and the irresponsible and clumsy anti-armed forces statements made by some its members. In the mean time it became increasingly plain in Paris which parts of Hungary would be taken away from the country.[1]

The Entente policies pulled the rug out from under Mihály Károlyi and in a matter of months his massive base crumbled. Budapest public opinion fell increasingly under the influence of the Communists sent from Moscow. Lieutenant Colonel Fernand Vix, the French head of the Allied Military Mission in Budapest, presented an Entente demand on March 20, 1919, to the government in Budapest that declared that Transylvania had been attached by the Romanians and Hungary had to give up additional territories in eastern Hungary. Károlyi rejected the demands and resigned. This made it possible for the Communists and the left wing of the Social Democrats to create a government on March 21, 1919. This was the Soviet Republic, the first implementation of a communist experiment in central Europe. It lasted for 133 days.

---

[1] Ignác Romsics, *Hungary in the Twentieth Century* (Budapest: Osiris, 1999), pp. 89–99.

In The Revolution, The Counterrevolution, And In The Government (1918–1921)

The Counterrevolutionary

Toward the end of November 1918 Pál Teleki became ill with the Spanish flu that was sweeping across Europe. It was during the days of his illness that he devised the idea of a new ethnographic map that would differ from all previous ones and would indicate not only the ethnic nature of the population but population density as well. In order to accomplish this, he left the mountains with very few inhabitants and mostly belonging to a minority, in white on the map and showed the nearby large masses of people as residents of the neighboring valleys. The central portion of Hungary became the standard and it was determined that one square millimeter should represent one hundred inhabitants. The map was prepared by Teleki with the assistance of Baron Ferenc Nopcsa, the Albania explorer and paleontologist. The map was known as the "carte rouge" because the Hungarian population was depicted in red and thus there was a large red area in the central portion of the map. The clearly significant Hungarian majority in the cities contrasted sharply with the multicolored or white areas of the peripheral areas. The idea and the technique were not really new. The technique was familiar to the international cartographic literature and Emmanuel de Martonne, the Transylvania expert of the French peace delegation, used a similar technique on the maps showing eastern Hungary. Teleki and Nopcsa finished their map at the beginning of January.[2] The work was the result of the cooperation of several agencies. These were the College of Applied Arts, the Hungarian Geographical Society, the Office of Statistics, and the Ministry of Commerce. A group of almost sixty graphic artists and a number of cartographers prepared the maps and the tables destined to be used at the peace negotiations.[3]

Teleki made the recommendation in the middle of January, 1919, that the Hungarian Geographical Society address an appeal to the geographical societies of the world protesting the predicted dismantling of Hungary. With Teleki's assistance, the appeal was drafted.[4] It is evident from the text that Teleki and his asso-

---

2 Jenő Benda, "A 'Carte rouge' históriája" [The story of the "Carte Rouge"], *Pesti Hírlap*, January 22, 1920. About the whole work see: Dániel Segyevy, "Carte Rouge 100: Teleki Pál vörös térképének hatástörténeti elemzése [Carte rouge 100: An analysis of the historical impact of Pál Teleki's red map]," REGIO, 26, no. 4 (2018): 114–179
3 Ignác Romsics, *The Dismantling of Historic Hungary: The Peace Treaty of Trianon* (Boulder, CO: Social Sciences Monographs, 2002), pp. 116–117.
4 "A Magyar Földrajzi Társaság szózata a világ földrajzi társaságaihoz" [Appeal of the Hungarian Geographical Society to the geographical societies of the world], *Földrajzi Közlemények*, nos. 7–10 (1918): 289–320.

ciates had a reasonable idea about the areas to be taken away from Hungary and in many instances their ideas were close to the plans being made in Paris. The politician in him, however, was not satisfied with the appeal. He believed that domestic propaganda was at least as important as making maps and appeals. He assisted in the creation of a new organization that could carry on the domestic propaganda he considered to be so important. At the beginning of 1918, the League for the Protection of Hungary's Territorial Integrity (TEVEL) was formed with Lajos Lóczy as its president. Teleki was deeply involved and after February 1919 he became the president.[5]

TEVEL was joined by a very large group of social organizations and at the first general meeting on December 15, they could speak about a membership of one million people. The league organized series of lectures, published propaganda material including postcards, brochures and posters, and tried to inform the representatives of the Entente who visited Budapest. Teleki enthusiastically participated in the hosting of all foreign visitors who were likely to have some influence in Paris at the Peace Conference. Teleki guided American delegates as well, one of whom was Major Lawrence Martin.[6] The count also welcomed and spent time with an old acquaintance from America, Captain Nicholas Roosevelt and with the visiting head of the British Military Mission in Vienna, Lieutenant Colonel Thomas Cuninghame.[7] He was also very busy in getting English-speaking experts to assist the Allied representatives. He was leaning heavily on the British and American acquaintances made during his trip in 1912. He sent three copies of his large ethnographic map abroad and wrote a memorandum in English that he sent to George C. Chisholm, a professor at the University of Edinburgh, in the hope that it would be read not only by the Scottish scholar but by the British diplomats as well. The latter were not overawed by the contents of the material. "There is nothing new in these papers" they wrote on the margin of the dossier arguing for the territorial integrity of Hungary.[8] Of the neighboring countries being established at the time,

---

5 Anikó Kovács-Bertrand, *Der ungarische Revisionismus nach dem ersten Weltkrieg* (Munich: Oldenbourg, 1997), pp. 50–52, and 55–61.

6 "Az amerikai bizottság tájékozódása" [The information gathering the American Commission], *Budapesti Hírlap* [Budapest News], January 17, 1919, pp. 3–4, and January 19, p. 4. See also Lawrence Martin, "Count Paul Teleki," *Hungarian Quarterly* 5, no. 2 (1939): 204–211.

7 "Az amerikai bizottság munkája" [The work of the American Mission], *Budapesti Hírlap*, March 1, 1919, p. 5; and Sir Thomas Cuninghame, "Between the War and the Peace Treaties," *Hungarian Quarterly* 5, no. 3 (1939): 422–423.

8 Comments of the British officials on the Teleki memorandum, London, February 8-10, 1919, The National Archives (Kew) (hereafter cited as TNA), Foreign Office (hereafter cited as FO), FO 371, vol. 3514, fol. 346.

In The Revolution, The Counterrevolution, And In The Government (1918–1921)

Teleki considered Yugoslavia, under Serb leadership, to be the most suitable for a "strategic partnership" with Budapest. At least, this is what he told the Austrian minister in Budapest.[9]

These diplomatic activities did not go unobserved by the left wing of the Hungarian political life. The TEVEL was attacked by the Socialist daily *Népszava* [People's Voice] in December 1918 and in the article it was stated that, "The activities seem unnecessary. The entire organization is considered to be harmful and is also suspect."[10] At the beginning of March, when the government believed the times to be appropriate for "tidying up" both the left and right wings, the aristocrats who hosted the Entente delegates were accused of counterrevolutionary activities[11] Teleki had good reason to heed these signs. His bailiwick, the National Office for Veteran Affairs came under the administrative control of the Socialist minister, Zsigmond Kunfi. The disabled had been a favorite target of Communist propaganda ever since the beginning of the 1918 Revolution. The Association of the Disabled, led by the Communists sent a representative to the National Office for Veteran Affairs on November 1, 1918. Of the leaders of that organization only Pál Teleki and his assistant Pál Petri remained at their post by February 1919.[12] On February 14, 1919, hundred and fifty disabled occupied the office, removed the officials and sent a delegation to the Office of the Prime Minister where the minister of public welfare promised them that their demands would be met. The Council of Ministers dismissed Teleki.[13]

In spite of the fact that the government relieved Teleki of his position, Mihály Károlyi maintained his confidence in Teleki and this is understandable on the basis of their similar backgrounds.[14] The two young men had the same teacher of French, Károlyi was present at Teleki's wedding and in the 1920s referred to Teleki, albeit

---

9   Tibor Hajdu, *Az 1918-as magyarországi polgári demokratikus forradalom* [The Bourgeois Democratic Revolution in Hungary in 1918] (Budapest: Kossuth, 1968), p. 182.
10 "Honmentés vagy ellenforradalom?" [Saving the country or counterrevolution?], *Népszava* [People's Voice], December 6, 1918, p. 1; and "A területi integritás hazug jelszava" [The lying slogan of territorial integrity], *Népszava*, December 5, 1918, pp. 1–2.
11 "A vendéglátó ellenforradalom" [The hospitable counterrevolution], *Népszava*, March 9, 1919, pp. 4–5.
12 Iván Bognár, "A Népjóléti Minisztérium és a Népjóléti Népbiztosság szervezete 1917–1919" [The organization of the Ministry of Public Welfare and of the Commissariat of Public Welfare 1917–1919], *Levéltári Közlemények* [Archival Reports], no 2 (1966): 308–309.
13 "A rokkantak elfoglalták a Hadigondozó Hivatalt" [The disabled have occupied the Office of Veteran Affairs], *Budapesti Hírlap*, February 15, 1919, p. 6 ; Bognár, "A Népjóléti Minisztérium," p. 309.
14 Count Paul Teleki, *The Evolution of Hungary and Its Place in European History* (New York: Macmillan, 1923), p. 133; and Count Michael Károlyi, *Memoirs of Michael Károlyi. Faith Without Illusion* (New York: E. P. Dutton, 1957), p. 124.

critically, as "Bóli," which was a nickname used only by family and close friends. It was a sign of President Károlyi's confidence in Teleki that a few days after Teleki had been relieved of his job, he was appointed to the Hungarian peace treaty delegation expected to depart soon for Paris and consisting mostly of left-wing experts.[15] That same day, February 19, a new party was formed under the leadership of István Bethlen, the Party of Hungarian Unity, a gathering of members of the traditional elite, disillusioned in Károlyi and forming the basis of a new, bourgeois, right-wing party organization. We do not find Pál Teleki among the founding members of this organization.[16] At the beginning of March 1919 the Külügyi Tanács [Foreign Affairs Council] was established. It had a similar composition as the peace delegation and was supposed to function as an advisory body for Hungarian foreign policy. The president was Oszkár Jászi, the former minister of nationalities, the majority of the members were Bourgeois Radicals, people close to them and financial experts. Teleki and one other could be viewed as right wing or being in opposition.[17] Teleki probably became a part of the council *in absentia* because at the very end of February or the very beginning of March he left for Switzerland.

It is not known when he decided that he had to represent the Hungarian affairs abroad. First he wanted to go to Great Britain but did not get an entry permit. On Károlyi's request and with his encouragement, he went to Switzerland. By this time there were significant Hungarian colonies in Berne and in the larger cities consisting largely of aristocrats, politicians surrounded by spies, adventurers and courtesans. Even though he insisted to his aristocratic partners that the mission was much against his wishes, he did not deny that he went to Switzerland on Károlyi's request to "study the situation" prior to going to Paris for the peace conference. He also declared that, "he did not believe that he would be useful but did not wish to be accused of standing aside in such difficult times."[18] He promptly made contact with Entente diplomats and after the Soviet Republic was established on March 21, 1919, he addressed an extensive memorandum to Sir Horace Rumbold, the British minister in Berne and through him to the officials of the Foreign Office.[19] In his

---

15 "Károlyi Mihály a békekonferencián" [Mihály Károlyi at the peace conference], *Budapesti Hírlap*, February 20, 1919, p. 2.
16 "Nemzeti Egyesülés Pártja" [The Party of National Unity], *Budapesti Hírlap*. February 20, 1919, p. 2.
17 "Tótország autonómiája" [The Autonomy of Slovakia], *Budapesti Hírlap*, March 9, 1919, p. 2; and Tivadar Batthyány, *Beszámolóm* [My Report] (Budapest: Athenaeum, [1928]), vol. 2, pp. 260, and 262.
18 Diary of Countess Gyula Andrássy, March 19, 1919, Gyula Andrássy Papers, box 1, t. 330, fol. 299, P4, MNL OL.
19 See Lajos Arday, *Térkép, csata utan. Magyarország a Brit külpolitikában 1918–1919* [Map after the Battle. Hungary in British Foreign Policy, 1918–1919] (Budapest: Magvető, 1990), pp. 79–111.

seven page memorandum Teleki struck a strongly anticommunist note although in this document he did not yet hold Károlyi responsible for the events. He emphasized that the democratic revolution initially enjoyed massive popular support and that Károlyi had complete confidence in Wilson's noble ideas. He blamed the president and the government for their optimism and passivity that kept them from reducing the territorial losses and resisting Bolshevization.

He explained about the recently installed rule of the Communists that it was based primarily on the inhabitants of Budapest and that their success in other areas was due only to the fact that they tried to exploit national sentiments. According to Teleki, should the Entente enter Hungary to overthrow communism it should make sure to declare itself to be the enemy of communism and not of the Hungarian nation. For this reason it was important that Serb, Czech or Romanian troops not be involved. Communism had to be overcome with Hungarian forces. According to the memorandum the Entente should promise that the anti-Bolshevik action of the Hungarians would modify the Entente's views vis-a-vis Hungary at the Paris Peace Conference. Teleki asked that the Entente assume a protective role over Hungary because Hungary could then again become one of the bastions of civilization in eastern Europe.[20] Another result of his stay in Berne was the publication of an English brochure that tried to prove, along with his map, that Transylvania, the Voivodina and its environs and Ruthenia were integral parts of Hungary.[21]

Teleki still hoped that he could go Paris with Andrássy to negotiate about the fate of Hungary but London was opposed.[22] When this became obvious, Teleki considered any further stay in Switzerland to be pointless and at the beginning of April 1919 he went to Vienna where a new counterrevolutionary center was set up. Many politicians of the old regime found refuge in the former imperial city.[23] These politicians, a number of emigrants and a large number of military officers established the Magyar Nemzeti Bizottság [Hungarian National Committee] under István Bethlen's leadership during April 1919. It was known by future generations as the Anti-Bolshevik Committee (ABC). Representing this organization, Teleki and Bethlen bombarded the Allied missions in Vienna, primarily the British and the

---

20   Report from Sir Horace Rumbold to Foreign Secretary Curzon, Berne, Apil 2, 1919. Addendum: Pál Teleki Memorandum to the Foreign Office, Berne, March 27, 1919, TNA, FO 371, vol. 3514, fols. 540–546.
21   Count Paul Teleki, *The Ethnographical Composition of Hungary* (Berne: Buhler and Werder, 1919).
22   Telegram from Sir Horace Rumbold, Berne, March 24, 1919, TNA, FO 371, vol. 3514, fols. 451–453.
23   Gusztáv Grátz, *A forradalmak kora* [The Era of Revolutions] (Budapest: Akadémiai Kiadó, 1992), p. 188.

French, with notes and memoranda. The principal discussion partners for Teleki and Bethlen in Vienna were old acquaintances, Cuninghame and the French high commissioner in Vienna, Henri Allizé. Their prime intermediary and money man, the reporter of the *Daily Telegraph*, Ellis Ashmead-Bartlett, who had surfaced in Budapest during the democratic revolution and who moved along the edges of journalism, adventure and subversive activities.

In April 1919, both Teleki and Bethlen were still convinced that Hungarian Bolshevism could be overthrown only with the assistance of international cooperation and as a preliminary to the overthrow of the Communist experiment in Russia. Thus they wished to establish a 60-100,000 strong Hungarian army that would have first cleansed Hungary and then Russia. In exchange for the Hungarian assistance outlined above they asked for a dignified treatment of Hungary, economic assistance and assistance with transportation.[24] At the end of March the highest Allied decision makers saw no prospect in this proposal. It was at this time that the Hungarian politicians in Vienna recognized the possibility of overthrowing the Soviet Republic in Budapest from within.[25] In the middle of April Georges Clemenceau, the French prime minister, and Stephen Pichon, the minister of foreign affairs, issued several ordinances that there would not be any territorial correction nor the establishment of an effective counterrevolutionary armed force in Hungary. General Paul de Lobit, the commander of the Armée de Hongrie, could only promise the politicians in Vienna that they could move to the French zone of occupation and that he would not stand in the way of them organizing an army. He would not, however, provide any money, arms or rations.

The Paris Peace Conference sent the South African General Jan Smuts to Budapest to negotiate with the Communist regime and when these talks ended in failure, it authorized the Czech and Romanian forces to continue their advance into Hungary that was halted at the beginning of the year.[26] Within two weeks the Romanian troops reached the line of the Tisza River and the Czech troops reached Ruthenia and also occupied Sátoraljaújhely, the valley of the Sajó River and Miskolc. The counterrevolutionaries in Vienna realized that they had to rely upon themselves. In the spring of 1919 Teleki was in daily contact with Allizé, the French High Commissioner, who made no secret of his opinion that after the peace treaty was signed all of central Europe, including Hungary, would be part of a French

---

24 Ignác Romsics, *István Bethlen: A Great Conservative Statesman of Hungary* (Boulder, CO: Social Science Monographs, 1995), pp. 122–125.
25 Grátz, *A forradalmak kora*, pp. 191–192.
26 Mária Ormos, *From Padua to the Trianon* (Budapest: Akadémiai Kiadó, 1990), pp. 234–239.

sphere of interest. He urged the politicians in Vienna to move to the south of Hungary, into the French zone of occupation [27] Allizé also believed that a significant portion of the Vienna counterrevolutionaries and the government formed in Arad by Count Gyula Károlyi at the beginning of May, was overly reactionary. The French diplomat, who kept careful track of the counts in the counterrevolutionary movement, had no problems with Teleki. Allizé considered him as one of the movers of the Vienna initiatives who made a very good impression on the Entente representatives.[28] The ABC expressed their confidence in the Károlyi government. They also decided that István Bethlen would be the Vienna representative of the Károlyi government and maintain contact with the Allied missions. It was decided that under the leadership of Teleki a large group should move to Szeged. This was the last meaningful activity of the ABC.

Teleki left for Szeged during the latter part of May and arrived there on June 2. The arrival of Teleki meant much to the politicians in Szeged, not only because it meant a unification of the forces but also because he arrived with three million crowns in his bag that was most helpful in getting the Szeged cabinet started on its way to become a government. The very next day Teleki sat in at the meeting of the government, was offered the position of minister of foreign affairs and took his oath on June 6.[29]

Szeged was a peculiar political enclave at this time. Even though the French military authorities in the city took a firm stand vis-à-vis the local officials of the Soviet Republic, they did support political pluralism, licensed publications and maintained good relations with some of the intellectual circles. The old civil administration was maintained in the city, the Moroccan Spahis organized colorful parades and the French infantry regiments organized soccer matches with the local teams. The clash of cultures caused some tensions. Some of the older, staid citizens took offense because some of French officers took Hungarian mistresses who did not hesitate to appear at their window in provocative clothes. The goats kept by the Spahis decimated the local gardens.

---

27 Béla Kelemen, *Adatok a szegedi ellenforradalom és a szegedi kormány történetéhez* [Data to the History of the Szeged Counterrevolution and the Szeged Government] (Szeged: Kelemen Béla, 1923), pp. 341.
28 Telegram from Henri Allizé, Vienna, May 18, 1919, Hongrie, vol. 28, fols. 141–142, Europe 1918–1940, Ministère des Affaires Etrangères, Archives Diplomatiques (hereafter cited as MAE AD); and Telegram from Henri Allizé, Vienna, May 19, 1919, Hongrie, vol. 28, fols. 145–146, Europe 1918–1940, MAE AD.
29 Kelemen, *Adatok*, pp. 209, 233–234, and 244.

With time increasing numbers of people arrived who fled from the Soviet Republic Hungary leaving all their goods and families behind under communist rule. This somewhat irresponsible group, filled with radical political ideas lived a very active social life in the Hotel Kass, in the boating clubs and in entertainment organized in the officers' clubs. The Szeged society was not enthralled by the policies held by this group and viewed the saber-rattling with some anxiety. Some of the old-fashioned, liberal leaders of the city did not understand political radicalism, the labor movement boycotted the ordinances of the government and the papers frequently made fun of the poor government infrastructure. The minister of foreign affairs, for instance, had his office in the chambers of the local court archives where the minister had to open a padlock every time a visitor appeared. In his office a chair was used to block the door since the door handles had been stolen.[30] The personnel of the ministry never exceeded thirty during the two months of its operations[31] Yet, the Ministry of Foreign Affairs appears to have had all necessary components. It sent messengers and secret envoys to the neighboring countries and to the European capitals and, from its own funds, supported the *Szegedi Új Nemzedék* [New Generation of Szeged] that represented the interests of the government and published Teleki's articles as well.[32] Szeged foreign policy had little elbow room and limited objectives. These were to have the government recognized, to gain a favorable position for the defeat of communism and the mitigation of the peace conditions to be imposed on the country. Teleki sent an unofficial representative to Paris to ascertain the likely peace terms. He endeavored to make contact with the Romanian politicians in Szeben [Sibiu] to coordinate anti-Bolshevik plans but these attempts were not received well.[33]

The minister of foreign affairs was most active in the direction of Belgrade and in the middle of June 1919 went to Belgrade, in the company of Vice-Admiral Miklós Horthy, the new minister of defense of the Szeged government, to negotiate with members of the Serb government and with the representatives of the Entente. This was presumably the first time that these two men worked together and they found each other very compatible. The vice-admiral also liked to draw and liked risque jokes. They were both great hunters, loved automobiles and had trav-

---

30 Fodor, *Teleki Pál*, p. 44.
31 Tárcafőkönyv [Main ledger], vols 1, pp. 11, 17, 20, and 23, A szegedi ellenforradalmi külügyminisztérium iratai [Papers of the Szeged Counterrevolutionary Ministry of Foreign Affairs], K 752, MNL OL.
32 Ibid., p. 38.
33 Report of Pál Teleki to József Somssich about the activities of the Szeged Ministry of Foreign Affairs, Budapest, August 30, 1919, Kiim., res. pol., cs. 2, 1919-4, K 64, MNL OL; and Kelemen, Adatok, p. 346.

eled enough in exotic places to have much to talk about. It was certainly a pleasant experience for Horthy to travel with a minister who engaged in politics when the nation was in danger but who always emphasized his being a scholar, rather than a stuffy professional politician.[34] The intimacy might have been strengthened by the fact that on the way toward Belgrade they had to sleep on the same billiards table in an inn, there being no other accommodation.[35]

In Belgrade they met with several members of the Serb government, with British, French and American diplomatic representatives and with Admiral Troubridge, Horthy's old acquaintance who was in charge of the Allied naval forces on the Danube. They negotiated with the deputy minister of foreign affairs who agreed to the Szeged government sending a permanent representative to Belgrade. The two men were very warmly received in the Serbian capital.[36] They had much less luck with the Entente representatives. H.P. Dodge, the American Chargé d'Affairs listened to the presentation of the two politicians very courteously but considered both of them unsuitable for a government function because neither of them was a democrat and both of them were "adherents of the ancient regime."[37] The British chargé d'affaires had reservations about the two visitors' statements concerning the horrors of the Bolshevik terror and did not respond to their complaints about Italy sending arms to the Budapest Soviet regime. Teleki again explained that the Transdanubian area would be better for the activities of the counterrevolutionaries but the diplomat made no commitments about this either. He expressed his sympathy for the victims of Bolshevism and thanked them for the visit.[38]

One month later Teleki was again in the Serb capital but the trip produced no results.[39] The Serb government was well intentioned toward a participation in an anti-Bolshevik campaign with Szeged but was willing only to recommend Hungarian participation to the Entente and could not insist that Hungary be a participant.[40] The two politicians also visited Teleki's old acquaintance Louis Gabriel Fontenay, the French minister, who had been consul general in Budapest before the

---

34 For the relationship between the two men, see Balázs Ablonczy, "Pancsovától a Sándor-palotáig. Horthy es Teleki" [From Pancevo to the Sandor Palace. Horthy and Teleki], *Rubicon* 12, nos. 1–2 (2001): 33–36.
35 Lily Doblhoff, *Horthy Miklós* (Budapest: Athenaeum, 1938), p. 212; and Kelemen, Adatok, p. 286.
36 Kelemen, *Adatok*, p. 286.
37 Zsuzsa L. Nagy, "Amerikai diplomaták Horthy Miklósról, 1920–1944" [American diplomats on Miklós Horthy, 1920–1944], *Történelmi Szemle* 33, nos. 1–3 (1990): 174.
38 Charles des Graz's report to Foreign Secretary Curzon, Belgrade, June 17, 1919, TNA, FO 371. vol. 3515, no. 93699/113.
39 Kelemen, *Adatok*, pp. 391, and 394.
40 Charles de Graz's telegram, Belgrade July 21, 1919, TNA, FO 371, vol. 3515.

war. Teleki outlined the foreign policy plans and goals of his government. The Szeged minister of foreign affairs declared that he wished to markedly improve his cabinet's relationship with the Serbs because the Hungarian public opinion had no resentment whatever against them and also because economically Hungary would be dependent upon them after the war. In contrast, Hungary was unwilling to accept any insult from the Romanians. Using South Russia and other international examples he asked that the Allies permit the move of troops to Transdanubia, to set up four to five divisions in the Szeged area, the left bank of the Tisza and in the Pécs area and that horses and arms be provided for an army of 100,000.[41] The request was not honored with a reply.

The minister of foreign affairs did not limit his activities to foreign policy but became active in Szeged in domestic affairs as well. At the time of his arrival he submitted an eight point proposal that was the work of the Vienna Committee but that actually reflected his own and István Bethlen's recommendations. According to these the Szeged government had to endeavor to obtain the Entente's recognition. He wished to address the situation of the unions, the Jewish question, the press and the wages. He wished to engage in propaganda asking that French troops occupy Hungary east of the Tisza River in the probable event of a Bolshevik revolution breaking out in Romania.[42]

This is the first time that the Jewish question was mentioned in any of Teleki's public statements. It was the shock of 1918-1919 and particularly of the Soviet Republic that triggered this reaction. Sixty percent of the membership of the Governing Council of People's Commissars was of Jewish origin, and this led him to the crude generalization that Hungarian Jewry, after having participated significantly in financial, commercial and intellectual occupations, was now endeavoring to take over the political powers and that the Soviet Republic was the "rule of the Jews."[43] In Teleki's thinking the statement against the Jews meant that the policies of assimilation and integration characteristic of the Dualist Hungary had to be revised. He believed that the Christian middle class was confronted by a Jewish middle class whose political goals diverged from what he considered acceptable. The "Jewish rule" equated with the Soviet Republic had to be prevented from ever

---

41   Memorandum from the Szeged government to the Entente Powers, Szeged, July 18, 1919, TNA, FO 371, vol, 3515, no. 111731/ 1193.
42   Kelemen, *Adatok*, p. 233.
43   János Gyurgyák, *A zsidókérdés Magyarországon* [The Jewish Question in Hungary] (Budapest: Osiris, 2001), p. 103.

recurring again by revising the concept of citizenship rights. It was from this notion that Teleki's ideas about numerus clausus and the anti-Jewish laws originated.

The Szeged Council of Ministers accepted the proposals of the minister of foreign affairs. Any effective action was, however, quickly negated by the increasing mistrust of the French officers and politicians in the Károlyi government. The prime minister was aware of this and repeatedly offered his resignation. After a prolonged crisis, Dezső P. Ábrahám formed a somewhat more left-wing government on July 12. Teleki kept his portfolio and after July 16 even held the office of minister of agriculture. He undoubtedly felt that the ratio of parties in the government turned out to be less favorable for him and in order to correct it he began to form a party himself. The emerging political group was going to have religion, morality and nationalism as its guidelines and would have relied primarily on Teleki's editorial in the *Szegedi Új Nemzedék* as its strategic program. In this editorial Teleki suggested that the imminent territorial losses and Bolshevism were only superficial dangers and that the real source of problems was much deeper. In his opinion liberalism was not national enough and leaned too much towards internationalism and that the new generation had to return to be truly Hungarian and feel Hungarian. "Sacred Egoism had to extirpate everything from the Hungarians that was not Hungarian, that could never be Hungarian and that did not wish to be absorbed by Hungarians."[44] The proposed party did not materialize because Szeged and the present government created an unfavorable environment for it.

After the failure of the offensive against the Romanians organized by the communist regime in Budapest, Teleki must have viewed the collapse of the system with considerable satisfaction, but had no confidence in the Gyula Peidl government composed of Socialist politicians. He regarded the labor union government as the same as its predecessor. On August 4 he participated in the organizational session of the Hungarian National Committee that was proposed as the parliament of the opposition government. Then, after the fall of the Peidl government, he repeated the necessity of the formation of a Hungarian unity coalition that was above parties or that included all the parties. He again called to the Hungarians to set aside all differences of opinion, all "isms" and to lead the country out of the cul de sac into which Bolshevism had taken it.[45] The next morning he flew to Siófok to

---

44 Pál Teleki, "Nemzeti egységet!" [National unity!] *Szegedi Új Nemzedék* [The New Generation of Szeged], July 2, 1919.
45 Pál Teleki, "Most tartsunk össze!" [Now let us stick together!], *Szegedi Új Nemzedék*, August 7, 1919.

get to Budapest avoiding the Romanians who had already entered parts of Transdanubia and also Budapest.

In the capital he negotiated with Archduke Joseph (József) Habsburg and with István Friedrich, the prime minister, who shaped the political situation in Budapest. He was also reunited with his family which had been stuck in Budapest. Teleki's negotiations were not designed to find some *modus vivendi* between the Szeged group and the Friedrich government that came to power by a coup on August 6. Teleki had given up on Szeged and the politicians who had stayed there.

Teleki came very close to the center of power. At the end of August 1919 he became the leader of the royalist Keresztény Nemzeti Párt [Christian National Party] that was an offshoot of the István Friedrich political group.[46] According to its published program, this party endorsed a democratic, national state that simultaneously eliminated the trends threatening the "Christian worldview". It demanded that franchise based on the amount of taxes paid be eliminated, that there be a universal and secret franchise, that the "press problem" be resolved, meaning that in place of the "Jewish press a Christian-national one be created by administrative fiat. It also wished to see a complete freedom of assembly and the right to organize. In its program, the party endorsed some form of land reform. Among the proposals of the party there were some with a socialistic orientation, such as mandatory old age pension, regularization of the affairs of widows and orphans, and the progressive taxation of large fortunes. In its emphasis on the fight against tuberculosis, sexually transmitted diseases and alcoholism Teleki's spirit was manifest.[47]

The party under Friedrich's leadership served Teleki as the basis for the rapidly increasing trend to unite the Christian parties. It was after consultation with Bethlen and with the concept of bringing together a Christian bloc that he accepted the invitation to the presidency of the party.[48] A few days after the party was launched, the new formation got into step with the Christian Agrarian Party and with some Christian-Socialist factions. The Paris Peace Conference sent the British diplomat, Sir George Clerk, to Budapest to prepare some acceptable political solution to follow the fall of the Communist Béla Kun regime. It was the culmination of his unification efforts that on October 26, 1919, the Party of Christian National Unification was born. In this way the Christian politicians hoped that they would be able

---

46 Jenő Gergely, *A kereszténysocializmus Magyarországon 1903–1923* [Christian Socialism in Hungary 1903–1923] (Budapest: Akadémiai Kiadó, 1977), p. 138.
47 See ibid., Appendix no. 11, "A Keresztény Nemzeti Párt Programja" [Program of the Christian National Party], Budapest, August-September, 1919.
48 Ibid., p. 150 n. 65.

monitor the increasing influence of István Nagyatádi Szabó's Smallholder Party, Hungary's most popular agrarian party and even counterbalance it if necessary. It was as the representative of this Christian bloc that Teleki appeared at the political discussions organized by Clerk.

Clerk, who later became British plenipotentiary in Prague, was close to Robert Seton-Watson's and Henry Wickham-Steed's *New Europe* circle during the war and it is therefore surprising that he developed an unexpected fondness for the Hungarian political class. He mentioned Horthy as the person whose "wisdom and influence" assisted in the formation of a coalition government. Clerk also wrote with undisguised affection that, "it was impossible not to look with sympathy as the representatives of a higher civilization are hopelessly persecuted by those who are just now learning the art of government."[49] At the initial negotiations at the end of October and the beginning of November, Friedrich promised everything, expressed his willingness to step down from power and to organize free elections. Horthy endeavored to pacify the left-wing parties and announced that the army would obey the new cabinet established after the departure of the Romanians. After the Romanians did leave in the middle of November, the prime minister refused to even consider resignation.[50] Compared to him, Horthy was a model of calmness and reliability. Teleki, who in the views of the British negotiators was the president of the Christian Bloc, participated in the preliminary discussions about the establishment of a new government, but never spoke. In those days he was satisfied with quietly informing Clerk and the diplomats accompanying him, about the foreseeable consequences of the peace treaty so humiliating for Hungary and about the atrocities inflicted on the Hungarians under foreign rule.

At last, in the middle of November a coalition government, consisting of groups from the Social Democrats to the Christian right, was formed by Károly Huszár and this cabinet was recognized by the Entente. Teleki ran in the elections scheduled for January 1920. He picked Szeged as his district and wished to convince both himself and also public opinion of the importance of the counterrevolution. He again had no opponent and thus could discuss his plans before a small local party elite at the Hotel Tisza on December 14, 1919. He emphasized that Szeged was important for him because this was the place where, "the only torch of national sen-

---

49 Report from Sir George Clerk, n.p., November 29,1919, TNA, FO 371, vol. 3517, fols. 354–357.
50 For the history of the Clerk mission see Arday, *Térkép csata után*, pp. 276–285; and György Ránki, "A Clerk-misszió történetéhez" [About the history of the Clerk mission], *Történelmi Szemle* 10, no. 2 (1967): 156–187.

timent shone far and wide in the sad days of Bolshevism."[51] In comparison with his earlier articles and speeches in Szeged and compared to the program of the KNP there was a change in that before his electors he put less stress on the desirable social aspects of the reforms even though his land reform proposal was still rather radical compared to the status quo. With his characteristic thorough preparation he spoke of the local issues of interest to the city but a new element was the forceful linking of the Jewish question to Bolshevism. He did not beat about the bush but declared, "In order for public law and order and everything it protected to collapse, extensive preparations were required. The worm of destruction was gnawing away at it for a long time and gradually it destroyed the national sentiment and slowly siphoned out Christian morality from our society."[52]

According to Teleki, this work of destruction found its wedge in the Jewry that assisted it in penetrating Hungarian life. These "Galician immigrants ruined us". They could not find a country here because this nationality did not have a country or any patriotic feelings where they came from. Love of the land where they lived never developed in this group."[53] In order to resolve the problem he called on the "patriotically inclined" Hungarian Jewry to engage in combat with the „non-patriotic Eastern Jewry".[54] The first electoral district of Szeged elected Teleki as its representative.

The politician was not an official member of the Friedrich government but on August 21, 1919, the short-lived head of state, Archduke Joseph Habsburg asked him to set up an office to prepare for the peace negotiations. Teleki became very active in continuing the work that was interrupted during the Soviet Republic. In the beginning Teleki had only two assistants with the work that began in the Ministry of Foreign Affairs and later moved to one of the wings of the Royal Palace.[55] Shortly, they were joined by a large number of associates and experts. Due to the Romanian occupation the work could not be all performed in one location because

---

51 Count Pál Teleki, *Gróf Teleki Pál programmbeszéde, melyet Szeged első választó kerületének Keresztény Nemzeti Egyesülős Pártja alakuló és képviselőjelölő nagygyűlésén mondott el, Szegeden, a Tisza-szálló nagytermében 1919. év December havának 14. napján* [The Program Speech of Count Pál Teleki He Presented at the Organizing and Nominating Meeting of the Christian National Unification Party, in Szeged in the Assembly Hall of the Tisza Hotel on the 14th day of December of the Year 1919] (Szeged: Tevel Nyomda, [1920]), p. 2.
52 Ibid.
53 Ibid., p. 4.
54 Ibid., 3–4.
55 Jenő Cholnoky, "Introduction" [Bevezető], in *Trianon. A Magyar béreküldöttség tevékenysége 1920-ban* [Trianon. Activities of the Hungarian Peace Delegation in 1920], ed. Magda Ádám and Győző Cholnoky (Budapest: Lucidus, 2000), p. 32.

the Romanian occupying authorities wanted to interfere with the Hungarian preparations for the peace negotiations. The officials and the experts worked in a number of locations throughout the city and in the various ministries. Teleki visited the various offices in a one-horse carriage, held meetings and then returned to the Royal Palace where he and his associates frequently shared the thin soup prepared in the former royal kitchen.[56]

In addition to the experts from most of the ministries, colleagues from the Central Statistics Office and a number of smaller specialist organizations participated in collecting the material.[57] It was in this organizational effort that some of the experts first appeared who later became important components of Teleki's career. István Csáky began his political career at Teleki's side, Imre Csáky, the future minister of foreign affairs, coordinated the collection of materials about Slovakia. The social politician Zoltán Bencs represented the Ministry of Education in these activities, Alajos Kovács, the statistician, organized the collection of and arrangement of statistical materials, Ferenc Fodor, the refugee professor from Karánsebes (Caransebeş), worked in the central office. All of them became important factors in Teleki's future personnel policies.[58]

With the beginning of October the activities entered a new phase. A great amount of material had been collected and the text of the Austrian Peace Treaty was published. It was likely that the Austrian treaty was going be a model for the Hungarian one in many of its articles and hence it became an important task to organize and analyze the material accordingly with the identification of the most important issues.[59] The materials developed at the ministries were discussed at a meeting of the undersecretaries of state and the two drivers of the peace preparations, Bethlen and Teleki revised them from a political and practical perspective. Then the materials were given to French- and English-speaking experts for translation.[60] By the beginning of December the Hungarian peace delegation was prepared, in spite of the unfavorable conditions, to receive the invitation to the Peace Conference. Among the more important members of the Huszár government there were several who wished to set conditions to the trip to Paris, such as the withdrawal of the Romanian troops from beyond the Tisza and the investigation of the

---

56 Fodor, *Teleki Pál*, p. 51.
57 Jenő Cholnoky, "Bevezető," in *Trianon*, ed. Ádám and Győző Cholnoky, pp. 32–34.
58 Ibid; and Emerich Csáky, *Vom Geachteten zum Geächteten. Erinnerungen*, ed. Eva Marie Csáky (Vienna: Böhlau, 1992), p. 278.
59 Jenő Cholnoki, "Bevezető" in *Trianon*, ed. Ádám and Győző Cholnoky, pp. 34–35.
60 Romsics, *Dismantling Historic Hungary*, p. 117.

serious injuries inflicted on Hungarians in the Successor States. The cabinet addressed several memoranda to the Entente decision-makers. Others claimed that the internal dissensions among the Allies and the changes in the situation in Southern Russia caused the Entente to lose all power in the region.[61] The decision-makers in Paris, however, made it clear to the government in Budapest that it was not in a position to set conditions.[62] For this reason the Council of Ministers decided on December 29, that it would send the Hungarian representatives to Paris even though the Hungarian demands were not met. Consequently the eight-car special train of the Hungarian peace delegation departed from the Eastern Railway Station in the morning of January 5, 1920. Among the seventy-three passengers, Pál Teleki was one of the leading personalities of the delegation.

In Paris the Hungarian delegation was practically interned in a fashionable Parisian suburb, in a less than fashionable hotel. According to one of the diplomats, the Hotel Château de Madrid was no better than a house of ill repute.[63] The members of the Hungarian delegation, including the seven chief delegates, hoped that using the preliminary memoranda prepared in Budapest, they might affect the decision-makers. They were not given the opportunity.[64] The members of the delegation were not allowed to go to Paris and all they could do was to go for walks in the neighboring Bois de Boulogne. Almost a week after their arrival the Hungarian peace delegation was able to submit its revised preliminary notes. This flood of paper caused a considerable consternation among the officials of the French Ministry of Foreign Affairs. It is most likely that the papers never reached the responsible politicians because it was only a few hours later that the representatives of the Supreme Council handed the Hungarian delegation the draft of the peace treaty in the Red Salon of the Quai d'Orsay. Georges Clemenceau, presiding, indicated to the Hungarian delegation that the leader of the Hungarian delegation, Count Albert Apponyi, would be given an opportunity on the following day, January 16, to present the Hungarian position in regard to the draft. The delegates anxiously returned to their lodgings to read the Allied peace conditions. Even though they were familiar with the broad outlines of the territorial and some other ordinances, they all hoped for a miracle. The miracle did not happen.

---

61 Ibid., p. 165.
62 Ádám and Győző Cholnoky, eds., *Trianon*, pp. 40–41.
63 Emerich Csáky, *Vom Geachteten zum Geächteten*, pp. 40–41.
64 Count Albert Apponyi, "Gróf Apponyi Albert beszámolója a békedelegáció tevékenységéről" [Report of Count Albert Apponyi on the activities of the peace delegation], in *Trianon*, ed. Ádám and Győző Cholnoky, p. 351.

When the delegation read the peace conditions its members were "shocked and appalled."[65] There was not much time for grieving because in less than one day they had to assemble and support with data the speech with which Apponyi tried to present the Hungarian perspective. From the point of view of the speech, the most important factor was Teleki taking his map and, in the early morning of January 16, drawing the new borders of Hungary, as proposed in the peace treaty, with India ink.[66] Apponyi's speech was not devoted entirely to the defense of Hungarian power politics and territorial integrity. The elderly politician did emphasize the historical unity of the Carpathian Basin and buttressed his position with economic and geographical arguments. He also explained his commitment to Hungarian cultural superiority. At the end of his speech he emphasized that that the Hungarian government would accept the decisions provided plebiscites would be held in the affected territories at some time in the future. He did not represent an ethnic perspective but was willing to accept the results of a plebiscite.[67]

On the request of the British Prime Minister David Lloyd George, claiming deafness, asked Apponyi to sit quite close to him so that Apponyi was able to pull the "Red Map" from his pocket and indicate the territorial implications of the Hungarian situation. This seemed to trigger some interest among the other British, French, and Italian politicians but then Clemenceau closed the session and the Hungarian delegates had to rely on the strength of the memoranda to be submitted in the future. Two days later the Hungarian delegation returned home where, on January 21 they informed the government. In his speech, Teleki emphasized that the borders were completely unrealistic, that cities were divided into two parts and that the lines were just like the ones the British drew in Afghanistan. It was here that he raised the question of the defense of the minorities and condemned the peace treaty on ethnic grounds. He indicated that the Hungarian documents under preparation would strongly support the ethnic perspectives.[68]

The peace delegation arrived back in Paris on February 11 and worked behind the scenes to get the peace terms modified. The Peace Conference refused to listen to Apponyi again and the delegates were limited to the submission of eighteen

---

65 Jenő Benda, *A béke kálvária-útján. Egy ujságíró naplója a párizsi békekonferenciáról* [The Road to Peace Calvary. The Diary of a Journalist at the Paris Peace Conference] (Budapest: Légrády, 1920), p. 78.
66 Apponyi, "Gróf Apponyi Albert beszámolója," in *Trianon*, ed. Ádám and Győző Cholnoky, p. 352.
67 György Litván, ed., *Trianon felé* [Toward Trianon] (Budapest: MTA Történettudományi Intézet, 1998), pp. 243–247.
68 Apponyi, "Gróf Apponyi Albert beszámolója," in *Trianon*, ed. Ádám and Győző Cholnoky, pp. 353, and 356.

memoranda. Most of the delegates left Paris by the end of February, having accomplished essentially nothing. The memoranda, again coordinated by Teleki, were more emphatic on self-determination and on the nationality problems although there was still some mention of Hungary's historic unity. In the memoranda the delegation began to favor the retention of the wholly Hungarian areas that were estimated, with some exaggeration, to cover 58,000 square kilometers. The proposal actually coincided with the ethnic boundaries in some areas, e.g. the Voivodina and environs and hoped to link the Székely Counties [Székelyföld] to Hungary with a corridor.[69]

Of the Hungarian actions undertaken to modify the peace terms, the one that was the most successful was the one for which the minister of foreign affairs had the least hope. Even prior to the collapse of the Monarchy, Teleki was in contact with the Kassa [Košice] attorney and land owner, Károly Halmos who, in turn, was an old acquaintance of Louis Loucheur, the French minister of reconstruction, and Paul Bignon, the French minister of the navy.[70] The young Count Andor Semsey, who owned estates at Semse [Šemša] in the Hungarian Highland (Slovakia) was the cousin of Louis de Robien, a French diplomat who was the secretary of the newly installed secretary general of the Quai d'Orsay, Maurice Paleologue. It was hoped that these relationships might prove a route to influential French personalities.[71] Teleki preferred, then and later, to avoid the traditional diplomatic channels and to use his own confidential advisers, French teachers, family acquaintances, distant relatives and people who were obliged to him. Semsey and Halmos established contact with Teleki during the autumn of 1919 and, at the beginning of 1920 they went to Paris where, with Baron Adolf Ullmann, the chief executive officer of the Hitelbank, who joined them later, they endeavored to attract an interest towards Hungary in French capitalist circles. Their activities were so successful that they were received on March 17, 1920, by Paleologue.

These discussions have a considerable literature and it can be said in summary that after the fall of Clemenceau's Minister of Foreign Affairs Pichon, the new leadership in the ministry of foreign affairs considered the possibility to replace its Czechoslovak-Romanian-Yugoslav-Polish orientation with a central European French network based on Hungary, Romania, and Poland. This would have bene-

---

69 Romsics, *Dismantling Historic Hungary*, pp. 143–144.
70 Diary of Countess Gyula Andrássy, March 19, 1919, Gyula Andrássy Papers, box 1, t. 330, fob 300, P4, MNL OL; and Romsics, *Dismantling Historic Hungary*, pp. 140–141.
71 Andor Semsey, "Az utolsó szó jogán" [Privilege of the Last Word] (typescript), fol. 4–5, Andor Semsey Papers, C/43, Ráday Levéltár [Ráday Archives] (hereafter cited as RL).

fited from French economic and commercial penetration. The Hungarian party offered to the French the takeover of the Hungarian Railway System on a rental basis, an option to build a free port on the Danube, a majority ownership of shares in a major bank (Hitelbank) and also in some industries. These offers were made to the Schneider-Creusot group and to several parties of the Union Européenne Industrielle et Financière.[72] In exchange for the Hungarian-French rapprochement Budapest wanted to keep the completely or largely ethnically Hungarian areas along the other side of Hungary's new borders.

Among other items, Hungary wanted to have a plebiscite in western Hungary, in the Banat, and in Ruthenia, for the multietnic inhabitants to determine the country they wished to belong to, autonomy in Transylvania for the Hungarian and German populations and the return of Hungarian property looted by the Romanian army. The French were cleverly vague in their response so that the Hungarians continued to hope that the territorial matters would be arranged satisfactorily. Teleki was initially deeply pessimistic. He wrote to the already gravely ill Lajos Lóczy, "We will be home by Easter but there is very little chance for not returning with the worst possible peace. Yet, the government will have to sign because otherwise Budapest will starve and the Vlachs [pejorative for Romanians] will again advance to the Tisza. I would even make these sacrifices but the majority would not."[73]

Teleki returned to Budapest at the beginning of April and there it had been an open secret ever since the beginning of March that he would assume the portfolio of foreign affairs in the Sándor Simonyi-Semadan government. The new cabinet took office in a changing domestic policy environment following the national parliamentary election, and after Miklós Horthy had been elected regent at the beginning of March. The universal and secret franchise completely changed the political image of the country. After almost fifty years of practically uninterrupted control the Liberal Party and its successor the Nemzeti Munkapárt [National Labor Party] established by previously liberal politicians ceased to exist. The various independence parties had equally little success. Victory belonged to two parties, the Smallholder Party, in existence since 1909 but so far on the margins of political life and the newly established KNEP [Christian National Unity Party]. The January 1920

---

72   Eric Bussière, "The Interests of the Banque de l'Union Parisienne in Czechoslovakia, Hungary and the Balkans, 1919–1939," in *International Business and Central Europe, 1918–1939*, ed. Alice Teichova and P. L. Cottrell (New York: St. Martins Press, 1983), pp. 399–410.
73   Letter from Pál Teleki to Lajos Lóczy, n.p. [Paris], March 24, n.d. [1920], Correspondence, Lóczy Papers, MBFSZ TtGy.

parliamentary election results forced the two most successful parties to form a coalition. Technically the elections were won by the Smallholder Party. Their victory became solid after the withdrawal of the Romanian troops and the elections held in June east of the Tisza River. The coalition government resulting from a delicate party balance included the party chiefs and had a singularly colorless prime minister in Sándor Simonyi-Semadam, a KNEP politician appointed on March 15, 1920. It was as the minister of foreign affairs that Teleki gave his maiden speech on April 26, 1920.[74]

Under the influence of the news coming from Paris he viewed Hungary's situation rather optimistically, although he did not expect any short-range changes.[75] Yet, this was not the central theme of the speech. He emphasized that Hungary had to fit into the new European order and, in order to accomplish this, he called for a national unity. He characterized the work of the peace delegation as being designed for opening the future and for collecting data, not for applicability to the moment. He considered the work accomplished as useful because, "recognition that this situation is insupportable and can not be maintained must come."[76] He was not willing to condemn the officials who came from the Ballhausplatz saying that he knew only good and bad diplomats. He chastised those who attacked Germany but expressed his willingness to cooperate with France.[77]

The diplomats serving in Hungary were pleased by the speech. According to the French High Commissioner Maurice Fouchet, Teleki's words did not show any affection for France but neither did they show any for Germany. As a perfect gentleman, Teleki made the same statement privately to Fouchet, that he did before the plenum of the National Assembly.[78] The London comments viewed the speech as "very interesting" but Thomas Hohler, the British High Commissioner in Budapest, who was sympathetic to the new regime, pointed out correctly that Teleki's domestic policy support was shaken by the fact that he and several of his landowner friends left the KNEP at that particular time to form their own Parliamentary group.[79] As soon as he had returned from Paris, Teleki endeavored to

---

74 Teleki, *Válogatott politikai írások*, ed. Ablonczy, pp. 51–64.
75 Ibid., p. 54.
76 Ibid., pp. 56–57.
77 Ibid., pp. 59–63.
78 Magda Ádám, ed., *Documents diplomatiques français sur l'histoire du bassin des Carpathes* (Budapest: Akadémiai Kiadó, 1999), vol. 2, pp. 515–516.
79 From Thomas Hohler to Curzon, Budapest April 30, 1920, PRO, FO 371, vol. 3522, fol. 130; and A W. A. Leeper's commentary on Teleki's April 26, and May 10, 1920, speeches, London, May 15, 1920, TNA, FO, vol 3523, fol. 27.

form a new government party and resigned from KNEP on April 22, with several of his friends, claiming that this step would promote the two government parties' coming together. This fact, combined with the information slowly trickling down about the Hungarian-French negotiations and the offers made by Hungary, turned a significant part of the representatives against the foreign policy conducted by him. It was a dilemma for Teleki whether he should go back to Paris for the signing of the peace treaty. It was evident that any politician whose signature appeared on the document was unlikely to have any political role in the future. The French chief delegate attempted to dismiss Teleki's concerns. It was he who talked the Francophil Teleki out of going to Paris and thus opened the door to Teleki's political survival. Fouchet believed that if the minister of foreign affairs would fall, there would be a renewal of anti-French policy and that the French economic plans would come to naught.

In spite of the Italian and British reservations and the secret Hungarian-French negotiations the final form of the peace treaty, accompanied by the so-called Millerand letter signed by the French chairman of the Peace Conference, arrived in Budapest on May 6. The peace conditions differed only on a few points from the proposal published in January. The value of the goods looted by the Romanian army was deducted from the reparations Hungary had to pay. Hungary was given ownership of the Hungarian-owned art treasures that were part of the Joint and Imperial collections in Austria. Romania and Yugoslavia were ordered to protect the minorities and it was decided that a Standing Waterway Technical Committee be established. The cover letter contained some nebulous promises and while emphasizing that, "the existing state of affairs, even though it might be thousand years old is not valid for the future if it was found unjust," it did not rule out the possibility of the League of Nations offering its services for the modification of the new frontiers, should the pertinent border commission declare them to be desirable.[80]

The weight of the cover letter was increased by a statement made by Maurice Fouchet and read before the regent, Miklós Horthy, the cabinet, and the principal delegates. In this the effective cooperation of France was offered in order to remedy the national and economic injustices of the treaty, provided of course, that the treaty was signed. All this was barely a pittance but the Hungarian government had no other choice. At the end of May it provisionally signed the option

---

80 Ignác Romsics, ed. *Magyar történeti szöveggyűjtemény* [Collection of Hungarian Historical Documents] (Budapest: Osiris, 2000), vol. 1, p. 139.

agreement about the Hungarian Railways and about the steel works in Pest and Diósgyőr, with the condition that this agreement might be submitted to parliament only if during the six months time limit set by Paris, meritorious steps were taken to change the regulations pertaining to territorial adjustments.[81] In a memorandum, dated one year later, the Quai d'Orsay freely admitted that the cover letter was needed to, "make it easier for Hungary to sign the treaty," i.e., make them swallow the bitter pill.[82] Led by these faint hopes and by the necessity to create consolidation Teleki and Apponyi argued in parliament for the acceptance of the peace treaty.[83] Even though there were quite a few voices against signing the treaty, the treaty had to be signed. On June 4, 1920, a few minutes before four thirty in the afternoon, Ágoston Benard, minister of welfare and labor and Alfréd Drasche-Lázár, minister plenipotentiary and envoy extraordinary, signed the Hungarian Peace Treaty in the Grand Trianon Palace in the gardens of the Palais de Versailles.

The territorial changes mandated by the treaty are well known. Not counting Croatia, the area of Hungary was reduced from 282,000 square kilometers to 93,000 square kilometers and the population from 18.2 million to 7.9 million, making it central Europe's smallest country. Its army was limited to 35,000 men. The country had to pay reparations. The new countries became the home of 3.3 million Hungarians, more than half of this mass in solid blocs, directly adjacent to the new borders. There was no social group or political party that considered this peace treaty acceptable. The proposals for improving it were various, ranging from armed reconquest to peaceful revision and from integral revision to modifications based on ethnic grounds.

After signing the Peace Treaty of Trianon it became obvious that the days of the Simonyi-Semadam government were numbered. The politically weak prime minister was unable to hold the coalition together. The three most likely candidates for the prime minister's post were Gyula Rubinek, the Smallholder party politician, István Bethlen, and Albert Apponyi. Teleki believed that if either Bethlen or Apponyi were to become prime minister, he (Teleki) would keep his portfolio.[84] The continuing crisis and the intervention of the Great Powers gradually eliminated all the candidates. During the first days of July the two government parties

---

81 Ádám, ed., *Documents diplomatiques français*, vol. 2, p. 617.
82 Memorandum, Paris, April 20, 1921, Hongrie, vol. 49, pp. 22-30, Europe 1918–1940, MAE AD.
83 Teleki, *Válogatott politikai írások*, ed. Ablonczy, pp. 65–88.
84 Letter of Teleki to Major Burrows the British liaison to the Hungarian peace delegation, Budapest, June 21, 1920, TNA, FO 371, vol. 4860, fol. 136.

agreed, after lengthy arguments, to the composition of the government. On July 7, Horthy asked Bethlen to assume the position of prime minister but he was unable to form a government. One week later, Bethlen was pleased to step down and recommended Teleki for the position. The former minister of foreign affairs entered the government party that very day and the following day Horthy designated him prime minister.[85] Bethlen presumably believed that if the situation would become clearer, he could assume the leadership of the country under more tranquil conditions. Teleki accepted the position as a penance. Bethlen was not alone in his view of the situation. Both the German and French diplomatic representatives in Budapest believed that Teleki's prime ministership would just prolong the transitional period by a few months.[86]

Teleki stayed. During the next nine months at least four attempts were made to bring him down, once he restructured the government, disarmed, pacified, bargained and pretended. His activities as head of the government are a little known chapter in Hungarian political history.

For the First Time at the Head of the Country

After the regent asked Pál Teleki to form a new government, the new prime minister had to face many serious problems. These included the flood of people coming from the occupied areas and the administrative problems this presented. A tangential issue was the new radicalism and anti-Semitism that appeared in some segments of Hungarian society and was shared by the new prime minister. It meant that the "Jewish question" would become part of the agenda. The problem of the landless agricultural workers and the pre-1918 land reform became increasingly pressing. The revolutions proposed radical solutions. The democratic revolution announced the distribution of land and land reforms, the Soviet Republic wished to establish large state-owned farms in the place of the expropriated large and medium-size estates. The Teleki government had to address all these concerns in some fashion. It appeared that August 1919 brought a new political group to power and there was no room for the former leaders of Dualism and of the 1918 Revolution. The activities of the right-wing, radical and anti-Semitic middle-class politicians managed, for a while, to cover up the fact that a new generation had taken over from the pre-1918 elite that was experienced in politics and in administration

---

85 Romsics, *István Bethlen*, pp. 128–129.
86 Ibid., pp. 109–110.

and that had contacts and experiences in foreign countries. It was this new generation, and Teleki particularly, that had to calm the social unrest, repair the tragic economic situation as rapidly as possible, reduce the isolation of the country and ratify the peace treaty. All this was made more difficult by the fact that there were still beatings and hangings going on in the unoccupied parts of the country, justified as the reestablishment of law and order. The military officers Iván Héjjas and Pál Prónay, led special detachments that in fact spread the so called White Terror.

Teleki announced his government on July 19. Initially he kept the foreign affairs portfolio. It appeared that the Smallholder Party had an almost monopolistic power position in the government because seven of the ten ministers were members of that party. The composition of the government suggested that the Smallholder Party had the same percentage representation in the government as the margin of their victory at the elections. This was far from the truth. István Nagyatádi Szabó, was alone in the government with his ideas about being the leader of all the peasantry.

Teleki gave his maiden speech as a prime minister in parliament on July 22. He compared Europe to an area devastated by earthquakes, the aftershocks of which were still occurring and where new quakes were likely.[87] Speaking about foreign policy, he explained that the government had good relations with Poland and asked the Great Powers to assist Poland currently in a desperate struggle with the Soviet Russian Red Army. He mentioned the economic discussions going on between Hungary and France and repeated his views announced in April that, "The Great Powers will now have understanding about the needs for change."[88] According to him the Millerand letter accompanying the peace treaty, hinting at future revisions, entitled Hungary to this opinion. He then turned from foreign policy to domestic policy and declared that his principal goal was the "reestablishment and maintenance of law and order." For those who were in doubt, he emphasized that he would oppose any move directed toward upsetting law and order, regardless of where it came from.[89] He also mentioned that, for him, gaining the goodwill of Europe was not a primary goal because the other countries "were completely wrong in their assessment of the White Terror."[90] He seemed to be inclined to be understanding about the labor problems and the trade unions. The latter would have to

---

[87] *Nemzetgyűlési napló, 1920–1922*, vol. 4, p. 6. The speech is included in Teleki, *Válogatott politikai írások*, ed. Ablonczy, pp. 89–119.
[88] *Nemzetgyűlési napló*, 1920–1922, vol. 4, p. 6.
[89] Ibid., pp. 9–10.
[90] Ibid.

be directed promptly toward their "responsibilities in representing the welfare of the workers" and toward economic self-adjustment. In connection with the above, he also presented his ideas about establishing military labor battalions for the "unreliable elements."[91] He promised that he would stop all arbitrary internments and spoke about the need to reform the administration.[92] He believed that decisions would have to be made about land reform as soon as possible and that when it was implemented elements of national improvements had to be the first consideration.[93] In later pronouncements it became evident that by "elements of national improvement" he meant the owners of large- and medium-sized estates. He gave numerous details about the plans for economic improvements. First and foremost he advocated economies, reduction of the number of government employees, the closure of unnecessary offices, better control of government expenditures, reduction of disbursements and a reduction in the number of automobiles available to the ministries. He was proposing a one-time major estate tax that he meant to impose on the most affluent. He wished to grant the minister of finance full authority in the area of economic management and economies.[94] About the „Jewish question" he said that there was a need for the "administrative protection of the interests of Christian society."[95]

The views demanding restrictions on Jews were largely limited to higher education. Limiting the number of students of Jewish extraction was one of the principal goals of the radical right. In the medical, legal and commercial curricula the ratio of Jewish students approached 50 percent during the war and consequently in some of the professions the ratio of Jews was above 40 percent as early as 1910. In medicine it was 48.9 percent, in law 45.2 percent, in journalism 42.4 percent, in commercial employment 42.7 percent and in veterinary medicine 40 percent. In general university studies the ratio of Jewish students was 30–33 percent.[96] Referring to the numerus clausus, demanded by many and to the regulation of admissions to higher education, the prime minister told the House that admissions would have to be controlled because the country had lost many of its centers of higher education. The introductory speech was well received by Hungarian domestic political circles and by the foreign diplomats.

---

91   Ibid., pp. 11–12.
92   Ibid., pp. 12, and 14.
93   Ibid., p. 14.
94   Ibid., pp. 12–14.
95   Ibid., p. 15.
96   Gyurgyák, *A zsidókérdés Magyarországon*, p. 83.

The National Assembly first addressed the extension of regental powers because Horthy had made this one of the conditions at the time of his election in March 1921. His endeavors were supported at that time even by royalist politicians. In February and indeed for another year after that nobody doubted Horthy's loyalty to the exiled king. The National Assembly voted to approve the regent's rights to prorogue parliament, to grant clemency and to send troops to fight abroad without preliminary approval of the legislature. This last step was justified by the proponents of the legislation and by the minister of justice as well as by the critical turns in the Polish-Russian war. Act XVII of 1920 became law on August 19. It was of no particular significance at the time, but it was on the basis of this law that, twenty-one years later, Horthy sent Hungarian troops against the Soviet Union, without preliminary approval of parliament.

Past and present critics of the period blame the prime minister for the introduction of corporal punishment. Hungarian criminal law had eliminated the use of such physical punishment in 1871. It was used again, for the first time, by Romanian troops of occupation in 1919. In the autumn of 1919 the minister of food supplies of the Friedrich government asked the commander of the Romanian troops for permission to use it. There were two laws enacted legalizing this form of corporal punishment. The Smallholders initially objected, but the National Assembly enacted the law on June 22, 1920.[97] The law affected a well-defined social group, the primarily Jewish wholesale merchants. The duration of Act XXVI of 1920 was limited to one year. Contrary to some historiographical claims, the law was used in some instances and the first one to receive corporal punishment was a pickpocket in January 1921.[98]

In the debate on the government program there came a moment when it became apparent that there were pitfalls ahead for the government. On July 30, an important member of the government party, in a question to a minister, mentioned an attack on a cafe in a Jewish neighborhood. The extreme right-wing groups, consisting of military officers and university students, known as the Awakening Hungarians [Ébredő Magyarok], who had been quiet prior to the signing of the Peace Treaty of Trianon became active again during the summer. On the evening of July 27 a group of twenty to thirty men invaded the Club Cafe on the Lipót Boulevard (today Szent István Boulevard) and assaulted the guests. Two of them died. Teleki, observing the concern of the representatives, immediately responded to the ques-

---

97 *Magyar törvénytár 1920* [Hungarian Law Code 1920], pp. 47–50.
98 *Pesti Hírlap*, January 28, 1921, p. 3.

tion and claimed that the event was only a public disturbance (and not an Antisemitic incident). He promised prompt and effective steps against the hooligans.[99] Early in August the perpetrators were identified tried and sentenced. All of them received jail sentences of up to twelve and thirteen years.[100]

These sentences started the process that led to the control of the racialists who had been forcing people in the street identify themselves if they were "Jews" or "Hungarians." They organized hate campaigns and engaged in street fights. The next step in this process was the bill "on the more effective protection of public law and order" presented to the Council of Ministers by the minister of justice on August 10. It was enacted by the legislature on March 16, 1921.[101] This then became Act III of 1921, that was designed to prevent both non-existent Communist, and rightist special detachment actions.[102] The last outrage committed by the Awakening Hungarians was a second invasion of the Club Coffee House and assault on the guests on October 5.

Prior to the ratification of the Peace Treaty there were a number of mass demonstrations. The members of the Awakening Hungarians participated in making people identify themselves in the street, beating up Jews and invading organizations labeled as being Jewish, e.g. the Freemasons. On an evening in November the members of a paramilitary organization killed a policeman who had come to the assistance of a victim assaulted by the hooligans. This was the climax. On pressure from the National Assembly the government took action and on the evening of November 10 the police, with military assistance, surrounded four hotels in Budapest, disarmed the special detachment members residing there and arrested many of them. Teleki was present at the raid. At dawn on November 11, soldiers surrounded a group of barracks in the suburbs where, in addition to displaced persons and building crews, the special detachment members were also lodged. There was gunfire and the soldiers shot four special detachment members. Subsequently, the prime minister issued an order that all organizations established after October 1918 had to have their bylaws revised and for the time being he banned all public meetings. The Budapest organization of the Awakening Hungarians was sus-

---

99 *Nemzetgyűlési napló, 1920–1922*, vol. 6, p. 118.
100 Tibor Zinner, *Az ébredők fénykora 1919–1923* [The Heydays of the Awakening Hungarians 1919–1923] (Budapest: Akadémiai Kiadó, 1989), pp. 70–75.
101 Minutes of the Council of Ministers, August 10, 1920, point 14 on the agenda, admin., box 128, K 27, MNL OL.
102 *Magyar törvénytár* (1921), pp. 8–11.

pended for behavioral irregularities.[103] Similar raids were promised for the rural areas and martial law was extended to all who committed similar actions. Teleki then proceeded to disband the special detachments. He did not do anything to the few groups whose leaders were exerting pressure on Horthy, e.g. Prónay and Gyula Ostenburg, but tried to limit their sphere of activities as much as possible. Teleki's actions resulted in public safety being very much improved in the country and the participants in attacks against Jews and assaults and robberies received their just punishment. The time of the atrocities and violence against the Jews slowly came to an end.

In addition to the restoration of law and order, the outrages of the special detachments brought another critically important problem of Hungarian society to the surface. By the middle of 1920 anti-Semitism and the Jewish question became a societal issue. Many demanded that the civil rights of the Jews be curtailed using the actions of Jews during the revolutions as a justification. The high incidence of Jews among the "war speculators" was also pointed out.[104] Yet, a number of writings and speeches produced during the counterrevolution, however, drew attention to the significant counterrevolutionary role of the Jewry. The anti-bourgeois hostility of the Soviet Republic in Budapest created a distinctly anti-Jewish trend in Budapest.[105] Furthermore, there were numerous Jewish victims of the Red Terror and numerous Jewish officers participated in the formation of the National Army in Szeged.[106] Rational arguments, however, had no place in the debates between 1919 and 1921. The Szeged officers, Christian intellectuals, extreme right-wingers, Awakening Hungarians, and neoconservatives kept on voicing indictments against the Jews.

The repression of Jewry was presented to public opinion as an attempt to do away with the intellectual proletariat. It was at the University Council meetings in Budapest in August-September 1919 a need for establishing a quota system for the students was raised. The overburdened medical faculty was at the helm of this proposal. The decidedly racial-religious implications of the issue were due to the position taken by the faculties of law and theology.[107] On the basis of instructions from

---

103 Zinner, *Az ébredők fénykora*, pp. 106–109.
104 Gyurgyák, *A zsidókerdes Magyarországon*, pp. 93–94.
105 Lajos Szabolcsi, *Két emberöltő. Az Egyenlőség évtizedei, 1881–1931* |Two Generations. The Decades of the Egyenlőség (Equality), 1881–1931] (Budapest: MTA, 1993), p. 281.
106 Ibid., pp. 282–283; and Gyurgyák, *A zsidókérdés Magyarországon*, pp. 111–114.
107 Katalin N. Szegvári, *Numerus clausus rendelkezések az ellenforradalmi Magyarországon* [The Numerus Clausus Ordinances in Counterrevolutionary Hungary] (Budapest: Akadémiai Kiadó,1988), pp. 96–101.

In The Revolution, The Counterrevolution, And In The Government (1918–1921)

István Haller, the minister of culture and education, the admission of Jews to the university was made more difficult during the first half of 1920. Haller submitted the bill to the National Assembly on August 13, 1920, as part of the presentation of the government program. On August 13, after committee discussions, The "Bill on Registration of Students at the University of Arts and Sciences, at the Technical University, at the Department of Economics of the University of Budapest, and at the Law School" was submitted to the legislature. Debates began three weeks later. The debate was closed on September 21 and the next day, on September 22, the National Assembly endorsed of Act XXV, 1920,[108] which came to be known as the anti-Jewish numerus clausus law. It required that the "proportion of students belonging to the various races and nationalities living in the country correspond to the proportion of those races and nationalities in the population of the country...."

The prime minister did not participate in the debate. One of the reasons was that between August 20 and September 15 he was ailing and could not attend cabinet meetings. When the bill was presented at the prime minister's residence, Teleki made no comments of merit. Yet we have ample reason to assume that the prime minister had no objection to the proposal. Definition of Jewry as race was also a familiar concept to him and this was indicated by his pronouncements made in Szeged during the summer of 1919. His ideas were very close to the majority views of the National Assembly and in some respects went even beyond them. In the treatment of the Jewish question, Teleki differed from the intransigent Christian politicians only in attitude but not in the assessment of the principles. In his speech to the electorate in Szeged, in October, he tried to explain his position. He cautioned all of them about engendering hatred, "because the preservation of the ethnic spirit is too sacred an obligation to be approached with hatred." He condemned generalizations in speaking about the Jews because many of them played an important, beneficial role during the revolution. He pointed out the extremely important role played by Hungarian Jews, for Hungary, in commerce, industry and economy.[109] At the same time he defended the act and in his arguments he distinguished between the integrated Jewry, "identifying themselves with national goals" and the newly immigrated and hence not assimilated "Galicians," who according to him were responsible for the revolution and that this justified the discrimination.

There is no doubt that the government did not entirely side with the intransigents and did not endorse the kind of anti-Semitic demands that would have upset

---

108 Gyurgyák, *A zsidókérdés Magyarországon*, pp. 117–123.
109 MTI news bulletins, vol. 1, October 10, 1920, fifth ed., K 428, MNL OL.

the fundamental economic conditions (large estates and capitalism).[110] Because of the numerus clausus law the number of Jewish students decreased at the universities in Budapest. The act made the social advancement of the Jewish petit bourgeoisie and their taking positions in the professions more difficult.[111] The young members of the Jewish upper classes and some of the Jewish middle class went abroad for their studies and returned from there knowing foreign languages, being well trained and made good contacts. Some of them never returned. Over the short range, the law, while contrary to the practices of the Dualism, to the freedom of education, to the emancipation of the Jewry and to the rules pertaining to nationalities, achieved its purpose. The radical, anti-Semite right wing generally felt, however, that the law did not go far enough, but the ratio of Jewish university students dropped from the earlier 30–34 percent to 10–12 percent and later to 8–10 percent and remained at this level, with minor variations until World War II.[112]

There was no other more isolated government in Europe in 1920 than the newly appointed Teleki government. It was isolated not only in a political sense but quite literally. Since June 20, 1920, the boycott on the transport of goods, announced by the International Federation of Trade Unions was in effect against Hungary.[113] The demands of the federation included the establishment of democratic rights in Hungary and the mitigation of the severe sentences imposed on the former leaders of the Soviet Republic who did not manage to escape.[114]

The most important consequences were on the relations with Austria. Hungary's most important link with the West, both on water and land, soon became blocked causing severe losses to Hungarian commerce. In Czechoslovakia the blockade eased up at the beginning of July and there was a way, through Bratislava [Pozsony], to circumvent the blockade on personal travel.[115] The Hungarian gov-

---

110 Zsuzsa L. Nagy, *Bethlen liberális ellenzéke* [Bethlen's Liberal Opposition] (Budapest: Akadémiai Kiadó, 1980), p. 34.
111 Rudolf Andorka, István Harcsa, and Rózsa Kulcsár, "A társadalmi mobilitás történelmi tendenciái" [The Historical Trends of Social Mobility], *Statisztikai Időszaki Közlemények* [Periodic Statistical Reports] 343, (1975): 13–39.
112 M. Kovács, Liberalizmus, radikalizmus, pp. 84–85.
113 Jenő Horvath, *A trianoni békeszerződés megalkotása és a revízió útja* [Creation of the Trianon Peace Treaty and the Path to Revision] (Budapest: MTA, 1939), pp. 201–202; Mária Ormos, "Francia-magyar tárgyalasok 1920-ban" [French-Hungarian negotiations in 1920], *Századok*, nos. 5–6 (1975): 931–932.
114 Máté Molnár, "A Nemzetközi Szakszervezeti Szövetség bojkottja Magyarország ellen, 1920. június 20.-augusztus 8." [The Boycott of the International Federation of Trade Unions against Hungary, June 20-August 8, 1920], *Századok*, no. 3 (1996): 641.
115 Ferenc Boros, *Magyar-csehszlovák kapcsolatok 1918–1921-ben* [Hungarian-Czechoslovak Relations in 1918–1921] (Budapest: Akadémiai Kiadó, 1979), pp. 253–257; and Molnár, "A Nemzetközi Szakszervezeti Szövetseg," p. 648.

ernment took steps, organized a counter-boycott and forbade the export of goods to Austria. The Vienna food supply was dependent upon Hungary and soon suffered from the effects of the ordinance.[116] In the end, the boycott proved to be a complete failure for its organizers. All personal and goods traffic was resumed with all the neighbors on August 8–9.[117] The Teleki government emerged much strengthened from this encounter, at least as far as domestic public opinion was concerned. Two months later Teleki spoke harshly about the organizers of the boycott when he addressed his electoral district. According to him "the boycott was directed against the fight of Christian Hungary against communism. It was organized by international elements outside of this country."[118]

The government weathered the first serious test of its strength but there were still many unresolved foreign policy problems. In July- August 1920 Hungary was for all practical purposes at war with all of its neighbors. It became the principal task for both Teleki, and for the new Minister of Foreign Affairs Imre Csáky, to control the unpredictable elements of Hungarian domestic policy, to eliminate the suspicions of the neighbor States and endeavor to free the country of the increasingly worrisome international isolation. During the summer of 1920 the international developments took a turn for the worse and during the second half of July, the Soviet Russian Red Army came within eighty kilometers, of the Carpathians. Teleki tried to point out the deplorable condition of the Hungarian army to the French, British, and Italian high commissioners in Budapest, and ask for assistance in rearming it.[119] Even though the request was not supported openly by the Great Powers, it gave a boost to the languishing Hungarian-French negotiations. Armed Hungarian assistance in Poland should have taken place at the end of July. On July 26, Teleki advised the representatives of the Great Powers in Budapest that if his government would not receive permission to station troops along the line of the Carpathians, Hungary would wish to declare a complete disinterest in the entire affair.[120]

The dilemma was made worse for the French by the announcement of the Prague government on July 31 that confirmed its neutrality in the Polish-Russian

---

116 Molnár, "A Nemzetközi Szakszervezeti Szövetseg," p. 648.
117 Ibid., p. 653.
118 MTI news bulletins, vol. 1. October 10, 1920, fourth ed., news no. 39, K 428, MNL OL.
119 Dezső Újváry and Ferenc Deák, eds., Papers and Documents Relating to the Foreign Relations of Hungary 1919–1920 (Budapest: Royal Hungarian Ministry of Foreign Affairs, 1939), vol. 1, doc. 523; and R. Butler, J. P. Bury, and M. E. Lambert, eds., *Documents on British Foreign Policy 1919–1939*, vol. 12, First Series (London: HMSO, 1962), doc. 198.
120 Ormos, "Francia-magyar tárgyalások," p. 936.

war. Maurice Fouchet, the French high commissioner in Budapest, discreetly supported the Hungarian plan and even the leaders of French foreign policies were considering the Hungarian proposal. On July 27, 1920, Maurice Paleologue, the Secretary General of the Quai d'Orsay, wrote, "The Hungarian government obviously made the offer to gain some benefit from it. It is possible, however, that events will take a turn where we will be forced to line up all possible help on the side of Poland. In the first line we are counting on our allies, but it is not impossible that we will accept the Hungarian offer to help against the peril threatening central Europe."[121]

Over the next few days, however, the direction of politics took a turn. Prime Minister Alexandre Millerand personally forbade the acceptance of the Hungarian offer. He also called on the Prague government, via the Quai d'Orsay, not to oppose the anti-Bolshevik coalition. In exchange for this, the Prague government was presumably promised that Hungary would be kept away.[122] It was as consequence of these events that the Czechoslovak-Yugoslav agreement came into being, in August 1920, and served as the origin of the Little Entente. The changes occurring on the Polish front, after August 16. made the Hungarian offer null and void for the French. Hungary thus could not send troops but did send equipment to vigorously fighting Warsaw.

The prime minister was determined to improve Hungary's foreign policy situation. In the middle of November Teleki had to personally disavow the attacks against Subcarpathia, planned by Iván Héjjas and his associates. Teleki stated that this plan against an area under Czechoslovak sovereignty was not in agreement with the plans of the Hungarian government.[123] He had to act similarly in the case of an action planned just before Christmas. Teleki gave the indignant special detachment leader to understand that if he started the action, he (Teleki) would so advise the Czechoslovak minister in Budapest.[124]

The Hungarian-Czechoslovak relations moved from an almost belligerent situation during the summer of 1920 and from continuous incidents along the border, to a quasi-frozen indifference by the end of the year. The careful exploratory moves in January 1921 and the Bruck negotiations in March 1921 were the first steps taken to improve the situation. After the initial steps, Teleki was prepared to engage

---

121 Paléologue's circular telegram, Hongrie, vol. 47, pp. 88–89, Europe 1918–1940, MAE AD.
122 Millerand's circular telegram, July 29, 1920, Hongrie, vol. 47, pp. 99–100, Europe 1918-1940, MAE AD.
123 Ministry of Foreign Affairs, res. pol., 1920-7-459, K 64, MNL OL.
124 Újváry and Deák, eds., *Papers and Documents*, vol. 1, doc. 882; and Minutes of the Council of Ministers, Budapest, December 23, 1920, topic 53 on the agenda, box 129, K 27, MNL OL.

in negotiations and hoped that territorial questions would also be discussed.[125] The Hungarian-Czechoslovak meeting took place on March 14-15 on the Austrian side of the Leitha River, in Bruck. Hungary was represented by the new minister of foreign affairs, Gusztáv Grátz, and by Teleki. Czechoslovakia by Edvard Beneš and by Rudolf Hotewetz the minister of foreign trade.[126] Even though Prague had announced that there would be no discussion of territorial matters, the Hungarian delegation did raise the matter. The Czechs refused to discuss it and the discussions were politically unproductive. The parties agreed on some pending interstate issues, but Prague refused to even listen to territorial adjustment matters. The views in Bucharest were the same.

It is a well-known fact and it is frequently mentioned in various documents that during the summer of 1920, with the knowledge and approval of the government, an extreme right-wing military officer group around the regent started discussion with an extreme right-wing military group in Bavaria. Teleki and Kálmán Kánya, the general secretary in the Ministry of Foreign Affairs, knew that the racist politicians were secretly meeting with the emissaries of General Erich Ludendorff and Bavarian Prime Minister Gustav Ritter von Kahr, but did not interfere with the negotiations.[127] The prime minister and the foreign policy leadership endeavored to make contacts at a higher level and sought contacts with the organizer of Weimar Germany's Reichswehr, General Hans von Seeckt and his circle. Teleki sent numerous hints to Berlin that "even though he was paddling in French backwaters" he did not wish to suppress his own political preferences or the traditional Germanophilia of Hungarian public opinion.[128] It is characteristic of the foreign policy game that when Teleki was ailing he was visited by the German consul general, but not by Maurice Fouchet.[129]

---

125 Minutes of the Council of Ministers, January' 12, 1921, no. 28 on the agenda, admin., box 130, K 27, MNL OL.
126 Endre Tóth, "Az első kétoldalú tárgyalások Csehszlovákia es Magyarország között (1921) Bruck an der Leitha (2. resz)" [The first bilateral negotiations between Czechoslovakia and Hungary (1921), in Bruck an der Leitha (Part Two)), *Forum*, no. 2 (2002): 59–75; and Gusztáv Grátz, *Magyarország a két háború között* [Hungary between the Two Wars] (Budapest: Osiris, 2001), pp. 44–47.
127 Data from 1920–1922, Kozma Papers, cs. l.fol. 1, K 429, MNL OL; and *Horthy Miklós titkos iratai* [The Secret Papers of Miklós Horthy], ed. Miklós Szinai and László Szűcs (Budapest: Kossuth 1972), pp. 33–38.
128 Egon von Fürstenberg-Stammheim to the Ministry of Foreign Affairs, September 26, 1920, R 74141, Politisches Archiv des Auswartigen Amts (hereafter cited as PA AA); and Charge d'Affairs Goos to the Ministry of Foreign Affairs, Berlin, August 31, 1920, R 30531, PA AA.
129 Egon von Fürstenberg-Stammheim to the Ministry of Foreign Affairs, Budapest, September 5, 1920, R 74194, PA AA.

Teleki and his minister of foreign affairs, Imre Csáky, both felt that the opportunities were becoming more limited. They were attacked on numerous occasions in Hungarian domestic policies because of the perceived unilateral French orientation.[130] Actually this orientation was not entirely sincere on Teleki's part and he confirmed this later in a confidential statement during the summer of 1921, "I have never been hopeful about the so-called French orientation"[131] In order for a new beginning to get under way, that Hungarian legations could be set up and that there be a faint chance to move forward, the government had to fulfill the last Great Power demand and ratify the Peace Treaty of Trianon. The majority of the National Assembly approved this on November 13, 1920 but not without major struggles and considerable dissatisfaction.

Even though the measures adopted by the 1918-19 revolutions were systematically reversed by the new system that came to power in August 1919, it was evident that the old problems, inadequately handled by the revolutions, had to be addressed. Ever since the Compromise, the most crucial problem in Hungary was land ownership. In 1920, 2,118,145 inhabitants of Hungary, that is 57 percent of the wage earners, lived from agriculture. One third of this enormous group owned no land property whatsoever.[132] All political forces agreed that a land reform was essential, but there were endless debates in the press and at the interparty conferences about the theoretical basis of receiving land, entitlement and the extent of the land reform. By July, 1920, the "Agrarian-Democratic" wing of the Smallholders, recommending a radical distribution of land and the political circles favoring the large estates, were deeply dissatisfied with the fighting that had lasted for more than six months and that was conducted in the press, at party conferences, between parties and in the National Assembly. The government conference meeting on July 25, 1920, made decisions about the essential components of the land reform in less than a day.

It was decided at the conference, attended by the prime minister, the ministers of finance, and of agriculture, and the party chiefs, that the basic principle of the distribution of land would be need. Widows, orphans and disabled veterans would have to make no payments for the land during the first year. According to the agreement one third of a large estate could be expropriated, provided that, "the remain-

---

130 Diary of Countess Andrássy, September 1929, Gyula Andrássy Papers, box 1, t. 330, fol. 480, P4, MNL OL.
131 Pál Teleki's summary of his Paris and London trip, to Miklós Bánffy. Budapest June 12, Minister of Foreign Affairs Papers, cs. 38, fol. 2, 1921- 266/res, K 58, MNL OL.
132 Gyula Konkoly-Thege, *Magyarország földbirtokviszonyai és a földreform* [The Conditions of Landed Property in Hungary and the Land Reform] (Budapest: Magyar Gazdaszövetség, 1925), table 3.

ing part was viable."[133] These principles truly represented a compromise between two points of view. Nagyatádi Szabó, the peasant politician fighting for radical reforms was not satisfied, but hoped to make some gains during the implementation process. The reluctance of the supporters of the large estates was partly due to the fact that their constituency and numerous agricultural experts believed that the reforms would lead to a catastrophic decline in agricultural productivity and to a fall in efficiency.[134]

István Nagyatádi Szabó submitted his bill on the "Enactment on the Appropriate Distribution of Land" to the National Assembly on August 18.[135] The general debate on the land reform legislation began on November 4. The representatives decided to hold daily eight-hour sessions to expedite the debate. On November 12, 1920, at the end of a painstaking session, the representatives stood, cheered and clapped their hands in recognition of István Nagyatádi Szabó.[136] Act XXXVI of 1920 was to be in effect for five years. It consisted of 11 chapters and 101 paragraphs. The critically important implementation order did not appear until six months later, in June 1921. Even though it was issued by Nagyatádi it did not seem to help those who wished to obtain land. The act contained 260 items and was so complicated that it was almost totally unworkable. Only relatively very few 10–15 acre mid-size estate parcels were created on the basis of this act and there was a huge number of dwarf holdings. The goal of the nonagrarian politicians was not the strengthening of the small-holder class but simply the defusing of social dissatisfaction.

In accomplishing the land reform a total of 1.12 million acres were distributed which rose to 1.275 million acres when the land given away in leasehold was included. This amounted to 8.5 percent of the total arable land in Hungary. The percentage of land that changed hands as the consequence of the law was approximately the same as in Poland but less than in Czechoslovakia (16 percent) and Romania (27 percent). We must add, however, that the generosity of the Successor States was almost invariably at the expense of Hungarian holdings. In Hungary 428,054 small holdings were created and 259,733 household plots. Of those who

---

133 Károly Mészáros, "A Rubinekkel kötött kompromisszum" [The compromise made with Rubinek], *Agrártörténeti Szemle* [Agrarian History Review], nos. 1–2 (1979): 49–50.
134 Minutes of the Council of Ministers, August 12, 1920, no. 4 on the agenda, admin., box. 128, K 27, MNL OL; and József Nagy, "A Nagyatádi-féle földreform lezárása és eredményei" [Closure of the Nagyatádi Land Reform and its results], *Agrártörténeti Szemle*, nos. 1–2 (1979): 45.
135 *Nemzetgyűlési napló, 1920–1922*, vol. 4, p. 534.
136 Ibid., vol. 6, p. 536.

became entitled to have land there were 300 thousand agricultural laborers who owned no land whatever.[137] Making this group into owners contributed greatly to the transient calming of Hungary and was an important component of the Teleki government's consolidation policies, even though most of the 1–2 acre parcels were not economically viable. Teleki did not participate in the debate and even in his public speeches avoided taking a strong stand in this matter. The idea of a land reform for social reasons was not unwelcome to him but he considered the mid-size (500-1000 acres) estate owners as the nationally supportive and sustaining element, both at that time and later.

The government was now past the two most difficult tasks, the ratification of the peace treaty and the land reform when, unexpectedly, Baron Frigyes Korányi, the minister of finance was given a vote of no confidence. His resignation was followed by the entire cabinet's. Public opinion was surprised but the political insiders knew that sooner or later this was inevitable.

The fact that it was the minister of finance who received the vote of no confidence was not an accident. The deterioration of the crown increased to as much as 60 percent in one month in 1920. During the spring the crown was stabilized by the Zurich Stock Exchange by using a Hungarian state symbol in the transactions, but from July to the end of the year the crown fell from 3.37 centimes to 1.15 centimes. The financial problems caused enormous social tensions and, compared to the prewar situation, almost every social group's standard of living declined by 60–90 percent. Compared to 1914 the prices had increased a hundred fold while the wages only rose by a factor of fifteen. The essential foods, milk, meat and vegetables were absent from the tables of most families and these families also lacked the funds for clothing and heating. Among the weakened population infectious diseases were devastating, particularly the influenza raging since 1918 and tuberculosis. Korányi saw the key to improving the fiscal situation in restricting the spending of the state agencies. Korányi stayed in the government after the beginning of August only by setting some rigid conditions and on November 10 he did resign because he found that his program did, "not meet with realistic understanding and support."[138]

After the vote of no confidence in December, the Council of Ministers was summoned promptly and Teleki announced that his government expressed its solidarity with the minister and that same day submitted the resignation of the gov-

---

137 György Ránki, ed., *Magyarország története 1918–19, 1919–1945* [The History of Hungary, 1918-1919, 1919-1945] (Budapest: Akadémiai Kiadó, 1976), p. 428.
138 Minutes of the Council of Ministers, January 4, 1921, pol., no. 1 on the agenda, box 129, K 27, MNL OL.

ernment to the regent.[139] Yet it was again Teleki who was asked to form a government and the new government was established on December 16.

"Now the real work will begin" wrote Teleki to his minister in Vienna whom he had invited to be the new minister of foreign affairs.

This spring is likely to be the hottest one we have seen yet, both domestically and in foreign affairs. I am unable to take on this dual battle and this duplicate work. Both activities overlap physically and no single person can perform both….In the Council of Ministers you would be a great comfort to me in the presence of the temperamental minister of finance and the minister of commerce whom I consider somewhat limited."

Teleki was thus courting the well-known expert.[140] The most important aspect of Gusztáv Grátz's activities as minister of foreign affairs was the negotiation concerning the sovereignty over western Hungary. The western segment of Hungary was given to Austria by the Paris Peace Conference and this was the only part of Hungary that, at the time of signing the peace treaty, was under Hungarian military and administrativecontrol. In connection with the Austrian demands, Teleki announced that the government would not yield the territory to Austria under any circumstances. When questioned about armed resistance, Teleki gave an even more definite answer. The Hungarian government would resist Austrian troops with full force and would resist the Entente forces as well even if the Entente plenipotentiaries would leave Budapest because of its resistance. Teleki refused to listen to some of his ministers, including the minister of defense who claimed that the area was not suitable for defense because it was a long narrow strip of land.[141] Pál Teleki's obstinacy was legendary. His personality lacked the inclination to weigh the relative forces and the careful assessment of risk and benefit.

The most important element of the new government was the appointment of the new minister of finance. Lóránt Hegedüs was an expert member of the peace delegation. His dynamism and his faith in his program had an effect on Teleki who, in his second introductory speech, skipped over the matter of the king, land reform, and judicial reform, and made the elimination of the economic difficulties the principal task of his government.[142] In the person of Hegedűs he acquired an expert

---

139 Minutes of the Council of Ministers, December 1, 1920, pol., no. 1 on the agenda, box 129, K 27, MNL OL.
140 Lajos Gecsényi and Péter Sipos, "Grátz Gusztáv emlékiratai" [The memoirs of Gusztáv Grátz], *Történelmi Szemle*, nos. 3–4 (2000): 329.
141 Minutes of the Council of Ministers, January 4, 1921, pol. no. 3 on the agenda, box 130, K 27, MNL OL.
142 *Nemzetgyűlési napló, 1920–1922*, vol. 7, pp. 209–212.

who not only held the confidence of the financial circles but who made his stabilization program credible and acceptable to the population of the country. This cabinet was composed of persons close to Teleki and the leaders of the two great political parties were left out.

In order to achieve financial stability it was essential to decrease the budget deficit and therefore Hegedűs took even more drastic steps than Korányi in curbing governmental spending. He introduced the universal 2 percent sales tax and showed great ingenuity in devising new consumption taxes. The most vigorous debate was about his introduction of the one-time special tax on large estates with which he tried to combine the stabilization of foreign exchange and the issues of the land reform.[143] After some favorable early signs the reform floundered. The deficit grew, the trade deficit increased and inflation got much worse. By the summer of 1921, Hegedűs had exhausted all his credit options and the economy took another nose dive. Hegedűs suffered a mental collapse and resigned from the Bethlen government. In the first half of 1921, at the time of the Teleki government, Hegedűs was a somewhat high-strung but credible person and he personified many hopes.

Subsequent to the ratification of the peace treaty, assessment of the monarchy issue became the watershed of Hungarian politics. The question of the ruler divided the Hungarian political elite albeit the groups had contacts with each other and exchanged views. In addition to the royalists, and the "Free King-Electors," there was a third group, numerically smaller but politically very influential, who believed that the "royal matter was not timely." The royalist ideas did have some societal support which included a significant percentage of the inhabitants of the mostly Catholic western Hungarian counties, most of the officer corps, almost every aristocrat, a huge majority of the Roman Catholic Church leadership, the Jewish bourgeoisie of Budapest and certain middle-class groups. The support for the Free King-Electors came from the Protestant areas, the Great Plain [Alföld], the Christian-Nationalist groups of the Budapest middle class, certain military officer organizations and the university students.

Pál Teleki was very careful to conceal his views. In public he always favored postponement of the royalty issue. The furthest he went was in October 1920 when he declared in Szeged, that, "The king of Hungary can only be a Hungarian king," meaning that Charles IV could be king of Hungary only because the Peace Treaty

---

143 Lóránt Hegedűs, *A pénz sorsa és misztériuma* [The Fate and Mystery of Money] (Budapest: M. Kir. Egyetemi Nyomda, 1938), p. 429.

of Saint Germain forbade Austria to restore the Habsburgs.[144] In statements to foreign diplomats Teleki considered it possible that Archduke József [Joseph] or his son, Archduke Albert [Albrecht] could be raised to the throne.[145] He evidently considered Charles to be the legal king but diplomatic considerations forced him to subject his personal feelings to foreign policy expectations. The fact that at the beginning of February 1920 the Great Powers categorically forbade the restoration weighed even more heavily than the domestic political tensions. The Conference of Ambassadors declared at their meeting in Rome on February 2, 1920, that, "although they did not wish to determine Hungary's form of government or constitution,...they could not agree that the restoration of the Habsburg dynasty was a matter for Hungary to decide alone and therefore they would not recognize or tolerate any kind of restoration."[146] Most parties, from the liberals to the racialists, however, agreed in the support of some form of royal rule. The government endeavored strongly all through the autumn to eliminate the question of the king from the political life of the country' and tried to prevent the administration and the officer corps from being immersed in this affair.

From his residence in Switzerland, Charles IV maintained an active correspondence with his followers in Hungary and with Regent Horthy. The king unmistakably indicated to Horthy that it was his intention to retake the throne at the earliest opportunity.[147] The cease fire agreement on the matter of the king came to an end with the ratification of the peace treaty on November 13, 1920. It was likely that the fragile government party composed from Smallholders and the KNEP would shortly be ripped apart by the conflict. In order to prevent this, Teleki stated at the time when the new government was established that both the immediate return of the king and his formal dethronement by a majority of parliament would represent a serious danger for the country.[148] Yet the matter of the king became one of the issues in the political crisis that erupted in February 1921. At the government party conference on February 2, 1921, the prime minister was voted down 58 to 62 when he asked the National Assembly to delay the consideration of the king ques-

---

144 MTI news bulletins, October 10, 1920, vol. 1, 5th ed, K 4289, MNL OL.
145 Ádám, ed., *Document diplomatiques français*, vol. 2, p. 199; and Elek Karsai, "Brit diplomáciai iratok az 1921. évi húsvéti királypuccs történetéhez "[British diplomatic papers concerning the royal coup at Easter 1921], *Levéltári Közlemények*, no. 1 (1968); and Athelstan-Johnson, deputy principal delegate's report to Curzon, November 2, 1920.
146 Adam, ed., *Document diplomatiques français*, vol. 2, p. 362.
147 Szinai and Szűcs, eds., *Horthy Miklós titkos iratai*, pp. 23–24.
148 Minutes of the Council of Ministers, December 16, 1920, box 129, pol., no. 1 on the agenda, K 27, MNL OL.

tion. The critically acute positions did not favor postponement of the issue and the government majority fell apart. On February 4, 1921, Teleki resigned from the party and with thirty-seven associates endeavored to establish a new government coalition on the ruins of united governing party that was formed in July 1920 by the Smallholders and KNEP.[149] The technique was an old one dating back to the Dualism and it was used successfully later by István Bethlen. Teleki was not successful in making his group the nucleus of a new unified party. The Smallholders and the Christian National Unity Party (KNEP) could no longer be held in the same organization and they were willing to rule only as a coalition. Both the Smallholder Party and KNEP were reorganized but it was likely that the peace would be short-lived. Events made it apparent that unless something dramatic happened, new elections would have to be called because the debates about the king would paralyze both legislature, and the government. The dramatic event was the Easter coup attempt by Charles IV that surprised everybody even though it was not entirely unexpected.

It cannot be determined what written or oral agreement induced Charles IV to leave Prangins in Switzerland on March 21, 1921, armed with the Spanish passport of his gardener, carrying a backpack, wearing dark glasses and a dark-colored moustache in order to regain Hungary's throne. The remaining French and British diplomatic documents contain no evidence on the part of the Great Powers in support of this action. Allegedly, before his departure, Charles IV had received the promise of the French prime minister that he would support the restoration of Habsburg rule in Hungary. According to the recollection of Queen Zita, the French sent emissaries made a verbal commitment that France would provide military and economic assistance, that the borders would be revised and that the Little Entente would be reined in.[150] Even if there was such an agreement it was worthless. Yet Charles wanted to believe in French support and it was with this idea that he started out for Hungary. In the company of a childhood playmate the former ruler went through Vienna and entered Hungary. He crossed the border at Pinkafeld [Pinkafő] and in the evening of March 26 he arrived to the Roman Catholic Bishop's Palace in Szombathely.

Some historians doubt that Pál Teleki being "accidentally" at nearby Ivánc was a pure coincidence. The American high commissioner, Ulysses Grant-Smith, was also present at the weekend snipe shoot. Yet it is hard to believe that Teleki would

---

149 "Felbomlott a kormánypárt" [The government party has fallen apart], *Népszava*, February 5, 1921, p. 2.
150 Gorden Brook-Shepherd, *The Last Hahsburg* (London: Weinfeld and Nicholson, 1968), 257–258.

have taken his family along for a coup and arrange it so that the representative of a country opposed to restoration was also present.

Teleki and his host Antal Sigray went to Szombathely that very night. The prime minister was devastated by the arrival of the king. "Teleki was shocked and worried about the possibility of a civil war and had great difficulties in preserving his equanimity,"[151] wrote an eyewitness. During their discussion Teleki suggested to Charles that he could turn back without anybody finding out about the events. Finally they all agreed that the king should hasten to Budapest and negotiate with the regent about taking over the power.

They agreed that Teleki would leave early the next morning and advise Horthy abut the arrival of the monarch and that Charles would start ninety minutes later. In the morning of March 27 the prime minister started for Budapest. His chauffeur got lost and then the car broke down. It is not likely that all this was done intentionally but Teleki's behavior gave rise to considerable suspicion. The foreign diplomats wondered why Horthy could not have been advised about the king's arrival by telephone.[152] The king did not wait for ninety minutes and started off with Sigray and a few officers in a powerful car for Budapest. His car was driven by the later famous desert explorer and even more famous movie hero (in the *English Patient*) László Ede Almásy. Charles reached Budapest around 1:00 P.M. and was driven immediately to the Royal Castle. After an initial shock Horthy, summoned from the luncheon table, received the king. The two participants in the discussion give different accounts of what took place.[153] The regent speaking of the likely attack by the Little Entente urged the king to leave. Seeing that Horthy would not yield, the king left the palace about 4:00 P.M. and returned to Szombathely. On his arrival there he claimed to be ill and refused to go further. Teleki arrived at the palace at the time of the royal audience. Horthy instructed him to return to Szombathely and convince the king to leave the country.

The neighboring states protested against the royal coup on March 29. Czechoslovakia and Yugoslavia considered it a *casus belli* and ordered a partial mobilization.[154] The Great Powers were more understanding vis-a-vis the government. On

---

151 Antal Lehár, "Egy katonatiszt naplója 1919–1921" [Diary of a military officer, 1919-1921], *História*, no. 11 (1993): 27.
152 Fürstenberg-Stammheim to the Ministry of Foreign Affairs, April 1, 1921, R 74188, PA AA.
153 Aladár Boroviczény, *A király és kormányzója* [The King and his Regent] (Budapest: Európa, 1993), pp. 93–96; and Miklós Horthy, *Emlékirataim* [My Memoirs] (Budapest: Európa, 1990), pp. 149–152.
154 Újváry and Deák, eds., *Papers and Documents*, vol. 2, nos. 265, 267, 268, 270, 273, and 274; and Gyula Juhász, *Hungarian Foreign Policy 1919–1945* (Budapest: Akadémiai Kiadó, 1979), p. 59.

March 28 the French, British, and Italian high commissioners discussed the situation and decided that there was no need for any strong steps to be taken and even calmed down the Yugoslav minister who was beside himself.[155] Under the pressure of the Entente powers and of the Successor States, the king left the country on April 5. As far as foreign policy was concerned, the event had one very real result. On April 23 the Czechoslovak-Romanian mutual assistance pact was signed and on June 7 a similar Romanian-Yugoslav pact. In contrast, it was very small solace that in the eyes of the Great Powers the Hungarian government looked good and had endeavored to act according to the stipulations of the peace treaty.[156]

The resignation of the Teleki government was just a matter of time and the royal coup was an opportunity for departure. After the great party agitations in February, relative calm descended on the National Assembly as well. The sessions of the Council of Ministers were devoted mainly to administrative matters. The royal coup put an end to the transitory calm but it contributed to the fall of the government only indirectly. It sharpened the antagonism between the two governmental parties over the most sensitive issue in Hungarian politics, the person of the head of state. Further development then brought to the surface some of the other issues such as the implementation of the land reform, the internments, and the assessment of the increasing power of the Smallholders.

Initially the leadership of the Smallholders gave a vote of confidence to the government.[157] On April 7, however, the papers published Charles IV's proclamation addressed to the nation. Teleki not only published it but even provided it with an introduction.[158] This produced new attacks against the government. Because of these attacks the minister of justice and István Nagyatádi Szabó both resigned. Consequently Teleki announced his resignation to Regent Horthy the same day, April 7, 1921. The regent refused to accept the resignation of the government.[159] At the Council of Ministers meeting on April 8, Teleki stated that the situation of the government was critical but that he still hoped to be able to establish a new cabinet.[160] Initially this endeavor was successful and he reached an agreement with the

---

155 R. Butler, .1. P. Bury, and M. E. Lambert, eds., *Documents on British Foreign Policy*, vol. 22, no. 66; and Mária Ormos, *"Soha, amíg élek"* ["Never as Long as I'm Alive"] (Pécs: Pannonia Books, 1990), p. 66.
156 R. Butler, J. P. Bury, and M. E. Lambert, eds., *Documents on British Foreign Policy*, vol. 22, no. 98.
157 József Sipos, "A Kisgazdapárt és aTeleki kormány lemondása" [The Smallholder Party and the resignation of the Teleki government], in *A Szegedi Móra Ferenc Múzeum Évkönyve 1978–1979* [Yearbook of the Szeged Ferenc Móra Museum 1978–19791 (Szeged: Móra Ferenc Múzeum, 1929), pp. 244–246.
158 *Nemzeti Újság*, April 7, 1922, p. 1.
159 Sipos, "A kisgazdapárt," p. 247.
160 Minutes of the Council of Ministers, April 8, 1921, admin. 71, box 131, K 27, MNL OL.

Smallholder Party. Agreement with KNEP did not come as easily. The members of KNEP felt that the concessions made to the Smallholders were excessive but eventually yielded on this matter. On April 12 it seemed that Teleki would be able to establish his third government. The next day, however, MTI, the Hungarian news agency, published Miklós Horthy's March 30 general military orders that the prime minister did not countersign. Within hours the battle between the two government parties flared up. Both parties agreed, albeit for different reasons, to make Teleki responsible for the general orders. The Smallholders complained that the order did not refer to Act I of 1920. The KNEP objected claiming that the regent placed the loyalty oath sworn to him in opposition to the loyalty oath sworn to the king. Now both parties demanded Teleki's resignation.[161] The tempest was partly due to the fact that the coalition agreement was reached contrary to the wishes of certain political forces, such as some Christian party members, royalists and others. These forces found the concessions made to the Smallholders to have been excessive and also wished to participate in the negotiations.[162]

The well-informed grey eminence of the period, Miklós Kozma, the president of the official news organization, MTI, believed that Teleki resigned because he lost his enthusiasm, was tired of the political back and forth and learned that István Bethlen was already picking his cabinet.[163] He urged Bethlen to form a government as early as December. On April 13, at 1:00 P.M. the prime minister handed in his resignation and this time the regent accepted it. The last Council of Ministers meeting was held the following day. Teleki "expressed his thanks for the unselfish and self-sacrificing support that the members of the cabinet were pleased to provide during the nine months of his prime ministership."[164]

The April crisis made Teleki detest party politics. This experience accompanied him the rest of his life. He became convinced that the great goals of the nation could not be entrusted to parties because they always gave precedence to their own narrow interests and ruined every worthwhile initiative. The balance sheet of his governance was impressive as far as domestic policies were concerned because the initial steps toward consolidation were clearly linked to his name. The reintroduction of corporal punishment and the numerus clausus law are clearly among the dark sides of his nine months. The establishment of law and order, the suppression of the special detachments and the attempts to reach economic stability, however,

---

161 Sipos "A kisgazdapárt," p. 255.
162 Ibid., p. 256.
163 Situation reports, April 1921, Kozma Papers. cs. 13,K429,MNL OL.
164 Minutes of the Council of Ministers, April 14, 1921, pol. no. 3 on the agenda, box 131, K 27, MNL OL.

were noteworthy activities. In foreign policy the Teleki government left behind a weighty inheritance. Some of the foreign observers gave the Teleki government cautious approval. According to the British high commissioner, "There can be no question that Count Teleki has danced on the tight rope of the political life in Hungary until he has tired his spectators; but it should not be forgotten that he has tided over many a difficult situation, and that Europe as a whole owes him a debt of gratitude for the firm attitude he maintained over the question of the return of the ex-Emperor Charles from Switzerland."[165] The German minister in Budapest believed that by playing a double-dealing game in the question of the king, Teleki lost the confidence of both the political elite and of the regent.[166] Later on Teleki stated that when on that April day he walked down from the Royal Castle and crossed the Danube on the Chain Bridge, he felt like a young man after high school graduation going out for a walk and twirling a cane.

A few years later he assessed his prime ministry more constructively. "I know that my governance can be justly criticized. There has never been an example in world history where, after great upheavals, like war and revolution, there immediately followed quiet, normal peaceful days accompanied by economic recovery." According to him, everybody who in such times accepted a position or participated in public life, "could be legitimately hanged if we measure him with the yardstick of absolute good or the measure of the nation's ultimate benefits." He added magniloquently, "How my role is judged is of no interest to me." He saw the shortcomings of his governance in the fact that he did not pay enough attention to economic matters. "What I consider the gravest omission of my governance is that we did not spend enough time on trying to raise the country from its restricted economic practices and bases. This, in my view, was the gravest error of the Teleki government."[167]

---

165 Thomas Hohler to Foreign Secretary Curzon, Budapest, April 15, 1921, TNA, Fo 371, vol. 6137, fol. 156.
166 Fürstenberg-Stammheim to the Ministry of Foreign Affairs, Budapest, April 24, 1921, R. 74188, PA AA; and Fiirstenberg-Stammheim to the Ministry of Foreign Affairs, Budapest, September 13, 1921, R74168, PA AA.
167 "Gróf Teleki Pál megjegyzései dr. Lengyel Ernő 'Ismeretlen ismerőseink' c. cikkére" [Comments by Count Pál Teleki on the article of Dr. Ernő Lengyel, "Our unknown acquaintances"], *Pesti Napló*, February 24, 1924, p. 3.

"Educating the Nation": Revision and Conservatism (1921–1938)

After stepping down from the leadership of the government, Teleki assumed further tasks as one of the most influential persons in Hungarian public life. In addition to his official position, a full professorship in the Faculty of Economics at the Budapest Science University, to which the regent had appointed him on December 30, 1919, he was the president or leader of some two dozen organizations, societies, associations, or clubs. The new government regularly sought out his opinion in matters of nationality policies and frequently entrusted him with information gathering or trips to foreign countries. During the 1920s he was in charge of the illegal government financing of Hungarian minority groups in the Successor States. At the same time he continued his geographer activities, established scientific institutes and pursued his foreign contacts. As one of the heads of the Teleki clan, he had to deal with problems of his relatives and endeavored to preserve the family inheritance.

It was during these seventeen years that he formulated his definitive worldview that later determined the policies of his second term as prime minister. One of its most important elements was constant emphasis on the education of the nation. Teleki wanted to produce a Hungarian elite of European standards that was imbued with a distinct sense of national obligation and a Christian spirit. This elite, in possession of all the intellectual offerings of Europe, would serve to renew the country through a variety of organizations and, having gained sufficient experience, eventually come close to the center of government power.

It is most significant that Teleki was present at all the various sites where this new Christian elite was undergoing training. The goal of the School of Economics was the training of a Christian, not Jewish, commercial and financial elite. The task of Eötvös College, which numbered only a very small percentage of Jews among its students, was the creation of a quality Hungarian teacher-training system, while the Boy Scout movement served to provide a Christianity-based education to large numbers of middle-class youngsters.

He saw Eötvös College as the model on the basis of which the education of the Hungarian elite would take place. The system, like the highly respected Ecole Normale Supérieure in Paris, that worked so satisfactorily abroad, was to be adapted to Hungarian conditions with an appropriate multidisciplinary approach to education and testing. According to his ideas the majority of the students engaged in these studies were to come from the lower middle classes, children of teachers and offsprings of public officials.[1] It was presumably the Christian nature of the college that appealed to him. The number of Jewish students was not only significantly below the ratio in general Hungarian higher education but was even well below the national percentage of Jews (5–6 percent).[2]

Teleki was not interested in renewing the Hungarian middle class with rural talents. For him the education of peasant boys and their advancement to the intellectual classes was not a major social policy goal. He was committed to the principle of moderate, step-wise progress and he did not believe in the political force of the smallholder group. He considered them to be suitable only for limited advancement and in his speeches the Hungarian peasant, while mentioned with respect and affection, was usually shown as the stereotypical manifestation of rural wisdom, occasionally as a good basis for society and as a synonym for the agricultural population. While apparently he did not pursue his prewar ideas about the doctrine of racial hygiene, he did insist that the influx of rural population to the cities had to be stopped. At that time this was mainly a problem of public health but after the revolutions it was colored by political innuendoes. Teleki believed that the rootless individual exposed to radical propaganda in the cities might become the source of all kinds of social

---

1   Tímea Kovács and Tibor Szabó-Pál, "Az Eötvös Collegiumba felvett hallgatók vallási, földrajzi és társadalmi hovatartozása a két világháború között" [The religious, geographic and social background of the students admitted to the Eötvös College between the two World Wars], in *Szabadon szolgál a szellem—Tanulmányok és dokumentumok a száz esztendeje alapított Eötvös Collegium történetéből* [The Spirit Serves in Freedom—Essays and Documents of Eötvös College Established One Hundred Years Ago], ed. László Kósa (Budapest: Gift, 1995), p. 65.
2   Ibid., 62. See also Victor Karády, "Le Collège Eötvös et l'Ecole Normale Supérieure vers 1900—Note comparatiste sur le formation d'intellectuels professionels," in *Intellectuels français, intellectuels hongrois XlllÈme-XXÈme siecles*, ed. Béla Köpeczi and Jacques Le Goff (Budapest: Akadémiai Kiadó, 1985), p. 250–251. According to him the Jewish students were interested primarily in careers in the free professions and thus the college, focused essentially on middle school teacher education, was outside their area of interest.

unrest and hence had to be kept in his original environment. His social policies were middle-class policies. Children of teachers and pastors, the sons of the penurious officials who fled to Hungary after the Peace Treaty of Trianon and children of war widows were the group that could be found in surprisingly large numbers in the Teleki initiatives. The politician considered them suitable to be the basis of a new middle class, filled with a nationalistic feeling, sharing his ideas about education and revision and being well educated with an international perspective.

He endeavored to reorient a number of organizations which he belonged to or lead them toward a conservative social reform. These included the Országos Kaszinó [National Casino], the Egyesült Keresztény Nemzeti Liga [United National Christian League] and the Senior Scouts. He presumably did all of this because the events of 1919 were frightening as they demonstrated the acute social differences. He found a superficial answer for the social tensions, for the problems arising from the inequalities of Hungarian social developments and for the spectacular, albeit transient achievements of a radical minority, the Communists: he made the Jewry into a scapegoat. The Hungarian middle class of Jewish extraction were in a competitive position and therefore a threat to the Christian elite that he envisioned and thus to the entire Christian middle class. He wished to assure the latter, by practicing discrimination, if necessary.

The most important task for the educated elite would have been the revision of the Peace Treaty of Trianon, accomplished according to the theoretical principles elaborated by Teleki. It was the cornerstone of his work in this area to make the Hungarian revision appear to be an overall European interest, i.e., the confrontation of the St. Stephen's principle [szentistváni gondolat] with the liberal nationality policies of assimilation of the nineteenth century.[3] He was always dissatisfied with propaganda and despised the news but never defined precisely what he would consider satisfactory. A complete revision, i.e. the return of all the territories removed from Hungary was his ultimate goal as a Hungarian but, starting with the first half of the 1930s, he frequently added that he knew that a compromise was inevitable and in the best interests not only of Hungary, but also of the neighboring countries and of Europe.

The tightly linked ideas of revision and national education were held together by Teleki's conservatism. His conservatism was a peculiar one, antiliberal, antipol-

---

3 A principle announced by St. Stephen, king of Hungary (997–1038), in a letter to his son, recommending patience with the foreigners. The medieval ideas were broadened by Teleki into a political doctrine, namely the promise of a patient nationality policy and autonomy to entice the former nationalities of Hungary to return to that country.

itics, imbued with Christian corporatism, committed to social reforms, open to new ideas such as the extreme right-wing authoritarian views and accepting the loss of legal equality as far as discrimination against the Jews was concerned. The tensions of his educational-political-aristocratic role causing radiating vibrations in his personality affected his former boy scouts and university students, and might well be the reason, in addition to his tragic fate, for the persistent impact of his persona. This was the most awkward period of his life to understand and describe because his interests were directed in so many directions simultaneously.

The Occasional Diplomat

Both Prime Minister István Bethlen and Minister of Foreign Affairs Miklós Bánffy, Transylvanian aristocrats like Teleki, counted on him even after his resignation. As early as the beginning of May he was getting ready for a trip abroad. It was his task to use his contacts in Paris and London and find out if there could be some mitigation in the enforcement of the Hungarian peace terms. It was at this time that the peace treaties were ratified in Paris, while in London this was to take place somewhat later. Teleki stated forcefully that he was led by three important matters, the question of minority rights, regulation of the western Hungarian borders and the remission of the reparations.[4]

The first official session of the Border Commission was scheduled in Budapest for the summer of 1921 and therefore Teleki explored the way in which the victorious powers interpreted the Millerand cover letter.[5] The head of the French mission in Budapest gave his superiors the following comments concerning the former prime minister, "The count was an honest man, a real scholar, clever parliamentary tactician and shrewd debater perhaps because of the Greek blood in his veins. What is more important, however, that this scholar implanted into an aristocrat will not urge his compatriots, after his return, to turn toward a German orientation."[6]

He arrived in Paris on May 15 and found an almost complete indifference, and even flippancy, vis-a-vis Hungarian affairs. At the end of May Teleki crossed the Channel and conducted discussions with high-ranking officials in the Foreign

---

4   Report from Pál Teleki to Minister of Foreign Affairs Bánffy about his trip to Paris, Budapest, June 12, 1921, Papers of the Foreign Minister's Cabinet, cs. 38, 1921-266 res. no. 6, K 58, MNL OL.
5   Political Division Chief Emmanuel de Peretti de la Roca's memo about his conversation with Pál Teleki, Paris, June 6, 1921, Hongrie, vol. 61, fols. 26–27, Europe 1918–1940, MAE AD.
6   Report from Maurice Fouchet to Aristide Briand, Budapest, May 14, 1921, Hongrie, vol. 61, fol. 13, Europe 1918–1940, MAE AD.

Office. In the early 1900s it was at a summer vacation in the Tatra Mountains, in the villa of Countess Sándor Teleki, that he first met Charles Rothschild and his wife, Rózsika Wertheimstein, who was a native of Oradea [Nagyvárad]. It was at their dinner parties and at other social occasions that he met men of the future and of the past. They included Herbert Henry Asquith, Lord Beaverbrook, and the two friends of Hungary in the House of Lords, Lord Newton and Lord Bryce, as well as geographers and businessmen.

In England the atmosphere for his discussions about Hungary was much friendlier than in France. He believed that in Great Britain there was much less sympathy for the Successor States than in France. He noted that there were a number of unfavorable comments about Romanian policies.[7] In the matter of the king, the British took a much stronger anti-Habsburg position than the French. For this reason Teleki, in his interviews with the *Daily Telegraph* and *Morning Post,* emphasized the question of the constitutional structure of the country and of the significance of the coronation.[8] He also sensed that there was considerable sympathy toward Horthy and that London considered that the transitional conditions that Horthy represented would remain stable for as much as ten years.

There was ignorance concerning minority rights and the only politician somewhat familiar with this matter, Robert Cecil, placed his trust in the legal remedial mechanism of the League of Nations. Teleki considered this ridiculous and berated Cecil in front of a large group. This was most ill advised because Cecil at that time was in line for the prime ministership.[9] In the matter of western Hungary the British diplomats expressed a disinterest but assured Budapest that they would not object to direct negotiations between Austria and Hungary. His British discussion partners believed that Hungary had already paid the reparations with the territories that she had lost. Teleki was so pleased with this striking sentence that he repeated it word for word every time he was asked about it.[10] The shapers of British foreign policy were impressed by Teleki's excellent command of the English lan-

---

7 Report from Pál Teleki to Minister of Foreign Affairs Bánffy about his trip to London, Budapest, June 14, 1921, Papers of the Foreign Minister's Cabinet, cs. 38, 1921-266 res., no 3, K 58, MNL OL.
8 See "Teleki gróf a királykérdésről" [Count Teleki on the matter of the king], *Nemzeti Újság* [National News], June 8, 1921.
9 Report of Charge d'Affairs István Hedry to Miklós Bánffy, London, August 2, 1921, Küm. res. pol. 1921-41-310, K 64, MNL OL.
10 Pál Teleki's report to Foreign Minister Miklós Bánffy on the trip to London, fols. 9–11, 38. cs., res. sz. 1921-266, K 58, MNL OL.

guage, the openness and honesty with which he spoke of the royal coup at Easter.[11] Some of the messages Teleki conveyed irritated the deputy foreign secretary. Alexander Cadogan resented the critical comments about minority agreements and he did not share Teleki's opinion that the Yugoslavs were delaying the evacuation of Baranya County. Cadogan also saw no chance for Hungary to further delay the transfer of Western Hungary that was due to take place in August 1921.[12]

Returning to Paris after the warm welcome he had received in London, Teleki was received much more cordially. Yet, there were no miracles and he never succeeded in seeing Philippe Berthelot, the grey eminence of French foreign policy. The minister of foreign affairs, Aristide Briand, and Raymond Poincaré, the former president of the republic, both advised Teleki that so far as France was concerned any modification of the peace treaty that was contrary to the interests of the Successor States was undesirable. So far as the matter of the king was concerned they were far less complimentary than London. Teleki believed that it was only the disapproval of the Little Entente that kept France from recognizing Charles IV. So far as the evacuation of Baranya was concerned he encountered the greatest understanding from the French politicians. When he met with the head of the Quai d'Orsay Political Division he experienced a cool and negative attitude vis-a-vis Hungary.[13] He was disappointed by the ratification debate that was going on at that time. He particularly disliked the persons and attitudes of the parliamentary reporters. The person presenting the issue to parliament first made some grandiloquent comments but then described Hungary in a very unflattering fashion. The person presenting the matter in the Senate was clearly totally disinterested in the matter.

At the end of the trip he summarized it rather bitterly by saying, "Regardless of how strongly we orient ourselves toward France, regardless of how much we expose ourselves, we will not succeed over the short haul to make French policies openly Hungarophil." He saw only one rather expensive way to gain their understanding, "It is my view concerning the French senators and representatives that they can be approached only with a risk-free business proposition and with presents. As soon as we are able to do so we will be able to counterbalance our enemies at least to some

---

11 Notes by Sir Cecil Harmsworth about his conversation with Teleki, London, June 3, 1921, TNA, FO 371, vol. 6139, fol. 166.
12 Notes by Alexander Cadogan, ibid., fol. 165.
13 Adam, ed., Document diplomatiques français, vol. 3, no. 258.

extent."[14] Returning to Hungary he could not speak quite so openly. Instead, he endeavored to disperse the illusions generated by the Millerand letter. He urged an end to the divisive tactics in order for the country to present a unified front to the world. He emphasized that, "only we can help ourselves." He told this to those who still harbored hopes that the principal goal of French foreign policy was the preservation of the status quo and not the fulfillment of Hungarian expectations.[15]

Teleki's unofficial diplomatic activities did not come to an end with the Western European trip. The start and relatively friendly atmosphere of the Bruck negotiations motivated Hungarian diplomacy to resume the discussion stopped by the first royal coup. Teleki and Minister of Foreign Affairs Bánffy went to Mariánské Lázně [Marienbad] for further discussions. Teleki told a British diplomat in Budapest: "We will now see once and for all whether Benes was a liar or not."[16] The Czechoslovak representatives sketched out a plan for a Czechoslovak-Hungarian-Austrian customs union that was received by the Hungarian representatives with some hesitation.[17] The latter were thinking in more concrete terms, such as the signing of a commercial agreement, the protection of minority rights and the freeing of political prisoners. They considered the customs union as a purely delaying maneuver. As far as the political prisoners and minority rights were concerned, the Czechoslovak minister of foreign affairs declared cynically that if necessary they would be pleased to revive the prewar Hungarian minority policies but that would be far less favorable for the Hungarians than the present situation. Beneš promised an amnesty for the Hungarian political prisoners and commercial cooperation, but was unwilling to agree to more than that. The Czechoslovak party was primarily interested in achieving a decision in practical matters (commercial, legal and financial), while for the Hungarians all this was merely a preliminary for a discussion of the political problems.[18] This was one of the experiences that made Teleki always skeptical of any central European agreement. For the public, however, he tried to emphasize the interdependency of the two countries: "The purpose of our meeting

---

14 Report of Teleki to Bánffy about the Paris trip, Budapest, June 12, 1921, cs. 38, fols. 4–18, res. sz. 1921-266, K 58, MNL OL.
15 Anna Szmrecsányi, "Gróf Teleki Pál nyilatkozik Az Estnek párizsi útjáról" [Count Pál Teleki speaks to Az Est about his trip to Paris), *Az Est* [The Evening], June 15, 1921.
16 Telegram from Deputy High Commissioner Athelstan-Johnson, Budapest, June 19, 1921, TNA, FO, 371, vol., 6140, fol. 12.
17 Juhász, *Hungarian Foreign Policy*, p. 61.
18 Endre Tóth, "Az első kétoldalú tárgyalások Csehszlovákia és Magyarország között, Mariánské Lázně, 1921" [The first bilateral discussions between Czechoslovakia and Hungary, Mariánské Lazně, 1921], part 2, *Forum* (Somorja/Samorín), no. 1 (2003): 51–56.

was…to adapt the theme of the Trianon peace treaty to life and to the cooperative existence of our two countries," because, "it [the peace treaty] is not a valid representation of all the details," and therefore the two nations would have to remove "some very painful thorns."[19] Within himself, however, he acknowledged the complete failure of the meeting.

At the end of June he returned to Budapest and started his preparation for a trip to America. He was scheduled to speak on the history and geography of Hungary to a select audience at the summer session of Williamstown University in Massachusetts. He left Budapest at the end of July 1921 and stepped ashore in the New World at the beginning of August. In Williamstown he addressed old American friends like Lawrence Martin, Isaiah Bowman, and W. M. Davis, an American audience and some European notables including Tommaso Tittoni, a prewar Italian minister of foreign affairs; Baron Korff, the former Russian governor of Finland; Stefan Panerotov, the Bulgarian minister in Washington; and others. His lectures were published two years later in New York with an introduction by Lawrence Martin.[20] Of the eight lectures the first dealt with the geography of the Carpathian Basin and the next three sketched Hungary's history from the beginnings to the First World War, with particular reference to the foundation of the country, the Turkish occupation and the economic situation prior to the World War.

In describing the decades after 1867, he emphasized the tolerant nature of the nationality policies and the large number of men from the minorities and from abroad who were elevated to the ranks of the nobility.[21] He mentioned the Vienna government as the block to the endeavors of the Hungarian reform movement and blamed it for politicizing the economic problems. The 1848-49 War of Independence that broke out after the rejection of the reforms had the outstanding characteristic that it encompassed and fused together all strata of society. He emphasized that it was only the Vienna government that called this war a revolution. The 1867 Compromise was the only possible way for the Hungarian political leadership when it realized that the West had abandoned it and that it had to rely on its own resources to achieve even a part of its 1848 goals. Yet, the situation after the Compromise still reflected the dominance of Vienna.[22]

According to Teleki, this unpopular system could be maintained by the government only by relying largely on the non-Hungarian electorate and by refusing

---

19 Quoted in ibid., p. 56.
20 Teleki, *The Evolution*.
21 Ibid., p. 123.
22 Ibid., p. 126–128, and 164.

any extension of political rights. This time he did not praise the Serbs or the Austrians. In his assessment of the 1918 revolution there was no longer any forgiveness or understanding. According to him the revolution was prepared by crypto-communists whose leader was Mihály Károlyi. He labeled the events between October 1918 and March 1919 as "Cold Bolshevism" and stated that the days of the "Hot Bolshevism" was merely a caricature of the antidemocratic procedures of the Russian Bolshevik Revolution. Using a clever rhetorical trick Teleki alleged that the Hungarian Soviet Republic was not overthrown by the Romanian army or by the Szeged counterrevolution but by the Hungarian peasants who refused to send food to the Bolshevik capital.[23] Addressing an American audience, committed to religious and economic freedom, Teleki discussed the antichurch actions of the Soviet Republic and the results of its senseless economic and commercial policies.[24] He claimed that the rise of anti-Semitic sentiments was the inevitable consequence of the Soviet Republic and that this sentiment was principally anti-Galician directed against the recently immigrated, non-assimilated group that was the driving force behind the revolution.[25] This statement, recurring regularly in his speeches, was not original with him. Both before and after 1914 conservative or agrarian politicians distinguished between the "old inhabitants" and the "Galicians" and called on the former to distance themselves from the latter both to make a point but also for no stated purpose whatever. In his lecture, Teleki briefly sketched the position of the various Hungarian political parties and spoke of the matter of the king as well. He claimed that the latter was not a real issue. In his final lectures he spoke mainly of the economic conditions in postwar Hungary and about the nationality problems that derived logically from the historical, legal and geographical conditions.

He listed the nationalities living in Hungary.[26] Discussing the behavior of the nationalities during the war he emphasized the loyalty of some Romanian politicians in Hungary. According to him, the nationality unrest had two reasons, the administration policies and agitation.[27] Speaking of the Magyarizing policies of the Hungarian government he admitted that the 1907 Apponyi Act approached the question in an unfortunate way but he criticized the sloppiness of the act and not its intent. He also regretted that the Hungarian political class was willing to

---

23   Ibid., pp. 134–136.
24   Ibid., pp. 138–140.
25   Ibid., pp. 140–142.
26   Ibid., pp. 148–152.
27   Ibid., p. 155.

equate knowledge of the Hungarian language with a Hungarian identity. He further concluded that the schooling of the nationalities in historic Hungary was better than in the homeland of the nationalities and that these nationalities lived at a higher standard than those in Romania or Serbia. Economically they occasionally lived at a higher level than the Hungarians.[28] The Romanian and Slovakian communities had many banks.

Speaking of the rumors of oppression he stressed that in the election districts of the ethnic areas, candidates who competed for seats, belonged to various organizations, including the radical nationalists and the government parties.[29] The allegedly Magyarizing administration had more experts from the nationalities in their ranks than in any of the free professions.[30] Teleki saw the mistake of the administration in the fact that it engaged in nationality politics along false principles. It was engaged in political and legal matters rather than in social and economic ones.

Teleki condemned the fact that the years of extreme economic liberalism were followed by protectionism and a blind faith in the omnipotence of the government that weakened entrepreneurial activities.[31] At the end of his presentation Teleki summarized the mistakes of the nationality policies with more severity than ever before or after. He faulted the lack of political sensitivity, the lack of recognizing the opportunities, the imitation of Western European ideals, the social insensitivity of the administration, the position of the state in county matters, the insistence on county autonomy, the inconsistency in the writing and implementation of successive legislation, the failure to monitor enemy propaganda and the occasional clumsiness and brutality of government interventions.[32]

After discussing the postwar economic situation of Hungary, Teleki returned to the nationality question. In a lecture entitled "The Racial or Nationality As Seen by a Geographer" he presented his own views as to how this problem could be resolved by a multidisciplinary approach and some territorial adjustments.[33] He sequentially listed the regions of historic Hungary that illustrated his concepts. These included the Banat, the seven Saxon-inhabited [Szászföld] Transylvanian counties, the eastern part of the Slovakia, Máramaros [Maramureș] and western

---

28 Ibid., pp. 157–163.
29 Ibid., p. 160.
30 Ibid., pp. 169–170.
31 Ibid., pp. 168–169.
32 Ibid., pp. 173–174.
33 This lecture was published in Hungarian as well. See Pál Teleki, *Európáról és Magyarországról* [On Europe and Hungary] (Budapest: Athenaeum, 1934), pp. 30–50.

Hungary. In all these there was an ethnic mix and they were all fairly isolated by hills, rivers or other natural barriers. With the exception of western Hungary they all turned toward the center of the Carpathian Basin economically. Their remaining in Hungary was indicated by the cultural orientation of their cities, the necessities of proper administration and historical tradition.[34] Teleki concluded that the nationality question could not solved by any universally applicable method and that every solution had to be individually tailored to a specific region. He viewed a modernized version of the traditional Transylvanian constitution as the principal concept for a number of local solutions. The fundamental principle contained federal elements, similar to the American and Swiss constitutions. It contained a joint parliament a jointly elected head of state, a territorial separation between the nationalities while, at the same time it assured individual autonomy, recalling the cultural autonomy proclaimed by the Austro-Marxists which meant that a person belonging to a nationality could be judged only by members of the same group. In Teleki's thinking, this approach would be suitable to remedy the mistaken nationality policies of previous regimes.[35]

He did not only sketch his ideas in theory, but he also buttressed them with maps and statistics that presented a detailed plan for the administrative reorganization of Hungary.[36] His plans, dividing the historic Hungary into twenty major regions, completely ignored the county system and proposed a new Hungarian administrative map based on the economic, geographic and nationality situation of the regions. The country would remain unchanged except for three minor regions. In half of the major administrative regions the Hungarians would be in majority but the seven major administrative regions with a nationality majority would not be viable without the regions where the Hungarians were in the majority. The plan demonstrated Teleki's increasingly pronounced regional-deterministic ideas. The geographic factors, both economic and physical, clearly predominated over the historical- administrative perspectives.[37] In Teleki's stated perspective geography represented a higher level of systematic arguments than even the traditional-administrative ones. The consistency of his views is shown by the fact that his thinking,

---

34 Teleki, *Válogatott politikai írások*, ed. Ablonczy, pp. 139–143.
35 Ibid., pp. 144–145.
36 Ibid., pp. 154–155.
37 Zoltán Vajda, "Területrendezési törekvések a magyar földrajztudományban a két világháború között" [Attempts for territorial rearrangement in the Hungarian geographical science between the two World Wars], *Földrajzi Közlemények*, no. 2 (1982): 92–94.

fixated on historic Hungary, was considered valid by him even in the 1930s otherwise he would not have included this lecture in the volume he published in 1934.

The American press devoted considerable attention to his trip and published extensive segments of his lectures, emphasizing the advantages that Hungarian explorations for oil might hold for the United States.[38] Another benefit of the trip was that he met President Warren G. Harding and Secretary of State Charles Hughes.

Returning to Hungary he had to deal with matters of graver nature than the theoretical ones. The matter of the king became a central issue again for a few days in October 1921. King Charles IV, learning from the failure of his last attempt tried to regain the throne with armed force. On October 23, at Budaörs, close to the capital, some regular troops and some hastily recruited university student units fought with the Carlist forces. The encounter led to a few deaths upon which the king ordered the cessation of fighting. A few days later he left Hungary for good. These days were tragic for Teleki. The friends of his youth and his political mentors, Gyula Andrássy, György Pallavicini and others were mostly siding with the king, while those politicians with whom he was linked since Vienna and Szeged, Horthy, Bethlen, Bánffy and others, took arms against the monarch. He held firm to his earlier statement and did not take a position in this matter, although a few years later he noted that deep inside he had condemned both sides. For a while he was estranged from a large part of the Hungarian aristocracy and his relationship to György Pallavicini became very tenuous. Countess Teleki had an even more difficult time, "The exaggerations of our royalist friends pushed my wife completely into the Bethlen circle," he wrote. Actually the push could not have been very hard since Countess Bethlen and Countess Teleki were cousins and intimate friends.[39]

In spite of all this, Teleki felt that he had to take part in national politics. Consequently he became a candidate in the 1922 election campaign. He had himself nominated in Szeged in the first electoral district as an independent but pro-government candidate. This time he did not have quite the same easy ride as two years earlier. He was opposed by another independent but opposition-supporting candidate, the former liberal Lord Mayor of Budapest. Teleki appeared in his district at the end of April and, at a well-attended party dinner and in the presence of his Brit-

---

38 "Teleki Says Aliens Ruined Hungary," *New York Times*, August 15, 1921; and "Teleki Thinks Oil May Save Hungary," *New York Times*, August 18, 1921.

39 About Teleki in the second royal coup, see, Béla Sarusi-Kiss and Ferenc Gáspár, "Teleki Pál közjegyzői letétbe helyezett feljegyzései a frankhamisításról" [The notarized annotations of Pál Teleki about the franc forgery issue], *Századok*, no. 4 (1999): 738–739.

ish friends, he announced that the Trianon treaty was bankrupt since it did not fulfill any of its promises. He stated: "This peace did more harm to the world than the war."[40] He opined that the peace treaties, hammered together in Paris, destroyed the natural economic units in central Europe. Restoration had to happen, he had repeated over and over again ever since 1920, because this situation could not be sustained and sober judgment would not permit that these conditions become permanent. At the same time he told his more prominent supporters at another dinner that his assuming a political role was unlikely to have lasting effects.

A government paper reported that, "He felt he was obliged to tell them, that in him the scholar was struggling with the politician and that he was unable to repress the scholar entirely even in the national interest because he was convinced that as a scholar he could do more for the country than as a politician." He stated that he had no personal antagonistic feelings vis-a-vis the government, Bethlen being an old and valued friend, and he justified his running as an independent by claiming that instead of playing party politics he was satisfied if he knew that somebody was an honest Hungarian who did not want to divide the city. He raised his glass to the city of Szeged and to the victory of the Christian national ideas.[41] He was not satisfied with party dinners alone and diligently visited his district, became acquainted with the electors, drank toasts and accepted requests to be a godparent. At the vote at the beginning of June, Teleki received 54.73 percent of the vote (5,385 ballots) against his liberal opponent.[42] This was a personal triumph because in a neighboring Szeged district, the Social Democrat, Gyula Peidl defeated his Unity Party [Egységes Párt] opponent in a tight race, though the latter party won parliamentary majority.

Even though his name came up regularly when a successor had to be found for Prime Minister István Bethlen's frequently changing minister of foreign affairs, he was either not chosen, or refused to serve.[43] He spoke only once in parliament

---

40 "Magyarország már megfizette a reparációt elszakított területeivel. Gróf Teleki Pál szegedi beszéde" [Hungary has already paid the reparations with the territories it lost. Count Pál Teleki's speech in Szeged], *Szózat* [Appeal], April 25, 1922.
41 "Gróf Teleki Pál Szegeden" [Count Pál Teleki in Szeged], *Szózat*, April 23, 1922; and "Grossbritannien und Amerika in Szeged," *Pester Lloyd*, April 25, 1922.
42 László Hubai, ed., *Magyarország XX. századi választási atlasza 1920–2000* [Hungary's 20th Century Electoral Atlas 1920–2000] (Budapest: Napvilág, 2001), vol. 2, p. 48.
43 For example, Minister plenipotentiary Jean Doulcet to Minister of Foreign Affairs Poincaré, Budapest, December 26, 1922, Hongrie, vol. 50, fol. 74, Europe 1918-1940, MAE AD; Minister plenipotentiary Carbonnel to Minister of Foreign Affairs Edouard Herriot, Budapest, March 6, 1925, Hongrie, vol. 51, fol. 7, Europe 1918–1940, MAE AD; and Minister de Vienne's telegram, Budapest, December 10, 1930, Hongrie, vol. 94, fol. 51, Europe 1918–1940, MAE AD.

before 1926 and completely ignored his district.[44] If asked about his absences he said, "I did not wish to be a representative. I am not a politician. My plans are not directed toward politics."[45] With disarming honesty, he told his constituency that a report had to be made only if somebody did something and that he had done nothing, mainly because he was away from Hungary most of the time. He gave this as the reason for being ill-informed about domestic policy matters He added that had he known that his tenure would last this long he would have resigned from his mandate.[46] When asked further, he explained, "As far as the true base of my convictions is concerned, it has not changed since I was prime minister and I see no need for a change."[47] He continued to think highly of Szeged, not necessarily as a place but as the city of the Szeged Idea, which encompassed a Christian-National, anti-Semitic, counterrevolutionary, and anti-Communist way of thinking.

Organizer and Ideologue of the Revision

Another motive for his disinterest in parliamentary politicking was that after he resigned from the prime ministership he became involved in other social endeavors. On the request of Prime Minister Bethlen he became responsible to the government for the affairs of the Hungarians who now found themselves in a minority situation in the neighboring countries.

In view of the imminent ratification of the peace treaty it was one of the primary tasks of the Bethlen government to make the activities of the associations and social groups engaged in irredentist propaganda less visible and to initiate a new way of approaching this problem. At a conference in May 1921 it was decided to stop or limit the support given to the openly irredentist organizations and to forbid the military organizations planning the reconquest of the lost territories.[48] The spy and conspiracy trials of the times, in Oradea [Nagyvárad], Cluj [Kolozsvár], Timişoara [Temesvár] and, shortly after the conference, in Petroşani [Petrozsény], clearly showed the detrimental aspects of this behavior. On the basis of the conference

---

44 For a prejudiced commentary on his parliamentary absences, see "Egy úr Dzsungáriából" [A gentleman from Dzsungária], *Népszava*, October 18, 1925, pp. 3–4.
45 György Vér, "Teleki Pál nem akar nyilatkozni a fajvédelemről" [Pál Teleki does not wish to speak about race protection], *Délmagyarország* [Southern Hungary], October 18, 1925, pp. 3–4.
46 "Tájékozatlanság" [Lack of information], *Délmagyarország*, October 20, 1925, pp. 1-2; and Teleki Pál beszámolója" [Statement by Count Pál Teleki], *Délmagyarország*, October 20, 1925.
47 "Gróf Teleki Pál megjegyzései" [Comments of Count Pál Teleki], *Délmagyarország*, October 20, 1925, p. 3.
48 Nándor Bárdi, "A Keleti Akció, I" [The Eastern Action, part 1], *REGIO*, no. 3 (1995): 97, 126, and n. 40.

deliberations, Bethlen submitted his proposal on May 27 concerning the unified direction of the domestic and foreign activities of the irredentist organizations, and the drastic reduction in the number of organizations involved in propaganda and irredentist activities. He wished to invite Teleki to be the head of the proposed new organization.[49] Antal Papp, a former financial director from Kolozsvár [Cluj] was appointed as his deputy and active administrator.[50]

The Council of Ministers endorsed the proposal on August 12, 1921, and Teleki became the head of the center in charge of the irredentist propaganda organizations,[51] the peculiarly named TESZ (Társadalmi Egyesületek Szövetségének Központja [Center for Alliance of Social Associations], which created or inspired groups working on individual territories.[52] Among the few people familiar with the organization it was known as the Teleki Bureau.[53] Teleki was not pleased and in 1921 and 1923 he announced at several meetings that the propaganda material prepared for use abroad were miserable. To be fair, he gave no directions whatever. He simply declared that the leaflets and brochures coming from the printers were "bad" and even when urged repeatedly, he refused to respond to the question as to how to improve them.[54] He was strongly opposed to the distribution of flyers and posters that had little beneficial effects and would not influence Western decision makers unless in a negative sense. The comment he made at the start of the information gathering for minority affairs is typical, "It all depends on people, not on any program and not on any paper organization."[55] This comment illustrates his entire problem-solving approach. He was unable to think in terms of organizations, plan along rational decision-making lines or follow the official path so important in Hungary. He rarely attempted to force his views on others, even when he was at the center of power. He preferred to set up a parallel organization and circumvent the

---

49 Dezső Nemes and Elek Karsai, eds., *Iratok az ellenforradalom történetéhez* [Documents on the History of the Counterrevolution] (Budapest: Kossuth, 1956–1959), vol. 2, doc. 25/a.
50 For Papp see, "Papp Antal dr. államtitkár" [Dr. Antal Papp, state secretary], *Hangya* [Ant], May 28, 1931, p. 3; and István B. Bernát, "A TESZK a revíziós propaganda egységéért" [TESZK for the unification of revisionist propaganda] (TESZK material 1920-1928), ms. 591/ 1987/1, pp. 4–5, OSZKK, fond 625 [Former Library of the László Teleki Foundation, Manuscript Division].
51 Nemes and Karsai, *Iratok az ellenforradalom történetéhez*, vol. 2, doc. 25/c.
52 The organization is frequently mistaken, even in specific studies, with TESZ (Társadalmi Egyesületek Szervezete) [Organization of Social Associations] and perhaps this was the intention of the founders.
53 Note from István Bethlen to Károly Andorffy, the head of the Housing Office, Budapest, June 24, 1921, cs. 1, t. 12, fols. 1-9, K 437, MNL OL.
54 Bárdi, "A Keleti Akció, I," p. 101. For the discussions between Dénes Sebess, Bethlen's confidant and Teleki, see Bernát, "A TESZK," p. 20.
55 Bernát, "A TESZK," p. 32.

office. He thought in terms of people and not in terms of models or organizations. His modern concepts were largely unenforceable in the Hungary of the 1920s and 1930s. Later, during his second term as prime minister this led to duplications and unclarified centers of authority.

The enormous amount of work done by TESZK cannot be dismissed. It is difficult to assess the amount of assistance rendered by this organization which played a major role in preserving the Hungarian institutions in Slovakia, Transylvania and, to a lesser degree, in Yugoslavia/Kingdom SHS.[56] On the basis of data from experts in this area it appears that the financial support might have reached between one tenth and one third of the Ministry of Foreign Affairs annual budget. The sums decreased until the middle 1920s but after 1926 increased again.[57] TESZK financed anything that related to the needs of the Hungarians beyond the borders. It collected data, analyzed the news, supported Hungarian parties beyond the borders, created independent positions in the Successor States to bring Hungarian political social and cultural matters into harmony, established Hungarian boarding schools for students from the neighboring states who studied in Hungary, supported their associations, financed commercial activities, handed out loans, welcomed foreign visitors and established a collection of books and other printed material in addition to a regular press archive.[58] Teleki did not de facto direct TESZK after 1924 partly because he spent extensive periods of time abroad and partly, presumably, because his advice was not followed. He still promised to carry on the propaganda activities, if, "there were funds and if the people followed orders."[59] At the same time he was looking for other structures.

A prime minister's order, issued in 1924, created the Hungarian Sociographic Institute, under the auspices of the Hungarian Academy of Science.[60] It was given

---

56 Extremely widely diverse data are in Bárdi, "A Keleti Akció, I," table 118; Report of the sums spent on the care of the lost territories in five years (In korona, gold korona and pengő), Papp Papers, Documents 5, PRMTKL and Antal Papp's summary of the expenses of the Teleki office, March 1, 1931, Papers of István Bethlen, cs. 9, B/9, dossier 1931, K 468, MNL OL.
57 Bardi. "A Keleti Akció, I," p. 121.
58 The organization of the Minority Library, notes of Antal Papp, Budapest, July 1, 1935, Papp Papers, Documents 5, PRMTKL.
59 Miklós Szinai and László Szűcs, eds., *Bethlen István titkos iratai* [The Secret Papers of István Bethlen] (Budapest: Kossuth, 1972), doc. 95.
60 Péter Niklay, "A Magyar Szociográfiai Intézmény szervezete és gyűjteményei" [The Organization and the collections of the Hungarian Sociographic Institute], in *A Magyar Társaság es a Falukutató Intézet évkönyve* [The Yearbook of the Hungarian Society and Village Research Institute], ed. Antal Bodor (Budapest: A Magyar Társaság, 1935), pp. 135–138; Sándor Krisztics, *Szociográfiai elméletek és eszmények* [Sociographic Theories and Ideals] (Budapest, 1942), pp. 17–28.

"Educating the Nation": Revision and Conservatism (1921–1938)

the task of preparing and implementing a sociological and sociographic assessment of post-Trianon Hungary. Its director was Sándor Krisztics who at the end of 1918 had been Teleki's intimate coworker in the League for the Protection of Hungary's Territorial Integrity. Teleki not only supervised the new institute but also taught the associates how to assemble a card catalog.[61] Because Krisztics was a professor at the University in Pécs, he appeared only once a week. All meritorious work was performed by the associates who shared Teleki's confidence even though some of them had been compromised at the time of the Soviet Republic. Due to the work starting at the beginning of 1927, in barely more than three years there was a card catalog of 400,000 items with data about the communities of the Carpathian Basin. By the end of the 1930s, the number of cards exceeded 800,000.

Under Teleki's direction several monographs about the villages were published on the basis of the card catalog of the Community Data Bank and of the collection of the Sociographic Institute. There was also an annual of „Hungarian government, and a social science bibliography". These were amplified later by a catalog of the local historic and descriptive literature. By the middle of the 1930s this bibliography contained almost ten thousand titles. Eventually the institute collected maps and catalogued the manuscripts and archival material. The modest budget of the institute confined its activities to a narrow field and there was not enough for the realization of novel concepts.

The Political Science Institute [Államtudományi Intézet], established in 1926 under the auspices of the Central Statistics Office, was given the task of being the workshop for proposals relating to revisions of the terms of the peace treaty, and to provide information to all the politicians, journalists and researchers who were studying the neighboring countries. The duty of the associates consisted of recording all data relative to the Hungarian minorities in the neighboring countries according to a coding system. The data contained laws and regulations, official gazettes, daily papers, news from the minority organizations and newspaper articles about these areas coming from abroad. A large number of the research fellows came from the territories annexed by the neighboring countries, spoke the language of that particular country and worked in complete secrecy. They were not allowed to publish under their own name.[62] The intensity of the work and the good spirits of the young people working there made Teleki enjoy himself in their com-

---

61 Letter from Pál Teleki to an unknown, Budapest, December 1929, Ms. 5300/524, MTAKK; and Pál Teleki to Imre Lukinich, Budapest June 23, 1928, Ms. 537/234, MTAKK.
62 András Rónai, *Térképezett történelem* [Mapped History] (Budapest: Püski, 1993), pp. 83–85.

pany. Due to the concentrated and carefully planned effort the card catalog of the institute contained 100,000 headings and 400,000 cards so that Teleki could feel free to recommend the material gathered under his supervision to the prominent figures of Hungarian scholarship. By this time the two Teleki institutes had an aggregate of over 900,000 index cards. At the beginning of the 1930s several dozen associates worked in the institute. The two workshops, but particularly the Political Science one, had collected material, produced expert essays, maps and tables that, at the end of the 1930s and in the period of the territorial revision (between 1938 and 1941), rendered inestimable service to Hungarian foreign policy.

In addition to national education, Teleki's other major activity that he pursued tenaciously and systematically, was his work on the modification of Hungary's borders. In his view the rights of Hungary to the lost territories could be justified by the "St. Stephen theory of statehood" (*szentistváni állameszme*).[63]

His views were arranged along two parallel paths. First came the Hungarian nation and particularly the national elite, which by virtue of its calling and obligations was to lead in the Carpathian Basin. The traditions and culture of the Hungarians was their base from which this leadership role devolved. The fact that the area was inhabited by a number of nationalities was attributed by Teleki primarily to the Ottoman occupation. To illustrate the present confining conditions, Teleki frequently referred to Transylvania where the Hungarians had withdrawn into their historic center, waiting to regain their strength, immersed in their own Magyarness, so that after the return of their ancient virtues they might again take their proper place in the direction of the region.

Secondly there was his view of nation and space, Hungarians and the Carpathian Basin that had an almost immovable, tight juxtaposition. This St. Stephen's concept of the state that Teleki developed for himself was suitable to replace the nationality policies of Dualism which were directed toward assimilation. As a politician, Teleki was prepared to offer the nationalities a new deal. In exchange for a tolerant nationality policy and for the religious and cultural identification of the nationalities he expected the recognition of the traditional Hungarian supremacy. In his concept there was room even for some territorial autonomy. But nothing could threaten the Hungarians' being in the leadership. His endeavors are shown

---

63 Holger Fischer, "Deutsch-ungarische Beziehungen in der Geographic der Zwischenkriegszeit," in *Technologietransfer und Wissenschaftsaustausch zwischen Ungarn und Deutschland*, ed. Holger Fischer and Ferenc Szabadváry (Munich: Oldenbourg, 1995), pp. 320–321.

by the steps toward the autonomy of the Subcarpathian Ruthenia that he took during his second tenure as prime minister.

According to Teleki, the St. Stephen concept on statehood was "new wine" in "old bottles" albeit it did not apply to the nationalities even at the time of territorial conquests. This ideology was the theoretical basis of Teleki the politician. The internationally famous scholar explored other venues in order to have the need for leveling among the nationalities accepted. From here it was only a small step toward the recognition of Hungarian cultural supremacy or, at least, toward some *primus inter pares* arrangement between the Hungarians and the other people of Central and Eastern Europe.[64] He had pointed out the differences between nations in his articles ever since the mid 1920s but presented this matter more fully in the German language Budapest newspaper, the *Pester Lloyd*, in 1931.

According to him the European national minorities could be divided into three groups, 1. Traditional, 2. Voluntary and 3. Forced minorities.[65] The traditional minorities included the Slovak, the Breton, Catalan and Flamand. The group of voluntary minorities included a large portion of the Serbs in Hungary, the Romanians in Hungary and a significant percentage of the Germans. The forced minorities were the ones confined to the countries established after World War 1. According to Teleki's calculation this group consisted of 15-16 million people as contrasted with 10-11 million traditional minorities and 2–2.5 million individuals who opted for a minority role voluntarily.[66] From this division he drew certain conclusions. In his view the traditional minorities and the voluntary minorities did not require any particular international legal protection. The former because the legal protection of the dictates and the Wilsonian League of Nations were artificial and did not consider the complex intertwining of national and cultural traditions and the evolved form of coexistence and the latter because their situation did not warrant it. The problems of the coerced minorities, however, demanded immediate legal remedies.[67] Even after the unfavorable reactions to his article, Teleki held firm to his position although he tried to tone it down and stated that there was no sharp dividing line between his three categories, and that there might be other categorizations

---

64 Ibid., p. 518.
65 Graf Paul Teleki, "Traditionelle, freiwillige und Zwangsminderheiten," *Pester Lloyd-Morgenblatt*, February 18, 1931, pp. 1–2. In Hungarian see "Hagyományos, önkéntes és kényszerkisebbségek" [Traditional volunteer, and forced minorities], in Teleki, *Válogatott politikai írások*, ed. Ablonczy, pp. 267–272.
66 Teleki, *Válogatott politikai írások*, ed. Ablonczy, p. 269.
67 Ibid., p. 270.

as well.⁶⁸ According to Teleki, the differing backgrounds required a different management approach.

The French minister in Budapest called Teleki's ideas "interesting speculations" and commented about their author that, "Teleki has withdrawn into his cave. Occasionally he emerges to give a lecture or publish an article. His pronouncements are always interesting because they come from a cultured mind even though his goals are different from ours."⁶⁹

The appearance of Teleki's article was related to the governmental mandate he received from Bethlen in 1931, according to which Budapest attempted to make Berlin agree that the Germans and Hungarians living in the Successor States should form a common front in their battle for their rights and for revision. The Germans, however, preferred to address the fate of the Germans living in Hungary.⁷⁰ Nothing much new emerged from the extensive discussions during the first part of the 1930s. In July 1932 the discussions were interrupted because the parties had different priorities. Berlin had commitments in other directions and resented Teleki's doctrinaire approach. He did not wish to hear about the problems of the German minority in Hungary and was willing to talk only about ecclesiastic matters as they related to them. His interest focused on the fate of the Hungarian minorities.⁷¹

His revisionist goals, in addition to the nationality matters, included another central issue, propaganda. He opposed the poster and leaflet campaigns considering them to be superficial, mainly because these appealed to the man on the street for whose goodwill he was not willing to fight. He also believed that this form of propaganda was not suitable to gain the support of the foreign decision-makers. It is not surprising, therefore, that while we find him among the officers of the Revisionist League, a mass organization practicing popular propaganda, established in 1927, his contributions were negligible. He was almost certainly correct when he believed that it was the flourishing periodical literature of the 1930s that was the best weapon in Europe. It was for this reason that he accepted a role in the creation of the foreign language periodicals clustered around the *Magyar Szemle* [Hungarian Review], first

---

68 Graf Paul Teleki, "Noch ein Wort zur Minderheitenfrage," *Pester Lloyd-Morgenblatt*, February 22, 1931, p. 5.
69 Report of Plenipotentiary Minister de Vienne to Aristide Briand, Internationale 1918-1940, vol. 588, fol. 60, MAE AD.
70 R 74178, passim, AA PA.
71 All the materials of these discussions are in "Gesandschaft Budapest," vol. 13, passim, in P24, AA PA. See: Ferenc Eiler: A kisebbségek kategorizálásának kísérlete, mint politikai fegyver a magyar-német kapcsolatokban (1930–1931) [The attempt to categorize national minorities as a political weapon in the Hungarian-German relations (1930-1931)] *REGIO* 27, 1. (2017), 41–71.

published at the beginning of the 1930s. He became the president of the editorial board of the *Nouvelle Revue de Hongrie* and a member of the board of directors of the *Hungarian Quarterly*. The two quality periodicals, reflecting the views and conservatism of the *Magyar Szemle*, were a very useful forum, from 1932 until the end of World War II, for the politicians and intellectuals in István Bethlen's circle.

That he assumed these positions had a background. Of the French and English brochures and propaganda publications produced by the various leagues and territorial protective associations in the 1920s, the only memorable one was the *Oxford Hungarian Review*, published between 1922 and 1924. After September 1923 it appeared under the name of *Anglo-Hungarian Review*. The carefully printed periodical edited by the British and created with the intensive cooperation of Teleki, was published by the Oxford League for Hungarian Self-Determination.[72] The periodical published the essays of noted Hungarian authors and of British authors committed to the cause of Hungary. Tele- ki was active in procuring writers for the periodical.[73] The experiment did not last long, the money ran out, enthusiasm flagged and the periodical came to its end. Only eighteen subscribers could be recruited.[74]

At the beginning of the 1930s the situation changed somewhat. The political climate improved after István Bethlen's visit to Paris and the financiers following Bethlen's political direction considered it worthwhile to publish a periodical in Budapest in French. The Société de la *Nouvelle Revue de Hongrie,* consisting of patrons of the periodical was formed and it soon became popular both in the country and abroad.[75] Louis de Vienne, the French minister in Budapest and a close observer of events, concluded that, "it was the best such publication in Central Europe."[76] The high level of the periodical was assured by the quality of the Hungarian contributors and by the well-recognized French publicists. The *Nouvelle Revue* was not directly involved in propaganda and only an occasional article addressed revision or the problems of the Hungarian borders. The emphasis was on quality Hungarian literature, on moderate foreign policy reviews, articles by Hungarian experts on a variety of subjects and on the contributions of well-known

---

72 Kovács-Bertrand, *Der Ungarische Revisionismus*, pp. 145–146.
73 Letter from Pál Teleki to Jenő Pintér, Budapest, July 2, 1922, Correspondences, OSZKK.
74 "Teleki Pál gróf előadása a propagandáról" [Lecture by Count Pál Teleki on propaganda], *Nagymagyarország* [Greater Hungary], February 1, 1929, p. 20.
75 See *Pester Lloyd-Morgenblatt*, January 17, 1932.
76 Report from de Vienne to Minister Louis Barthou, Budapest, May 14, 1934, Hongrie, vol. 147, Europe 1918–1940, MAE AD.

French authors. Teleki also contributed a few times.⁷⁷ Yet his role was an exception and a great source of annoyance to József Balogh, the editor. Teleki was always late and even after vigorous reminders handed in his contributions well after the deadline.⁷⁸ Because of his connections, reputation and rank, he could recruit authors from abroad and maintain a liaison with the Ministry' of Foreign Affairs. He received the French dignitaries visiting Budapest and found out if they would be willing to support revision. It was evident for Teleki that the Société was a tactful, and therefore successful, propaganda organization. He did not publish in the *Hungarian Quarterly* but occasionally received the British guests of the periodical.

In Teleki's views the rank order of revision-national education-propaganda evolved as follows: 1. If the nation, or its opinion-forming leading classes, were mature enough to regain the lost territories, (national education), 2. If the world recognized and acknowledged the legitimacy of the Hungarian position (principle of the three types of minorities and the importance of clever propaganda), 3. If the former nationalities and national public opinion accepted the idea of a "new alliance" (the St. Stephen state ideology), then 4. the revision might take place, not as an independent event but encompassing a complete revision of the "European individual, of Europe's structure and Europe's new balance... It also meant that there must be the recognition that the peace treaties were not *noli me tangere* [do not disturb] and that they were not immutable."⁷⁹

In the matter of a complete or ethnic revision, Teleki was first vague but then quite definite: "Our national position must be the complete, integral, revision... We know, however, that in the reconstruction of Europe we will have to make sacrifices and will have to yield in some areas and territories which we would never have yielded voluntarily. Being an ancient political nation, this is what our sober political good sense tells us," he said in 1934.⁸⁰ Thus, even though he claimed in a number of instances that "ethnic revision was not consistent with our ideas," as a realpolitiker he was willing to accept the fact that a total revision was not possible. For

---

77 Paul Teleki, "Considérations sur l'évolution de l'Europe," *Nouvelle Revue de Hongrie*, no. 5 (1932): 323–331; Teleki, "Avant-propos," *Nouvelle Revue de Hongrie*, no 7 (1933): 643–645; Teleki, "Problèmes du Danube—problèmes de l'Europe," *Nouvelle Revue de Hongrie*, no. 2 (1934): 113–117; and "A propos d'une carte ethnique," *Nouvelle Revue de Hongrie*, no. 1 (1937): 21–26.

78 A good example is the grievance associated with the special publication about the World Jamboree, in Letters of the Editor to Pál Teleki, Budapest, May 4, and June 9, 1933, Papers of the *Nouvelle Revue de Hongrie*, József Balogh Papers, fond 1/3067, fols. 27835- 27838, OSZKK.

79 Teleki, "Európa az újonnan alakuló világban," [Europe in the newly forming world], in *Európáról és Magyarországról*, p. 145.

80 Gr. Teleki Pál, "Magyarország és az európai politika" [Hungary and European politics], *Fiatal Magyarság* [Young Hungary], May, 1934, p. 83.

him a modification of the borders on geographic and economic grounds was the fixed minimum. According to his public utterances, he came to this conclusion in the first half of the 1930s and held on to it until the end of his life.

In the School of Economics

When Teleki resigned as prime minister in the spring of 1921, he already had the position that served as a base for the realization of his goals in public life. On December 30, 1919, Teleki had been appointed a full professor at the School of Economics of the Budapest University (today: Corvinus University of Budapest). The newly established school was assembled with the goal to create and educate a Christian middle-class elite that could successfully compete in commerce and finance with the Jewish preponderance then considered to be oppressive. The school was established over the protest of the rest of the schools of the university and it was largely due to Teleki that it survived. Initially, since he was mainly involved in politics, he did not teach.

In the academic year 1921–22 he returned to the School of Economics and lectured on economic and transport geography.[81] The new university had great need of his reputation and influence and it is thus not surprising that on June 8, 1922, Teleki was elected dean of the school. It was one of the duties of the dean to direct the move of the faculty into its new, presumably permanent, quarters.[82] In his program as dean he considered the move to an independent facility and the improvement of relations with the prominent old home institution, Péter Pázmány (Budapest) University, as his principal goals.

The fact that he continued to be interested in the prewar Hungarian plans about the East and the Balkans is shown by his involvement with the maintenance and reorganization of the Oriental Institute. "Because there is a major calling for the Hungarian politician, the Hungarian merchant and even the Hungarian farmers in the East."

According to him the principal task of the School of Economics was "the education of citizens to be economic leaders" and therefore he encouraged his colleagues that at all exams the greatest severity be practiced in order for the greatest faculty in the country to avoid the accusation of producing an intellectual proletariat.[83] It is

---

81 June 24, 1921, fob 314, no. 14 on the agenda, 5 a, vol. 1, Budapesti Corvinus Egyetem Levéltára [Archives of the Corvinus University of Budapest] (hereafter cited as BCEL).
82 About his election, see June 8, 1922, fol. 156, no. 1 on the agenda topic, 5 a, vol. 1, BCEL.
83 Ibid. vol. 3, Pál Teleki's introductory speech as dean, September 22, 1922, ad 3624/1922. ikt. sz., 5.a, vol. 3, BCEL

evident that from the perspective of the faculty his deanship had strategic significance. In the midst of financial and educational problems, he should have supported the ailing institution with his political standing and lead it into the "Promised Land" of a new and permanent building. This would have required enormous tact, activity and persistence. It was not his fault that he could not bring it off.

During the summer of 1922 he complained to Jenő Cholnoky about an infection and fever.[84] Barely one month after his inaugural speech, the vice-dean announced at a faculty meeting that Teleki was seriously ill and that Ferenc Fodor would take over his teaching duties. At the end of 1922 Teleki underwent surgery and had one kidney removed. His family believed that he acquired the disease while at the front and that he had neglected it.[85] It is more likely that the tuberculosis that he might have picked up at the front progressed to renal tuberculosis eventually causing renal failure and bladder contractions. Consequently he had great difficulties in voiding. There was no cure for the disease at that time and therefore during the last nineteen years of his life he had to catheterize himself three times each day, regardless of where he might be. With a clever arrangement he sterilized the necessary equipment in the desert, sleeping car or on board ship. In this way he could move around freely "like anybody else."[86] Such long-term self-catheterization is rare even today and required an almost superhuman discipline. The physical discomfort, despondency and the dramatic decline of his prospects produced a severe depression in the man who was only forty three years old at the time. Active participation in politics was not a possibility.

He seemed to recover rapidly and a few days later appeared briefly at a faculty meeting. He expressed his gratitude to the substitute lecturers and received the good wishes of the faculty.[87] During the spring he attended some of the faculty meetings. On April 12 he welcomed the faculty to its new home but it was already an open secret that he had requested permission to retire from his professorship and wished to leave the School of Economics.[88] He communicated his position in a

---

84 Letter from Pál Teleki to Jenő Cholnoky, Budapest, July 22, 1922, Scientific and Official Correspondence until 1931, box 3, Cholnoky Papers, MFMA.
85 János Kubassek, "Gróf Teleki Pál utolsó napjai—ahogyan veje Gróf Zichy Nándor látta" [The last days of Count Pál Teleki—as seen by his son- in-law, Count Nándor Zichy], *Napi Magyarország* [Daily Hungary], March 4, 2000; and Fodor, Teleki Pál, pp. 92–93. I gratefully acknowledge the assistance of Dr. Miklós Vanik, urologist at the Szent János Hospital in Budapest.
86 Letter from Pál Teleki to Andor Teleki, Budapest, December 10, 1931. cs. 1, t. 1, Teleki-Degenfeld Papers, P 2026, MNL OL.
87 January 21, 1923, no. 1 on the agenda, 5.a, vol. 3, vol 13, BCEL.
88 April 12, 1923, no. 1 on the agenda, 5.a, vol. 3, vol 13, BCEL.

very depressed letter to his faculty colleagues and to Kuno Klebelsberg, the minister of culture and education. He was in doubt about a rapid recovery and spoke of future operations. "I am in a state of insecurity," he wrote, "and don't know whether I may have to keep to my bed for a long period of time... Consequently I can not, in clear conscience, continue to hold a chair and jeopardize the education of the students. I need not say that this was a very difficult decision for me but I have no choice." He recommended that Ferenc Fodor be his successor and only requested that as an emeritus professor he might give an occasional lecture. He thanked his colleagues for their support and warm friendship.[89]

The school and the minister refused to consider his retirement. Instead they gave him a one year leave of absence and Teleki, who had regained most of his spirits, responded that he might need only about half that time for a complete recovery.[90] He did not even use six months of the leave of absence, but 1923 was a year of many days of sickness and of getting used to painful and unpleasant daily procedures. At the end of the year he again felt that he could not tolerate the burden of teaching. He again wished to resign from the School of Economics and wished to work with Jenő Cholnoky on the School of Humanities. Later he gave up even on this. He wrote Cholnoky,

> My conscience bothers me greatly....It is a pity that you encouraged me so. I was right when I resigned from the School of Economics. I am not crazy, I just procrastinated because it is very hard for me to give up my professorship and the work that goes with it. My life has been broken in half. Everybody should see this, but it had to happen because what was dilettantism so far would have become humbug. Perhaps some day I might go back to it. I must seek some work to earn a living but if I have enough spare time and regain my equanimity and can continue my studies that I do not wish to give up, perhaps in ten years I can produce something and arrive at a point where I can ask for reinstatement with conviction and confidence. I know that there are ignorant professors but that is no reason why every fool could be professor.[91]

---

89 Letter from Pál Teleki to the faculty. April 6, 1923, and his letter to Kunó Klebelsberg the same day, box 45, 958/1923 ikt. sz., BCEL.
90 June 5, 1923, no. 2 on the agenda, 5.a, vol. 3, BCEL.
91 Letter from Pál Teleki to Jenő Cholnoky, n.d. and n.p. (probably at the end on 1923), Cholnoky-Teleki correspondence in separate dossier, Cholnoky Papers, MFMA.

He wrote to the School of Economics in December 1923 that it was not a serious engagement but an unnecessary courtesy toward others that constantly and completely impeded his serious work. He stated that he was "regressing and that neither his intellectual abilities nor his training were such to make up for his deficiencies." Consequently he reached the conclusion that he would resign his professorship.[92] The faculty and the minister convinced him to stay on and Teleki now did take advantage of the leave of absence and did not teach in 1924.[93] The wide swings of his mood and his feelings of inadequacy were much improved by rest and by a trip to Finland during the summer of 1924. After Finland he returned to Pribékfalva. He had time to consider the events of the last few months and his future. He shared his thoughts with his old friends.

> Finland and the life here at home where I mow the lawn in the morning, then ride and, in the evening, play tennis has much improved my health. Concerning the chair, good manners keep me from doing anything and I don't want to do anything anyway. Believe me it will be better if I don't become a professor at your place. I could not do it justice. I saw this in Finland, where I have learned a great deal, but I found that I was a very long way from being satisfied with myself. Furthermore my financial situation would demand that I withdraw from all public service and enter some commercial enterprise, such as a paint factory....[94]

He did not abandon the scholarly activities for a paint factory. On his return from Finland he found an invitation from the League of Nations to participate, as an expert, in determining the Turkish-Iraqi border.

The Mosul Episode

The Great Powers were concerned with the Mosul vilayet of the Turkish Empire even during the war. Under the Sykes-Picot agreement of May 1916 between Great Britain and France, the area would have fallen under French, Russian, and to some

---

92 Letter from Pál Teleki to the dean of the School of Economics, Budapest, December 30, 1923, G 603, R 3486/963, Egyetemi Könyvtárés Levéltár, Kézirattár [University Library and Archives, Manuscript Department].
93 January 30, 1924, no. 5 on the agenda, 5 a, vol. 4, BCEL, and February 28, 1924. no. 3 on the agenda, 5 a, vol. 4, BCEL.
94 Letter from Pál Teleki to Jenő Cholnoky, Pribékfalva, August 30, [1924], Cholnoky-Teleki special dossier, Cholnoky Papers. MFMA.

extent, Arab control to serve as a buffer between the territories to be acquired by Great Britain and the furthest point of the Russian Near East penetration after the war. In 1917, however, the Soviet government published the hitherto secret agreement. The discrepancy between what the Allies said and did, e.g. promising independence to the Arabs and secretly dividing the area between them, plus the furor of the Arabic world nullified the proposal.[95]

In May 1920 the Peace Conference decided that Iraq would be a British Mandate under the League of Nations and that until the promised independence Great Britain would be in charge of the administration of the kingdom.[96] The Sèvres peace treaty prepared for Turkey awarded the Mosul vilayet to Iraq. Turkey, however, did not sign the peace dictate and started an armed conflict. This fight was successful and the Entente had to revise its peace plans for Turkey. The Peace Treaty of Lausanne, signed in July 1923, left the fate of the areas with Muslim population but without a Turkish majority open. This was the case for the Mosul vilayet that the Turks were unwilling to give up.

Lord Curzon, the British Foreign Secretary, and Mustapha Ismet Pasha, the leader of the Turkish delegation, agreed that if direct Turkish-British negotiations about the fate of the Mosul vilayet were not successful within nine months that matter would be referred to the League of Nations.[97] The Turks argued for retaining the territory by claiming that that the British statistics were wrong and that the Kurds who represented the majority of the inhabitants and the Chaldeans who represented a large minority wished to live with the Turks and that the region had no connection whatever with Baghdad.[98] The British insisted that the Kurds had no intention to live with the Turks and added that the same could be said about the large Arab population of the region.[99] They emphasized that they had occupied the territory during the war, that there were a number of economic, strategic and geographic arguments for it to remain with Iraq and that therefore a plebiscite was not

---

95 Elizabeth Monroe, *Britain's Moment in the Middle East 1914–1956* (London: Chatto & Windus, 1964), pp. 32–34, and 53.
96 Geoffrey M. Gathome-Hardy, *A Short History of International Affairs* (London: Oxford University Press, 1942), p. 116.
97 William Stivers, *Supremacy and Oil. Iraq, Turkey and the Anglo-American World Order, 1918–1930* (Ithaca: Cornell University Press, 1982), pp. 141–142.
98 "Question de la frontière entre la Turquie et l'Iraq," pp. 14-15, and 58, C.400 M.147. 1925.VII., ENSZ Letéti Gyűjtemény [UN Collection], Országgyűlési Könyvtár [Parliament Library] (hereafter cited as OK), 14–15, and 58.
99 Ibid., p. 75.

desirable.[100] The negotiations did not succeed and therefore the matter came before the Council of the League of Nations in August 1923. At a session in Brussels, in October, the council drew a line separating Turkey from Iraq. This line generally coincided with the northern border of the Mosul vilayet. This line, known as the Brussels Line, separated the two countries until the final determination of the border.[101] For different reasons, both countries rejected this line. The Turkish government would have liked to have a plebiscite in the area (approximately 8,900 square kilometers), while Baghdad laid a claim to 3,500 square kilometers north of the Brussels Line.[102] The options for a final decision were referred by the Council of the League of Nations to a commission consisting of three members.[103]

Teleki's name was first mentioned at the end of September 1924.[104] Teleki accepted the task with pleasure although he was concerned that his prewar contacts with and affection for Turkey and his presidency of the Turanian Society might make him vulnerable. Knowing all this, the League of Nations still picked him. He was the first member of the commission and the date of his appointment was October 20, 1924.[105] The other members of commission were Albert Paulis, a Belgian colonel and colonial entrepreneur, and the chairman was Carl Einar Thure af Wirsen, the Swedish minister in Bucharest.

Teleki engaged in feverish activity to familiarize himself with the literature on this issue. The League of Nation delegation, complete with secretaries, interpreters and international officials set out on December 25, 1924, and traveled through Istanbul, Ankara, and Damascus to Baghdad. In Konya they met the Turkish head of state.[106] The delegation arrived in Baghdad on January 16, 1925, and, after consultations there, arrived at the end of the month in Mosul, the center of the disputed territory. They left on March 23 after having traveled several thousand kilo-

---

100 Records of the Council of the League of Nations, Geneva, January 23, 1923, Societe des Nations, vol. 600, fols. 106–107, MAE AD; and "Question de la frontière," p. 16.
101 Garthorne-Hardy, *A Short History*, p. 116; István Klinghammer and Gábor Gercsák, "Der ungarische Geograph Pál Teleki als Mitglied der Mossul-Kommission," *Cartographica Helvetica* 19, no. 1 (January 1999): 18–19.
102 "Question de la frontière," p. 56.
103 Aryo Makko: Arbitrator in a World of Wars: The League of Nations and The Mosul Dispute, 1924–1925. *Diplomacy and Statecraft*, vol. 21 (2010), Issue 4, 631-649.
104 Anonymous report to Sir Eric Drummond, September 20, 1924, Section politique-Political Section, Registry 1919–1927, Section 11 (Politique- Political), R 605, 1919-1927:11/39416/25888. League of Nations Archives- Archives de la SDN (hereafter cited as LONA-ASDN).
105 Notes for the Head of the Political Division, Geneva, October 20, 1924, Societe des Nations, vol. 601. fol. 78, MAE AD.
106 "A főcserkész mesél" [The Chief Scout tells a story], *Magyar Cserkész* [Hungarian Scout], January 1, 1926, p. 2.

"Educating the Nation": Revision and Conservatism (1921–1938)

meters by train, car and plane. They interviewed several hundred people and then returned to Europe in order to prepare their report based on their local experiences and assembled documentation, and make a recommendation for the final location of the Turkish-Iraqi border.

For Teleki these months were full of novel experiences. First of all, and unbeknown to him, he got immersed into a political turmoil that seriously harmed his reputation. His person was somewhat suspect right from the beginning because of his alleged sympathies toward Turkey. It was also a cause for suspicion that in Istanbul and Ankara he was seen repeatedly in the company of high Turkish officials who were well known for their hatred of Great Britain.[107] If this would not have been enough, one of the secretaries of the delegation, the Italian Marcello Roddolo, was on a secret vendetta against Teleki and accused him to the British officials of everything imaginable.[108] In addition, Teleki made things worse. In Baghdad, for instance, he stated before unhappy Iraqi ministers that he did not trust any of the interpreters selected by the Great Powers because these countries were interested only in the Mosul oil. This was why he used only the Dutch interpreter who was certainly not prejudiced. As it turned out J. H. Kramers knew Turkish, but his knowledge of Arabic was limited to a very narrow literary field and was practically useless in Mosul.[109]

The reputation of the Hungarian scholar, who appeared before the king of Iraq in a Boy Scout uniform, was not enhanced by his publicly contradicting the ministers and telling them that according to his views in the Middle East religion was the only determinant of identity and nothing else mattered. This conviction came to him at the time of the Paris peace negotiations. He frequently stated that the nationality data of the Carpathian Basin could be monitored with religious statistics and that the nationality mix in the Near East was even more complex than in central Europe. The Iraqi Prime Minister Yasin Pasha was shocked and told Teleki

---

107 Notes of Gertrude Bell, High Commissioner Dobbs' advisor. Baghdad, January 19, 1925, Secret, TNA, FO 371, vol. 601, fols. 187–190. The author of the note, the archeologist-traveller considered Teleki first as „danger" but later corrected herself and added: „Teleki is as clever as he can be and most interesting to talk to." However, she considered the Hungarian politician as a threat for the British politics. See: Letters of Gertrude Bell to his father, Sir Hugh Bell, Baghdad, January 21, 1925, and to her stepmother, Dame Florence Bell, Baghdad, January 28, 1925. Gertrude Bell Archive, University of Newcastle, http://gertrudebell.ncl.ac.uk/ (Last visite: September 23, 2022)
108 Telegram from High Commissioner Dobbs, Baghdad, January 19, 1925, TNA, FO 371, vol. 10823, fols. 183–184; and telegram from High Commissioner Sir Henry Dobbs to Colonial Secretary Leopold Amery, Baghdad, January 22, 1925, TNA, FO 371, vol. 10824, fols. 161–175.
109 Letter from High Commissioner Dobbs to Leopold Amery, Baghdad, January 22, 1925, TNA, FO 371, vol. 10824, fols. 134–137.

that he was voicing the Turkish point of view and that, in fact, in Iraq all of them were Iraqi patriots first and Sunnis or Shiites only second.[110]

The suspicion of the British was increased when upon arrival Teleki said that a plebiscite was a possibility. For both London and Baghdad this sounded like a Turkish argument. The conflicts continued. Teleki picked a quarrel with the other secretary of the delegation, a Frenchman, Horace de Pourtalès. Then, on January 27, 1925, in Mosul Teleki and Jawad Pasha, the Turkish delegate, skipped out of the building designated for the negotiations in order to walk around the streets of the city. The Turkish officer was in uniform and this led to an unexpected development. A large group of people started following the two men. Opinions are divided whether the group was hostile and meant to harm the two men or whether they wished to express their friendship to the Turkish officer. In any case, the police brutally broke up the demonstration. Teleki protested, but he did not deny that he had skipped out on his own.[111] This little episode clearly demonstrates his occasionally faulty, inconsistent assessment of the situation and his confusion about what was possible, what was permitted, and what was proper. This occurred particularly when he was in a new environment without adequate points of reference. This is the only way his statements in Baghdad and the Mosul affair can be explained.[112]

Toward the end of the mission Teleki found out that London and Baghdad had lost confidence in him. This upset him and he asked his friend the Hungarian Minister in London to let the Foreign Office know that he (Teleki) was willing to go along with the British point of view as far as possible. Baron Ivan Rubido-Zichy was very uncomfortable with this request but complied. His British audience was not impressed by his friendly intercession and told him, somewhat maliciously, that there was nothing they could do. They even commented, for internal use, that they understood Count Teleki's endeavor to salvage his reputation but that the Hungarian politician "Can hardly have expected that we could seriously give a reply to his question." There were some who went even further and said that Count Teleki was a little nervous which was not surprising because his methods in Iraq revealed his lack of tact and discernment. All of them, however, were pleased to note that Teleki

---

110 Ibid; and "A főcserkész mesél," part 2, *Magyar Cserkész*, January 15, 1926, p. 17.
111 "Row in the Streets of Mosul," Bagdad Times, February 5, and February 6, 1925; Abstract of a telegram from High Commissioner Dobbs in Iraq, Baghdad, January 19, 1925 TNA, FO371, vol. 10823, fols. 190–195; and Major H. I. Lloyd, British Administration inspector in Mosul to High Commissioner Dobbs. Mosul, January 27, 1925, TNA, FO 371, vol. 10823, fol. 203. Teleki's version of the event was accepted in the "Question de la frontiere," p. 8.
112 For the suspicions about him see the letters of Gertrude Bell of January 21 and 28, February 25 and March 4, 1925 from Baghdad. The Gertrude Bell Archive. http/Avww.gerty.ncl.ac.uk/.

had changed his earlier views about the way the Mosul matter should be arranged.[113] By the time the news of the dissatisfaction with Teleki reached Budapest the matter was resolved.[114]

As soon as the local activities began with interviews with the inhabitants local officials and merchants the scandal quieted down. During the next month and a half the three delegates met with eight hundred people. In the interim Teleki became ill and had to be flown to Baghdad.[115] He had surveyed Erbil and its environment and soon learned the nature and peculiarities of the predominantly Kurdish area. He was so enchanted with the geography, ethnic composition and cultural diversity of one of the cradles of civilization that he decided to write a book about the Mosul mission. His activities gained the grudging recognition of the British officials, particularly when they found out that he had rejected the idea of a plebiscite. They recognized that the other two members of the delegation were completely under his influence because the Hungarian count was the most vigorous and active of the three and that the addresses in Mosul that he brought with him from Budapest did not reflect any Turkophil prejudice. He also performed completely unprejudiced work in his mapping of the conditions.[116]

After the return the report was prepared and June and July 1925 were intensively busy. They worked for eight, ten and even fourteen hours per day. Teleki wrote to his former interpreter, "We are working like camels."[117] Because he felt that the maps of the two antagonists were not based on adequate statistics, he prepared his own map, according to the methodological principles derived from the preparation of the "Red Map" and based on the data he collected at the scene.[118] The public report was published on August 7, 1925. It was long and exhaustive. After describing the work and the methodology of the commission he discussed not only the geographical, geological and climatic characteristics of the region but

---

113 Chief of Section Thomas Spring-Rice's report on his discussion with Ivan Rubido-Zichy, April 2, 1925, and the attached comments on the documents, TNA, FO 371, vol. 10825, fols. 52–53.
114 Ferenc Kiss, "A félhivatalos Anglia kifogasolja gróf Teleki Pál moszuli magatartását" [The semiofficial Britain is critical of Count Pál Teleki's behavior in Mosul], *Az Est*, August 2, 1925.
115 "A főcserkész mesél," part 2, *Magyar Cserkész*, January 15, 1926, pp. 17–19.
116 Foreign Office Division Chief Thomas Spring-Rice's commentary on High Commissioner Dobbs's report. London, n.d., TNA, FO 371, vol. 10825, fol. 5; Report of High Commissioner Dobbs in Iraq to Leopold Amery, Baghdad, January 29, 1925, TNA, FO 371, vol. 10824, fol. 193; and Iraq High Commissioner Dobbs to Leopold Amery, February 2, 1925, TNA, FO 371, vol. 10824, fol. 134.
117 Letter from Pál Teleki to J. H. Kramers, Geneva, July 13, 1925, cs. 1, dossier-A, fols. 20–21, K 37, MNL OL.
118 Klinghammer and Gercsák, "Der ungarische Geograph," pp. 19–20.

its ethnography as well.¹¹⁹ Here a decision had to be made. There were four different statistics available to the commission, which of them would be used to arrive at a conclusion? At the end, Wirsen, Paulis, and Teleki chose the data gathered from the 1922–1924 census conducted by the Iraq government.¹²⁰

Attempts were made to describe Mosul, having about ninety-eight thousand inhabitants, from a nationality-statistical perspective but this was not easy. They believed that the city was principally Arab with minimal Turkish or Kurd influence although in the near future the Kurds streaming in from the countryside would likely become significant. In its general conclusions, the commission recommended that the Brussels Line be accepted, with certain modifications, as the border between the two countries, because it was a very good border.¹²¹ Emphasizing the importance of not only the ethnographic factors but of the economic, geographic and strategic factors as well, the commission recommended that the region remain with Iraq. The economic factors included commercial routes and markets with their environment while the geographic factors were hydrography, climate, arable area, etc. The report considered the possibility of a Kurd establishment because with the easily assimilated Turks and the related Yesidi Kurds would have a 70 percent majority.

Yet the commission rejected a plan based entirely on ethnography.¹²² It recommended that the Kurd language be used in instruction and administration and also that the region be under Iraqi authority with an extension of the British mandate.¹²³

The Council of the League of Nations discussed the report at its September 2, 1925, session and accepted it. Turkey did not agree with the decision and requested the International Tribunal in The Hague for an expert opinion. The tribunal ruled that the Council of the League of Nations was entitled to render a decision and in December 1925 it was ruled that the region south of the Brussels Line would remain under British administration and that the Kurds were entitled to some form of autonomy. Even though the Turkish government was outraged about the decision, the Mosul question was settled in June 1926, for a while at least, by a tripartite, British, Turkish, and Iraqi negotiation.¹²⁴

---

119 "Question de la frontiere," pp. 20–24, 30–53, and 53–56.
120 Ibid., p. 33.
121 Ibid., p. 74.
122 Ibid., p. 57.
123 Ibid., pp. 88–89.
124 Stivers, *Supremacy and Oil*, pp. 165–166; and Gathorne-Hardy, *A Short History*, p. 116; and Péter Kovács, "Paul Teleki et le règlement de l'affaire de Mossoul dans la Société des Nations," *Miskolc Journal of*

Teleki was not pleased even though the ruling was according to the recommendations of the commission and in the best interests of Great Britain and that it brought international scholarly approval. The Swiss professor, Emile Chaix truly devoured the report that he called "the best present for my library" and "a model."[125] Isaiah Bowman wrote Teleki from New York, "Both the maps and the text are gripping" and the work that produced them was "admirable."[126] The eminent American professor published a panegyric about the report in the journal that he edited and mentioned only Teleki among the members of the commission.[127] Yet the political and international debate about the summary and the disinterest shown in Geneva about the Hungarian minority problems induced him to question the meaning of Hungary's membership in the League of Nations, before the plenum of the National Assembly.[128] This was his only parliamentary speech between 1922 and 1926. He did not agree with the way the minority question was handled, condemned the slowness of the council and called the statements about disarmament and security hypocritical. "This is *our* disarmament and *their* security," he said.[129]

According to him the international organization had come to a crossroads and, Hungary had to consider whether to follow the League on its path. He recognized the economic advantages of the League of Nations loan but pointedly asked, "Is this why we must decide to stay in or not?"[130] Prime Minister Bethlen rejected Teleki's proposal. The press picked it up and thus Teleki, in a speech to the electors in Szeged, had to deny that he recommended leaving the League and also had to make a disclaimer to the British minister in Budapest.[131] That this step was a considered one but was probably born of desperation is shown by the fact that later Teleki participated in the work of several League of Nations agencies. He was even

---

International Law 1, no. 2 (2004): 156–187 (http://www.uni-miskolc.hu/~wwvvdrint/ 20042kovacsl.htm).

125 Letter from Emile Chaix to Pál Teleki, December 1, 1925, Papers of Pál Teleki, cs. 1, dossier-A, fols. 22-23, K37, MNL OL.
126 Letter from Isaiah Bowman to Pál Teleki, New York, September 17, 1925, Papers of Pál Teleki, cs. 1, dossier-A, fol. 58, K37, MNL OL.
127 [Isaiah Bowman], "Geography and Boundaries in Mosul," *The Geographical Review* 16, no 1 (January 1926): 143–144.
128 "Érdekes beszelgetés Teleki Pál és Baross János között a népszövetségi kérdésről" [Interesting conversation between Pál Teleki and János Baross on the League of Nations Question], *Pesti Napló*, October 16, 1926; and Papp, ed., *Teleki Pál országgyűlési beszédei*, vol. 1, pp. 272–282.
129 Papp, ed., *Teleki Pál országgyűlési beszédei*, vol. 1, p. 274.
130 Ibid., p. 281.
131 Report from Colville Barclay to Foreign Secretary Austen Chamberlain, Budapest October 31, 1925 TNA, FO 371, vol. 10778, fols. 98–101; and "Teleki Pál gróf beszámolója" [Count Pál Teleki's report], *Délmagyarország*, October 20, 1925, p. 2.

elected to the membership of the Commission Internationale de Coopération Intellectuelle, in 1937.[132] He did not participate in the activities because he had other obligations and barely two years later, under Teleki's prime ministership, Hungary retired from the League of Nations. The autumn 1925 newspaper polemics are dwarfed by the huge scandal that was developing in Budapest and in which Teleki had a starring role.

Political Tempests

Arisztid Jankovich, a retired colonel was arrested on December 14, 1925, in Amsterdam after he tried to exchange two forged thousand franc notes in a change bureau. When the detectives came he was engaged in trying to put several more forged bills into his socks. In his hotel room suitcases full of forged notes were found. Jankovich's comrades were György Mankovich, a hosiery manufacturer and journalist, and György Marsovszky, journalist, former gunnery officer, long distance racer and former parliamentary secretary to Gyula Gömbös.[133] At the police station Jankovich tried to avoid questioning by showing a Hungarian diplomatic courier passport and the Ministry of Foreign Affairs in Budapest attested to the validity of the passport.[134]

The scandal rapidly reached international notice and, based on Jankovich's confession, the originators of the forgery came to the attention of the French and Dutch police. It became known in Hungary with some delay because Imre Nádosy the commander in chief of the National Police knew about the forgery, was the one who gave Jankovich the diplomatic passport and initially tried to cover it all up. After he was dismissed, the Hungarian investigators went to work. Relying on information from Amsterdam they arrested Prince Lajos Windischgraetz, the former minister of public supplies, and a leading figure of the royalist group. Dezső Rába, the prince's secretary, and Gáspár Kovács, his valet, were also arrested and disciplinary process began against some officials in the Institute of Cartography. Initially the French government did not raise the issue of the responsibility of the Hungarian government and the personal responsibility of Bethlen and even put

---

132 Extract of the minutes of the May 27, 1937, meeting of the Council of the League of Nations, R4026, 1933–1946:5 B/29069/5884, LONA-ASDN.
133 Mária Ormos, "Hamis frankokkal teli bőröndök" [Suitcases filled with forged francs], in Skandalum. Magyar közéleti botrányok 1843–1991 [Hungarian Public Scandals, 1843–1991], ed. András Gerő (Budapest: T- Twins, 1993), pp. 175–193. And David Petruccelli: Banknotes from the Underground: Counterfeiting and the International Orderin Interwar Europe. *Journal of Contemporary History* 2016, vol. 51 (3), 507–530.
134 Karsai and Nemes, eds., *Iratok az ellenforradalom történetéhez*, vol. 3, docs. 114/a, and 114/b.

the breaks on the furious politicians in Prague.¹³⁵ By the middle of January 1926 the attitude of Paris changed. Seeing the reluctance of the Hungarian government, the increased diplomatic pressure from the Little Entente, and the activities of the emigrants of the 1918 revolution, the Quai d'Orsay raised the question of the responsibility of the head of government. In parallel with the investigation, a parliamentary committee was appointed that heard the prime minister and the other Hungarian politicians who could be shown to be involved in the forgery.¹³⁶

Teleki had very bad premonitions as early as the first days of January 1926 and offered to the Prime Minister's Office that he would take full responsibility for the whole affair. It is unlikely that he would have made this offer absent of serious pangs of conscience. As he said, "I knew that they would involve me."¹³⁷ Then Teleki left for a long lecture tour in Germany and by the time he returned the tempest was in full force. The parliamentary opposition, Liberals, royalists and Social Democrats believed that the time had come to make Bethlen fall and the developments of the international scene seemed to favor it. Teleki was seeking political support. On February 17, 1926, prior to the hearing by the parliamentary committee he joined the government party and stated at a party dinner that, "today all honest Hungarians must line up behind István Bethlen."¹³⁸ In a document written several weeks later and deposited with his notary, Teleki said that he entered the government party because of his patriotic fervor and because Bethlen particularly asked him to do so.¹³⁹ It is likely that the motives for this action were both defensive and patriotic. No other independent representative followed his footsteps.

Teleki's reputation received a fatal blow from a letter written by an old friend. Count Imre Károlyi, Teleki's former codirector in the MARTA automobile factory in Arad, published an open letter in the February 6, 1926, issue of the *Pester Lloyd* that raised Bethlen's responsibility and, without mentioning any names, spoke of another person, "about whose conscience I wonder. How can he sleep when Lajos Windischgraetz and László Gerő [map maker and military officer who actually did the forging of the francs] have sat in a dirty jail for weeks? Those two did not even know each other until this person introduced them to each other for

---

135 Ignác Romsics, "Franciaország, Bethlen és a frankhamisítás" [France, Bethlen and the franc forgery], *Történelmi Szemle*, no. 1 (1983): 68–69.
136 For the committee, see Karsai and Nemes, eds., *Iratok az ellenforradalom történetéhez*, vol. 3, doc. 137.
137 Sarusi-Kiss and Gáspár, "Teleki Pál," p. 742.
138 "Újra meghallgatja a frankbizottság Bethlen Istvánt es megidézik Teleki Pál grófot es Gömbös Gyulát" [The Franc Committee again questions István Bethlen and summons Count Pál Teleki and Gyula Gömbös], *8 Órai Újság* [8 O'clock News], February 14, 1926.
139 Sarusi-Kiss and Gáspár, "Teleki Pál," p. 740.

them to cooperate."[140] The somewhat theatrical statement was certainly incorrect in one area, it is unlikely that Teleki slept well during these weeks.

He had no choice among the increasing attacks and even before the hearing of the parliamentary committee he went voluntarily to the police and behind closed doors he gave them his version of the story. He maintained this version, with minor modifications, until the end of the affair.[141] He mentioned the letters of Pallavicini and Károlyi as the principle causes for his having gone to the police. A few days later Imre Károlyi also presented his version. He learned about Pál Teleki's involvement from a secret document, but was unwilling to reveal the origin or content of the document.[142]

In postwar Europe large-scale money forging was a frequent crime that was used repeatedly by both the victors and the vanquished. Between September 1924 and April 1926 there were 192 known forgery cases in Europe and these were published regularly in the *Marques caractéristiques* that specialized in this matter. The Hungarian franc forgers had substantial contacts in Germany. A German expert, Arthur Schultze was the one who, becoming acquainted with Prince Windischgraetz, first laid out the technical possibilities of the forgeries in Hungary. He was the one who introduced Gerő to the technical aspects of the forgery. After the scandal exploded Schultze could not be found but when he reappeared he confessed to the German authorities. He could not answer any further interrogations because he suffered a nervous collapse, was confined to a mental institution where he died very promptly of a gastric hemorrhage.

This was not the only German contact. The plates used for printing also came to Hungary from Germany, presumably from Eugen Trautmann, a Munich map printer whose office specialized in the production of peculiar materials. The paper used in printing the notes presumably also came from his office. In his confession Trautmann named Teleki as the person who had come several times to his office to talk to him.[143] Teleki claimed that it was during his first prime ministership that Windischgraetz came to him and indicated that he would like to forge the notes of a foreign country. First he claimed that he would destabilize the French economy with forged francs. Very soon it became evident that this argument was untenable.

---

140 Quoted in ibid., p. 744 n. 78.
141 "Teleki Pál gróf szenzációs vallomást tett a rendőrségen a frankhamisítók előkészületeiről" [Count Pál Teleki makes sensational admissions about the preparations of the franc forgers], *Újság*, February 16, 1926.
142 Confession of Imre Károlyi (copy), Budapest, February 26, 1926, Papers of István Bethlen, cs. 18, dossier B/20, K 468, MNL OL.
143 Ormos, "Hamis frankokkal," pp. 178–179.

Even assuming that every one of the 3,000 thousand franc notes was perfect, the 30 million unbacked francs would have been insufficient to cause any real damage to the French economy. It was worse than that. The most thorough search found only 4,400 good forgeries and more than half of the total was of very poor quality. According to a later explanation this money was going to be used for patriotic purposes and the perpetrators claimed that they wanted to influence the 1925 Czechoslovak elections.

When Windischgraetz first went to see Teleki, the latter advised him not to engage in forgery. He introduced him to László Gerő the trained map maker and printing techniques expert to convince him that the forgery could not be successful. Gerő reported his discussions and Teleki relaxed in the belief that the forgery was not possible. Teleki so advised Prime Minister Bethlen who, in turn, told Police Chief Nádosy to keep an eye on the matter. They did not speak about it again.[144] He knew nothing about any further collaboration between the prince and Gerő. The government party majority of the committee accepted the somewhat illogical explanation and accepted that Gerő did not meet Windischgraetz in 1921 but that they met by chance one or two years later.[145] In a minority report, the opposition representatives named Teleki as the principal agent between the government and the forgers.[146]

Later, in his deposition before the court, Teleki modified this by saying that their first meeting was in 1922 and thus not during his prime ministership. He considered Imre Károlyi's attack undignified and he was so upset by his old friend's letter and by Dezső Rába's deposition stating that Teleki had served as the contact between the prime minister and the forgers that, after a consultation with István Bethlen, he decided on a counterattack.[147] Even though he was dissuaded from starting a libel suit against Károlyi and Pallavicini, he sent a message to the royal-

---

144 For the official version see, "Teleki Pál gróf szenzációs vallomása"; "Teleki Pált kihallgatja a parlamenti bizottság" [Pál Teleki is questioned by the parliamentary committee], *Népszava*, February 16, 1926, p. 5; and "Gróf Teleki Pál nyilatkozik a rendőrségi és parlamenti vizsgálóbizottság előtt tett vallomásairól" (Count Pál Teleki speaks about his testimony before the police and before the parliamentary committee], *Pesti Napló*, February 18, 1926.

145 Az 1922. június 16.-ra összehívott nemzetgyűlés nyomtatványai. Irományok [The publications and documents of the national assembly elected on June 16, 1922. Papers], vol. 17, no. 1028. *A frankhamisítás bűnügyspacepolitikai hátterének megvizsgálására kiküldött parlamenti bizottság jelentése* [Report from the parliamentary committee established to investigate the franc forgery crime] (Budapest: Pesti Konyvnyomda, 1926), pp. 180–183.

146 Ibid., appendix 1, pp. 192–193.

147 "Rába Dezső tegnap délután súlyosan terhelő vallomást tett Teleki és Gömbös ellen" [Dezső Rába yesterday afternoon made weighty accusations against Teleki and Gömbös], *Esti Kurir* [Evening Messenger], February 17, 1926.

ists saying, "Yes I have a trump in my hand but I will play it only when I consider it timely and not when you want to force it out of my hand."[148] He called Rába's deposition a phantasm.[149] He also announced that he would not again respond to attacks and to the vindictive press campaign.

A month and a half later, at Easter, he thought about the issues more calmly and made some notes that he deposited with a notary. By this time he was certain that in the trial being prepared he would serve as a witness and not as a defendant and that the French did not wish to haul him in front of a tribunal on the basis of the additional investigations.[150] Teleki was very apprehensive about the trial scheduled for May, thinking that it would prove the "hardest nut to crack" because the "ideas of gentlemanliness are different inside a prison" and he mentioned the prince and his secretary by name as men who would certainly talk.[151] Among the papers deposited there are two very important ones. In one of them he related his role in the franc affair. The other one is a memorandum prepared for Bethlen in which he summarized the conclusions drawn from the case and the way he wished to handle it.

Three conclusions can be drawn from the notes that have surfaced only recently:

1. In the summary, Teleki presented a very unfavorable picture of Bethlen whose inapproachability and indifference during the critical days affected him very painfully. He claimed that he and Bethlen were not as close to each other as it was assumed by many. According to him the prime minister handled the affair badly during the first days and then he was swept away by the events.
2. Teleki knew considerably more than what he stated before the police and the court. He intentionally kept in the dark his meetings with Gerő and Nádosy and the frequency of their meetings. He did not mention that he had informed Bethlen in great detail.
3. Teleki was perhaps somewhat less involved or guilty than it was suspected at the time and since, but he was much more deeply involved politically than permissible.

---

148 "Teleki Pál szerepe és a kormány politikai felelőssége [The role of Pál Teleki and the political responsibility of the government], *Pesti Napló*, February 28, 1926.
149 "Teleki Pál gróf tiltakozása Windischgraetz fantazmagóriái ellen" [Count Pál Teleki's protest against Windischgraetz's phantasm], *8 Órai Újság*, February 25, 1926, p. 4.
150 Report of Inspector Royere, March 2, 1926, dossier: Rapports et pièces, F7 Police générale, vol. 14766, Archives Nationales (Paris).
151 Sarusi-Kiss and Gáspár, "Teleki Pál," p. 756.

Teleki's central role is very probable. Assessing his relationships with the suspected people we can find instructive connections. It was Teleki who appointed Nádosy as National Chief of Police in August 1920 and both of them were directors of the same social club, the National Casino. He knew László Gerő well from the Boy Scout movement and this was no secret even then. Teleki tried to cast a shadow on this relationship in order to protect the youth movement. Imre Károlyi made a witty comment to the British minister concerning Teleki recommending Gerő, "This is like if we wanted to talk somebody out of buying a pair of shoes by making him meet the best shoemaker in town."[152] The quip is very telling.

Among the officials of the Institute of Cartography, the workshop of the forgeries, there were a number of Boy Scout officers. In addition the maps of the Mosul Committee were made there during the spring and summer of 1925. Teleki was a regular visitor at the institute. It was Teleki who sponsored Lajos Hajts, the director of the institute until the end of 1924, for membership in the Hungarian Geographical Society in March of 1917. It was Teleki who called Gábor Baross, one of the accused, to join him in the National Office for Veteran Affairs, also in 1917. The acquaintance he maintained with Eugen Trautmann makes it credible when the frequently untrustworthy Windischgraetz claims that Teleki was the link between the government and the forgers.[153]

The suspicion is made stronger by the fact that Teleki was no stranger to unusual and risky political maneuvers. The trial brought out some surprises and some additional malfeasances but the defendants loyally played out their assigned roles and therefore received very light sentences. The judgment took full account of Teleki's deposition and completely exonerated him. The Royal Hungarian Court indicated that it considered the patriotic motives as mitigating circumstances.[154] At the Appellate Court Rába also withdraw his accusations against Teleki who thus could stand *pro forma* free and clean before public opinion.[155] István Bethlen's cabinet survived its severest trial but in the long run the forgery affair was very harmful for Hungary and Teleki's role was not forgotten in Paris. Teleki summarized the events

---

152 Report of Sir Colville Barclay to Foreign Secretary Chamberlain, Budapest, February 17, 1926, TNA, FO 371, vol. 11366, fol. 15.
153 Ludwig Windisch-Graetz, *Helden und Halunken. Selbsterlebte Welt- geschichte 1899–1964* (Vienna: Wilhelm Frick Verlag, 1967), p. 145; and Mária Ormos, *Egy magyar médiavezér: Kozma Miklós* [Miklós Kozma: A Hungarian Media Tsar] (Budapest: PolgART, 2000), vol. 1, pp. 134–136.
154 Lajos Windischgraetz and codefendants, fols. 30–33, 41,79–80, and 100, Papers of the Budapest Criminal Court, 193/1926, VII. 5. c., Budapest Fővárosi Levéltár (Budapest Capital City Archives) (hereafter cited as BFL).
155 Karsai and Nemes, eds., *Iratok az ellenforradalom történetéhez*, vol. 3, doc. 166.

as follows, "Although I never thought very highly of humanity it was just this year that I found out what swine they were."[156]

The case was a good reason for Teleki to give up all parliamentary politicking for a while. When on Prime Minister Bethlen's request Regent Horthy prorogued parliament on November 15, 1926, Teleki did not again appear as a candidate. He had the opportunity for a new distinction. On January 7, 1927, the Council of the School of Economics elected him to represent the council in the newly established Upper House of Parliament. He was reelected on the same basis in 1934, this time with no opposing votes and in absentia. He spoke mainly on issues related to education and cultural matters. Yet, these speeches revealed that he was distinguished from the large group of members by having a comprehensive, albeit not fully worked out, scheme for national education and by being to the right of most of them, particularly during the 1930s. In this chamber he did not have to worry about loutish representative behavior or rude and sarcastic comments. At the same time his preexisting social and political standing assured him of a proper position in the Upper House that was designed to be a stabilizing element of the system. His conservative reform ideas found a relatively large audience without having to go through the torture of a parliamentary election. It was here that he had the opportunity to defend the actions of his first government when he spoke against amending the numerus clausus law.

The Bethlen government, under pressure from international public opinion, the League of Nations, and some Jewish organizations, and perhaps also because of conviction, wished to amend Act XXV of 1921, the numerus clausus law.[157] The Minister of Culture and Education Kuno Klebelsberg had hinted about such amendments as early as the autumn of 1926. In the autumn of 1927, Bethlen officially announced at the government party conference that the act would be amended so as to eliminate, "those ordinances that had caused serious resentment and displeasure in a group of Hungarian citizens and which were also discussed before the League of Nations."[158] The announcement was followed by a great uproar. The right-wing and extreme right-wing politicians and organizations were furious. Behind the unrest of the university students objecting to the amendments Teleki's figure seemed to loom. Teleki attempted to coordinate the activities of the students and he made no secret of this, being the person who transmitted the petition of the student organizations to the president of the Upper House.

---

156 Sarusi-Kiss and Gáspár, "Teleki Pál," p. 748.
157 Andor Ladanyi. "A numerus clausus-törvény 1928. évi módosításáról" [About the revision of the numerus clausus act in 1928], *Századok*, no. 6 (1994): 1117–1148.
158 Gyurgyák, *A zsidókérdés Magyarországon*, p. 128; and Ladányi, "A numerus clausus-törvény," p. 1126.

In the debate on the numerus clausus law the former prime minister presented his views in a longer address and in a brief comment. In the Upper House debate there were fifteen speeches. Of these three were against amendment, all by university professors with Teleki being one of them.[159] In his speech he tried to justify his sharply discriminatory and rigidly anti-amendment position with statistics. He cited data about the Jewry participating in commerce, finances and industry in numbers far above their ratio in the population.[160] He committed himself to the preservation of the anti-Jewish regulations. While he condemned the beating of Jews at the university, he stated that these were frequently due to offensive behavior and to provocations and for these he held the press responsible.[161] His position was clear, "This is a racial struggle."

He considered Jewry a race and vigorously warned against Hungary becoming increasingly Jewish.[162] He at length argued that the Jewry was incapable of assimilation and buttressed this statement with a reference to the paucity of Jewish-Christian mixed marriages. He also argued that assimilation in this instance did not mean lining up along national culture and the political community but a complete dissolution, denominational melding and the giving up of the entire Jewish culture. According to him the unjust peace conditions were also due largely to the fact that Hungary could not assimilate its minorities and if this were repeated with the Jews the consequences might be similar.[163]

In response to comments about his earlier activities he explained that his work in preparing for the peace treaties was not all his and that he included in the expert material of the delegation everything that supported the position of the government and of the peace delegation. These included the statistics that numbered the Jews among the Hungarians.[164] At that time this was in the country's interest. His statement was unworthy and he was justly accused of cynicism. In this instance Teleki's position was inflexibly doctrinaire and he was the most rigorous opponent of any mitigation in discrimination.

The amendments were eventually accepted by both houses. The racial discrimination section was removed and the emphasis was more on social composition. The

---

159 Levente Püski, *A magyar felsőház története* [History of the Hungarian Upper House] (Budapest: Napvilag, 2000), p. 40.
160 Teleki, *Válogatott politikai írások*, ed. Ablonczy, pp. 190–191, and 192–193.
161 Ibid., pp. 193–194.
162 Ibid., p. 194.
163 Ibid., p. 200.
164 Ibid., pp. 203–204.

minister of culture and education was charged with supervising the implementation of the act.[165] Teleki never agreed with the mitigation and during his second tenure as prime minister he took credit for the numerus clausus.

Teleki was an anti-Semite. He admitted this albeit he used complex distinctions to rationalize his position. "I have complete respect and admiration for the excellent qualities of the Jewry, do not wish to repress these in any way and I am not an anti-Semite in that sense. I respect the Jews individually and Jewry collectively particularly those who behave accordingly and make this evident. This is admirable. We just demand a place for us that is appropriate for our ratio and weight."[166] Teleki also praised the "respectable cohesive strength" before which; "he dipped his flag with respect."[167] He seemed to admire Jews for the properties that were the basis of their alleged rule and preponderance. Not only for the intellectual qualities developed in the ghetto *Inzucht* [inbreeding] but also for the cohesiveness that derived from it and which was the barrier for the upward mobility of the Hungarians. It was for this latter reason that he considered himself to be an anti-Semite although this was not stated in his address. Yet it can be deduced from his comment: "We only ask for more space...we do not repress." Which was a clear discriminatory standpoint coloured with cynicisme, turned into racial politics during his second premiership.

Teleki's anti-Semitism was not the expression of some instinctive and long-felt antagonism. He never referred to youthful injuries or traumas and did not try to make the question subjective. It is more likely that for him the 1918–1919 revolutions showed the failure of the assimilation policies of Dualism and that the "inmigrant Jews in Hungary supported destruction." Later, his stand against the Jews became a complementary element in his ideas about building up the nation. In his view the Jews, and the majority of the Jewish middle class, in the light of 1918–1919, represented the greatest barrier to his plans for building up the nation and the society.[168]

Workshops of the Elite: Eötvös College, Boy Scouts, and Youth Movements

Besides the School of Economics, the Eötvös College, and the Boy Scouts were the pillars of his program for the education of an elite. The full name of the former one was: Baron József Eötvös College. It was founded in 1895. The idea came from the physicist Loránd Eötvös who functioned for a short while as minister of cults and

---

165 Gyurgyák, *A zsidókérdés Magyarországon*, pp. 129–131.
166 Teleki, *Válogatott politikai írások*, ed. Ablonczy, pp. 203–204.
167 Ibid., p. 189.
168 Gyurgyák, *A zsidókérdés Magyarországon*, pp. 310–313.

education. He was thinking of a residential high school teachers college, modeled on the Ecole Normale Supérieure that would overcome the painful deficiencies of the university education.[169] At the turn of the century there were already a number of collegians, scholars and writers, who became the leaders of Hungarian intellectual life. The establishment reflected the spirit of Hungarian liberalism. The graduates were imbued with respect toward a blend of democratic and paternalistic principles and toward individual achievements. This spiritual background was not necessarily a good letter of recommendation during the first few years after the revolutions. In the autumn of 1920, the minister of cults and public instruction asked the prime minister to assume, temporarily, the role of chief administrator.[170] Teleki assumed this task with energy and enthusiasm.[171]

For the protection of the institution the Association of Alumni of Eötvös College was established[172] and they created a new set of rules for the association. Teleki was indefatigable when he worked on the improvement of the financial and administrative aspects of the institution. He pestered ministers and secretaries of state, or intrigued against them. Several times, unsuccessfully, he intervened to improve the miserable salary structure of the institution. He was the one who submitted teaching appointments, salary adjustments, petitions, the roster of students to be admitted and their qualifications. He extended his authority and demanded the right to determine which of the foreign exchange students may live in the building.

His personal involvement was manifest in other areas as well. He frequently participated in the selection of students and personally quizzed them in history and geography even though the college had a number of well qualified staff persons.[173] He participated in the frolics of the students, played soccer with them and tolerated their teasing. It was because of his personality that he was unpleasantly

---

169 Domokos Kosáry, "Az Eötvös Collegium történetéből —Az első évtizedek: 1895–1927" [From the history of Eötvös College, the First Decades 1895–1927], in *Tanulmányok az Eötvös Kollégium történetéből* [Studies from the History of Eötvös College], ed. József Zsigmond Nagy and István Szíjártó (Budapest: Eötvös József Kollegium, 1989), pp. 9–12.
170 Letter from István Haller to Géza Bartoniek, Budapest, October 9, 1920, Papers concerning the College's curators, box 88, dossier 185, Mednyánszky Dénes Könyvtár és Levéltár [Dénes Mednyánszky Library and Arhive of the College Eötvös] (hereafter cited as MDKL); and proposal from Kuno Klebelsberg to Miklós Horthy, Budapest, April 16, 1923, cs. 161, t. 25, no. 1923-25-13382, K 636, MNL OL.
171 About his years as a curator see: Imre Garai: Teleki Pál, a báró Eötvös József Collegium curatora [Pál Teleki, the curator of the Eötvös College], in *Gyermekek, tanárok, iskolák. Tanulmányok a 90 éves Mészáros István tiszteletére.* [Children, teachers, schools. Essays in honor of István Mészáros on his 90th anniversary], ed. András Németh, Béla Pukánszky (Budapest: ELTE Eötvös Kiadó, 2017]
172 Kosáry, "Az Eötvös Collegium történetéből," p. 29.
173 Faculty reports, June 11, 1937, box 54, dossier 102, MDKL.

affected when the institution under his supervision became involved in a minor domestic policy scandal. The police discovered a number of illegal Communists among the studentsin the early 1930's. They included the children of prominent parents and some of them were admitted on Teleki's personal recommendation.[174] The conspiracy was completely nonsensical. The task of these students consisted of passing out leaflets, participating in illegal seminars and distributing Communist propaganda products. They did not participate in any learning activities that would lead to illegal activities. It is characteristic of the entire affair that the reason it became known was that one of the participants left his notebook among the propaganda leaflets in the university. The attacks which appeared instantly in the press damaged the reputation of the college and, in addition, those who had previously attacked the institution because of its enlightened spirit and liberalism, now found their suspicions vindicated. In *Magyar Kultura,* a Jesuit publication, it was stated that the college produced "atheistic weeds and moral corpses from healthy-minded, Christian, Hungarian youth".[175] The student body distanced itself from the "Communist conspirators," presumably on the urging of the provost and director, and rejected the recent attacks.[176] The provost recommended that the arrested students be expelled.

Later on, Teleki still continued to be firmly, albeit more cautiously, involved in the affairs of the college. He continued to be on cordial terms with the successive directors and, during his second term as prime minister he took advantage of this connection. Many of the former collegians worked for the Prime Minister's Office, on Teleki's request, during his second prime ministership.

Although his moves toward national education did not initially turn intentionally toward the training of an elite, his later steps were clearly in that direction. Besides the School of Economics, and Eötvös College, it was the Boy Scout movement that gave him an area where he was most active and with which his name is most firmly linked in public opinion.

The ideas of the legendary B-P [Lord Baden-Powell] quickly surfaced in Hungary. The most important parts of his book, *Scouting for Boys,* appeared in Hun-

---

174 András Tombor, "Az 1932-es kommunista szervezkedés a Collegiumban" [The 1932 Communist oplot in the Eötvös College"], in *Szabadon szolgál a szellem*, ed. Kósa, p. 129.
175 János Léber, "Bolsevista diákok" [Bolshevik students], *Magyar Kultura* [Hungarian Culture], July 5, 1932, pp. 45–47; quoted in Éva Deák, "Az Eötvös Collegium viták és támadások kereszttüzében [The Eötvös College in the crossfire of debates and attacks], in *Szabadon szolgál a szellem*, ed. Kósa, p. 139.
176 "'A jobb jövő felépítésében nekünk is szerepünk lesz'—A Báró Eötvös József Collegium ifjúságának nyilatkozata" [We will have a role in building a better future. A proclamation of the youth of the Baron József Eötvös College], *Nemzeti Újság* [National News], June 21, 1932.

garian translation in 1909 and the formation of Boy Scout troops began. The organizations started along multiple lines but in 1913 the single, united Boy Scout-Sentry Alliance was established.[177] The organization had approximately five thousand members but because of the war was unable to accomplish much. The late summer-autumn of 1919, after the end of the revolutions, saw the regulation of a number of matters. It occurred to the highest managing group of the Boy Scout movement, the National Executive Committee, that the organization, numbering fifteen thousand members, needed a central figure similar to Robert Baden-Powell in Great Britain, who, since 1920, was the chief of the scout movement in the world. Ferenc Fodor, who was Teleki's assistant at the School of Economics, mentioned Teleki's name as a possibility. The former prime minister was not unacquainted with the Boy Scout movement. His son, Géza, was a member of the Boy Scout troop at the Piarist High School. The National Executive Committee chose Teleki on May 19, 1922, and their request was forwarded to the Council of Ministers one week later. According to a submission by the minister of culture and education the person filling the position of chief of scouts was a dignitary appointed by the regent either for life or at least for a long term. Having this highest endorsement, he would represent the principle of respect in the Boy Scout movement and would be able to represent the movement best both in the country and abroad. It was the task of the chief scout to support the activities of the alliance at the highest level, represent the scouts both in the country and abroad and, as president of the Grand Council of Scouting, be the most powerful societal supporter of the Boy Scout movement.[178] Because of his illness, Teleki could not hold the position for long. He asked the regent Horthy on March 22, 1923 to be relieved. This was about the same time that he began to think about resigning from the faculty of the School of Economics as well.[179]

The Boy Scout movement was one of the most important, obvious components in his ideas about national education and can be characterized by identification with the imperatives of Hungarian national goals, namely, duty, and the development of culture. By Hungarian national goals he meant the continuing interaction between Hungarians and Europe and everything that derived there from. A former superior and later university colleague wrote, "It was said many times and some-

---

177 Ferenc Gergely, *A magyar cserkészet története* [History of the Hungarian Boy Scout Movement] (Budapest: Göncöl, 1989), pp. 13–25.
178 Extract from the Minutes of the Council of Ministers Session on May 26, 1922, Papp Papers, Documents 7, PRMTKL.
179 F. Gergely, *A magyar cserkészet története*, p. 51.

times mockingly that he always taught. In fact he did just this always and everywhere. In him the intentions of being an influence on others was strong. It was this that made him an educator."[180] This national education program was his basic public life endeavor, one which he assumed most willingly.

For him the interaction of Hungary and Europe did not mean primarily the acceptance of cultural or artistic movements but rather the methodology of problem resolution, culture in its everyday context and receptivity toward European ideas. He hoped that a new elite, having a broad perspective, might implement a reform that was designed to transform Hungarian society from the ground up in a conservative direction. On the basis of its French model, but well adapted to Hungarian circumstances, the Eötvös College was well suited to perform its dual function, produce a well educated group of high school teachers and turn out a new generation of scholars. The Hungarian Boy Scout movement was originally based on a British model, but after 1919 it was also based on a strong religious foundation, endeavoring to give high school students a strong nationalist education. Teleki never viewed the Boy Scouts as a mass movement. The elite organization, having over fifty thousand members in its peak years, and almost 1,000 troops, represented only a fraction of Hungarian youth. Its leaders were opposed to the influx of large masses. Even though there were some troops consisting of apprentices or workers, whose importance Teleki recognized, the majority of the Boy Scout troops were composed of high school students, who, after the comprehensive exam, almost automatically became members of the middle class and hopefully would eventually produce the leaders of Hungarian society.

The second major element of Teleki's "national education project" was duty as an independent virtue. The principal features were:

1. Duty toward the country which was expressed as three parts. The recognition of the blows and tragedies inflicted upon Hungary, principally Trianon, and letting the civilized world know about it. The next level was the responsible representation of treaty revision abroad. The third level of duty for each new generation was an honest appraisal of self and country.
2. Duty toward the church and a morally pure life.
3. Duty toward Europe. This meant primarily a consistent anti-Bolshevism.

---

180 Sándor Imre, *Gróf Teleki Pál és a felső oktatás ügye* [Count Pál Teleki and Higher Education], (Budapest: Királyi Magyar Egyetemi Nyomda, 1943], p. 11.

The third major element of the national education scheme, derived from the first two, was the emphasis on culture. In achieving a satisfactory level of culture Teleki did not consider the schools as the only base and his ideal was an all encompassing, not age-related education. He opposed every form of fragmented and specialized education and castigating "paper and pencil" education was one of his favorite and recurring themes.

For Teleki, Boy Scouting produced the type of person who was the man to transform society, who was trained to lead and was ready to lead and who was replaceable by others like him. According a striking image he used, "The Boy Scout movement was like a nursery where people come to buy a tree. One leaves with a fruit tree, one with an ornamental shrub, the third one with an oak tree and the fourth one with enough trees to start a small forest."[181] The Eötvös College, the School of Economics, and the Boy Scouts were the three massive cornerstones of Teleki's mighty national education edifice.

In the Boy Scout movement, however, he did not consider the youth as the most important component. He thought that the true possibilities for national education were with the former Scouts (the so-called "Rovers") whom he tried to pull together into an organization ever since the end of the 1920s. He declared in 1928, "We must create a Boy Scout society of men in order to permeate our social life with Boy Scout ideals because the country needs this."[182] He was opposed to all forms of association-mongering and to all forms of "bylaw making and amending."[183] He opposed any legal definitions or restrictions placed on the duties and obligations of the Boy Scout movement, claiming that the "form was not essential." This actually made his work harder because in the absence of any regulations, in just about every contested matter he had to go to a minister or to some other high-ranking patron for clarification and action.[184]

The successes achieved at the 1924 Copenhagen Boy Scout Jamboree motivated the leaders of the Hungarian movement to demonstrate to Hungarian public opin-

---

181 József Koszterszitz, *Emlékbeszéd gróf Teleki Pálról* [Memorial Speech about Count Pál Teleki] (Budapest: Hungarian Boy Scout Association, 1941), p. 10.
182 Records of the General Meeting of the Hungarian Boy Scout Association, November 4, 1928, box 10379, fob 41, X 10379, MNL OL.
183 "Vissza az eredeti cserkészethez" [Back to the original scouting], *Vasvármegye* [Vas County], January 12, 1937, p. 3; and "Teleki Pál gróf a magyar cserkészet feladatairól" [Count Pál Teleki about the tasks of the Hungarian scouting], *Budapesti Hírlap*, January 12, 1937.
184 "A Magyar cserkészet jövője és az Almásy-Frobenius vita Teleki Pál gróf megvilágításában" [The future of Hungarian scouting and the Almasy-Frobenius debate, as seen by Count Pál Teleki]. *Vasvármegye*, September 11, 1934.

ion and to the world the successful trip of the Boy Scout troops at a major national troop review. They planned a National Gathering at which eight thousand Boy Scouts, about 40 percent of the current membership, would give an accounting of the character- and society-building strength of the movement. Organization took almost all the efforts of the Boy Scout movement during 1925.

The encampment was a great public success in spite of the fact that the Budapest liberal and Social Democratic opposition, and their newspapers, spoke disparagingly of the encampment that was in operation from July 9 to 23, 1926. There were many visitors and the work of the Boy Scout movement became known to much of the population. Teleki was less pleased. He thought that the concessions went too far, condemned the lack of organization and the bourgeoning of competitiveness at the expense of "Boy Scoutishness." The notes and comments surviving from the encampment justify Teleki's opinions. The food was scarce and of poor quality, the buffet was too expensive for the rural Boy Scouts and there were numerous complaints about the scanty clothing worn by the visitors. There were not enough latrines dug and trash and garbage removal was not arranged adequately.

According to the leaders of the movement a national review would not be repeated. The results were not proportional to the efforts expended on organization and solicitations or to the offensive comments. In fact there were no more general encampments between the two wars. Yet visits to foreign encampments and domestic camping continued. It signified the world-wide recognition of Hungarian Scouting that Lord Baden-Powell, the international head of scouting, visited Hungary in May 1928. The troops of the Budapest Boy Scout district welcomed him on the Üllői Road soccer field of the Ferencváros Club. B-P was very pleased with what he saw and declared, "The whole world knows how good the Hungarian Boy Scouts are."[185] Even though Baden-Powell told his British associates that he was very pleased with his visit, and thanked Teleki for his reception in a particularly warm note, he categorically refused to issue a supportive statement about Hungarian revision demands. He was not pleased by the Boy Scouts on the Üllői Road presenting a tableau vivant of historic Hungary[186]

---

185 "'Az egész világ tudja, milyen kiválóak a magyar cserkészek' — mondotta tegnap Sir Baden-Powell tábornok, a világ főcserkésze" ["The whole world knows how excellent the Hungarian scouts are," said yesterday the world's chief scout, General Sir Robert Baden-Powell], *Új Nemzedék* [New Generation], May 8, 1928.
186 Letter from Baden-Powell to Lord Rothermere, May 19, 1928, General Hungary 1924-1938, TC/50, The Scout Association Heritage Collection, London-Ching- ford, Gilwell Park (Hereafter cited as SAHC); Letter from Baden-Powell to Pál Teleki. Budapest, May 10, 1928, And F. Gergely, *A Magyar cserkészet története*, p. 152; for the refusal, see Baden-Powell to Frigyes Kaposi Molnár, the international secretary

"Educating the Nation": Revision and Conservatism (1921–1938)

A Hungarian Boy Scout delegation of more than eight hundred members attended the World Jamboree, held in 1929 in Arrowe Park next to Birkenhead. Teleki, as principal organizer, was in a difficult position. Perhaps on the basis of Baden-Powell's Budapest experiences or because of the Rothermere campaign supporting Hungarian revisionism, the International Boy Scout Bureau asked the Hungarian association not to mention the matter of Hungarian frontiers' revision in any context and not refer to it verbally, in writing or in demonstrations. In the paper of the Boy Scout officers Teleki wrote an article in July 1929 in which he tried to convince the Boy Scout leaders that, "Our task is not to introduce Hungary's fate but to live a Hungarian life at the jamboree. Not everybody is interested in our fate. Those far away do not care, become bored with repetitions and eventually we lose their goodwill... Trianon, integrity or revision, must not be discussed in writing, verbally or by pictures." It seemed the Boy Scout officers understood the expectations of the chief scout.[187] Yet, that is not what happened. In spite of the undeniable success of the Hungarian troops, Teleki reaped many unpleasant and annoying experiences from the Birkenhead Jamboree.

Among the 25–30,000 Boy Scouts from different countries, the almost military discipline and friendliness of the Hungarian troop made a good impression. Teleki very much enjoyed living in a tent with the boys, participate in their competitions, polished his boots and got wet in the rain. At the same time he was under attack from the leadership of the international Boy Scout organization. Hubert S. Martin, the director of the International Boy Scout Bureau and in private life an official in the Foreign Office, accused the Hungarian troop that, in spite of their solemn promises, it practiced irredentist propaganda at the jamboree. The lost territories were illustrated on banners and the Hungarian Boy Scouts distributed post cards with revisionist texts to the audience. Teleki claimed that the latter was done on individual initiative and took no responsibility for it.[188] Criticism directed toward him did not stop and it was particularly the French representative, Count Marty, who mentioned critically the Hungarian Boy Scouts' participation in irredentist

---

of the Boy Scout Association, April 29, 1928, TC/50, SAHC. All those letters are downloadable from the Lord Baden-Powell Papers database of the Brigham Young University, Digital Collection: https://lib.byu.edu/collections/lord-baden-powell-papers/, last visite: 23 September, 2022)
187 Teleki, *Válogatott politikai írások*, ed. Ablonczy, pp. 222–223.
188 Letter from Hubert S. Martin to Baden-Powell, London, November 14, 1930, TC/50, SAHC.

gatherings. The British leaders agreed with his comments but later regretted the vehemence of their earlier reactions.[189]

The results achieved by Hungarian scouting and by Teleki personally, proved to be poisoned fruit. The former prime minister was elected to the highest administrative body of scouting, the nine-member International Council. This contributed greatly to the reputation of Hungarian scouting but within the council Teleki was assigned the problems of Scouting in Germany. After World War I the scout troops in Germany varied widely both geographically and as far as their worldview was concerned. While there was only one, central Boy Scout organization in Hungary, there were about eighteen of them in Germany. Bringing them together and integrating them into the international association proved to be an impossible task and remained that way. This task occupied most of Teleki's time when he was in Germany visiting relatives and friends.

A few years later Hungary gained the right to organize the 1933 Boy Scout World Jamboree. At the time, this was arranged in private and also later in public, Teleki was opposed to having it in Hungary. He was worried about the "inner contents" of Hungarian scouting from the excess of publicity and the showiness of the event.[190] Yet in the spring of 1931 he wrote several letters to Prime Minister Bethlen urging that the government shoulder the responsibility for arranging for the World Jamboree.[191] Teleki was present at International Boy Scout Conference in Baden where the participants assigned the jamboree to Hungary. By this time the economy of the country was faltering and this made any government support doubtful. Even after the decision was made Teleki could not participate with full force. He was tortured with misgivings, saw his own role in the international movement to be in trouble and was concerned about the provocations accompanying the event. We know from another letter that this summer was particularly difficult for him.

He had no time for rest. For four weeks after the Baden meeting he was showing American experts around his country and he was also very concerned as to how he could perform his fourth term as dean, participate in the unification of the university and deal with the withdrawal of much financial support. During the sum-

---

189 Letter from Baden-Powell to Pál Teleki, December 3, 1930, and Teleki's response, Budapest, January 24, 1931, TC/50, SAHC; and letter from Baden-Powell to Hubert S. Martin and to Lord Hampton, Gilvell Park, September 13, 1931, TC/50, SAHC.
190 Béla Witz, *Emlékezzünk Telekire!* [Let Us Remember Teleki!] ((Budapest?]: n.d.), part 2, pp. 4–5.
191 Ferenc Gergely, Cserkész világtábor Magyarországon (Gödöllő, 1933) (Boys Scout world camp in Hungary (Gödöllő, 1933)], *Századok*, no. 6 (1981): 1219–1220.

mer he had a minor nervous collapse that he could not get over quickly. Yet, at the beginning of September, the Boy Scout leaders gave him his confidence back, convinced him of the importance of the occasion and asked him to become the commander of the jamboree.[192]

Gödöllő came quickly to the fore in the organizers' thinking. The fact that there was good transportation and that it was relatively close to Budapest were in its favor and it was also important that the Crown Properties and Miklós Horthy offered the area, free of charge, for the world gathering. Teleki traveled all over the country and in lectures and articles popularized the idea of the jamboree. He emphasized that only about one eighth of the costs would be carried by the government and that the balance would have to be produced by the encampment itself. He told the scouts that not all of them could be present in Gödöllő.[193]

The prime minister appointed Teleki as a government commissioner for the jamboree at the beginning of the summer of 1932 and created the Jamboree Council that guaranteed the public support and societal patronage for the event.[194] The organizers had to deal with everything: press releases, marking the encampment sites, building a road network, warding off of increasingly inane proposals, providing of financial support and judging the Boy Scout porcelain designed by the Herend Factory.[195] Even though the government granted only 250,000 pengő toward the total budget of the jamboree of 2–2.5 million pengő, the organizers of the jamboree received support in money and goods from a number of ministries, and companies, the community of Gödöllő and the city of Budapest. In obtaining such a support Teleki played a key role. On June 17 there was a national Pál Teleki Jamboree Alert to bring the event to the attention of the public, the national dailies gave it prime space on the front page, the *Nouvelle Revue de Hongrie,* with Teleki as the chairman of the editorial board, brought out a special issue and the *Magyar Cserkész* [Hungarian Scout] and the *Fiatal Magyarság* [Young Hungary] published articles in foreign languages. The jamboree became a particular opportunity for the Hungarian Boy Scout movement. The attention of the international community was focused on Hungary. It was clearly a major success. Foreign leaders spoke with approval about the success of the World Jamboree and emphasized Hungarian hos-

---

192 Letter from Pál Teleki to Baden-Powell, Budapest, September 21, 1931,TC/50, SAHC.
193 Count Pál Teleki, A IV. világ jamboree [The Fourth World Jamboree], special edition of *Testnevelés* [Physical Education], nos. 1–2 (1932): 7.
194 Pester Lloyd-Morgenblatt, June 12, 1932; and "Konstituierung des Jamboree-Rates," *Pester Lloyd-Morgenblatt*, March 18, 1933.
195 F. Gergely, "Cserkész világtábor," pp. 1227–1229.

pitality. The problems encountered by the organizers never surfaced. Baden-Powell was also very satisfied with the Gödöllő jamboree.[196]

The jamboree lifted one worry off Teleki's shoulders. In June 1933 Nazi Germany disbanded the Boy Scout movement, so that in the organization he had to deal only with the occasional problems of the emigrant movement.[197] The principal organizer, who became as popular as Baden-Powell, was awarded the highest distinction, the "Silver Wolf" medal for the success of the enterprise. He was not satisfied. He noted many tactless acts by the public, found the market atmosphere excessive and, felt that the shops that were set up and that provided much of the revenue were ten times more numerous than he would have liked to see. From a scouting perspective the encampment was not as successful as it could have been, but it was undoubtedly a triumph for the country. His overall impression was not "black and white" but rather an "almost white gray".[198] Market atmosphere or not the encampment did not meet the financial expectations and closed with a deficit of almost eighty thousand pengős.[199]

The jamboree played a significant role in Teleki's life. In later speeches he frequently stated that he managed the organizational matters with the help of a few Boy Scout officers and a few hundred scouts, practically without any remuneration. Gödöllő showed him that by the means of some sacrifices and individuals working together for a common goal could replace the clumsy, expensive and complex governmental activities. Individual initiative could become routine and national commitment could produce funds. It was almost certainly thus with the jamboree but Teleki forgot that the frequently despised government apparatus supported the project with several hundred thousand pengős.

This was not the end of Teleki's participation in the Boy Scout movement. He participated in international Boy Scout conferences and maintained a role in the Hungarian movement. The problems of the movement became more serious during the ensuing years. Teleki at times vehemently argued against playing "parliament" and "fussing with bylaws" at the meetings of the National Administrative Committee. At the 1936 November General Meeting he gave voice to his dissatisfaction

---

196 Letter from Baden-Powell to Sir John Simon, London, August 12, 1933, TNA, FO 371, vol. 16786, fol. 72.
197 Gesandschaft Budapest, karton 124, VıI/15, passim, PA AA.
198 D.S., "Teleki Pál gróf, a gödöllői tábor parancsnoka a Magyarságban nyilatkozik a jamboree eredményeiről" [Count Pál Teleki, the commander of the Gödöllő camp, speaks in Magyarság about the results of the jamboree], *Magyarság* [Hungarianness], August 13, 1933, pp. 7–8.
199 F. Gergely, "Cserkész világtábor," p. 1243.

"Educating the Nation": Revision and Conservatism (1921–1938)

about the militarization and the departure from the Baden-Powell ideals. The new bylaws were accepted with minor modifications, the revolt was put down but Teleki, upset over the "rebellion" angrily resigned from his honorary position as chief of scouting.[200] On request, he withdrew his resignation and at the last World Jamboree before World War II, in Vogelenzang, Holland, he again appeared as a member of the Hungarian delegation and as a member of the international Boy Scout leadership. The Holland Jamboree also had its own scandal. Otto von Habsburg, the son of the last king of Hungary, Charles IV, visited the scouts and came to see the Hungarian delegation. His appearance and Teleki's behavior at the time were sharply criticized by an extreme right-wing paper.[201] In view of Teleki's position in the question of the king and his assessment in royalist circles ever since the royal coups, it can be imagined that he made the preparations with excessive zeal.[202]

In spite of the attacks and failures, Teleki relied on the Scouts even after his return to politics and, wherever possible, helped them along. He regularly referred to the national education potential of scouting and was proud of the popularity and accomplishments of the movement. Although he was unable to prevent the increasing influence of the military on the governance of scouting, he used "his boys" for many tasks that he did not wish to entrust to government agencies. The Boy Scout movement was perhaps his major achievement. He had nothing to do with its initial appearance in Hungary but its spread, the direction of its development and its educational goals reflected his ideas. Contemporary public opinion assessed Teleki largely on the basis of the Boy Scout movement. Had he been asked what was closest to him in education, he would surely have answered, "the youth movement," primarily because he achieved a prestige there, second to none.

If we compare Teleki's national education ideas to a three nave cathedral, the School of Economics, the Eötvös College and the Boy Scout movement, this enormous edifice had a number of transepts and numerous support pillars.

---

200 F. Gergely, *A magyar cserkészet története*, pp. 221–223; "Súlyos vádak a Cserkész Szövetség ellen—Teleki Pál gróf lemondott" [Serious charges against the Boy Scout Association—Count Pál Teleki resigned], *Reggeli Újság* [Morning News], November 23, 1936; and "A cserkészek ellenzéki vezére kilépett a Cserkészszövetségből" [The opposition leader of the Scouts resigns from the Boy Scout Association], *Reggeli Újság*, December 7, 1937.
201 "Ottó főherceg látogatása a vogelenzangi jamboreen" [The visit of Archduke Otto at the Vogelenzang Jamboree], *Összetartás* [Unity], August 29, 1937.
202 Pro memoria Ottó királyi hercegnek a vogelenzangi jamboree táborban tett látogatásáról [Memorandum on Royal Prince Otto's Visit to the Vogelenzang Jamboree Camp], August 3, 1937, Papp Papers, Documents 7, PRMTKL.

Of these it was primarily the *Fiatal Magyarság* and its circle that stood close to the Boy Scout movement. It supported the young scouts with full force. The young intellectuals who wrote articles for this journal, and who later became well known, indicated that a demanding but very talented young generation was getting ready to enter Hungarian life. The journal was edited by Teleki's faithful right-hand man, Ferenc Fodor. Among the young men turning toward sociography there were several, who in Fodor's and probably Teleki's views, fell away from the conservative ideals of making society better and became imbued with radical ideas dictated by the current political fashions.[203] Until 1939 Teleki published nine signed articles in the journal that was published on twenty pages every month. The few pages of each article reflected Teleki's views that he had elaborated much more extensively in other publications. Even though the appearance of this journal was very modest, it meant much in the Rover Boy Scout movement particularly since every troop was obliged to subscribe to at least one copy.

The first issue of the journal, in 1931, published a long essay with the title of, "Young Hungarians: Ideas and Resolutions," that summarized the tasks of the Rover Boy Scout movement. The authors were Teleki and some officials of the Boy Scout movement as well as György Oláh, the later extreme right-wing journalist and parliamentary representative, and Zsolt Aradi, the writer and a leading figure of the right wing of the Catholic reform movement. In this essay the authors distanced themselves from party politics, from irredentism that manifested itself only in empty verbiage and even from Turanism because that was a negative concept that surrounded simple facts and modest scientific conclusions with the glittering dust of fantastical dreams.[204] It also drove the ideas of Hungary into a labyrinth of the old inactivity of mirages and dreams. The pages of the journal were shared by skeptical and antiliberal views demanding the regulation of the Jewish question with demands for land reform, village-life studies and national independence.

Teleki's articles, published in this journal, furnished data for these programs and circumscribed politics and the Boy Scout movement. He did not approve of the ambitious programs and of the minute detail work in resolving societal problems.

---

203 Ferenc Fodor, "Elsodort falvak?" [Villages swept away?], *Fiatal Magyarság*, no. 3 (1935): 41–42; Ferenc Fodor, "A falukutató mozgalom kritikája" [Criticism of the village life study movement], *Magyar Szemle* [Hungarian Review], May, 1937, pp. 23–33.

204 "Fiatal Magyarság—Eszmék és elszánások" [Young Hungarians — Ideas and Resolutions], *Fiatal Magyarság*, February, 1934, pp. 27–29.

He felt that a thorough acquaintance with the field was clearly a precondition.[205] He rejected the "theoretical and numerical equality" because that only produced envy and wished to replace it with "equal rights to happiness."[206] He summarized the program for the Rover Boy Scouts in four points: patriotism, religiosity, a sense of national duty and social responsibility. He always emphasized the importance of activity, recognition, service, and living and confessing one's faith.[207]

This was the most important youth group of the 1930s. It followed Teleki's program and, with a modernizing trend, opened windows in many directions, but could not really become an organization with character and an independent worldview. In November 1938 it endeavored to change but this came to nothing, serving only the goals of the daily politics of the time. Later it could address a wide audience from communist fellow-travelers to the extreme right wing. Even though it could not be developed into a true generation, the contributors to the journal and the Rover Boy Scouts became a unique source of coworkers for Teleki.

This was not the only youth organization Teleki was active in. His name appears as president-teacher of the Székely [Sekler] University and Higher Education Student Association in the 1920s. It is perhaps from this that the frequently found mistake was made that listed Teleki as a Székely count. It was on his initiative that the elders of the above organization established the Association of Transylvanian Men [Erdélyi Férfiak Egyesülete]. Even though Teleki described the members of the association as the representatives of the Transylvania concept who had escaped to Hungary and whose divergent individual trends he melded together into an unbreakable *fasces*, in fact the members were nationality politicians who were either already successful, or at the beginning of their career but with definite views of the matters.[208] By the beginning of the 1930s it became apparent that this association could not fulfill the organizational tasks for the generation that the politician envisioned. The younger representatives of the leading group could not make themselves understood by Teleki and this led to mutual suspicion, estrangement and even resentment.[209]

---

205 Pál Teleki, "Irány a fiatal magyarságnak" [Directions for young Hungarians], *Fiatal Magyarság*, February, 1934, p. 22; and Pál Teleki, "Cserkészférfi feladatok a mai nehéz világban" [Adult scout duties in today's difficult world], *Fiatal Magyarság*, November 1931, p. 118.
206 Teleki, "Cserkészférfi feladatok," p. 119.
207 I. B. [Iván Boldizsár?], "Rá kell ébrednünk mulasztásunkra, amit a kisebbségi magyarsággal szemben évek óta elkövettünk!" [We must become aware of our many-year-old neglect of the Hungarian minorities!] *Nemzeti Újság*, December 25, 1934, p. 4.
208 Count Pál Teleki, "Előszó" [Foreword], in *Az Erdélyi Férfiak Egyesületének évkönyve 1928-1933* [Yearbook of the Association of Transylvanian Men] (Budapest: EFE, 1933), pp. 3–5.
209 Miklós Mester interview. Prepared by János Gyurgyák and Tamás Varga in 1986. no. 45, pp. 13, 27–28, 40–41,48, 55, 60, 76, 77, 142, and 144, Veritas Intézet Oral History Archívuma [Oral History Archives

Representing Hungary abroad with dignity was one of Teleki's persistently voiced ideas and the Foreign Affairs Committee of the Hungarian Student Association [Magyar Egyetemi és Főiskolai Hallgatók Országos Szövetsége], a partly social and partly official organization, provided Teleki with an ideal framework for his activities. It was also an important consideration that this organization conformed perfectly to Teleki's ideas according to which Hungary should be represented abroad by a young elite whose education had been guided by him. The idea of representing Hungary was so firmly embedded in his thinking that, in various forms, it was consistently present throughout his career. The managing director of the organization was a former pupil and, with his assistance Teleki, guided the affairs of the association for two years personally instructing the young men prior to their going abroad.[210] Even during his second prime ministership, he belived that a true Christian national policy could be implemented through the association and not through government or other formal institutions.[211]

The politician did not, however, endeavor to heal the problems of the Hungarian intellectuals and of society in general, by gathering the young intellectuals into an organized unit. He wished to perfect his great task from above, by reforming the system of instruction and education and by the proper orientation of the groups considered to be the leading strength of society. The natural base for this was thought to be the Countrywide Casino [*Országos Kaszinó*], the middle class, gentry membership of which could be recruited for some national improvement scheme. This social organization was established in 1883 as a counter to the National Casino [Nemzeti Kaszinó] which was the gathering place of the aristocracy. Géza Teleki was one of the three directors from 1892 until his death. In respect for his father, Pál Teleki was also elected to be one of the directors in January 1920 and, due to the trust of the membership, he was reelected in 1927.[212] Teleki had a poorly defined but persistent national educational plans for the casino. It had between 1,800 and 2,300 members, coming from the upper middle classes, land owners, law-

---

of the 1956 Institute] (hereafter cited as OHA); Miklós Asztalos, "Arcok fénnyel és árnyékkal" [Faces with light and shadows], Miklós Asztalos Papers, box 2, fol. 119–120, fond 301, OSZKK.

210 Béla Padányi Gulyás, *Vallomás egy elsülyedt világról* [Confessions about a Sunken World] (Munich: Aurora Könyvek, 1975), pp. 41–54.

211 "Gróf Teleki Pál miniszterelnök a helyes keresztény és nemzeti politikáról beszélt" [Prime Minister Count Pál Teleki speaks about the proper Christian and national politics], *Magyarország* [Hungary] (mornig edition), May 26, 1940, p. 3.

212 Lajos Halász, ed., *Az Országos Kaszinó ötvenéves története, 1883–1932* [The Fifty-Year History of the National Casino] (Budapest: Országos Kaszinó, 1932), p. 82.

yers, physicians, higher government officials, former ministers, secretaries of state and university professors.²¹³

Being removed from active daily politics in 1925-1926, he wanted to activate the well-intentioned, jovial membership. He planned a series of lectures in 1926 through which he wanted to inaugurate a new era in the old establishment believing that it had major tasks and serious responsibilities vis-a-vis the Hungarian nation and Hungarian society.²¹⁴ He wanted to accomplish this task through more frequent membership meetings and indicated the topics that he considered worthy of consideration. These included the concerns of the middle class, the nationality frictions, the social obligations of society, Trianon and the Hungarian minority problems, foreign propaganda, foreign policy education and matters related to the press. The members of the casino agreed and were pleased to listen to the lectures delivered by Teleki and his associates and honestly participated in the debates. Teleki was usually present at the lectures, contributed to the discussion, commenting on the issues according to his standards and individual perspective. On the press matter he stated that it was "our youth that should work for the press" and not the Jewish middle class or the sons of the lower bourgeoisie. The lectures had no real effect except that, after the middle of the 1930s, the casino hosted the meetings of the Boy Scout officers. Other than that, the life of the casino reverted to the usual peaceful ways of the past.

Since 1911 Teleki had been a member of the Hunnia Boating Club, a sporting organization linked to the Countrywide Casino with many ties. In 1925 he became a director of the club.²¹⁵ The mellow old sporting club, established in 1882, was the gathering place of those members of the Christian middle class who enjoyed rowing, tennis, and bridge. They wore a distinctive uniform, a bluejacket, plus knee pants and t-shirt with a square neck and all this in Neapolitan red and Berlin blue. They also had an impressive boathouse and clubhouse. No wonder they were the envy of all other similar clubs. The membership included the names that accompanied Teleki throughout his life. According to the annual reports of the club, Teleki never rowed an inch between 1920 and 1924 or between 1929 and 1941 but for him the club, with its very high annual fees, had a different significance. In his talks to

---

213 Gabriella Eőry, "Az Országos Kaszinó tisztikara és tagsága, 1883–1943 [The officers and members of the Countrywide Casino], *Korall*, no. 17 (September 2004): 80–83.

214 Dr. gróf Teleki Pál előadása a "Magyar társadalmi politikáról" (Lecture by Count Pál Teleki on "Hungarian social polices"], *Az Országos Kaszinó évkönyve az 1926. évről* [Yearbook of the Countrywide Casino for 1926] (Budapest: Országos Kaszinó 1927), p. 131.

215 Minutes, Papers of the Hunnia Boating Club, box 1, 1907-1926, fol. 269, X. 248, BFL.

the plenum of the club he discussed the calling of the educated middle class, its role and its tasks.[216] The Hunnia Club was a pillar of that distinctive upper middle class group that selected the Countrywide Casino as the site of its formal gatherings, did their politicking in the United Christian National League, put their money into the First National Savingsbank [Pesti Hazai Első Takarékpénztár], and engaged in sports at the Hunnia Boating Club. Their separateness was palpable. They did not mingle with the Jewish upper classes in any of these venues and considered themselves politically to be "one hundred percent right wing".[217]

For Teleki the casino represented a social obligation derived from tradition. He also had a large number of other offices, for which he volunteered or which he accepted after lengthy solicitation. Most of these were related to government functions. Even Teleki could not keep track of all of his various memberships or titles. He was a member of the National Physical Education Council, the National Natural Science Council, the National Higher Education Council and a number of committees of the Hungarian Academy of Science. This latter included the Oriental Committee and the Ethnology-Ethnography Committee.[218] In addition he was the president of the Scholarship Council and of the Collegium Hungaricum Association. After 1934 he was the lay president of the St. Ladislaus Society [Szent László Társulat] which was established to provide Hungarian Catholics in foreign lands with spiritual support, schools and priests. His offices imposed an incredible amount of work on him. He tried to live up to his commitments but in most instances his contributions were limited to a hasty and brief visit and speech or the writing of a foreword to a publication. The continuous rush occasionally produced anguished statements. In 1936 he complained to an acquaintance, "Two or three more years and I will be completely ground up."[219]

The National Public Education Council [Közoktatási Tanács] was the advisory body to the minister of culture and education. Before it, invited experts, grade school, high school and teachers college instructors presented their ideas or commented on proposed legislation. After the death of Albert Berzeviczy in March 1936 some members of the Hungarian Academy of Sciences and the Minister of Culture and Education Bálint Hóman came up with the idea of electing Teleki to head up the academy. He did not wish to accept the position although it would have meant great prestige

---

216 Obituary, Minutes of the Board, April 5, 1941, Papers of the Hunnia Boating Club, box 2, X. 248, BFL.
217 Eőry, "Az Országos Kaszinó tisztikara," pp. 82–83.
218 Jánosné Fráter, A Magyar Tudományos Akadémia állandó bizottságai [The standing committees of the Hungarian Academy of Science] (Budapest: MTA Könyvtára, 1974), pp. 129, and 321.
219 Letter of Pál Teleki to Bálint Hóman, Budapest, Nov. 5, [1935?], fond 15/1541, OSZKK.

and the recognition of his scholarly career. It was a peculiar decision because this appointment should have put an end to his frequent doubts about his own calling and abilities. He gave his reasons in a letter to Hóman. "I could not do justice to this position for reasons of both health and finances....I did accept the other one [Public Instruction Council] and will work hard in it because I believe that youth is worth working for....To take on the academy in addition would be impossible and unconscionable. I prefer to work for the young than for the old scholars of the academy." He then went on to convince Hóman to take the position himself.[220] Eventually Archduke József Habsburg became the president of the Academy of Sciences.

Teleki's activities on the council caused considerable aggravation to the expert members. His haphazard and authoritarian behavior offended many of them. One of them, who liked Teleki, was unhappy to see how Teleki's improvisations occurred regularly and that in his activities a lack of self-criticism was frequently paired with amateur willfulness. He wrote, "I was increasingly sad to see that he, whom I valued so highly because of his honest openness, knowledge and goodness, became a subject of ridicule through his blunders."[221] He worked there for less than two years. In August 1937 he was relieved of his position, allegedly on his own request, by Miklós Horthy, who appointed Bálint Hóman as his successor. He never considered his activities to have been a failure. He frequently talked about them but he never talked about his resignation/dismissal.

Political Views

Teleki's ideological ties and spiritual structure can best be defined by conservatism. His conservatism was open toward the radical new ideas of the times and thus toward the extreme-right, totalitarian ideologies. The turning point in his ideas came at the time of the 1918–1919 revolutions that completely reversed his previously atheistic, or at least religiously indifferent, reform-oriented liberalism. Conservatism was his answer to the revolutions, the dismemberment of the country, and to the recognition of the ills of Hungarian society. His relationship to a mass democracy is well illustrated by the strongly restrictive, conservative interpretation of freedom and democracy characteristic of the *Fiatal Magyarság*. This was not the result of a conscious, political, philosophical training. A reference to the popular

---

220 Ibid.
221 Zoltán, *Ki voltam....Egy kultuszminisztériumi államtitkár vallomásai* [Who Was I....Confessions of a State Secretary of the Ministry of Education] (Budapest: Országos Pedagógiai Könyvtár es Múzeum, 1998), pp. 204–207. The quote is from p. 206.

author of The *Decline of the West* suggests that Oswald Spengler's all-encompassing approach to learning and culture affected him deeply. Yet the influence of Max Nordau, the essayist, journalist and publicist, who was born in Hungary and who, incidentally, was of Jewish extraction, was even greater, with his work saturated with cultural pessimism.[222] Lashing out at the degeneracy of the masses and the damage they had done were the central themes of Nordau's extensive works and the same ideas are present in Teleki's thoughts about social politics.

Another philosopher who had influenced Teleki was Hermann von Keyserling, the Baltic German idealist philosopher, and the founder of the "School of Wisdom." They had good personal relations and there is a police report that in the spring of 1933 they spent all their free time together in Paris.[223] Keyserling's works, critical of the culture of the day, were organic and mystical, thinking in terms of Europe, of continent and of centuries. They were very popular at the time but are essentially forgotten today. "Thinking in terms of historical eras" was a favorite expression of Teleki's as well and he was convinced that the present had to be judged by the past.[224] Keyserling was in Budapest in 1925 and, according to the newspapers, the principal thrust of his lecture was castigating the "mass man."[225]

Teleki's statements frequently appear to be taken from a politics textbook they conform so closely to the well known elements of conservative discourse. He stressed, to the point of boredom, that one could not plan in a routine fashion, that there were no two identical situations and that every problem had to be studied individually. It was though he wished to prove Karl Mannheim's ideas about the conservative mentality. According to Mannheim, "Conservative reformism consists in the exchange (substitution) of certain individual facts for others ('improvements')....To experience and to think concretely now comes to signify a specific mode of conduct, a desire to be effective only within the particular immediate environment in which one is placed and a total aversion to all things that are merely 'possible' or 'speculative.'"[226] This drive toward individuality is the conclusion of Teleki's sociopolitical work, written at the lime of World War I. He tried to imple-

---

[222] Teleki referred to Nordau in his numerus clausus speech. See Teleki, *Válogatott politikai írások*, ed. Ablonczy, p. 194.
[223] Confidential report fragment, Ministry of Foreign Affairs, Political Section, misc. documents, cs. 469, no number, 1933, K 63, MOL.
[224] "Új Európa—Új Magyarország—Új elit" [New Europe–New Hungary–New Elite. An interview with Count Pál Teleki], *Pesti Napló*, December 25, 1934, p. 7.
[225] "Der zweite Vortrag des Grafen Keyserling," Pester Lloyd-Morgen- blatt, May 8, 1925.
[226] Karl Mannheim, *Conservatism: A Contribution to the Sociology of Knowledge* (Collected Works, vol. 11) (New York-London: Routledge, 1986), p. 88.

ment it in his teaching but frequently got lost in its details. Robert Nisbet, discussing the thinking of the conservatives, emphasizes that, "Basic to conservative politics is its view of the role of history. History reduced to its essentials is no more than experience over abstract and deductive thoughts in matters of human relationships. This is on what trust in history is founded." Tradition was important because, "the present is not free...to remake the social structure as fancy or a 'spirit of innovation' might dictate."[227] His social sensitivity did not mean that there were all-encompassing inclinations toward benevolence in Teleki's character. In fact whenever he could, he deplored self-centered benevolences and the associated practice of "society mongering."[228] He wanted land reform and believed that the government should think in social terms because he considered these essential for a healthier national organization. In contrast to many of the period's conservatives, he felt and appreciated the centrifugal forces in Hungarian society. He was socially conservative in the sense that he saw the nation and society as a larger unit waiting for order and wanting education. He lived as a symbiotic unit with the environment created for him and he fulfilled his destiny in the framework of tradition and historicity.

He continually condemned the external manifestation of the interwar technical developments, the flashy and false advertisements, the flood of moving pictures and their continuous machine gun-like hammering on the people's consciousness.[229] Industrialization, urbanization, rapid industrial developments and such external signs as the building of tenements and the hunt for electors were, for him nothing but *"culte de l'incompétence,"* the direct consequence of the activities of the massman.[230] The man of the day was an individual, the captive of false ideas, whose drive for independence threatened the nation, that great and organic unit. The proliferation of individuals who were superficial, without better education, were always involved in the events of the day and getting all their knowledge from newspapers was frightening for him and he rejected the rule of political democracy.

According to Teleki, real democracy was the societal democracy, the traditional and harmonic rule of interests and values. His democracy was a type of meritocracy. The conservative has a built-in suspicion about the institutions of democracy and does not believe that the masses are capable of making the right decisions. For

---

227 Robert Nisbet, *Conservatism: Dream or Reality* (Minneapolis: University of Minnesota Press, 1986), p. 23.
228 For the societies see Papp, ed., *Teleki Pál országgyűlési beszédei*, vol. 1, p. 383.
229 Teleki, *Európáról és Magyarországról*, pp. 189–193; and Teleki, *Válogatott politikai írások*, ed. Ablonczy, pp. 301–304.
230 Teleki, *Válogatott politikai írások*, ed. Ablonczy, p. 303–304.

Teleki, decision making should be left to those who, because of their knowledge, training and commitment, were better able to handle problems appropriately. The decision-making processes are handled according to competencies and not mass desires. Planners and executors were in their position because of merits and ability and not on the basis of mass decisions or a false sense of equality. The system of equal rights, or as he put it, the exaggeration of equal rights, and its role in society were labeled by him as "egotistical and superficial lies."[231]

He saw education as the initiator of change. Not education in schools or in institutionalized instruction, but in the family and in the broader human community with the aim of moral improvement. As he explained at the Paris meeting of European intellectuals in 1933, "This is what we have to strive for in education. Our first task is to raise a moral elite. In education we must endeavor to emphasize values and quality rather than quantity, numbers and mass culture."[232] Characteristically it was the Boy Scout movement that he mentioned as an educational organization in which raising the national character could be side-by-side with activities: competition with cooperation.[233] In parallel with this education, "We must promote the respect of values and of authority" because the equality of men must be respected only as far as this occurs in nature as well.[234] Man is a biologically shackled person and thus the order of society can not be very different from the order in nature. The fact that "the newborn come into this world with very different capabilities" and that this leads to differences in abilities, potentials and possibilities, was the cornerstone of conservative political thinking.[235] His statements were unlikely to produce any resentment at the Paris meeting because the other intellectuals were even cruder in their interpretations. For example, Aldous Huxley's *Brave New World*, published about this time, states that, "The present life style of European society has sunk to baseness." Teleki differed from Paul Valéry, who was present in Paris, by believing that in spite of the masses the necessary moral and spiritual renewal was helped along by two factors, tradition and nationalism. Teleki's conservatism was Central European, antiliberal, anti-Semitic and, in some instances, antiparliamentarian.

Teleki's interpretation of tradition started out with the recognition that, ever since the war, Europe was in an economic and values crisis when "No period needs

---

[231] Ibid., p. 306.
[232] Ibid.
[233] Ibid., p. 305.
[234] Ibid., p. 307.
[235] Ibid., p. 309.

to sense a historical perspective, meaning the true understanding of and attention to tradition, as much as the great periods of mankind."[236] What he meant was that tradition was nothing but the understanding of and paying attention to the historical perspective. About the same time he spoke of this more precisely: "Tradition is nothing but the living and continuous linkage of past, present and future, i.e. life itself that is stronger than any mind and any logic."[237]

For him nationalism was identical with patriotism[238] and was a part of tradition and perhaps its most important constituent. Their interrelationship was obvious. Tradition assures the historical framework of patriotism and the latter proves, strengthens and keeps alive the traditions. It is not and can not be of itself because there is no explanation for it being stronger than mind and logic. No doctrine or abstract theory can render the flow and branching of life itself, only nationalism can do that, the ideal, "emanating from the soul of the nation," coeval with it and inseparable from it. Nationalism, preserving its unity of content, explains tradition and tradition legitimates nationalism. There can be no change in the reality of the content of nationalism.

This redefinition of nationalism appeared in his writings in the 1930s but the Hungarian aspects of it were already developed in 1928 in an article in *Budapesti Szemle* [Budapest Review], entitled, "National Spirit—National Culture." The writing is part of his developing antagonism with Klebelsberg. It is not known when their relationship deteriorated. Teleki followed the future minister in the National Office for Veteran Affairs and in 1920 they cooperated in creating the dissident group designed to be the basis of a new majority party. Klebelsberg was also a lecturer at the School of Economics, undoubtedly with Teleki's knowledge and approval. What was the antagonism about? Was it the unworthy successor in the chair of his father? Were there conceptual differences in their assessment of culture? Was it political resentment over the numerus clausus? In the absence of sources, there is no answer to these questions.

An unreliable memoir from a knowledgeable person claims that Teleki was offended because Klebelsberg kept him from directing Hungarian cultural policy.[239]

---

236 Count Pál Teleki, "Hagyomány és forradalom" [Tradition and revolution], *Katholikus Szemle* [Catholic Review], February 1934, p. 115.
237 "Teleki Pál Wekerle emlékserleg-beszéde" [Pál Teleki's Wekerle Memorial Cup speech], in *Az Országos Kaszinó Évkönyve az 1934. évről* [Yearbook of the Countrywide Casino for 1934] (Budapest, 1935), p. 172.
238 Teleki, *Válogatott politikai írások*, ed. Ablonczy, p. 318.
239 István Milotay, *Egy élet Magyarországért—Ami Horthy emlékirataiból kimaradt* [A Life for Hungary—What Was Left Out of Horthy's Memoirs] (Budapest: Gede Testvérek, 2001), p. 148.

At the beginning of the 1920s the scholar already made sarcastic comments about the minister of culture and education.[240] In 1927 he spoke about the legislative proposal on scholarships for the Hungarian institutes abroad and for the purposes of higher education. He expressed his reservations about the minister's ideas and also argued with Klebelsberg's plans to gather the universities into one organization.

In 1928 the relationship between Teleki and Klebelsberg became very tense, presumably over the issue of mitigating the numerus clausus rules. In addition, on May 4, 1928, during the debate on the budget, Klebelsberg's commented on the quality of the university professors, the decline of their scholarly activities and on the level of their level of performance. He added threateningly, "I will force the refreshment of professorial knowledge" and he thundered from his ministerial chair: "Today I only caution, today I only ask those whose divine spark has become extinguished, that they change or depart."[241] Teleki was incensed. In connection with Klebelsberg's neonationalism, Teleki's students could venture to say that the Klebelsberg ideas about cultural superiority were simply, "a stripped slogan."[242]

On the basis of the ideas impressed on him during his childhood, and also by the strength of his rationality, he came to the realization that religion, as society- and nation-building force, was the most effective protection against Bolshevism and other destructive ideas. In light of this it is instructive to see how he commented on the authoritarian political systems between the two World Wars. In 1933, in Paris, he believed that European public opinion was slowly turning against the excesses of freedom and against individualization and this assumption justified for him the advance of the dictatorships about which he said nothing either good or bad. "Of these dictatorships those will be successful that can give credence and confidence in a goal."[243] The initial results and dynamism of National Socialist Germany were first appealing to him precisely because this type of credence and confidence. Teleki met Adolf Hitler in 1928.[244] He was also very interested in the march of the Hitlerjugend in Berlin in 1932.[245] His early acquaintance with the

---

240 Pál Teleki's calling card to Zoltán Felvinczi Takács when the art historian was appointed to be a head government councilor, Felvinczi Takács Papers, A2664, Archives of the Ferenc Hopp East-Asian Art Museum.
241 *Képviselőházi napló*, vol 12, 1927–1932 (Budapest: Athenaeum, 1928), p. 118.
242 *Fiatal Magyarság*, February 28, 1936.
243 Teleki, *Válogatott politikai írások*, ed. Ablonczy, p. 310.
244 Diary of Bálint Hóman, fol. 63, the Szálasi trial, parts 9-10, V- 19430/3, ÁBTL.
245 Letter from Pál Teleki to Gyula Farkas, October 2, 1932, Gyula Farkas Papers, box 2, dossier of the correspondence between Pál Teleki and Gyula Farkas, Seminar fur Hungarologie, Humboldt Universität, Berlin (hereafter cited as SH-HU).

leading politicians of National Socialism is attested by the laudatory comment about him in the *Völkischer Beobachter*, "He belonged to those few statesmen who at the time when National Socialism was not yet in power, were interested in us and sought contacts with our leading personalities." This article does not necessarily refer to Hitler, but that Teleki had good contacts with the Munich University circles which were already imbued with National Socialism is beyond doubt. It is also certain that at the end of 1933, Teleki commented very favorably on the results of the German "national revolution."[246]

For him the new Germany was proof of what could be achieved with faith and will. In education, a matter very close to his heart, Germany implemented a series of recommendations that "were long overdue, but that the systems that are derived from the false freedom ideas of liberalism and that have hampered so much progress in Europe, did not permit to become reality. I have seen it particularly in the area of social assistance what it meant when instead of the eternal talk and endless compromises of committees and councils, an organization goes to work, established for that purpose and consisting of young people."[247] In the National Socialist model he saw things that he thought could be transplanted to Hungary. He was particularly impressed with the youth labor camps. On his trip to Germany in autumn of 1933 he became acquainted with Count Gottfried von Bismarck-Schönhausen who at that time was a National Socialist Reichstag deputy and, provincial councilor. He belonged to the circle of SS leader Heinrich Himmler, and his cousin was married to Hermann von Keyserling. The National Socialist count, who worked in the Stettin [Szczecin] *Regierungspräsidium,* became friendly with Teleki and invited him to visit a youth labor camp on the shores of the Baltic Sea, because, as Teleki had said, he would have liked to bring the experiences gathered there to fruition in Hungary.[248] He did go and mentioned his impressions even years later. In 1938 he encouraged the formation of similar camps in Hungary.

This sympathetic attention was neither rare nor surprising at that time. Even Winston Churchill was anxious to meet Hitler and some of the British conservatives of the day turned to Germany with a certain amount of confidence. Teleki's views about nationality policies turned him rapidly against the dynamism of National Socialism because it initiated an ever increasing German national propa-

---

246 "Graf Paul Teleki über die Probleme des Donauraums," *Völkischer Beobachter*, December 3, 1933.
247 "Teleki Pál Gróf Berlinben nyilatkozik az új Németországban szerzett benyomásairól" [Count Pál Teleki speaks in Berlin of the impressions he gathered in Germany], *Magyarság*, December 16, 1933.
248 Minister Hans Georg von Mackensen to the Ministry of Foreign Affairs, Budapest, January 8, 1934, R 74195, PA AA.

ganda in Hungary of which he strongly disapproved. In 1934 he moved that the German exchange students be no longer domiciled in the Eötvös College because they were engaged in National Socialist propaganda.[249] He took strong steps against the *Volksdeutsche* student movement at the School of Economics and finally in 1937 he spoke of his misgivings in the Upper House.[250]

"Nevertheless, Hungary, true to her old traditions, since the war became organized on a Christian and national basis, followed a Christian and national path. Every government proclaimed the same and in the heart of the entire nation this view prevailed. Regretfully I see dangers for the country in both of these paths, the Christian one and the national one,… because it is undeniable that in Hungary there is a strong pro-German agitation by both Hungarian citizens and by people who are not Hungarian citizens."[251]

His concerns were only about the National Socialist propaganda conducted in Hungary and concerning the German nationals. He continued to speak of Germany with approval because 1933 gave the German people something to believe in and this, according to him, was "the greatest possible act in these days of chasing after material goods."[252]

If there was a dictatorship which was successful in its fight against the „excesses of freedom" and which gained Teleki's approval, it was the Portuguese one. In October 1933 he spent some days in Portugal and learned something about the system.[253] He believed that in the clerical- corporative structure he found a tool that would awaken the Christian and national characteristics of the Hungarian political system, that would protect against the totalitarian endeavors and that would transform the inheritance of liberalism and of parliamentarism according to the requirements of the times.

The above comments attest to the fact that between the two wars there was in Hungarian political life an antiliberal, conservative, right-wing, socially sensitive trend. It was leaning toward the clerical-corporative state and was willing to accept the withdrawal of equal rights under the law. The scholar-politician was one of the

---

249 Letter from Pál Teleki to Minister [of Education] Bálint Hóman, April 21, 1934, in *Szabadon szolgál a szellem*, ed. Kósa, p. 200.
250 About the School of Economics see the interview with Sándor Barcs, obtained by Ferenc Kubinyi in 1987, no. 81, p. 36, OHA.
251 Teleki, *Válogatott politikai írások*, ed. Ablonczy, pp. 338–339.
252 "Teleki Pál megnyitó beszéde" [The opening remarks of Count Pál Teleki], *Liga Értesitő*, November-December 1937, p. 80.
253 Letter from Pál Teleki to Andor Teleki, Madrid, October 2, 1933, Teleki-Degenfeld Papers, cs. 1, t. 3, fol. 76, P. 2026, MNL OL.

distinct representatives of this trend. In view of this, the often seen statement in the historical literature that speaks of the Bethlen-Teleki group as the informal leaders of the Horthy era must be revised. The careers of István Bethlen and Pál Teleki do show similarities as far as ancestry and political background are concerned, They were both Transylvanian, counts, conservatives, fundamentally oriented toward the West and more or less anti-Nazi. The similarities, however, frequently obscure the essential differences between their perspectives. Bethlen was less sensitive socially, opposed land reform and anti-Jewish legislation and the 1940 constitutional reform. From the turn of 1940–1941 he opposed the foreign policy of the prime minister and from the beginning of the 1940s found his way back to Eötvös-type liberalism.[254] The personal relationship between the two men was not as close as suggested by a number of comments. Bethlen respected Teleki's knowledge and honesty but did not think much of his "childish behavior," romanticism and idealism. Teleki stayed away from the social circle dominated by Bethlen. Occasionally he did appear at dinners of the *Magyar Szemle* Association, did minor favors for the periodical, but wrote only one article for it.[255]

Teleki was rarely present in Horthy's entourage. Occasionally he sent the regent letters and recommendations, but it is only after 1938 that there is any evidence of their discussing political issues. At the time of their working together in 1919-1920 there clearly was mutual trust and sympathy between them. Teleki proposed Horthy for an honorary doctorate by the School of Economics and the regent reciprocated by awarding him the Corvin Chain in February 1931. It was the highest recognition awarded to persons most highly esteemed by the Hungarian intellectual and artistic world.[256]

Geography, Homeland Studies, and the Study of Village Life

In his article, written for the *Budapesti Szemle* at the end of the 1920s, entitled "Nemzeti Szellem—nemzeti kultura" [National spirit—National culture][257] he

---

254 Romsics, *István Bethlen*, pp. 352–361; and *Képviselőházi napló*, 1935–1940, vol. 13 (Budapest: Athenaeum, 1937), pp. 64–65.
255 Pál Teleki, "Az európai probléma" [The European problem], *Magyar Szemle*, no. 3 (1931): 209–220. About their disparities see: Balázs Ablonczy: Bethlen István és Teleki Pál konzervativizmusa. [The Conservatism of Pál Teleki and István Bethlen] In: Romsics, Ignác (ed.) *A magyar jobboldali hagyomány* 1900-1948. [The Tradition of the Hungarian Right] Budapest: Osiris Kiadó, 2009. 167-185.
256 The School of Economic's Memorandum to the Regent Horthy on March 14, 1930, box 22, registration no. 417-1930, BCEL.
257 Teleki, *Válogatott politikai írások*, ed. Ablonczy, pp. 206–220.

alluded to an important concern and something that pointed toward his second tenure as prime minister. He stated that knowledge of one's country, i.e. what one must know about one's country, was a buttress of national feeling.[258] Knowledge of one's country was not some form of science for him, composed of rigid categories but a powerful conglomerate of geography, ethnography, history, sociology, statistics, and botany.[259] In an approach toward resolving the social problems of the country, he believed that the most important element was their recognition. He stated that we can help only where we understand. Among the goals of the *Fiatal Magyarság,* sociographic work was one of the key issues. As early as 1934, the periodical published a special issue on sociography.[260]

One month later, at a general Village Life Conference, Teleki outlined the directions and significance of studying village life. Accordingly:

1. Directing and assisting the village spiritually and physically.
2. Make the village more familiar with higher society.
3. The careful expert analysis and presentation of the village as a social unit from the perspective of its particular life and social conformity.[261] He believed that the conditions were met and therefore he organized a lecture in his department on the recently published *Elsüllyedt falu a Dunántúlon* [A Vanished Village in Transdanubia]. This was a volume, published in 1936, in which the results of the work of the 312th Rover Scout Troop in the south of Hungary were reported and to which Teleki wrote a foreword.[262]

He did this even though he knew that the last few sentences of the volume were a devastating indictment of the large estate (latifundium) system. Teleki read every work entrusted to him very faithfully and it is extremely unlikely that he had omitted to do so in this case.

In connection with the notion of knowledge of one's country it must be asked what aspect Teleki's work in geography contributed to the rigidity of his ideas. Between the two World Wars, Teleki was very much in the center of geographic

---

258 Ibid., p. 213.
259 Ibid., pp. 213–215.
260 *Fiatal Magyarság,* November 1934.
261 F. P., "A magyar 'falumunka' mozgalom" [The Hungarian "Village Work" movement], *Fiatal Magyarság,* June 12, 1936.
262 Count Pál Teleki, "Előszó" [Foreword], in *Elsüllyedt falu a Dunántúlon—Kemse község élete* [The Vanished Village in Transdanubia—the Life of Kemse Village], ed. Peter Elek and others (Budapest: Sylvester Irodalmi és Nyomdai Intézet, 1936).

activities although he began to distance himself from organizational affairs. Because of his illness, he resigned in 1923 from his position of secretary general of the Hungarian Geographical Society and assumed the much less onerous position of vice president.[263] There was an increasingly dissatisfied group in the society that tried to get rid of Cholnoky as president and considered Teleki as a likely replacement. He, however, always declined such invitations.[264] These events affected the relationship between the two friends. During the 1920s there was a cooling off, they met less frequently and their letters became more formal. Teleki appeared less regularly at the board of directors meetings.

Foreign honors were showered on him. In 1923 he was elected as an honorary member to the Gesellschaft für Erdkunde, in Berlin, and in the 1920s he also became a member of the Athens, Madrid, Florence, Rome, and Sofia geographical societies. He was one of the most regular contributors to the *Földrajzi Közlemények*. Between 1918 and 1941 he wrote more than one hundred pages in this periodical and was among the twenty most diligent contributors.[265] His department regularly published the work of young scholars who received their doctorate with Teleki and he was also one of the editors and frequent contributor to the *Földrajzi évkönyv* [Geographic Yearbook] that annually published popularizing articles and small maps. He did not consider it to be below his dignity to edit a textbook for high school teachers under the auspices of the Didactic Section of the Hungarian Geographical Society. In this textbook he wrote a chapter entitled, "Continuing Education for Geography Teachers."[266]

The majority of his geographical work was performed during these years, but as his admirers and analysts of his work have noted, his work was very uneven and the greatest and most demanding work, the Thünen-type representation of the theory of concentric agricultural productivity with maps, was never published in book form.

The first decades of the twentieth century gave the geographers new opportunities. Geopolitics and political geography, as new anthropo-geographic areas, opened up new vistas. Both his good relationships with the internationally known practi-

---

263 Records of the April 26, 1923, General Meeting, p. 12, 1923/10, MFT IL.
264 Letter from Pál Teleki to Lajos Ilosvay, Budapest, May 5, 1926, Ms5289/345, MTAKK.
265 Róbert Győri, "Magyar gazdasagföldrajz a két világháború között" [Hungarian economic geography between the two World Wars], in *Geográfia az ezredfordulón* [Geography at the Turn of the Millenium], ed. József Nagy Nemes (Budapest: ELTE Regionális Földrajzi Tanszék, 2001), p. 65.
266 Dr. Count Pál Teleki, "A földrajztanár továbbképzése (és a legfontosabb földrajzi irodalom)" [Continuing education for geography teachers and the most important geographic literature], in *Modern földrajz és oktatása* [Modern Geography and How to Teach It], ed. Pál Teleki and György Vargha (Budapest: Studium, 1923), pp. 156–163.

tioners of these areas as well as his own inclinations made it easy for him to move in this direction. Because definitions were wide open, Teleki was able, between 1920 and 1940, to reformulate his geographic priorities which were the politically dependent part of his scholarly activities.[267] Elaborating this interest served the purpose of buttressing his studies of the questions that were of interest to him, e.g. revision, imperialism, British Empire and League of Nations, from a geographic perspective and the answers he arrived at. Relative to Hungary, in writing about the interdependence of area and state he went so far that later analysts held his views to be deterministic. According to his approach, the space allocated to the Hungarians was clearly the Carpathian Basin.[268] His activities in economic geography did not come to an end and it was at this time that his magisterial two-volume lecture notes were published.[269] He did not write the book. It was written by his assistants on the basis of his lecture notes. It was still a unique accomplishment in the scholarship of the day. According to a later reviewer of his work, "the author created the masterpiece of Hungarian geographic synthesis."[270]

In this part of his life the Great Plain [Alföld] became a central metaphor of his geographic region categories.[271] The concept of the "plains" became for him the concept for the Hungarian people and was imbued in his speeches with mystical and historical qualities. In one of his speeches as prime minister he said, "The plains culture has a deep world of thought. It is far-looking, deeply meditative, mystical but sharply observant, carefully deliberate, taciturn and expressive with little material and small creativity."[272] The final crystallization of concept of region and its quasi organic transformation can be seen in his speech as president at the Technical University in 1937.[273] "The subject of geography, the region, is a creation not limited by human frailty," he said and then continued,

---

267 Zoltán Hajdú, "Teleki Pál a földrajztudós" [Pál Teleki the geographer], in *Teleki és kora: a Teleki Pál emlékév előadásai* [Teleki and His Time Presentations of the Pál Teleki Commemorative Year], ed. István Csicsery-Rónai and Károly Vigh (Budapest: Occidental Press, 1992), pp. 156–163.
268 Ferenc Koch, "Teleki Pál gazdaságföldrajzi munkásságának bírálata" [Critique of Pál Teleki's activities in economic geography], manuscript, Library of the Geographical Research Institute of the Hungarian Academy of Science.
269 Count Pál Teleki, *A gazdasági élet földrajzi alapjai* [The Geographic Basis of Economic Life] (Budapest: Centrum, 1936), vols. 1–2.
270 Győri, "Magyar gazdaságföldrajz," p. 78.
271 Pál Teleki, "Bevezető" [Introduction], *Széphalom*, no. 1 (1927).
272 "Vigyázzunk a magyar lélekre! Gróf Teleki Pál nagy beszéde a jász-kun kongresszuson" [Let us take care of the Hungarian soul! Count Pál Teleki's major address at the Jász-Kun Congress], *Nemzeti Újság*, August 17, 1939, pp. 3–4.
273 Count Pál Teleki, "A tájfogalom jelentőségéről" [On the significance of the region concept], *Budapest Szemle* [Budapest Review] 247 (November 1937): 129–141.

AH science is human…and even narrower than that because it is always moving within the confines of human understanding.…Even if some sciences are able to confine their results to a closed circle of logic they can still not define and give real truth, free-standing by itself. They can give only a relative, finite reality that is composed of reason we humans can understand.[274]

It was in this speech that he gave the ultimate summary of his geographic credo, "For me geography exists not for itself and not as a useful object, but as a tool for the achievement of higher moral and intellectual goals."[275]

The Everyman

After the surgery at the end of 1922, "his face changed in a remarkable way and he aged prematurely," wrote Ferenc Fodor.[276] His lines became deeper, his face was thin but from this tortured face a pair of grey eyes shone with their effect enhanced by the heavy, horn-rimmed glasses that he now wore all the time. Few could stand up under his stare. His face frequently dissolved into a sarcastic-cynical smile that was strengthened by raised shoulders and widespread arms. Surviving pictures show that when he was bored he did not care who knew it and his posture reflected this. He sprawled in his chair, at home or at a meeting, and listened to the speaker with eyes half-closed or shut. When he was thinking, it was evident to the observer. He pushed out his lower lip, held his chin between the thumb and forefinger of his left hand, pushed his cheek with his other hand and stared wordlessly into the distance.[277] Some of his gestures became famous and even foreign observers knew that he was not telling the truth when he was rubbing the lobe of his right ear with the thumb and forefinger of his left hand.[278] When he was in a good mood, his "faithful hunting dog" face broke into a thousand wrinkles, he threw back his head and shook with honest mirth.[279] He liked to participate in jokes and pranks. He drew caricatures, including of himself, wrote poems and, in male company liked bawdy humor some of which would have made a teamster blush. He was pleased to be

---

274 Ibid., pp. 132–133.
275 Ibid., p. 141.
276 Fodor, *Teleki Pál*, p. 93.
277 Ibid., p. 94.
278 Jean Mistler, Le jeune homme qui rôde (Paris: Grasset, 1984), p. 96.
279 Tüdős, "Rongyok," vol. 2, p. 205, Ms. 10907/11, MTAKK.

invited to give a humorous toast and to make somewhat dated puns.[280] On one occasion, when he did not wish to be disturbed in his office at the university, he put a piece of paper on his door on which he drew a cross and wrote, "Pál Teleki is dead. Please go away, reverently and quietly."[281]

He did not change much although with time his body became leaner and two deep lines from the nose to the corners of the mouth were indications of his suffering. At the end of the 1930s he also had much trouble with his teeth. His daily calendar for 1939 shows several visits to the dentist.[282]

Teleki had trouble expressing himself and he was a bad speaker. He had painfully long pauses between his lengthy sentences and frequently took so long, searching for the proper expression that the audience felt sorry for him. At such times he had an awkward smile on his face and nervously tugged at his moustache and adjusted his vest.

In spite of his illness, medical supervision and daily painful procedures, he lived a full life. He rowed with the Boy Scouts, fenced, albeit less and less frequently because of time constraints, took stairs three at a time, shared Spartan accommodations with the Boy Scouts and, if necessary, washed in the river.[283] He was a heavy smoker and there are many photographs showing him with a cigarette in his hand. He actually preferred a cigar and for many years smoked two cigars each day. He had no other harmful habits and used alcohol very moderately.

In addition to his physical ailments he suffered from recurring, deep depressions. He viewed his values and prospects with deep pessimism and, after 1923, these periods became longer and more severe. At one of the worst periods, in 1929, he made a will and asked his secretary and his family that he be buried with the simplest possible ceremony and that no one accompany his coffin. We know of at least one mental breakdown at the beginning of the 1930s but there are innumerable reports about gloomy statements to friends and acquaintances about his imminent demise.[284]

---

280 Teleki's toast "His Excellency Uncle Anti," no date, Papp Papers, Documents 7, PRMTKL; Tibor Zsitvay, *Magyarország 1921–1941* (Hungary 1921–1941], ed. Péter Sipos and Tamás Csiffáry (Budapest: Palatinus, 1999), pp. 532–533.
281 Dr. Gy. Sz., "Ha Magyarországot tanulmányozzuk, vegyük elő Európa térképét..." [If we study Hungary, let's look at the map of Europe], *Esti Kurir*, December 24, 1940, p. 5.
282 1939 daily calendar, Pál Teleki Papers, cs. 3, dossier p, K 37, MNL OL.
283 Fodor, *Teleki Pál*, p. 94; and Bassola, *Ki voltam...*, p. 146.
284 Letter from Pál Teleki to Baden-Powell, Budapest, September 21, 1931, TC/50, SAHC. About his statements see Bassola, *Ki voltam...*, pp. 206–207; and Diary of Bálint Hóman, part 9, fol. 57, and 82–83, Szálasi trial, parts 9–10, V-19430/3, Állambiztonsági Szolgálatok Történeti Levéltára [Historical Archives of State Security].

His greatest help in the management of his affairs came from Péter Incze (1896–1960), the slightly mischievous and always good-humored private secretary whom he had engaged as a law student at the beginning of the 1920s.²⁸⁵ Teleki was usually disappointed in his choices but Incze was a major exception. The clever private secretary took care of his personal correspondence, managed the household expenses that tended to be mismanaged by Countess Teleki and supervised the servants. Teleki regarded Incze as an equal partner and frequently asked for his opinion in political matters and the secretary frequently dared to contradict his boss.²⁸⁶ Their relationship became even closer when Incze got married and Teleki was one of the witnesses, presenting a pair of Gobelin-covered armchairs to the young couple. After the wedding Incze moved from the József Nádor Square palace and Teleki's financial situation deteriorated to the point where he was forced to dismiss Incze in 1935.²⁸⁷ Their good relationship did not come to an end and when Béla Imrédy asked Teleki to recommend a good private secretary, he was happy to recommend Incze and eventually inherited him back from Imrédy when he followed him as prime minister.

Teleki had three expensive hobbies, books, autos, and his somewhat unusual sporty clothes which he had hand-tailored in Vienna. The first thing that impressed all who entered the palace on the József Nádor Square was the enormous library.²⁸⁸ His love of books was shared by his wife who was primarily interested in Western literature. He did not always have enough money for cars. During his first prime ministership, he had to sell his large touring car because his position imposed too many financial burdens.²⁸⁹ After 1928 he again had a car and he used it to visit the Boy Scout camps in the Bükk Mountains.²⁹⁰ In the letter announcing Incze's dismissal in 1935 he complained again, "I have no money for cars or cabs."²⁹¹

---

285 Oral communication from Lászlóné Szepes, née Margit Incze, October 2, 2002; and Rónai, *Térképezett történelem*, pp. 52–61.
286 Rónai interview, no. 53, vol. 1, pp. 460-462, and 468, OHA.
287 Letter from Pál Teleki to Bálint Hóman, Budapest, November 5, n.d., fond 15/1541, OSZKK. See Teleki's recommendation letter to State Secretary Tibor Pataky, n. d., fond XIV.307, BFL. Downloadable here: https://bparchiv.hu/sites/default/files/atoms/files/hu_bfl_teleki_levelek_6-7.pdf (Last visite October 2, 2022)
288 Padányi-Gulyás, *Vallomás*, p. 120; Béla Kornitzer, "Gróf Teleki Pál elárvult dolgozószobája" [The deserted study of Count Pál Teleki], *Pesti Hírlap*, December 25, 1941, p. 9.
289 Cholnoky, *Vár ucca 17*, p. 302.
290 Letter from Ferenc Fodor to his wife, Vira Fenczik, Nagyvisnyó, July 9, 1928, Fodor Papers, private collection.
291 Letter from Pál Teleki to Bálint Hóman, Budapest, November 5, no year, fond.15/1541, OSZKK.

He lived a very puritanical life. He was not concerned about traveling in third class, eating mediocre food, and staying in flea-infested rooms. The furnishings of his house were also modest and the sparseness of the dining room was depressing to the guests.[292]

He was not the master of the house, it was his mother. The respect in which the widow of Géza Teleki was held in the family was enormous. Her son not only looked in on her every time he left the house, but when he was abroad he cabled her every day.[293] He discussed not only family matters with her but political ones as well. One of the signs of the distinction in which she was held was that in her presence only German was spoken. At the dinner she sat at the head of the table and the rhythm of the meal was adjusted to her convenience. As soon as she laid down her fork, the dinner was over.[294] As the countess became older her eyesight failed and she left her three room apartment less and less frequently. Yet, still, her rather shrieky voice was heard ordering the servants about.

Other than her personality, there was another reason for dominance. During the 1930s her income was greater than that of her son and daughter-in-law combined. Her houses and shares assured her and her family of a comfortable existence. She also knew that the survival of the Teleki family depended on the real estate coming from the Muráti inheritance. According to the tax rolls of 1932, Dowager Countess Teleki paid 3,960 pengős tax after an income of 41,363 pengős while her son paid 2,040 after an income of 29,260 pengos. It was Pál Teleki who paid the property tax of 364 pengos due on her estate of 308,734 pengős, representing the value of two or perhaps three buildings in Budapest. In the district, her income was not among the largest ones and not even among the first fourteen. Successful lawyers, living in that district made about half that amount per year.[295] The houses owned by his mother were managed by Teleki.

After lengthy discussions his financial status was put in order in 1926 and he received not only the money due to him as a former prime minister but he also received the differential increment of his salary as professor, retroactive to 1924.[296] This was a considerable sum even in those days of inflation. In the fall of 1926 he

---

292 Bassola, *Ki voltam...*, p. 138.
293 Kornitzer, "Gróf Teleki Pál elárvult dolgozószobája."
294 Verbal communication from Lászlóné Szepes, née Margit Incze, October 2, 2002; Bassola, *Ki voltam...*, p. 138; Komitzer, "Gróf Teleki Pál elárvult dolgozószobája."
295 B.K., "A Lipótváros adótávlatból" [The Lipótváros seen through the tax rolls], *Pesti Napló*, July 2, 1932, p. 3.
296 Minutes of the Council of Ministers, September 24, 1926, no. 40 on the agenda, box 153, K 27, MNL OL.

was given four hundred fifty million, six hundred eighty crowns and his monthly salary was quadrupled from seven million two hundred thousand to thirty million. After the financial reorganization and the introduction of the pengő on November 1, 1927, he was in the top bracket at a monthly salary of about 1,200 pengős.[297]

This was not his only source of revenue and, according to the custom of the times, he was active in commercial life. He was on the Board of Directors of the Pesti Hazai ElsőTakarékpénztár [First National Savings Bank of Pest], This was a major financial institution, allegedly the third largest in Budapest which served almost exclusively a Christian middle class clientele with solid and conservative business practices. Teleki was on the board of directors of the bank since 1925 and had served, since 1921, on the board of an affiliate institution, the Hazai Bank, Inc. After 1929 he was the president of Magyar Wayss and Freytag Building Company, owned by the bank.[298] In 1938, when he became minister of cults and education, he resigned from all these positions.[299] The Wayss, and Freytag Company was one of the oldest road-construction companies and Teleki was a shareholder of the company as well. In 1936 he presided over the board of directors with 200 shares of 32 pengős par value.[300] He also had 100 Hazai Takarékpénztár shares and he received an annual dividend of 3 to 14 pengős per share. We do not know whether he received any compensation for his positions in the bank or the construction company but it seems likely because we know that the bank had a stipend for its board of directors. The board received a percentage participation in the profits of the bank. In 1934 this was 6 percent. The papers reveal that in the 1930s Teleki and the other members of the board of directors received 3,140 (1938) to 4,340 (1930) pengős that was usually credited to their account at the beginning of the year.

Adding up all his additional income and his salary, he received a considerable sum. Because of his many activities and frequent travels Teleki was nevertheless under considerable financial stress. He was also affected by the economic crisis. And in 1930 he took a quarterly 500 pengős advance on his annual compensation

---

297 Documents of his salary question, b. 6, box 45, BCEL.
298 Statement of additional faculty income for the period ending on March 31, 1932, b 5, box 25, registration number 1919–1931/32, BCEL.
299 Letter from Pál Teleki to Pál Szécsi, the President of the Hazai Bank, Budapest, May 18, 1938, Hazai Bank Papers—Directorate, cs 1, t. 2, Z 931, MNL OL; Minutes of the June 28, 1938 Board of Directors Meeting, cs. 13, t. 32, Z 100, MNL OL.; and Annual Report for 1938, p. 15, Papers of the Pesti Hazai Elso Takarékpénztár Egyesület, cs. 12, Z 23, MNL OL.
300 Minutes of the October 31, 1936, Meeting, Papers of the Hazai Bank—Secretariat, cs. 13, t. 32, Z 100, MNL OL.

at the Hazai Bank.³⁰¹ He commented to one of his nephews, "There is practically nobody here who was not on a slope toward bankruptcy and nobody, with the possible exception of a few rich Jews, who does not have to reduce his standard of living."³⁰² He not only looked after his mother's and his own affairs, but he had to look after and find jobs and livelihoods for his wife's and the entire family's needy, unworldly or just deprived relations. He helped nephews who had lost their job find new jobs or he fought to get their articles published or have their Hungarian citizenship awarded. Later, during his second prime ministership, he tried to get them into parliament as representatives. With Tibor Teleki, the keeper of the crown, and the representative of the Gyömrő branch of the family, he presided over the annual family gathering. He not only tried to assist the Telekis but he also worked for the members of his wife's family. And if this would not have been enough there was also the estate in Transylvania.

In spite of Teleki's protests, the Romanian land reform left him only a fifty acre park and sixteen acres of arable land of the Pribilești [Pribékfalva] estate, so that he had to spend money on it and also pay the almost two dozen servants and employees over the summer.³⁰³ Teleki and István Bethlen were among the landowners for whose compensation the Hungarian government engaged in an eight year legal battle with Romania in the so called "Optant Dispute."³⁰⁴ In contrast to Bethlen, however, after 1922, Teleki regularly returned to his old administrative district of Transylvania, Kővárvidék [Chiorana], and spent several weeks there each summer. He visited all the relations in the area, participated in the afternoon teas and in the other activities of the reduced post-Trianon Transylvanian Hungarian society.³⁰⁵ The chateau remained his property and the weeks spent there each summer were his real relaxation. He painted in the park, took photographs, rode, played tennis, read and, if the spirit moved him, mowed the lawn. Occasionally he took a shotgun and came back with a duck or coot.

---

301 Documents of the September 26, June 26, March 27, and December 18 Board of Directors Meetings and Receipts, Papers of the Hazai Bank - Directorate, cs. 1, t. 2, Z 931, MNL OL.
302 Letter from Pál Teleki to Andor Teleki, Budapest, December 18, 1931,Teleki-Degenfeld Papers, cs. 1, t. 3, P2026, MNL OL
303 Report from Thomas Hohler to Foreign Secretary George Curzon, Budapest, August 25, 1922, TNA, FO 371, vol. 7703, ff. 218-221.
304 See: Antal Berkes: The League of Nations and the Optants' Dispute in the Hungarian Borderlands. Romania, Yugoslavia, and Czechoslovakia. In: Peter Becker, Natasha Wheatley (eds.), *Remaking Central Europe. The League of Nations and the Former Habsburg Lands.* (Oxford: 2020, Oxford UP). 283-314.
305 Count Sándor Degenfeld, "A Degenfeld család kalandos útja Svájcból Magyarországra" [The adventurous journey of the Degenfeld family from Switzerland to Hungary], *Korunk*, no. 12 (2002): 24–25.

He rarely received guests at Pribékfalva. Every Sunday he walked down the tree-lined path to the Uniate church to hear a Mass. In the 1920s he contributed considerable sums to the repair of the church. After the service he chatted in Romanian with the farmers. If he wished to hear a sermon in Hungarian, he drove to [Nagybánya] Baia Mare where he made confession and took the sacrament with Canon Károly Pakocs.[306] We have only fragmentary information about his faith but everything seems to indicate that during the last two decades of his life Teleki's faith was very deep and totally sincere.[307]

Even the summers did not suffice, however, for complete relaxation. During the year, including the summer, he had to travel abroad on a number of occasions on both official and semiofficial missions. According to a report of the School of Economics at the beginning of the 1930s, Teleki attended more conferences and consultations and made more trips between 1921 and 1931 than all the other members of the faculty combined.[308] At times he simply said that he had to have some rest, but he was also sick several times and in the autumn he usually had a feverish illness. In 1924 he was not sick until the Mosul mission in 1925. We come across a number of requests for leave of absence in 1933, 1935, 1936, and 1937. These requests were always met by the school and administration.

During Easter or in the summer he frequently visited his Greek relatives in Trieste, Gerasdorf (in Austria, near Wiener Neustadt) or Marseilles. He was frequently in Berlin, Munich, Hamburg, London, and Paris. Kandersteg, in Switzerland, hosted the Council of the International Boy Scout movement. In July 1931 he summered in St. Gilgen am Wolfgangsee with his family and it seems that he was very fond of the Baltic, vacationing there in 1924, 1930, 1931, 1933, and 1934. He visited the United States for the third time in 1935 and for the last time in 1937 when he participated in meetings organized by the Carnegie Foundation. When he was in the United States in 1935 he was awarded an honorary doctorate at Columbia University, while during his last visit he sent a peace message to the world over the radio. Due to problems with the radio transmissions this speech could not be

---

306 In writing about the days in Pribékfalva I relied on conversations conducted on September 9, 2001, with Ioan Botez, veterinarian, Vasile Buie, former estate gardener, and Ioan Micașin Pribékfalva [Pribilești].
307 Béla Witz, *Teleki vallásossága* [Teleki's religiosity] (Budapest: Középponti Katolikus Kör, 1943).
308 Memorandum of the School of Economics to the VKM. Budapest, October 27, 1931, b. 5, box 24, registration number 456-1931/32, BCEL.

heard in Europe.[309] Later as a minister and prime minister he was Horthy's guest in Kenderes and Gödöllő.

He traveled both for pleasure and for scholarly reasons to Normandy, and Brittany in France (1926–1927). In 1928 he was in Greece and visited Athens, Mycenae, Nauplion, Delphi, Argos, and Thessaloniki. He even got to Crete because he wanted to see the excavations in Knossos.[310] It seems that his 1933 autumn trip to Iberia was a tourist excursion. He always prepared himself carefully for these trips, read a great deal and always took his camera. He included the better photographs among the illustrations of his books. He even published some of his wife's better pictures taken in Greece in his university lectures for 1936. He enjoyed traveling by car but preferred the train. As prime minister he frequently sat in the engine cabin of the Lél motor train sitting on an uncomfortable bench chatting at length with the engineer.[311] Aboard ship he suffered sea sickness and was therefore afraid of sea travel. His fear of flying was well known among his underlings at the time of his second prime ministership.[312]

On these trips he frequently traveled with his wife and, more rarely, with his daughter Majcsi. While the ladies were shopping, he went to museums and galleries. His relationship with his children was tenuous. One of the tutors of the children considered both Géza and Mária to have been neglected children.[313] Yet Teleki took his daughter into society and tried to introduce her to society life. At the same time, young Géza, afflicted with all the problems of the early teens was interested only in ice hockey and led a lonely existence at home. The father was proud of his son's early accomplishments in geography but when Géza eventually became a university professor he admitted that he preserved few memories of his father. Teleki's relationship vis-a-vis his children became increasingly embittered when the marriage of both of them ended in failure.

---

309 -n -k, "Egy magyar tudós amerikai kitüntetése" [The American honors to a Hungarian scholar], *Társadalomtudomány* [Social Science], no. 4 (1935): 300–301; "Teleki Pál Gróf békeszózata az amerikai közönséghez" [Count Pál Teleki's speech on peace to the American public], *Budapesti Hírlap*, November 12, 1937; and "Gróf Teleki Pál békeszózata az amerikai rádióban" [Count Pál Teleki's peace speech on American radio], *Pesti Hírlap*, November 12, 1937.

310 Letters from Pál Teleki to Béla Procopius, Budapest, March 9,15, and 24, 1928, Béla Procopius Papers, Dossier on papers and letters about the lecture of Count Pál Teleki in Athens, box 2, t. 10, P 545, MNL OL.

311 Kálmán Konkoly, "Nyolc év magyar történelem a 'Lél' ablakaiból" [Eight years of Hungarian history as seen from the windows of the "Lél"], *Magyarország*, November 24, 1943, p. 7.

312 Béni L. Balogh, *A magyar-román kapcsolatok 1939–1940-ben és a második bécsi döntés* [Hungarian-Romanian Relations in 1939–1940 and the Second Vienna Award] (Miercurea-Ciuc: Pro Print, 2002], p. 209 n. 2.

313 Bassola, *Ki voltam...*, pp. 137–140.

"Educating the Nation": Revision and Conservatism (1921–1938)

During the 1920s and 1930s he rarely saw his children because his many and varied interests frequently took him away from home. In contrast to his wife, Teleki was an early riser and therefore they slept in separate bedrooms. When at home, the countess rarely got up before noon. The politician had been up and about since seven, exercised, had breakfast and scanned the newspapers. He preferred the Catholic papers.

After reading the papers he attended to his business in town. His university lectures were usually scheduled to begin at ten, although in some years they began at nine. In 1925 he had no lectures on Mondays and used those days for other matters.

The university needed Teleki. It is evident from the papers preserved in the dean's office that they turned to him when they had to negotiate with the ministry about the future of some departments, like foreign affairs or administration, both among the premier departments of the school. His standing was shown by the annual ritual of awarding both domestic and foreign scholarships. Compared to his colleagues, Teleki made few recommendations but his nominees almost always received the requested scholarship.

He was an excellent teacher, but a poor lecturer. He frequently wandered off, spoke in a monotone, and had the bad habit of continuing to talk after the time had expired.[314] He did capture many, however, with his lectures, illustrated with maps, slides and drawings, and replete with anecdotes and political asides. His students became devoted and determined fans. He usually appeared at the St. Nicholas Day party of the geography students and, when the mood became mellow, danced with the girls. He did not like to be addressed at the university as Excellency although as a former prime minister he was entitled to this form of address. If he gave a business card to a person in one of the scholarly disciplines he usually crossed out the word "Count" on the card and he usually signed with just his name. When he answered the telephone he always announced himself simply as Teleki.[315] When he was tired, nervous or disappointed in his students, he could become quite rude. On such occasions, his consciously assumed cordiality disappeared and when a student addressed him as professor, he growled, "Why don't you just call me Uncle Paul."[316] Much to the misfortune of his students he belonged to that unfortunate group of examiners who expected the examinee to guess what he was thinking about and be able to follow the examiners unstated thoughts. If a candidate turned to the wrong

---

314 Rónai interview, no. 53, pp. 165–166; Sándor Barcs interview prepared by Ferenc Kubinyi in 1987, no. 81, p. 35. OHA; and talk with Imre Kovács, in Tibor Huszár, *Beszélgetések* [Converssations] (Budapest: Magvető, 1983), pp. 85–86.
315 Personal communication from Béla Erődi-Harrach, Jr., November 22, 2000.
316 Ferenc S. Szabó interview, prepared by Endre Babus in 1987–1988, no. 110, pp. 76–77, OHA.

map, the exam was over. If a candidate said something silly, Teleki slowly pushed his glasses onto his forehead, glared at the students with his penetrating gray eyes and made it evident to the increasingly-red-faced student that the end had come.[317] The modest professorship on Szerb Street became the starting point for the large-scale informal network through which Teleki directed his students and proteges to the various key points of Hungarian public life and culture. Initially these people were supported only by his personal standing and by the influence of the institutions he controlled. Between 1939 and 1941 Teleki attempted to transfer this network to the political arena but was only partially successful in so doing.

Teleki tried to arrange his schedule so that he was free between noon and three, so that he could return to József Nádor Square for lunch with his family. It was here that he saw his children and the conversation was in English after the dowager countess retired. An English lady was hired to live in the house and maintain the family's competence in the English language. After lunch he took a nap to make up for the short night. It happened occasionally that his employees did not wish to or forgot to wake him up. After the nap he returned to the university or attended to a political or business obligation. Occasionally he had several of these and this was usually not the end of his day. In the evening he frequently had to attend dinners and even after dinner he had to see people or devoted his time to writing. Because of his many contacts, there were frequent visitors at the Teleki Palace: foreign diplomats, Boy Scout leaders, university colleagues, pupils, relatives, and travelers. The visitors were almost unanimous in describing him as an appealing, pleasant host and a remarkably informed scholar who, at times, engaged in an endless monologue.

He did not like the movies, but did occasionally accompany his wife to the theater out of a sense of duty. He read much, but whether he read much fiction is not known. It is characteristic that when he attended the Book Fair in 1940 he was not interested in contemporary literature and asked only that the work of the White Stag, a Hungarian posing as a Native American author, be dedicated to him.[318] Even as an older man he enjoyed the stories of Karl May, a trait his politician friends considered to be juvenile. He went to bed well after midnight but did not sleep well.

---

317 Kálmán Nyikos, "Teleki Pál a tanár" [Pál Teleki the teacher], *Magyar Nemzet*, April 5, 1941, p. 6.
318 "Teleki miniszterelnök és Csáky külügyminiszter látogatása a Könyvnap sátraiban" [Prime Minister Teleki and Minister of Foreign Affairs Csáky visit the booths of the Book Fair], *Magyarország* (evening edition), June 3, 1940, p. 6.

Back into Politics (1938–1941)

Just as he felt after the prorogation of parliament in 1904, or after the Romanian invasion of Transylvania in 1916, Teleki felt in the spring of 1938 that Hungary was again confronted with trials and that therefore he had a role at the cutting edge of politics. At the beginning of the year he participated in the background discussions on the possible consequences of the first anti-Jewish legislation to be introduced. The fundamental turning point in international politics was the Austrian Anschluss. He presented his views on the pages of the government newspaper a few days prior to Hitler's entering Vienna. He admonished the nation to recapture its ancient sobriety or "have we departed from it too far both in blood and spirit?" He followed by writing, "The related peoples of two friendly nations have united and this was proper according to both history and nature." He further said that changes were taking place in the world that would affect several generations and for which the nation had to gather strength from the past and from its ancient good sense. There is, he wrote, need for more confidence and this perseverance and strength can be found in the people of the Hungarian villages to whom one must turn with interest.[1]

Imrédy's Minister of Education

He did not wish to remain idle, events affecting generations were taking place. When after Kálmán Darányi's resignation Béla Imrédy formed a government, Teleki accepted the portfolio of Culture and Education on May 14, 1938. He knew Imrédy from the Countrywide Casino and from the Hunnia Boating Club. The

---

1   Count Pál Teleki, "Magyarok legyünk" [Let us be Hungarians], *Függetlenség* [Independence], March 20, 1938.

fact that he retained his chair at the university suggests that he did not view his ministership as a long-range involvement. The liberal opposition to the government welcomed his appointment.[2] In his introductory address before the staff of the ministry, Teleki emphasized that he did not come as minister for a specific task but as "an old Szeged fighter" because, as he stated, "issues must be addressed with firmness and rigor."[3] He mentioned that the most important task was to eliminate favoritism from Hungarian middle and higher education.[4] Even though this was an old idea of his, he was still willing to help friends, acquaintances and proteges. We have a number of letters of recommendation that he wrote at this time and also answers to letters of recommendation.

He presented a detailed program on June 11 in the House of Representatives when he spoke during the budget debate on the allocations to his ministry. He referred to himself primarily as a "minister of education" who wished to educate not only the youth in school but the entire country.[5] He endorsed the importance of theoretical training and within that he emphasized the importance of the humanities.[6] On the other hand, as the first of the Hungarian ministers of culture and education, he wished to place the government support of folk culture at the forefront of his endeavors. He promised to promote education outside of the schools, the cataloging of ethnographic monuments and the elevation of ethnography into the curricula of the schools of education. He mentioned that collecting folk music and ethnography were important parts of his plan and he also wished to get the university students involved in village life studies. He told the National Assembly that he wanted to set up Scandinavian-type open air folk museums. Under the attraction of István Győrffy's ethnographic research ideas that formed a core of Teleki's middle class policies, he hastened to declare, "We must shape and conserve Hungarian traditions based primarily on folk traditions and we must save what we have left of Hungarian traditions, whether folk traditions or middle-class traditions."[7]

The Unemployed Intellectuals Committee, established in 1937, came under the jurisdiction of his ministry. In 1938 the National Emancipation Foundation,

---

2   "Szakítás" [Rupture], *Esti Kurír* [Evening Messenger], May 17, 1938, p. 5.
3   "Gróf Teleki Pál fogadtatása a kultuszminisztériumban" [The reception of Count Pál Teleki in the Ministry of Cults and Education], *Néptanítók Lapja* [Teachers' Journal], June 1, 1938, p. 425.
4   Count Pál Teleki, "Protekciós levelet nem olvasok el!" [I will not read a letter asking for favoritism], *Függetlenség*, May 17, 1938.
5   Papp, ed., *Teleki Pál országgyűlési beszédei*, vol. 2, p. 4.
6   Ibid., p. 15.
7   Ibid., p. 19.

designed to assist the smaller Christian establishments toward independence, was melded into the above. As an intellectual committee, the two organizations became the most important factors in the implementation of the social policy program of the first and later of the second anli-Jewish legislations under the slogan of "changing of the guard" meaning the displacement of Hungarian Jewry. The committee acquired an increasingly broad spectrum of activities and a rapidly growing number of employees. Its leader was Ministerial Councilor István Kultsár, one of the mysterious figures of Hungarian governmental Jewish policies, who fled in 1945 to South America and thus avoided prosecution. He became an important collaborator. Teleki considered his person and his task so important that, after he became prime minister he moved the Kultsár Committee over to the Prime Minister's Office.

It was an early project of his ministerial activities to organize one of the greatest international events held in Hungary in the 1930s, namely the Eucharistic World Congress. As a devout Catholic and as minister of education he actively participated in this major event. On May 23 he welcomed the arriving Cardinal Pacelli, the future Pius XII, who was the papal legate to the congress.[8] The event had certain similarities with the Gödöllő Jamboree, with Berlin forbidding the German and Austrian faithful to attend.

After the budgetary debates, the summer was spent in travel within the country. He visited a lot of the institutions under his jurisdiction. According to some scattered references he engaged, with his usual impetuosity, in a large number of affairs. He wished to set up a national quality assessment system for all middle school teachers. He wished to eliminate favoritism. On the basis of his experiences during the summer, he wished to set up a large-scale government-supported and coordinated village life study and sociographic program. Teleki's priorities were as follows: in Tata the ethnic German problem and the living conditions of the miners; in the Great Plain the village and its borders, assessment of economic life, and production methodology, the matter of involvement with commerce, and the study of influences impacting on the village, such as policies, parties, motion pictures, newspapers, schools, radio, and Jews living in the area. Village opinions and their view of the world were all part of his research proposals. As a minister he rendered two characteristic decisions. One was the authorization of using Boy Scout

---

8   Jenő Gergely, *Eucharisztikus világkongresszus Budapesten* [Eucharistic World Congress in Budapest] (Budapest: Kossuth, 1988), p. 119.

and Levente (paramilitary youth organization) emblems in school,[9] and the other was a thundering letter, dated September 11 to the semiofficial publication of public instruction: "It has come to my attention that an enlarged portrait of me is being offered by unauthorized persons to the directors of the schools. I have never authorized anybody to do so and I instruct all addressees to refrain from purchasing such portraits."[10] Based on the political system of Dualism he felt that he must become a Member of Parliament. Hence, at the beginning of September he put his name down as the candidate for the mandate of a deceased representative from Tokaj in northeastern Hungary. At the end of an intensive campaign he was unopposed and he attributed this to the "uniform enthusiasm with which the population of the Hegyalja (Foothill of the Tokaj Mountain] endorsed Béla Imrédy's reform policies."[11]

The turns of European politics brought it about that the government needed Teleki as the ideologue of revision rather than as an educator and teacher. Since the beginning of the summer Hitler's Germany had increased the pressure on Czechoslovakia. The problem of the Sudeten Germans living on the border between Germany and Czechoslovakia were the excuse for Germany's demands. The minority problem becoming a European problem was very significant for the Hungarian government. It was hoped that the approximately nine hundred thousand to one million Hungarians who lived in Czechoslovakia might come under Hungarian control again. The Munich Agreement signed by Germany, Italy, Great Britain, and France on September 29, 1938, legitimized the attachment of the areas, inhabited by German majorities, to Germany. An appendix to the Munich Agreement demanded that the Polish and Hungarian minority issues in Czechoslovakia be regularized by the concerned countries through a three months negotiations program. If the issues remained unresolved the reconvened four- power conference would place the issue on its agenda.[12]

The Budapest government, under Imrédy's leadership together with Horthy, rejected Hitler's call to provoke its northern neighbor with weapons and thus to initiate open warfare. At the same time, however, they allowed insurgent groups to cross the border to initiate sabotage and chaos in Czechoslovakia. Because of the

---

9 *Néptanítók Lapja*, June 15, 1938, p. 504.
10 Ibid., October 1, 1938, p. 802.
11 Count Pál Teleki, "Minden program központjában az ember áll" [Man is the center of all programs], *Esti Újság*, September 13, 1938, p. 13.
12 Dénes Halmosy, *Nemzetközi szerződések 1918–1945* [International Agreements 1918–1945] (Budapest: Gondolat, 1983), p. 446.

haste and poor supervision, extreme right-wing elements appeared among the insurgents. At the same time, immediately after Munich, the Hungarian government expressed its willingness to negotiate the issues. After some hesitation, Komarno [Komárom] was designated as the site for the Czechoslovak-Hungarian negotiations. Teleki was a member of the delegation and the steamer Zsófia carried the delegation and some very large dossiers from the Institute of Political Science. In Budapest, the offices of the institute were manned around the clock in order to be able to answer any question at any time.[13]

The Hungarian territorial demands reflected the compromise, accepted „in the interest of Europe, the neighbors and Hungary" which limited the territorial adjustments largely on an ethnic basis. Taking the 1910 census as the base, the Hungarian delegation demanded the transfer of 14,153 square kilometers with 1.09 million inhabitants of whom 848,969 or 77.9 percent were Hungarian. Budapest asked for twelve cities which had a Hungarian majority in 1910 and for 812 villages of a total of 830, also with a Hungarian majority.[14] The Czechoslovak party played for time. It considered the possibility of a minor territorial adjustment and although the territory offered increased from day to day, it was still much less than what the Hungarian delegation demanded. During the five days of negotiations the minister of education played a key role. He was excited and thrilled. He had to account for fifteen years of preparatory work before the representatives of the Hungarian government. He could show that his concepts were, in fact, valid.

Czechoslovakia was represented almost exclusively by Slovaks with materials assembled in a great hurry. The leader of the delegation was Minister Plenipotentiary Jozef Tiso, the future Slovak prime minister. The official language of the meeting became Hungarian because every member of the Slovakian delegation spoke it. In his speeches Teleki demonstrated his superiority and frequently urged the Slovaks on, occasionally rather rudely. "Let your experts come here... the entire Czechoslovak material is in my hands and I will let you have it. I have your statistical material from 1930. We can start negotiations with your experts immediately... Call them on the phone to be here tomorrow." He called one of the Slovak border adjustments a bad joke. At another time he remarked that they had not come to wheel and deal and what had been suggested was not a conciliatory position.[15] He insisted on a border adjustment on an ethnic basis rejecting all economic, geo-

---

13   Rónai, *Térképezett történelem*, pp. 124–126.
14   Gergely Sallai, *Az első bécsi döntés* [The First Vienna Award] (Budapest: Osiris, 2002), p. 88 n. 174.
15   Quoted in ibid., pp. 88, 96, 94, and 93.

graphic or transportation arguments. The Czechoslovak delegation promised more and more but it was still not enough. Tiso and his colleagues played for time and their politicians were in Berlin seeking help against the Hungarian endeavors, with some success.

The negotiations ultimately failed and came to an end on October 14. As a good-will gesture, two small towns were returned to Hungary at the beginning of October and the Hungarian military triumphantly entered Ipolyság [Šahy] and the formerly detached part of Sátoraljaújhely. A little more than a week later a Slovakian offer, made through Berlin, almost followed the ethnic line and met the Hungarian demands. Yet, the larger cities of the territory, Bratislava [Pozsony], Nitra [Nyitra], Košice [Kassa], Užhorod [Ungvár], and Munkačevo [Munkács] would have remained in Czechoslovakia and for this reason Budapest rejected the offer.

The failure of the Komárom negotiations, Imrédy's belligerence, and the pressure of public opinion excited by the press and by extreme- right propaganda created a very tense atmosphere in Budapest by the end of October. The extreme-right Arrow Cross activists violently attacked the "incompetent government" which could not accomplish a revision. The Arrow Cross activists clearly represented a segment of public opinion. The government lacked true mass support, the Ncmzeti Egység Pártja [Party of National Unity] (NEP) was about to disintegrate because of the "miraculous revolution" announced by Imrédy in September and because of his increasingly overt anti-parliament ideas. Within one month Teleki had the opportunity to show what he could do, this time in domestic politics.

The idea of Fiatal Magyarsag Movement and of the various Catholic organizations demonstrating together and even forming a unified organization did not originate with Teleki but he endorsed the endeavor.[16] The organizers drafted a proclamation that was published in the newspapers and chose to call the organization the "Anonymous Hungarian." The Fiatal Magyarság Movement, the St. Imre College and other organizations called a mass meeting for October 16 on Szabadság Square in Budapest. There were approximately 10–12,000 demonstrators who voiced primarily progovernment policies and anti-extreme right-wing demands.[17] The purpose was to give the government the opportunity to claim that it had mass support. In its November issue the *Fiatal Magyarság* published the national political ideas

---

16 István Kiss, "Visszaemlekezés a Táj- és Népkutató Központ kiállítására" [Recollection of the Region and Folk Study Center's exhibition], *Ethnographia*, no. 4 (1984): 607–610.

17 András Papp, "Vasámap megmozdult a névtelen fiatal magyarság" [On Sunday the anonymous Hungarian youth made a move], *Reggel* [Morning], October 17, 1938, p. 5; and *Új Nemzédek* [New Generation], October 18, 1938, pp. 1–2.

and determinations of the Fiatal Magyarság [Young Hungarian] Movement.[18] In the document, signed by Ferenc Fodor, Teleki's *aide de camp*, the demands were a strong national state, accelerated development, social reform, the restitution of authority, the establishment of an economic parliament for the professional organizations, rejection of liberal capitalism, the improvement of the middle classes with rural elements, the banning of multiple job holdings, the national supervision of capital, the control of unjustified amassing of money and land reform. According to the proclamation, the Jews had to be treated as foreigners and eliminated from the economy and culture unless they had shown on an individual basis that they had identified themselves with Christianity and with the national goals. The Hungarian "soul" had to be cleansed from "Jewish contamination."[19] This proclamation and the demonstration quieted the Arrow Cross agitation but had little other effect and the movement largely died in November.

Teleki had to distance himself from his pupils who were active in the Anonymous Hungarian Movement when the scandal about the exposition of the Region and Folk Study Institute erupted. The institute was created by a Ministry of Culture and Education ordinance on October 19. Teleki wished to assign many of his pupils to this institute which was under the directorship of István Györffy, the professor of ethnography and Zoltán Magyary, the administration expert and professor of law. The new institute was destined to become the official base of the new village study endeavor.[20] The first public activity of the institute was an exhibition in the Károlyi Palace at which the various groups presented their work. On the wall of the palace enormous posters illustrated the inequalities of Hungarian land ownership, the mass of landless peasants, the proliferation of entailed land and its undesirable consequences.

Immediately after the opening of the exhibit on November 21 turmoil exploded. The traditional political and social elite and the representatives of large estates and of capital vigorously protested against the trend of the exhibit and his message. Within two weeks Teleki closed the exposition and then ordered that the institute be disbanded as well. Prior to that he summoned the organizers and for more than hour berated them.[21] The harangue ended with the famous words, "and now, I am

---

18 Reprint from the November 1938 issue of *Fiatal Magyarság*.
19 Ibid., p. 6.
20 János Almási, "Az 1938-as Táj- és Népkutató Kiállitás és politikai viszhangja" [The 1938 Region- and Population Study Exposition and its political repercussions], *Elmélet és Politika-Információs Szemle* [Theory and Political Information Review], no. 2 (1986): 107.
21 Kiss, "Visszaemlékezés," p. 611.

going back to my social class."[22] The scandal about the exhibition gave the right-wing opposition a good opportunity to demonstrate its social sensitivity. The exhibit was instructive for two reasons, it is evident that Teleki bowed to political pressure when he closed the exhibition and did not act out of conviction. He was convinced that some type of land reform was necessary and was thinking in terms of ten to fifteen years after which the large estates would survive, reduced but functional. It also shows Teleki's style and insight that although he disavowed his pupils, and some of the pupils disavowed him, none of the organizers of the exhibit had any serious trouble because of their involvement.[23]

Because the Hungarian and Czechoslovak parties could not reach an agreement, it was a German-Italian arbitration panel that decided the fate of the areas of Czechoslovakia inhabited by Hungarians. On November 2, 1938, the First Vienna Award returned to Hungary the southern segment of Slovakia, inhabited mostly by Hungarians. Eleven thousand nine hundred and twenty-seven square kilometers with one million sixty thousand inhabitants were returned. According to Hungarian statistics the percentage of Hungarians in this area was 84, while the Slovakian statistics claimed that the ratio was 57 percent. Teleki celebrated by marching into Komárom in Boy Scout uniform. This was done to honor the Boy Scouts of the Komárom Benedictine Gymnasium who demonstrated in favor of the Hungarian delegation at the time of the negotiations. His task was not finished. He was the head of the Hungarian delegation on the Hungarian-Slovak Border Committee. As far as his activities were concerned, András Rónai, his former pupil and collaborator emphasized Teleki's emphatic, expert and, vis-a-vis the Slovaks, magnanimous position. One of the Hungarian negotiators, the leader of military intelligence, was much less complimentary. "Teleki fusses around," he wrote, "he meddles with the drawing of the Munkács border, is helpless, rigid and professorial. His principle is that the border should not divide any large estate and this makes an agreement almost impossible."[24]

His work on the Border Committee was made more difficult by the November government crisis. Imrédy reorganized his government and replaced several conservative ministers, including justice, industry, agriculture and defense. In their place he chose politicians who were committed to radical, right-wing reform policies.

---

22   Huszár, *Beszélgetések*, p. 127.
23   Ibid., p. 131.
24   Rónai, *Térképezett történelem*, pp. 137–141; and the *Diary of Rudolf Andorka*, January 2, 6, 23, 27, February 15, and 25, 1939, entries, X 7497, MNL OL. For the Border Commission see Sallai, *Az első bécsi döntés*, pp. 173–202.

They were Antal Kunder, András Tasnádi Nagy, Mihály Teleki, a distant relative of Pál Teleki, and Andor Jaross as minister without portfolio for the reannexed Highland [Felvidék). These changes were displeasing to a significant part of the government party. The conservative-liberal, moderate Catholic politicians who had survived Prime Minister Gyula Gömbös's housecleaning were disturbed by the plans of the prime minister that wished to convert the government party into a totalitarian mass party and also wished to introduce a governance by edict.[25] When it became evident on November 22–23 that the attempts of the government to get those parts of Subcarpathia that remained under Czechoslovak rule back to Hungary failed because of a German and Italian veto and that the prime minister persisted in his plans to reorganize parliament in a spirit more in tune with the new trend, they went on the attack.

On November 22, fifty-four deputies, including former ministers and secretaries of state, resigned from the NEPand they were followed by four others. Counting those who had left earlier, a total of sixty-two deputies resigned from the government party and on November 23, they joined the opposition and cast a no confidence vote against the prime minister.[26] Teleki was very critical of the dissidents because, according to him they brought the country into danger by opening the arena for Arrow Cross action.[27] He participated in organizing a student demonstration in front of the Parliament in support of the prime minister. Between November 24 and 27, Horthy consulted with Teleki about resolving the crisis. The minister of culture and education opposed the resignation of the government and recommended a variety of legal maneuvers. It seems likely that it was Teleki who convinced the Regent to retain Imrédy.[28] On November 27 Horthy asked Imrédy to form a new government. Seeing these developments and under German pressure, Kálmán Kánya, the minister of foreign affairs, resigned and was succeeded by his chief of the cabinet, István Csáky. It is likely that Teleki's support was effective. He had worked with Csáky in Szeged in 1919 and their relationship had strengthened over the years.[29]

---

25 Notes by Prime Minister Béla Imrédy on November 13, 1938, in Péter Sipos and András Sipos, eds., *Imrédy Béla a vádlottak padján* [Béla Imrédy in the Dock] (Budapest: Osiris-BFL, 1999), pp. 497–501; Zsitvay, *Magyarország 1921–1941*, pp. 362–373.
26 Péter Sipos, *Imrédy Béla és a Magyar Megújulás Pártja* [Béla Imrédy and the Party of Hungarian Renewal] (Budapest: Akadémiai Kiadó 1970), pp. 70–72.
27 *Andorka Diary*, November 24, 1938, entry, X 7497, MNL OL.
28 P. Sipos, *Imrédy Béla*, p. 22.
29 György Ránki, Ervin Pamlényi, Lóránt Tilkovszky, and Gyula Juhász, eds., *A Wilhelmstrasse és Magyarország* [The Wilhelmstrasse and Hungary] (Budapest: Kossuth. 1968), no. 167.

The opposition, however, found a way to remove the weakened Imrédy from the government. In order to deter him from proposing the second anti-Jewish law to parliament, Károly Rassay, the head of the liberal opposition presented documents showing that Imrédy had Jewish ancestors. The prime minister first denied the allegation but then handed in his resignation to Horthy. According to a well-informed politician of the day, it was Ferenc Keresztes-Fischer who recommended Teleki to Horthy's attention.[30] The assumption is strengthened by the fact that Teleki went back and forth between the Sándor Palace and the Regent's Office in the company of the minister of the interior. In persuading the minister of culture and education to take the position István Bethlen, Smallholder leader Tibor Eckhardt and, perhaps, the former Prime Minister Gyula Károlyi might have had a hand.

At the Head of the Government. First Steps in Foreign and Domestic Policies

Teleki took over Imrédy's entire cabinet and invited Bálint Hóman, the historian and university professor, former director general of the National Museum, to take over the chair in the Ministry of Culture and Education where he had actually preceded him. The forces within the cabinet seemed to be reasonably well balanced although the apparent harmony soon came to an end. The prime minister was the balancing wheel between the warring factions and this very shortly began to sap his energies. He could totally rely on Ferenc Keresztes-Fisher the gray eminence of Hungarian politics. Csáky and Hóman belonged to the right wing. Initially, in awkward situations, the personal attachments were stronger than the ideological relationships. The Minister of Agriculture Mihály Teleki was the distant relative of the prime minister who valued family relationships very highly. Mihály Teleki's right-wing sympathies and his devotion to Imrédy became manifest only during 1940. The Minister of Defense Károly Bartha was Horthy's nominee as Horthy regarded defense matters as his personal arena. Thus Bartha was untouchable. Even so, Teleki could get along much better with Bartha than with Henrik Werth, the chief of the General Staff, with whom Teleki's relationships became impossible after just a few weeks.

---

30 Zsuzsa L. Nagy, *Egy politikus polgár portréja. Rassay Károly (1886–1958)* [The Portrait of a Civic Politician, Károly Rassay (1886–1958)] (Budapest: Napvilág Kiadó, 2006); and Zsitvay, *Magyarország 1921–1941*, pp. 487–490.

Lajos Reményi-Schneller, who was a member of every cabinet from March 1938 until the spring of 1945 was the model of a technocrat, committed to social reform and increasingly far right-wing. He obliged Teleki by always being able to come up with the money for Teleki's reform plans and for rearmament while keeping the budget reasonably balanced. The prime minister even thought that Remenyi-Schneller might become his successor.[31] Antal Kunder, the minister of commerce and industry also held an important portfolio for which Teleki had more far-reaching plans than his predecessors. In spite of their frequent meetings there was no personal relationship between them. Andor Jaross, the minister for the Highland [Felvidék], without portfolio, was pushed increasingly to the side because he proved to be unable to deal with the nationality issues that were of key importance to Teleki. Jaross's loyalty to Imrédy made any cooperation with him very difficult. Andras Tasnádi Nagy, the minister of justice, was confronted with a very complicated problem. It was his responsibility to present the second anti-Jewish law, inherited from Imrédy, to the National Assembly. In spite of all these problems, Teleki was received with enthusiasm by public opinion. Widely divergent politicians and intellectuals spoke approvingly of the new prime minister.[32]

In his program presentation of February 22, 1939, Teleki assumed the program of his predecessor. After a lengthy historical introduction he spoke of the most important features of his legislative program, including the anti-Jewish legislation. "Let no one believe," he said, "that the submission and implementation of such an act was not a painful process. In order to maintain the national characteristics among the leadership of the country we must not only do what everybody recognizes as being essential, but the nation must also decide to take some grave step... Let no one think, here in this country or abroad, where it had been said, that this law was prepared under German pressure or any other influence."[33] If anybody thought that Teleki would withdraw the proposed legislation, he was disappointed within a few days, when the prime minister declared, "This will be our last battle with the Jews."[34]

In his introductory speech he stated about the land reform and the formation of small landed properties that,

---

31 Szinai and Szűcs, eds., *Horthy Miklós titkos iratai*, p. 234.
32 Sándor Hunyadi, "Teleki Pál miniszterelnök bemutatkozó beszéde" [Introductory speech of Prime Minister, Pál Teleki], *Magyarország*, February 23, 1939, p. 7; Endre Bajcsy-Zsilinszky, "Mit várunk Teleki Páltól" [What do we expect from Pál Teleki?], *Magyarország*, February 19, 1939, p. 3; and Gusztáv Grátz, "Gróf Teleki Pál" [Count Pál Teleki], *Pesti Napló*, February 26, 1939, pp. 1–2.
33 Teleki, *Válogatott politikai írások*, ed. Ablonczy, p. 353.
34 "Egyesült a Keresztény Községi Párt és a NEP fővárosi szervezete" [The Christian Municipal Party and Budapest organization of NEP are united], *Pesti Napló*, March 1, 1939, p. 11.

> I believe and trust that the successors to the Hungarian nobility that could abdicate its ancient privileges to elevate the serfs in order to strengthen the nation, will now understand that in the interest of further strengthening the nation we need a distribution of land that will broaden and strengthen the society of those who belong to the land and which includes the nobility and the old land owners....Also, transferring the land that is currently held by individuals who are strangers and whom no tradition links to the land to Hungarian and more reliable hands, is evidently the duty of every Hungarian government.

This was a reference that he wished to link the land reform legislation to the anti-Jewish one.[35] He came out for the continuation of rearmament known as the Győr Program, spoke of the protection of the farmers, the introduction of social legislation, public instruction matters and the problems of the reattached Highland.

Turning to foreign policy, he emphasized that in its foreign relations Hungary wished to rely on the Rome-Berlin Axis and that with their support of the first phase of the revision, "Chancellor Hitler and Prime Minister Mussolini had inscribed their names forever onto the pages of Hungarian history." He left no doubt about some further tasks of Hungarian foreign policy and again emphasized, "The highest goal of Hungarian foreign policy is the assurance of the continuation of our national life and the realization of our legitimate demands," i.e. revision. He emphasized Hungary's good relations with Poland and urged that good relations be maintained with Hungary's neighbors. He mentioned the democratic Great Powers only in passing. In conclusion, he spoke of national sovereignty, "We respect the rights and views of all countries, large or small, but in exchange we demand the same degree of respect for the thousand year-old Hungarian national way of life and structures that do not harm anybody and that can include the most modern ideas and principles."[36]

The speech was received in the House in various ways. The leader of the Smallholder Party, Tibor Eckhardt recalled conversations held with Teleki over twenty years and hoped that the goals remained the same.[37] Speaking on behalf of the Social Democrats, Károly Peyer indicated that because the government wished to continue the policies of the previous government, the Social Democrats could not support it with their votes. At the same time he said, "there was a pleasant tone" in Teleki's speech and that it was the voice of a scholar of European standing. He also

---

35 Teleki, *Válogatott politikai írások*, ed. Ablonczy, p. 356.
36 Ibid., pp. 359–362.
37 *Képviselőházi napló, 1935–1940*, vol. 21, pp. 512–514.

hit the bull's eye when he said that the prime ministers usually had more trouble with the followers than with the opposition.[38]

Antal Sigray, an independent opposition member, was a childhood friend of Teleki and yet had some serious reservations and blamed the prime minister for wishing to deprive the Jews of their rights. In the name of the opposition liberals, Károly Rassay announced that, while he was not distrustful vis-a-vis the person of the prime minister and indicated that they would be his supporters in the social and economic reforms, he expressed his doubts that the anti-Jewish legislation would accomplish anything useful. He concluded by saying that because of the government's adherence to earlier policies his party could not support the government program.[39] The dissident representatives expressed their confidence. János Vázsonyi, a Democratic Party representative, in a stern and dry statement reminded the government that their position on the Jewish question was untenable and warned them that they would have to be accountable before the court of history.[40]

A solidly hostile tone was struck only by Kálmán Hubay, in the name of the Arrow Crossists. He demanded that Szálasi be released from prison and that the ban on *Magyarság* be lifted.[41] When on February 3, 1939, the extreme right wingers threw hand grenades at the synagogue on Dohány Street, the minister of the interior banned the activities of the extreme right wing Hungarian National Socialist-Hungarist Movement effective February 24. More than 120 party offices were closed, 150 members were detained, and 43 political leaders were interned. The only paper of the movement, the *Magyarság* was shut down on February 5.[42]

These steps of the government and the parliamentary echoes made a good impression in the West. According to the French minister in Budapest, "Teleki is more of a scholar than a man of action," who would guard Hungary's independence vis-a-vis Germany and while not very enterprising or belligerent, he had acquired merit by his good relations with Western scholars and for setting up a French high school in Gödöllő.[43] The British diplomats were more cautious. They recognized Teleki's role in the dissemination of British culture as minister of culture and education, and knew his friendship toward Great Britain. They received the reports

---

38 Ibid., pp. 520–524.
39 Ibid., pp. 528–531.
40 Ibid., pp. 536–538.
41 Ibid., p. 531.
42 Laczkó, *Nyilasok, nemzetiszocialisták 1935–1944*, Margit Szöllősi-Janze, *Die Pfeilkreuzlerbewegung in Ungarn. Historischer Kontext, Entwicklung und Herrschaft* (Munich: Oldenbourg, 1989), pp. 124–125.
43 Pierre Guerlet to Minister of Foreign Affairs Georges Bonnet. Budapest, February 20, 1939, Hongrie, vol. 95, p. 24, Europe 1918-1940, MAE AD.

from their minister in Budapest about Teleki's brave first political steps, his Puritanism and adherence to tradition with some reservations. They did acknowledge with relief that the new prime minister would be a much more pleasant negotiating partner than his predecessor and that his Germanophilia was much less evident.[44]

The *Times* and *Daily Telegraph* highlighted those comments from Teleki's speech that seemed to suggest that he was anti-German, namely the friendship with Poland, the adherence to parliamentary traditions and the conciliatory tone. The Rome papers saw mainly the adherence to the Axis in the prime minister's speech while the response of the German press was markedly lukewarm. Hitler was so discourteous that he did not even respond to Teleki's introductory telegram and this was viewed as a favorable sign in London.[45] The German diplomats in Budapest were very reticent in their comments on Teleki becoming the prime minister. They saw that he held the regent's confidence, was a realpolitiker who would be able to carry the anti-Jewish legislation through the House and who then would call for new elections to have his policies evaluated.[46]

At the same time the government took unmistakable steps toward Berlin and on February 24, 1939, formally joined the Anti-Comintern Pact. The step was first discussed in various European capitals and the decision was announced by István Csáky on January 13.[47] Consequently the Soviet Union announced that it would discontinue its direct diplomatic relations with Hungary, recalled its representative from Budapest and invited the Hungarian government to do likewise.[48] The decision came as a surprise to Hungary and at the Ministry of Foreign Affairs on Dísz Square they were distressed that Germany and Italy who did not break diplomatic relations with the Soviet Union did not protest against the step taken by Moscow or at least call back some of their diplomats from Moscow.[49]

---

44 Comments from R. L. Speaight London. February 17, 1939, TNA, FO 371, vol. 23112, fol. 121; and Charge d'Affairs Gascoigne to Foreign Secretary Halifax, Budapest, February 27, 1939, TNA, FO 371, vol. 23112, fols. 167–173.
45 "A világsajtó Teleki Pál gróf programbeszédéről" [The world press on the program speech of Count Pál Teleki], *Budapesti Hírlap*, February 24, 1939; László Zsigmond, ed., *Diplomáciai iratok Magyarország külpolitikájához 1936–1945* [Diplomatic Papers to Hungary's Foreign Policy], vol. 3, Magyarország külpolitikája 1938–1939 [Hungary's Foreign Policy], ed. Magda Ádám (Budapest: Akadémiai Kiadó, 1970), p, 486; Gascoigne to Halifax, Budapest, February 27, 1939, TNA FO 371, vol. 23112, fols. 167–173.
46 Charge d'Affairs Karl Werkmeister's report, Budapest February 17, 1939; and Minister Otto von Erdmannsdorff reports, February 23, and March 1, 1939, R 103787, PA AA.
47 Juhász, *Hungarian Foreign Policy*, p. 150.
48 Ádám, ed., *Magyarország külpolitikája 1938–1939*, p. 421.
49 Ibid., pp. 479–480.

The passivity of the new allies was an indication at the onset of the Teleki regime that even though Hungary was among the first to join the international Anti-Communist Pact, its participation had no effect on its standing among the nations. This was a good lesson for the future as well. Hungary also decided to withdraw from the League of Nations. Preparations for this step were initiated during the Imrédy regime and were due to both the urging of Germany and the disillusionment with the Geneva organization. The withdrawal took place officially on April 11, but Hungary remained a member of some of the smaller League of Nations structures.

Subcarpathian Ruthenia

In the remaining area of the Czechoslovak state Germany had initiated so much domestic political activity that a new international conflict arose. Budapest was primarily concerned about the Subcarpathian issue. This has come very close to a government crisis at the end of November 1938 when Hungary was not allowed by Germany and Italy to occupy the area below the northeastern Carpathians.

The Subcarpathian question was one of the cornerstones of Teleki's revisionist ideas. Actually the large majority of the population in this area known as Ruthenia was not Hungarian because the predominantly Hungarian areas had already been returned under the First Vienna Award. The mineral wealth, its mountainous topology, and drainage conditions of the region, however, gave it a key role in Hungarian foreign policy. Its repossession would have created a common border with Poland and Teleki had always pointed out the importance of adequate water supplies going to the Great Plain from the rivers originating in the Subcarpathian area. It was Teleki who believed after November 1938 that the Great Powers would not be swayed by the historical arguments to accept the idea of the Ruthenia's return but by the modern economic and political geography arguments that would correct the one-sidedness of the ethnic approach. Thus at the turn of 1938–1939 the Hungarian diplomats had to bring up matters, distant from their background, and regale their British, Polish, German, Czech, American, and Italian negotiating partners with problems of Carpathian lumbering, the Tisza River water level, salinization and karst development.[50] The results were not convincing. "The British charge d'affairs... clearly did not understand my explanations.... got nowhere with him" noted János Vörnle, the minister's permanent deputy concerning his discussion with his British

---

50 See ibid., pp. 508–514, 520–521, 526, 538–540, and 555–556.

discussion partner.⁵¹ This episode illustrates how science and politics became intermingled in Teleki's mind and, even more so, the limitations of this way of thinking.

In the end the decision was not made on a geographic basis. Even though the Hungarian government kept the Subcarpathian issue on the table in Berlin, Hitler's behavior was eventually influenced by the endeavors of Czechoslovakia to regain its initiative in Slovakia. The Czechslovak government introduced military rule and on March 10 dismissed the Tiso government. The same day Teleki explained in the Council of Ministers meeting that Hungary was prepared to reconquer Subcarpathian Ruthenia, without German consent if Slovakia proclaimed its independence or German troops marched into Czechoslovakia.⁵² There was no need for such belligerence. On March 13, Döme Sztójay, the Hungarian minister in Berlin, transmitted Hitler's message that Germany had no objection if Hungary occupied the Subcarpathian Ruthenia. Berlin only stipulated that Hungary had to act within twenty-four hours or Germany would recognize the self-styled Ruthenian government sitting in Chust [Huszt].⁵³ The decision caught the government by surprise and Werth, the chief of the General Staff claimed that it would take a week to mobilize sufficient military strength to occupy the area. This procrastination probably confirmed the opinion of the prime minister that this general was a stupid, inflexible officer with whom no collaboration was possible.⁵⁴

The deadline given by the Germans was fixed and thus on March 14 a force, largely composed of untrained recruits, crossed the border in the Užhorod, Mukačevo and Beregovo area and began its advance toward the ridge of the Carpathians.⁵⁵ On March 15 Hungarian troops entered Chust and Prime Minister Avgustin Voloshin and the members of the cabinet fled to Romania. By the evening of March 17 the Hungarian troops overcame all the scattered resistance and reached the passes in the Carpathians where they made contact with Polish frontier guards. A few days later the Hungarian troops attempted to expand the occupied area toward the west and, the Slovak-Ruthenian border being undetermined, on March 23 they started an attack to secure the Ung[Uh] Valley rail line and its foreground. During this engagement, referred to in the Slovak literature as the "Little War,"

---

51 Ibid., pp. 513–514.
52 Juhász, *Hungarian Foreign Policy*, p. 153.
53 Ibid;, p. 551 n. 68; and Macartney, *October Fifteenth*, vol. 1, p. 332.
54 Lóránd Dombrády, "Akiről nem beszélünk: Werth Henrik" [About whom we will not speak: Henrik Werth], *Hadtörténeti Közlemények*, no. 1 (March 2004): 99–101, and 118–119.
55 Csilla Fedinec, *A kárpátaljai magyarság történeti kronológiája* [The Chronological History of the Subcarpathian Hungarians] (Dunaszerdahely: Fórum Intézet, 2002), pp. 318–323.

(Malá vojna) there were aerial battles, artillery and tanks were used and the Hungarian planes bombed the Spišská Nová Ves [Igló] airfield.[56]

The territorial occupation, referred to in the Hungarian foreign policy and military jargon as the "small solution" was done with German acquiescence.[57] "Small solution" implies that there could have been a "large solution," meaning that if the circumstances had permitted it, the Hungarian troops would have tried to occupy the High Tatra-Lučenec [Losonc] line that the large number of Hungarian politicians, including Teleki, would have accepted as the optimal border. In the end the parties sat down to the negotiating table in Budapest on March 28 and by the beginning of April they determined the final Slovak-Hungarian border that assigned to Hungary the eastern Slovak areas occupied during the three days in March. The Western echoes were favorable. French public opinion calmly accepted the occupation of Subcarpathian Ruthenia and in London it was felt that it was better if the Hungarians occupied the area than if the Germans had done so.[58]

Ten days after the territory had been regained, the prime minister traveled to Subcarpathia [Kárpátalja]. Accompanied by his associates he covered the area in three days. In his speech, announcing the recovery of the region and stating that the territory had returned to the "Thousand-Year Hungary," he intimated that he wished to give the territory some form of autonomy.[59] He summoned a group to the ministry on March 18 to discuss this matter. Those who spoke at the conference were in general agreement that there was a need for some form of autonomy in the territory, based on a minority principle but there were wide differences of opinion as to how this could be accomplished and what its final form would be.[60] This meeting was the opening move in the long process that was supposed to serve the preparation of Subcarpathian Ruthenia's autonomy. In the fall of 1939, the prime minister personally drafted the introduction to the legislative proposal.

The Subcarpathian matter had an aspect that was in the closest possible relationship with a problem that was engaging the attention of Hungarian domestic policies. This was the "Jewish question". With Subcarpathia a very large number

---

56 István Janek, "Az elfelejtett háború. A szlovák-magyar kis haború története 1939 márciusában" [The forgotten war. The history of the Slovakian-Hungarian small war in March 1939), *Történelmi Szemle*, nos. 3–4 (2001): 299–313.

57 Ádám, ed. *Magyarország külpolitikája 1938–1939*, pp. 672–673.

58 Ibid., pp. 655–656; and György Barcza, *Diplomataemlékeim 1911–1945* [My Memories as a Diplomat] (Budapest: Europa-História, 1994), vol. 1, pp. 407–408.

59 Papp, ed., *Teleki Pál országgyűlési beszédei*, vol. 2, pp. 118–119.

60 Géza Vasas, "A ruszin autonómia válaszútján (1939 marcius–szeptember) [At the crossroads of Ruthenian autonomy (March-September, 1939) 1, *Aetas*, no. 4 (2000): 64–70.

of Jews returned under Hungarian control. Their role in the economic life of the community and their undeniable demographic weight made the government back off to some extent. Yet, in the spring of 1939, with the first anti-Jewish legislation having been enacted, the government was preparing additional legislation to curtail the rights of this Hungarian Jewry.

The Second Anti-Jewish Law

The outline for the legislative proposal came to the Teleki government from its predecessor. This does not mean, however, that Teleki as minister of cults and education did not have a controlling role in drafting the proposal. He wrote most, if not all, of the preamble of the bill and he so stated it before the House.[61] The preamble makes it clear that the author went beyond denominational definitions and considered Jews as a racial entity. He believed that the Jews were different on a "racial, philosophical, spiritual, intellectual and emotional" basis and not just on a religious one. It was the millennia-old history and historical determinism that was the cause of Jews's inability to create an intimate relationship with the land. Its members were prone to extremes and were practically incapable of being assimilated. Teleki, the author of the preamble wrote, "Only repeated cross breeding with other people and a firm conviction linked to a solid determination might modify and soften these characteristics even though they might not be entirely eliminated."[62] The preamble to the act mentioned that similar legislation had been enacted in a number of European countries and that this was not only a stimulus to do likewise but also a warning. If Hungary took no protective measures, the Jews expelled from among the two hundred million people surrounding Hungary, would flood the Carpathian Basin.[63] He then stated that Hungary was located on the border between East and West and that the Eastern unassimilated Jews were treated by the Hungarians according to Western customs that were used in the countries where there was no noticeable difference in clothing, behavior and language. Teleki blamed the liberal era and the weakness of the Hungarian commercial class for allowing the percentage of the Jews to rise so high in certain occupations and he buttressed his reasoning with his usual geographic arguments. The country was a continental one and it was the absence of ports that was responsible for the weak-

---

61 Teleki, *Válogatott politikai írások*, ed. Ablonczy, p. 354.
62 *Országgyűlési nyomtatványok 1935–1940*, vol. 9, *Felsőházi Irományok* [National Assembly Publications 1935–1940. Upper Chamber Papers] (Budapest: Athenaeum, 1939), vol. 9, no. 408, pp. 299–300.
63 Ibid., p. 300.

ness of the commercial enterprises. He indicated that the regulations of the first anti-Jewish legislation were unsuitable and easily circumvented. The 20 percent participation permitted in some occupations proved to be too generous.[64] The prime minister explained about the citizens belonging to the Israelite denomination that "Jewish" was not identical with "Israelite" and went well beyond it.[65] This placed the act on a solid racial basis.

The writer of the preamble defined the goal of the act as making the acquisition of Hungarian citizenship more difficult, limiting the activities of the Jews in public life, and banning Jews from public office, press, theater, motion picture directing, and all licensed occupations. The act restricted the ratio of Jews to 6 percent in the professions of law, engineering, medicine, press, theater and motion pictures, and to 12 percent in other intellectual endeavors. The act "empowered the government to promote the emigration of the Jews."[66] This was a clear indication of what the writers, and Teleki particularly, had in mind for those who did not meet the criteria listed above, including "no proof of loyalty to the nation" and "lack of a firm conviction linked to a solid determination" and "rejection of repeated cross breeding."

Teleki's views are even better illustrated by the letter that he sent to a British journalist a few days before his appointment, knowing full well that the addressee was not the only one who would read the letter. In the ten page missive to John E. Keyser he stated that the anti-Jewish acts were not enacted under German pressure.[67] Hungarian anti-Semitism was not a copy of the German one, but had historical roots, existing already in the era of liberalism and that 1919 (made and led by Jewish propagandists) just gave it another push. It was also not a copy of German anti-Semitism because it would never be so cruel even if the Hungarian act would be identical with the German one or even more strict thanks to "our happily Oriental temperament." After quoting extensively from the preamble that he had written, Teleki stated that twenty years earlier, when he was prime minister, he recommended that the Jews choose between their Hungarian compatriots and between "your Oriental coreligionists" and that the Hungarian Jewry opted to choose their brethren swarming in from the East. The "flux" had no basis in fact and it was an absurdity to confront the "patriotic" Jews with such a choice. Teleki claimed that

---

64 Ibid., p. 301.
65 Ibid., pp. 302–303.
66 Ibid., "Indoklás" [Preamble], p. 303.
67 Letter from Pál Teleki to John E. Keyser, Budapest, February 13, 1939, TNA, FO 371, vol. 23112, fols. 153–162.

the Jews were not only a biological race but an ideological race as well that would be essentially incapable of being assimilated. Biological race or blood was not all that important because eight or nine of every ten Jews could be identified on the basis of their appearance. The ideology and behavior, shaped by their millennial isolation, and their moral code was the real danger, according to Teleki, threatening Hungarian intellectual life, economy and morality. By the last one he meant that the middle class becoming more "Jew-like" would assume the value system of the Jews.

According to his opinion the legislative proposal was not good and too complicated but suitable for defusing the emotional tension produced by the mood of the masses. The prime minister likened it to an appendectomy that was painful but necessary for the health of society. While he gave it much thought he could not do anything other than support the legislation and the government. He said this three days before he became prime minister. Teleki also said that he had seen for many years the bad influence that the Jewish mentality, so different from the Hungarian one, had on the aristocracy and on the middle classes, the pillars of the nation. This is an important letter because in none of the letters to Hungarians had the prime minister stated his thoughts on the Jewish question this honestly. He was undoubtedly sincere in what he wrote but the concern about the nation and the intent to prevent social tempests, in practice meant a deprivation of rights, exclusion, and marginalization. This is not so only in retrospect but was seen clearly at the time by a number of thoughtful politicians as became evident during the debate in the House.

The legislative proposal for the second anti-Jewish law was introduced by the Teleki government at the first session of the House following the formal introduction of the government. The debate lasted for almost two months and there was a bitter struggle in both chambers. The debates were held in an atmosphere of verbal aggression with the Arrow Crossists and the right wing of the government party trying to intimidate the opposition by screaming at them and attempting to drown them out. In the name of the liberals, Károly Rassay spoke to the proposal and said that "under the guise of a racial theory it attacked those who already belong to a Christian denomination." He also noted the implementation problems of the act that produced an agitated response from Tasnádi Nagy, the minister of justice.[68] Károly Peyer and Manó Buchinger rejected the proposal on behalf of the Social Democrats. The latter stated that the anti-Jewish law served no other purpose but to create jobs for a few thousand golden youth from Christian middle classes at the price of ruining hundreds of

---

68 *Képviselőházi napló, 1935–1940*, vol. 22, pp. 116, and 119.

thousands."[69] Gusztáv Grátz, a former minister in the Teleki government, and a liberal-conservative thinker also condemned the ideas of the prime minister but it was János Vázsonyi, who in his dynamic address, most clearly and effectively condemned the anti-Jewish legislative proposal, "I will not wear the yellow star and will not volunteer for the ghetto," he summed up his prophesy.[70]

The dissidents were divided and the position of the Smallholder Party was ambivalent. The leader, Tibor Eckhardt, supported the position of the government and demanded an immediate ban on all immigration and the national registration of all Jews, while many others in his party rejected the proposal. The opposition representatives stood firm against the government representatives, many of whom had a bad conscience and who entered the House only for a vote. The prime minister did not comment during the debate and left it to the minister of justice, Tasnádi Nagy, not, however, because he did not agree. According to Tasnádi Nagy, the prime minister was of the opinion that "whose grandparents were Jewish, is a Jew."[71] The scholar was convinced that his rigidity was in the service of Hungarian society.

The House concluded the debate by the end of March, accepted the proposal on its third reading and, on March 27, sent it to the Upper House for endorsement. Here the members resisted vigorously even though certain minimal amendments had been made in the debates and in committee deliberations.[72] At the committee discussions, beginning on March 31, and later during the plenum of the Upper House the resistance of the members focused on the matter of the ones who had accepted Christianity and were baptized. They wished to accept a date up to January 1, 1939, in contrast to the proposal's date of January 1, 1919. They also wished to set up an Upper House commission to grant exemption to 150 people and classify them as Christians who would otherwise come under the law. They also wished to increase the categories of those who would be exempt.[73]

At the plenary session between April 15 and 18, Teleki finally spoke mainly to overawe his reluctant colleagues with his authority.[74] He again emphasized that the government was not under any pressure when it endorsed the proposal. He asked the members to accept the proposal before them without any amendments and attacked

---

69 Ibid., p. 282.
70 Ibid., p. 310.
71 Trial transcript, July 11, 1946, Criminal Trial Transcripts, Budapest People's Court, Nb. 7937/1950, Documents of the András Tasnádi Nagy Trial, fol. 146, XXV, 1 a, BFL.
72 Record of the deposition by János Makkai, March 24, 1945, Criminal Trial Transcripts, Budapest People's Court Nb 8147/50, Documents of the János Makkai Trial, fol. 38, XXV, 1 a, BFL.
73 , p. 116
74 Teleki, *Válogatott politikai írások*, ed. Ablonczy, pp. 377–389.

the simplistic interpretation of the St. Stephen ideas. He reiterated what he had stated in the preamble that there were indeed "Christian Jews."[75] He also admitted the deprivation of rights, claiming the higher interests of the nation and castigated liberalism at considerable length.[76] He stated proudly that he did not yield to the urgent requests of exempting certain categories and claimed that the reason for his stance was "protection and not persecution."[77] He also stated that he was the most radical member of the former cabinet in judging the mixed marriages and the transmission of characteristics, without wishing to debase anybody by so doing. He offered some accommodation but rejected the idea of any amendments.[78] Tasnádi Nagy promised that the amended proposal sent back to the Lower House would be considered there with dignity. It soon became evident that the minister of justice misled the Upper House opposition and the majority of the government party rejected the mitigations. In this the leaders of the party were accessories and assistants.[79]

A joint committee of the two houses met to iron out the differences. Sándor Wekerle, former minister of finance, a good friend of Teleki's, was the mediator and had a role in reaching an agreement. In the debated section on dates of conversion the date of August 1, 1919, was eventually accepted and in this a role might have been played by Teleki. While in Budapest between two trips abroad, he mobilized his old friend, the statistician Alajos Kovács, who enjoyed a good reputation and who certainly was not friendly toward the Jews. During the debate Kovács submitted his hasty analysis of the different effects the dates of 1919 and 1939 would have. According to him there were approximately ten thousand people still alive who converted prior to August 1, 1919, and that with their children of about 2,700 they represented a total of about thirteen thousand people. In contrast, those converting prior to the end of 1938, with their children represented a group of approximately 50–52 thousand and were 25–26 percent of all the "Jewish Christians." This made the date unacceptable.[80] The opponents of the proposal finally had to be satisfied with some minor amendments and even some of these were voted down by the House.[81] The members of the Upper House conceded.

---

75 Ibid., pp. 378–381.
76 Ibid., pp. 382–384.
77 Ibid., pp. 386–388.
78 Ibid., pp. 388–389.
79 Püski, *A magyar felsőház története*, p. 117.
80 Letters from Alajos Kovács to Pál Teleki, April 24, and April 26, 1939, Alajos Kovács Papers, VB. 09345, fols. 1-3, KSHK.
81 *Képviselőházi napló, 1935–1940*, vol. 22, p. 621.

It was the prime minister's responsibility under the enacted law to define scientifically who was to be regarded as a Jew and in this it went far beyond denominational criteria. Teleki intended the text to be straight forward but the exceptions, exemptions and time frames made the interpretation and implementation of the act very difficult. Whoever had one parent or two grandparents of the Jewish faith at the time the law was enacted was considered to be a Jew. The law closed the door toward assimilation and left only a tiny opening for the children born after May 5, 1939, who were baptized after birth, whose parents were baptized at the same time and whose family had lived in Hungary in January 1849.[82] Groups were exempt for meritorious service such as frontline duty during the war, university professors, participants in the 1918-1919 counterrevolutionary movement, clergymen of Christian denominations, Olympic champions, and royal and national secret councilors. The act left most of the original sections of the law intact, including the expulsion of the Jews from the artistic, economic, intellectual and financial life of the country, from higher education, and from public service. The second anti-Jewish legislation was the basis of all later anti-Jewish regulations. What the first act did not specify, the second one did, namely who had to be regarded as a Jew. This was further refined by the third act and the 1944 deportations to Auschwitz were based on these categories.

It is necessary to state, however, that Teleki did not know of the Holocaust and had no way of foreseeing it. He was a convinced anti-Semite who, while torn internally, always represented a radical albeit unacceptable, point of view in the Jewish question. He wished to establish hegemony for the Christian middle class and cleanse it. The anti-Jewish legislations sponsored by him were responsible for marginalizing the Hungarian Jews with the support of government policies. The coarsening of the political discourse on the Jewish question inevitably brought about the coarsening of the press and of public opinion. It made the social position of the Jews a desirable and attainable quarry and the same was true, later on, of Jewish property and even Jewish life. In this Teleki was guilty, his perspective is indefensible. It was a deadend for Hungarian conservatism from which, short of a radical turn around, there was no way back to the European traditions.[83]

---

82 Gyurgyák, *A zsidókérdés Magyarországon*, pp. 145–146.
83 Ibid., p. 313.

The 1939 Elections

Prior to the completion of the discussions of the anti-Jewish legislation, Teleki had to undertake two trips that had become mandatory ever since Gömbös was prime minister. They were trips to Rome and to Berlin. On the invitation of Benito Mussolini, he went to Rome on April 18, 1939, accompanied by Foreign Minister István Csáky. The Italian government confirmed that it was firmly committed to Hungarian revision and urged that Hungary continue its allegiance to the Axis Powers. The prime minister could take with him as a present to his host the report that Hungary withdrew from the League of Nations, effective April 11. The two parties harmonized their policies vis-a-vis Yugoslavia and the Hungarian leaders, in contrast to Foreign Minister Count Galeazzo Ciano and Mussolini, were seriously concerned that a potential German-Polish conflict could escalate into a world war.[84] Teleki did not say much and made a favorable impression on his Italian negotiating partners while the same could not be said about his minister of foreign affairs. Ciano considered Csáky to be an empty-headed clown who orated endlessly about facts for no purpose whatever.[85]

The Berlin visit caused a larger echo. The extreme right wing of the government party had advised the National Socialist circles that Teleki was a puppet in the hands of the anti-German Minister of Interior Ferenc Keresztes-Fischer and that they wished to replace Teleki with Daranyi and thus further tighten the ties with Germany. In other words, that Teleki was a lightweight.[86] According to the record, Teleki was very taciturn during the Berlin visit. He responded to Hitler's word cataract with a handful of words and relinquished the conversation to Csáky who was happy berating the British and the Americans.[87] That same day, during a discussion with Foreign Minister Joachim von Ribbentrop, Teleki spoke only once, when he said that the rumors about a Warsaw-Budapest-Belgrade-Rome alliance were not true. He was silent also when the German minister spoke about the importance of a Romanian-Hungarian minority agreement. Concerning the parliamentary rep-

---

84 László Zsigmond, ed., *Diplomáciai iratok Magyarország külpolitikájához 1936–1945* [Diplomatic Papers to Hungary's Foreign Policy], vol. 4, Magyarország külpolitikája a II. világháborő kitörésének időszakában 1939–1940, ed. Gyula Juhász [Hungarian Foreign Policy during the Period of the Outbreak of World War II 1939–1940] (Budapest: Akadémiai Kiadó, 1962), p. 182.
85 Malcolm Muggeridge, ed., *Ciano's Diary 1939–1943* (London: William Heinemann, 1947), pp. 73–74.
86 Arno Schickedanz, head of Alfred Rosenberg's staff to Obergruppenführer Wilhelm Brtickner, Hitler's SS Adjutant, Berlin April 24, 1939, Aussenpolitisches Amt der NSDAP, Band 51, fols. 8–10, NS 43, Bundesarchiv.
87 Ránki, Pamlényi, Tilkovszky, and Juhász, eds., *A Wilhelmstrasse és Magyarország*, no. 208.

resentation of the German minority in Hungary, he said that he wanted to take that step-by-step although as a Transylvanian he was fully aware of the importance of the matter. It was Csáky who kept talking to the Germans.[88] At their second meeting he limited his remarks to pointing out the lack of Hungarian responsibility for the Slovak-Hungarian incidents.[89] It is characteristic of the meeting that no agreement or pact was signed. The only purpose of the visit was to reinforce the obligations of the Hungarian government toward the Axis and Teleki unenthusiastically made such a statement in his toast.[90] There was only one apparent benefit of the visit. Teleki became convinced that the next target of Germany would be Poland and that this would lead to a European war, as he had already explained in Rome. This might have been the reason for his continuous ill humor. At the same time he sent his confidant and childhood friend, Prince György Festetits, to England to enlighten London about the goals of Hungarian foreign policy.[91] Returning from Germany, he took advantage of Horthy's permission and prorogued the House with a regental fiat and called for new elections.

The prime minister had a difficult time. He had participated in the inauguration of the extreme-right Magyar Élet Mozgalom [Hungarian Life Movement] of Prime Minister Imrédy at the Vigadó concert hall, but after he himself became prime minister and thus the head of the government party, the movement became a nuisance. He solved the problem by melding the movement into the ragged NEP [Party of National Unity] in February. The new group now took the name of Magyar Élet Pártja [Hungarian Life Party] (MÉP).[92] Finally, to complete the unification, the Budapest organization of the government party united with the previously independent and extreme right-wing Keresztény Községi Párt [Christian Municipal Party].[93] At this time Teleki announced that the dissidents who left the old party in November 1939, would not be taken back into the new party. In order to show their support some prominent extreme right wingers also joined the party. Rejecting the dissidents was a serious strategic mistake by the prime minister and

---

88 Ibid., no. 209.
89 Ibid., no. 210.
90 Macartney, *October Fifteenth*, vol. 1, p. 349.
91 Letter from Pál Teleki to György Festetits, April 16, 119391, György III. Festetits Papers, cs. 1, t. 2, P255, MNL OL.
92 "A Nemzeti Egység Pártja egyesült a Magyar Élet Mozgalommal" [The Party of Hungarian Unity joined with the Hungarian Life Movement], *Pesti Napló* February 23, 1939, p. 11.
93 "Egyesült a Keresztény Községi Párt és a NEP [Nemzeti Egység Pártja] fővárosi szervezete [The Christian Municipal Party and the NEP (Party of National Unity) fused], *Pesti Napló*, March 1, 1939, p. 11.

made the further shift of the party to the right inevitable. The Imrédy circle enjoyed a disproportionate influence in the organization.

The MÉP followed a model of an authoritarian mass party and its organization enveloped all of Hungarian society. Every ten electors were monitored by a "corporal" and every five corporals were supervised by an "organizer." Every elector had to be visited by an activist regardless of party affiliation, provided he or she was not Jewish. The party directives signed by Pál Teleki, the "National Party Chief," stated in its introduction that every Hungarian citizen over twenty-one years of age and of blameless life might belong to the party provided he or she was not Jewish.[94] The militarized organization was ubiquitous and every elector was visited by the corporal every week and even more frequently during election campaigns. The corporal kept records about the electors.[95] The MÉP demanded land reform, the development of an infrastructure, family and child protection, protection of cottage industries, a uniform and just regulation of labor and capital, the elimination of Jewish economic and intellectual influence, regulation of the press, the banning of multiple simultaneous positions and social reforms. It was with this militarized party, involved in reforms and voicing modern slogans that the prime minister had to enter the election campaign, one of the most difficult ones of the entire Horthy era.

Ballots were secret for the first time since 1920. The government had a good chance. Teleki was popular because of the territorial revisions and, perhaps, because of the anti-Jewish legislation. Ferenc Keresztes-Fischer was firmly in control of the administration, rapidly replaced a large number of the county prefects (főispán) after the change of government, and, just to be sure, redesigned the electoral districts a few weeks prior to the elections. In the campaign the minister of the interior gave the opposition very little leeway. Administrative interference disrupted the meetings and campaign of the dissident parties. Great pressure was brought on the Smallholders, liberals, and Social Democrats, but the heaviest pressure was exerted on the Arrow Crossists. The extreme right, reappearing as the Arrow Cross Party, did not run candidates in significant areas of the country because the nominees were not acceptable or because the party was unable to come up with the required 2,000 to 3,500 pengős security deposit.[96] The Arrow Cross newspapers were banned during April and May and a number of their leading functionaries were interned.[97]

---

94 *A Magyar Élet Pártjának szervezeti felepítése és szervezési utasítása* [The Structure and Organizational Directives of the Party of Hungarian Life] (Budapest: Stádium 1939), p. 4.
95 Ibid., pp. 9, and 11–12.
96 *Képviselőházi napló, 1939–1944*, vol. 1, p. 64.
97 Szöllősi-Janze, *Die Pfeilkreuzlerbewegung in Ungarn*, pp. 151–152.

The prime minister demanded a vigorous campaign. He not only spoke at the usual election meetings and gave interviews to the papers but, contrary to his usual practice, supported candidates, whose return he considered to be important, with personal appearances. It was in Debrecen that he made the comments that caused the greatest surprise in the election campaign. Speaking of party financing, on May 20 he told his audience that he knew that, "money is flowing into the country that no Hungarian who was loyal to his country must touch."[98] His statement about the "rolling marks" was immediately picked up by the government and opposition press who joined in attacking the Arrow Crossists. It is difficult to establish the truth in Teleki's statement. There undoubtedly was some money coming from Germany and the Arrow Crossists evidently shared in it. Yet, if they had spent all the money the prime minister was talking about on the election, is it likely that they could only run a candidate in 60 percent of the electoral districts?[99]

Teleki, while traveling through the country and writing articles about the necessity of a rapid and thorough national and Christian reform, had to take care of his own district. After Tokaj, he returned to Szeged, which he had represented earlier in his career, to demonstrate that the Szeged Idea was alive and well. He spoke in the theater in Szeged, spoke at party dinners and listened to the paprika growers demands for electric lights.[100] The Pentecost elections on May 28–29 resulted in the greatest government triumph between the two wars. In Szeged the MÉP list received almost 55 percent of the votes and of the three seats two went to the government party. Of the 260 seats 187 went to the government party and three to the affiliated United Christian Party, while the Arrow Crossist and other extreme right-wing parties received only forty-four mandates. It was a cautionary signal, however, that they did receive 30 percent of the total votes. The left-wing opposition of the MÉP, the Smallholders, the liberals, and the Social Democrats together gathered only twenty-four mandates.[101] Endre Bajcsy-Zsilinszky, the prominent opposition representative, who barely made it into the House spoke of the defeat, saying, "They treated us badly, not so much the government as the enraged electorate that could not accept Teleki's nobler and more humane ideas."[102]

---

98 Count Pál Teleki, *Beszédek 1939* [Speeches 1939] (Budapest: Stádium, n.d.), p. 111.
99 Szöllősi-Janze, *Die Pfeilkreuzlerbewegung in Ungarn*, pp. 214–220.
100 Ferenc Vásárhelyi, "Korszaknyitó programot adott az országnak gróf Teleki Pál Szegeden" [Count Pál Teleki gave the country a new program in Szeged], *Az Est*, May 9, 1939, pp. 1–3.
101 István Pintér, "A kényszerpályára szavazó ország—1939" [Voting for the path the country is forced to take—1939], in *Parlamenti választások Magyarországon 1920–1998* [Parliamentary Elections in Hungary 1920—1988], ed. György Földes and László Hubai (Budapest: Napvilág, 1999), p. 199.
102 Letter from Endre Bajcsy-Zsilinszky to Miklós Kozma, June 16, 1939, box 12, dossier 5, fol. 681, K 429, MNL OL.

Political Undertow

The prime minister was triumphant. "I am happy," he declared in a newspaper article. While he said that he was not in favor of secret ballots he felt that the country had voted for the right side, for constitutional continuity and for the national and Christian Hungarian way.[103] Actually the situation was far from rosy. Imrédy and his followers largely took over the control of the MÉP candidate selections and this was the reason for the massive change in representatives that fundamentally changed the configuration of the government party, for the second time in one decade. Of the representatives elected in 1931 on the United Party ticket only nineteen remained in the government party and of Gyula Gombos's 170 member NEP group only twenty-seven remained in the House. The representatives of capital and of the large estates disappeared. Their place was taken up by a group of the new Christian money men who came either from the socially conscious youth movements or from a professional background, medicine, engineering, and economy, and wished to start a political career.[104] The average age of the representatives was two years less than in 1931 and dropped from 50.7 to 48.76. Examined in more detail it appeared that the age distribution changed. The number of representatives under forty years of age almost doubled, from twenty-six to fifty-four, albeit in a House larger by fifty representatives than the previous one.[105] Of these many were right-wing or receptive to right-wing ideas. The representatives were better educated than the ones in 1935. Of the elected and not appointed representatives 159 (61 percent) had a university degree, 28 (11 percent) had a commercial degree and 20 representatives had a high school education only. There were only 49 representatives who did not finish secondary education.[106]

Teleki's endeavors to get his own people into parliament were only partially successful. In spite of his failures he managed to organize the government party faction, known in the literature as the Laky-Bencs group whose only link was Teleki

---

103 "Teleki Pál cikke az alkotmanyfolytonosság győzelméről" [Article by Pál Teleki on the victory of constitutional continuity], *Nemzeti Újság* [National News], June 2, 1939.

104 Péter Sipos, Miklós Stier, and István Vida, "Változások a kormánypárt parlamenti képviseletének összetételében" [Changes in the composition of the government party's parliamentary representation], *Századok*, nos. 3-4 (1967): 616–617.

105 Figures based on László Lengyel and Gyula Vidor, *Magyar országgyűlési almanach 1931–1936: ötszáz magyar élet* [Hungarian National Assembly Almanac 1931–1936: Five Hundred Hungarian Lives] (Budapest: Globus, [193?]); and István Haeffler, ed., *Országgyűlési almanach. Az 1939–1944. évi országgyűlésről* [National Assembly Almanac. On the 1939–1944 Session] (Budapest: Haeffler I., 1940).

106 Pintér, "A kényszerpályára szavazó ország," p. 206 n. 35.

himself. It seems likely that the group was never larger than 20-25 people.[107] He got some of his university colleagues and some Boy Scout leaders into parliament as well as some of his favorite public servants and relatives, including his son-in-law. The group did not have very clear ideas and initially the supporters of radical social reforms did not find it contrary to their principles to attend the meetings of the evolving Imrédy group. When, in the spring of 1940, it became evident that there was a conflict between the two wings of the MÉP, this group stood solidly behind the prime minister. He could count on several of the appointed Highland representatives and the ones from Subcarpathia were loyal to him. The biggest problem was the small size of the group. In size and intellectual preparedness it was similar to the Imrédy group but was much smaller than the strong agrarian group of the middle-sized estate owners (100–1,000 acres) or the majority of the government party who strongly pulled toward the right and who sympathized with Germany.[108] It could be seen that the House was dominated by an antiestablishment group that considered the Upper House a conservative and feudal anachronism.

The policies of the prime minister were further impeded by the fact that he did not have a press that was completely on his side. The government papers were either under the influence of the right wing or had minimal effect on national policies. They included the *Új Magyarság* [New Hungarians], *Függetlenség* [Independence] and to some extent *Esti Újság* [Evening News] and *Pester Lloyd*. The opposition liberal or Social Democrat papers could not be expected to support the head of the government. Contrary to popular belief, the liberal-conservative *Magyar Nemzet* [Hungarian Nation] was not close to Teleki. The situation changed when the government laid a heavy hand on the Est Company which published the liberal-conservative papers. The distinguished *Pesti Napló* [Journal of Pest] was discontinued and the *Est* [Evening] was replaced with the government paper renamed *Pest*.

The first session of the new National Assembly, on June 12, 1939, indicated to all outsiders that the times had changed. The MÉP and one of the smaller national socialist parties appeared in traditional Hungarian dress to emphasize the historic dimensions of the reforms to come. The representatives of the Arrow Cross Party arrived in their party uniform. All of them wore green shirts and Sam Browne belts and the leader greeted the surprised House with the Nazi salute. In the ocean of black and green garb the dark or light civilian suit appeared to be unpatriotic.[109] In

---

107 P. Sipos, *Imrédy Béla*, p. 121. He estimates their number at fifteen, although it was probably larger.
108 Ibid., pp. 122–123
109 "Összeült az új képviselőház" [Reassembled the New House of Representatives], *Új Magyarság*, June 13, 1939, p. 1.

his speech on June 19 the prime minister reiterated his February program. New elements were the compulsory labor service, the dams regulating rivers in Subcarpathia, the Árpád Bridge on the Danube to be completed in 1944, and the eight-year elementary school. This last item was strongly opposed by the Arrow Crossists who claimed that it would destroy the higher elementary schools.[110] He also announced that he would like to have a new House rule adopted which had been on the table in August. The right to ask questions was limited, the detailed discussion of legislative proposals was referred to committees thus significantly reducing the rights of the opposition. The immunity of members was curtailed and all of these items were instituted to speed up the work of the House.[111]

Teleki found little joy in the new National Assembly. The Arrow Crossists attacked continuously from the first day on, for election abuses, the curtailment of the Arrow Cross press, the multiple positions and the "rolling marks" comment. At the August session they attacked the prime minister on social issues and because of the alleged corruption of his relatives and ministers. The head of the government lost his patience and at a party dinner in August sharply attacked the disrespectful and coarse language of the Arrow Crossists which lacked good taste and social tact.[112] He proposed the regulation of their press.[113] The government attempted to bridge the unproductive and dangerous parliamentary debate by issuing ordinances. A number of continuously revised ordinances were issued during the summer of 1939 about the implementation of the second anti-Jewish legislation.

This was the last summer of peace. On September 1, 1939, the war broke out.

In the Shadow of the War

The German-Polish conflict did not come as a surprise to the prime minister. He knew very well, ever since the Berlin visit, that Poland was the next stop on Hitler's itinerary. The Hungarian government, and Teleki personally, did not wish to do anything against Poland.

The prime minister valued the Polish-Hungarian association and the friendship between the two countries. In addition to personal motives his decision was motivated by strategic considerations. He was seeking for foreign contacts and neigh-

---

110 Papp, ed., *Teleki Pál országgyűlési beszédei*, vol. 2, pp. 134–138.
111 *Képviselőházi napló, 1939–1944*, vol. 1, pp. 527–530; Sándor Pesti, *Az újkori magyar parlament* [The Modern Hungarian Parliament] (Budapest: Osiris, 2003), pp. 158–161.
112 P. Sipos, *Imrédy Béla*, p. 132. Also in Papp, ed., , vol. 2, pp. 179–180.
113 Papp, ed., *Teleki Pál országgyűlési beszédei*, vol. 2, pp. 180–184.

bors who could represent a balance vis-a-vis Berlin and maintain the possibility of an independent decision in the presence of German pressure and open up vistas for Hungarian foreign policy seeking independence.[114] When he felt that the European political situation was pointing increasingly toward war he endeavored to communicate his reservations to the Axis Powers. On July 24 he sent two letters to Rome and to Berlin. In one he assured Hitler and Mussolini of his solid commitment to the Axis but indicated that this attachment "could not damage our sovereignty and could not introduce impediments in the realization of our national goals." He recommended that representatives of the three countries, Germany, Italy and Hungary, discuss, as soon as possible, "those problems that might arise from the most effective cooperation of the three countries."[115]

This enigmatic composition concealed the plans involving Romania and also served to make the second letter more acceptable. In the second letter Teleki stated bluntly that for moral considerations Hungary would not engage in military action against Poland.[116] Count Ciano was correct when he noted in his diary that, "I vaguely suspect that the first letter was written in order to launch the second."[117]

Hitler was incensed. At the beginning of August Csáky had to explain the letters to the Führer and to Ribbentrop. Following the customary and enraged monologs by Hitler, Csáky had to withdraw both letters in writing.[118] While Csáky was trying to salvage the situation in Berlin, Teleki advised London via Minister György Barcza, his former student Judit Márffy-Mantuano, Lady Listowel, and William Goode, the former economic advisor to the Hungarian government, that Hungary would engage in no action against Poland and would preserve its neutrality. If Germany were to invade Hungary, the Hungarian army would offer "nominal resistance." There ensued a lengthy discussion in the Foreign Office about the interpretation of that expression.[119] At the same time Hungary prepared to mobilize its forces against Romania and in the middle of August Hungarian troops deployed east of the Tisza River. The tensions eased up only at the beginning of

---

114 Gyula Juhász, *A Teleki-kormány külpolitikája 1939–1941* [The Foreign Policy of the Teleki Government 1939—1941] (Budapest: Akadémiai Kiadó, 1964), p. 34.
115 Magda Ádám, Gyula Juhász, and Lajos Kerekes, eds., *Magyarország és a második világháború* [Hungary and the Second World War] (Budapest: Kossuth, 1959), p. 244.
116 Ibid., p. 245.
117 Muggeridge, ed., *Ciano's Diary 1939–1943*, p. 118.
118 Juhász, ed., *Magyarország külpolitikája*, pp. 408–409; Memorandum of Woermann to Hitler and Ribbentrop, Berlin, August 10, 1939, 61176, fol. 138, BA [Bundesarchiv], PA AA; and Memorandum for State Secretary Ernst von Weizsäcker. Berlin, August 9, 1939, R 29784 (microfiche No. 1265), PA AA.
119 Memorandum from Sir Orme Sargent on his conversation with Minister Barcza, London, August 27, 1939, TNA, FO 371, vol. 22977, fols. 262–263.

September when, after the British and French declaration of war, it became evident that there could not be another international Munich conference about the central European questions.

The day the war broke out, September 1, 1939, the Hungarian government held a special meeting of the Ministerial Council. The members of the cabinet listened to Hitler's radio address. Following this, Teleki read his proclamation to the Hungarian people in which he announced that the special powers authorized by Act II of 1939 would go into effect.[120] The right to meet and gather would be curtailed, the press would be censored, the owners of motorized vehicles had to register them with the army, a commissioner for mobilization was appointed, price control was introduced and certain goods were sequestered.[121] A number of other ordinances addressed such minutia as curtailment of markets, the ownership of messenger pigeons and the hours of operation for the stores. The war affected the country in other ways as well. On September 9, Ribbentrop called Csáky at his home and asked if the Hungarian government would be willing to grant transit to German troops operating against Poland, on the Kassa-Nagyszalánc [Slanec]-Velejte [Veľaty] rail line. The next day, Teleki, Csáky, Bartha and Werth met with the Regent and all agreed that such permission could not be granted by Hungary.[122] Mainly because it would involve the transit of Slovak troops as well and that could not be allowed. Another major consideration was the fact that it would result in a declaration of war from Great Britain, France and Poland and thus entry into the World War. After the Council of Ministers assured the Regent and the minister of foreign affairs of their support, Csáky went into the next room and called Ribbentrop, telling him the Hungarian government's negative response.[123]

One day later, in response to a similar request by the Slovak government, the Hungarian government simply and with insulting firmness said no and even threatened Bratislava that it would consider any infringement of the border as a war-like aggression.[124] The matter was of no particular strategic significance to the Germans because by September 9, their troops stood before Warsaw and, starting from Silesia and East Prussia, cut Poland in two. The otherwise limited capacity line would have been useful only for the transport of the wounded and perhaps might have

---

120 September 1, 1939, box 202, K 27, MNL OL.
121 RT 1939. vol. 2, nos. 347-353, 355-356, 360-361, and 410.
122 Juhász, *Hungarian Foreign Policy*, p. 163; Czettler, *Teleki Pál és a magyar külpolitika*, pp. 58–60; and Macartney, *October Fifteenth*, vol. 1, p. 367.
123 September 10, 1939, box 202, K. 27, MNL OL.
124 Juhász, ed., *Magyarország külpolitikája*, p. 508.

been used against the Polish troops stationed in Galicia. Teleki and his ministers were aware that Berlin was getting ready to irrevocably compromise Hungarian foreign policy and the Germans never forgot Hungary's "perfidy." At all of the future revisionist discussions the September 1939 Hungarian refusal was brought up over and over again. Ribbentrop did not fail to mention that it was Germany that had given the railway line in question to Hungary.[125]

The German-Polish war meant a much more serious problem for the Teleki government than the disapproval of the Great Powers. First, there was only a trickle, but soon after the September 17 Soviet attack there was a flood of Polish refugees across the common border in Subcarpathia into Hungary. Among the refugees there were intact military units with their weapons, women, children, old men, and the staff of an observatory with their telescopes.[126] The minister of the interior reported on September 22 that the number of refugees had reached ten thousand and that the facilities made available were no longer adequate.[127] His requests were regularly repeated throughout 1940. By the end of spring 1940, the Hungarian government had spent more than five million pengos for the sustenance of the refugees. It must be emphasized that these numbers refer to the civilian refugees whom the Ministry of the Interior was keeping track of. The soldiers who were in a majority were cared for by the Ministry of Defense and there were undoubtedly many who found a refuge with friends and relatives. The expert literature cites varying numbers about the Polish refugees. The lowest estimate was forty thousand[128] and the highest one was one hundred thousand.[129] The most likely number is between seventy and ninety thousand. It is to the great credit of the Hungarian government, led by Pál Teleki, that it welcomed the Polish refugees and helped them to reach Western Europe, in opposition to the hostile comportment of Berlin and the crudely phrased attacks of the Hungarian extreme right. Until July 1940 there were Polish consulates in Budapest and Ungvár. There was a Polish legation in Budapest until December 31, 1940, there was a Polish Institute, three dozen Polish elementary schools and, after the autumn of 1940, a Polish high school in Balatonboglár. During these years this was the only Polish high

---

125 Ibid., p. 413.
126 Juhász, *Hungarian Foreign Policy*, p. 164.
127 Minutes of the Council of Ministers, September 22, 1939, no. 11 on the agenda, box 202, K 27, MNL OL.
128 Ágnes Godó, *Magyar-lengyel kapcsolatok a második világháboruban* [Hungarian-Polish Relations during World War II] (Budapest: Zrínyi, 1976), p. 88.
129 Károly Kapronczay, *Akkor nem volt Lengyelország* [At That Time There Was No Poland] (Budapest: Magvető, 1992), p. 64.

school in Europe because the Germans closed all Polish high schools in the occupied area and in the Generalgouvernement.[130] There were a number of organizations, in addition to government agencies that handled Polish refugee matters and even after the diplomatic offices were closed, Hungary was an important focal point of Polish underground movements. Several historical works and sources mention that Teleki sent a Hungarian legion to the assistance of Poland and the Germans also suspected that this had taken place. Even though a few Hungarian volunteers fought along with the Poles, there is no evidence for or against the claim that the Hungarian government was involved.[131]

Social Reform Policies

The outbreak of the war served as a way for the government to impose a *treuga dei* [Truce of God] on public life. The only ones who did not accept it were the Arrow Crossists who resented that Teleki had not accepted their demands. Kálmán Hubay, their principal policy maker, announced at the end of September that the party would not participate in legislation. On October 10, the debate on what was proposed as the framework for the land reform started without Arrow Cross participation. The issue was the creation of small holdings for tenant farmers and of homesites. The opposition felt that the proposal was too modest and the goals were too narrow. Speaking for the Smallholders, Tibor Eckhardt announced that they would not accept the legislation.[132] The proposal was also opposed by the Social Democrats and the various non-Arrow Cross national socialist groups. György Apponyi, a member of the Rassay liberal opposition group, indicated that in spite of some concerns he would vote for the proposal. This was awkward for the prime minister because it seemed to support the claims of the right wing of the govern-

---

130 Károly Kapronczay, "Teleki és a lengyelek" [Teleki and the Poles], in *Teleki Pál és kora*, ed. Csicsery-Rónay and Vígh, pp. 124–127.
131 Romsics, *Hungary in the Twentieth Century*, p. 200; Macartney, *October Fifteenth*, vol. 1, p. 251; and unknown writer to the German Foreign Office, Vienna, September 10, 1939, R 104139, PA AA; The summary of Gauamtsleiter Helmut Triska, Berlin September 11, 1939, R 104139, PA AA. The subject is studied from Polish sources by László E. Varga, "Orlowski budapesti lengyel követ visszaemlékezései" [Memoirs of Orlovski, Polish minister in Budapest], *Századok*, no. 6 (2003): 1392–1395, and documents nos. 4–6, 8-10, and 12–15.and recently: Ákos Bartha: Törzsökösök, rongyosok, turániak. Németellenes magyar fajvédelem, 1938–1945 [Rootsotckers, ragged guards, turanians. Anti-German Hungarian racist movement, 1938-1945](Budapest, Ludovika, 2023), pp. 113-127.
132 *Képviselőházi napló, 1939–1944*, vol. 2, pp. 168–179, 399, and 433–439.

ment party and of the extreme right wing of the opposition that the proposal was favoring the anti-reform forces and was acceptable even to a liberal count.[133]

The radicals on the right wing of the government party still supported the prime minister. The proposal was accepted and transmitted to the Upper House in November. It was criticized by the majority of the conservative-liberal members even though it contained numerous amendments favoring the mid-sized and large estates. This was due to the fact that the prime minister, was more flexible than at the time when the anti-Jewish legislation was debated and did not wish to exert force to push the land reform through. During the debate, Teleki got into a newspaper debate with Bethlen.[134] Even though they discussed domestic policy matters, this was the third time that they crossed swords. The subjects, anti-Jewish legislation, the new House of Representatives and the land reform, clearly indicated where the paths of the two politicians diverged.

Because of lengthy committee deliberations, the act was proclaimed only in April 1940. The detailed preamble clearly showed that the land of Jewish owners would be used far in excess of the percentage they represented. This land reform would have been by far the most extensive property legislation of the Horthy era. The extremely complex implementation regulations envisaged the use of 100,000 acres per year with the distribution of 1.5 million acres over a period of fifteen years.[135] This was only one of the social reform proposals that Teleki government made. Still, in September 1940, the government submitted a legislative proposal about the pension of the widows of agricultural workers. The debate on legislation modifying certain public health regulations concerning protection against tuberculosis and sexually transmitted diseases started in December. The legislation proposed an increase in the number of hospital beds, mandatory treatment of some diseases and a number of other important public health measures.[136] Barely a month later, in January 1941, the House debated minimal wage legislation. There was an unlikely combination of support from the Arrow Cross, liberal, and Smallholder representatives, while the Social Democrats opposed it.

In addition to intensive social legislation, the prime minister found a way during the autumn to get rid of his unsatisfactory ministers. In July he appointed his university colleague, József Varga to be minister of industry and in October he also

---

133 Ibid., pp. 227–232.
134 "Gróf Bethlen István kritikája—Teleki miniszterelnök válasza Bethlennek" [Criticism of Count István Bethlen—Prime Minister Teleki's response], *Pesti Hírlap*, November 23, 1939, pp. 3–4.
135 *1940. évi törvenycikkek* [1940 Acts] (Budapest: Franklin, 1941), pp. 7–42.
136 Act IV of 1940, in ibid., pp. 48–76.

made him minister of commerce and transportation in lieu of Antal Kunder. He also dismissed his minister of justice. He realized during the debate on the anti-Jewish legislation that Tasnádi Nagy did not perform well and became confused even by legal questions posed in the House. In addition he could not be counseled and at the Council of Ministers meeting raised issues like the director of the Kispest textile factory being paid too high a salary. This must have seemed like an open rebellion to Teleki who was frequently prejudiced in favor of his family members; the name of the head of the textile factory was Count János Teleki.[137] Tasnádi Nagy was replaced by László Radocsay, the former prefect of Komárom County. The former minister of justice was kicked upstairs and became the president of the House of Representatives. It was known early in the autumn that the position of Andor Jaross, minister without portfolio, would be concluded soon. The prime minister had indicated in October 1939 that the tasks of the Jaross ministry would come to an end. Teleki also took the most important task of that ministry, the Highland estate adjustments under his own control.[138]

During the first year of Teleki being in office his entire operational methodology became obvious. Teleki attempted to transfer to politics his former students and followers who gained their experience in association and organization activities and in whose education he had participated between 1921 and 1938. The personal involvement of the prime minister is an indication of the importance he assigned to this group. He met with them more frequently than with his ministers and almost as much as with all the high government functionaries together. About one fifth of all his administrative time was spent in their company. His ideal was "scientific" governance where political perspectives could be excluded and all decisions were made on the basis of recommendations from content experts.

Among his guests in 1939 there were many university professors and experts from institutes that he had organized. Of the ten most frequently consulted collaborators only three were ministers in 1939. They were Keresztes-Fischer, Csáky and Kunder. The inner circle also included Ferenc Zsindely, the secretary of state in the Office of the Prime Minister, Béla Kovrig, the social politician and social policy councilor, and Tibor Pataky, who was the head of the Nationality Department of the Prime Minister's Office and who served every prime minister between 1920 and 1944. Other than the minister of the interior he was Teleki's most frequent vis-

---

137 Minutes of the Council of Ministers, July 7, 1939, no. 30 on the agenda, box 201, K 27, MOL.
138 Loránt Tilkovszky, *Revízió és nemzetiségpolitika Magyarországon 1938–1941*]Revision and Nationality Politics in Hungary], pp. 77, and 83.

itor. We know very little about this leading figure of Hungarian nationality policies and it is typical that the biographical dictionary does not give the year of his death.[139] In accordance with traditional Hungarian political practice, the prime minister frequently asked for his opinion prior to making any serious decision. Of the former prime ministers Teleki saw Imrédy most frequently with Móric Esterházy, a childhood playmate, a close second. He saw Daranyi more often than Bethlen. Teleki's close relationship to Esterházy is shown by the fact Esterházy was assured a position even in the much modified government party. Bethlen appeared rarely on the prime minister's appointment calendar and the former ministers and advisors of Bethlen were also rare visitors to the Sándor Palace.[140]

In December 1939 the House took up the budget to bring the state's budget year into conformance with the calendar year. The budget envisioned expenditures of 2.690 billion pengős, a revenue of 2.563 billion and a deficit of approximately 130 million pengős that was much increased by the events of the ensuing year.[141] The rearmament program and the infrastructure expenditures continued. The budget of the commissioner for intellectual affairs increased thirty-fold in comparison to the previous year (60,000 to 1,800,000). There were 290 employees in this office of which one hundred were working on the implementation of the anti-Jewish legislation alone.

The budget was accepted but Teleki could not rest even then. The deficit increased from month to month and in June 1940 the minister of finance reported in confidence to the Council of Ministers that by May the deficit had reached 277.7 million pengos which was one and one half times as much as predicted.[142] The reasons for the deficit can be found in the flooding that occurred in the spring of 1940 and in the disproportionately large expenditures on rearmament. The cost of living index also rose. It went, for a four member family, from 102 in July 1939 to 108.3 in June 1940.[143] The demands for defense expenditures could not be resisted by the prime minister or the minister of finance. In order to cope with the increasingly

---

139 About Pataky's life see: Csilla Fedinec: Az ismeretlen eminenciás I.: Pataky Tibor élete (1888-1921) [The Unknown Eminence: Tibor Pataky's Life] and ibid: Az ismeretlen eminenciás II. Pataky Tibor élete (1921-1953). *Kommentár* [Commentary] 10, (2015), no. 1-2., and 3-4. pp. 97-109, and pp. 1-20. .
140 Our calculations are based on the appointment diary found in cs. 3, dossier P 3, K 37, MNL OL. For a detailed analysis see Balázs Ablonczy, "A kegyelmes úr napjai — Kísérlet Teleki Pál miniszterelnök határidőnaplójának elemzésére" [The days of his excellency—an attempt to analyze Prime Minister Pál Teleki's appointment calendar], *Korall*, no. 17 (September 2004): 193–207.
141 Act XVII of 1939, in *1939. évi törvénycikkek* [The 1939 Acts] (Budapest: Franklin, 1940), pp. 186–208.
142 June 7, 1940, no. 23 on agenda, box 209, K 27, MNL OL.
143 July 26, 1940, no. 16 on agenda, box 212, (1913=100), K 27, MNL OL.

threatening deficit, the government considered an increase in taxes, partly by modifying the structure of taxation but also by an across the board rise in taxes. It was for this purpose that the National Assembly debated a legislative proposal about modifying societal taxes, direct taxes and taxes on bonuses, royalties and other income. The government also increasingly took advantage of the opportunities granted by the banknote printing presses. Yet, at the turn of 1939–1940 Hungary was not in a state of war. Because of the economic activities related to the war the economy was booming and unemployment had decreased. Thanks to the good harvest in 1938 the price of agricultural products increased, the agrarian squeeze decreased and wages rose.[144] All this would have been encouraging had war not raged in Europe.

Neutrality or Revision?

In striving for independence and taking advantage of the inconsistencies in German foreign policies, it was an important element in Hungarian foreign policy to offer aid to Finland, which was attacked by the USSR in the Winter War. Ever since his first visit in 1924, Teleki was very sympathetic toward Finland but this was only one of the reasons for his current action. Sending the Hungarian legion and shipping arms could be accomplished because Germany, technically an ally of the Soviet Union ever since the signing of the Ribbentrop-Molotov treaty, could not and did not want to stop the independent Hungarian action. Teleki's ideas were received warmly in Paris and in London and, oddly enough, went along with the condemnation of the Soviet Union by the League of Nations and its call for assistance for Finland. In October 1939 the Hungarian government reopened its legation in Moscow and the returning Soviet envoy again became active in Budapest. These initiatives did not affect the relations between the two countries. The organization and departure of the 361 member Hungarian legion for Finland is evidence of Teleki's administrative habits. The administration and the defense apparatus were essentially excluded and the prime minister arranged the entire affair through personal contacts. The legion departed at the beginning of February 1940. Even though they arrived after the hostilities had been concluded, the sympathy toward the volunteers and the propaganda value of the enterprise justified Teleki's ideas.

---

144 Ránki, *Magyarország története*, vol. 8. pp. 1005–1006, and 1008–1011.

The success convinced him that it was possible to govern with much looser structures than what the ministries considered essential.[145]

At this time Teleki believed that his foreign policy was successful and that the country could not only stay out of the war but that eventually revision might also take place. First of all against Romania but later perhaps against Yugoslavia as well. The diplomats serving in the Hungarian capital were generally complimentary about Teleki's activities. Hungarian neutrality caused a pleasant surprise in Western Europe, "The Hungarians are behaving splendidly" enthused a Foreign Office official in September[146] This same official, in another comment, clearly pointed out the limitations of the Hungarian-British relations. When a few days later Csáky talked to the British Minister in Budapest, Owen O'Malley and told him that if the Germans violated Hungarian neutrality, Hungary would resist but would not be able to sustain this for more than a week and would thus expect British and French assistance. In response, the Foreign Office stated that, "We have never promised Hungary any assistance. In the light of recent events, the fact that we can not give direct military assistance does not mean that no resistance is necessary. Promise of assistance means we will assist in the creation of a free Hungary after the war." This was indeed plain talk.[147]

The British minister was also very sympathetic toward the Hungarian dilemmas. In his memoirs he writes with respect about the Hungarian prime minister whom he compared to Antonio Salazar and Eamon De Valera because all of them were devout Christians, bright, patient and flexible but "in certain matters of principle inflexible and incorruptible." He emphasized Teleki's passionate dedication to his country and religion.[148] He believed that, "there was nobody in current political life that could equal Teleki in intelligence, honesty, courage and skill."[149] In the autumn of 1939 the French minister also wrote very understandingly about the Hungarian revisionist goals and did not exclude the possibility that Teleki could become Horthy's successor.[150] The German minister who was not one of the Nazi

---

145 Gábor Richly, "Magyar katonai segítsegnyújtás az 1939–1940-es finn-szovjet háborúban [Hungarian assistance in the 1939–1940 Finn-Soviet war], *Századok*, no. 2 (1996): 403–444.
146 Comment on Minister O'Malley's telegram from Budapest, September 14, 1939, TNA, FO 371, vol. 23114, fol. 41.
147 Telegram from O'Malley, Budapest, September 18, 1939, Comment by Sir Walford Selby, TNA, FO 371, vol. 23114, fol. 55. For the British-Hungarian relations of the time see András D. Bán, *Hungarian-British Diplomacy 1938–1941* (London: Frank Cass, 2004), pp. 77–92.
148 Sir Owen O'Malley, The Phantom Caravan (London: John Murray, 1954), pp. 204–205.
149 Report of Minister O'Malley, April 23, 1940, TNA, FO 371, vol. 24427, fol. 177.
150 Minister Pierre Guerlet to Foreign Minister Edouard Daladier, Budapest, November 13, 1939, Hongrie, vol. 192, fols. 65–67, Europe 1818–1940.

diplomats also wrote with sympathy about the policies of the Hungarian government.[151] The Polish minister, Leon Orlowski, always spoke of Pál Teleki with the greatest approval.[152]

There was one person with whom, right from the beginning, he failed to make proper contact. The American minister, a former condensed milk manufacturer and Democratic Party donator, was not nearly as simple-minded as Teleki believed him to be. Teleki believed that Minister John F. Montgomery belonged to those who could be made to understand Hungary with a story from his Boy Scout and teacher background. Montgomery was bored by Teleki's stories[153] and even though he was on excellent terms with the Hungarian elite of the days, the picture he formed about the prime minister never improved. "I should like to say that he was a great statesman but I am sorry that I can not," he wrote, "He considered himself very clever. Often he mentioned his Greek grandmother, always saying, 'You know the Greeks are a clever people'.... As I knew his intense hatred of national socialism and all it represented, I said nothing further, although I believed then and I believe now that his overconfidence in his own cleverness had much to do with what happened later."[154]

In the favorable foreign policy situation the prime minister could engage in the work he considered to be his most important task. Ever since he established his government he gave evasive answers about Hungary's revision demands vis-a-vis Romania. Hungary's revisionist successes to date did not come when and how Teleki would have preferred them. He called the First Vienna Award "not entirely according to our ideas" because in the Belvedere Palace the Germans and the Italians reached their decision on an ethnic basis alone.[155] In the case of Subcarpathian Ruthenia, the Great Powers ignored Teleki's ideas about economic geography and hydrography when they gave the Hungarian government a free hand or, at least, looked at the Hungarian territorial acquisitions with benevolent neutrality. At the turn of 1939–1940 he began to draft the plans for the proposed reattachment of

---

151 Otto von Erdmannsdorff, "Die politischen Ereignisse in Ungarn während der Zeit von Mai 1937 bis Juli 1941," Bd. 2, fols. 40–61, Otto von Erdmannsdorff, Nachlass 48, PA AA.
152 László E. Varga, "Orlowski Leó budapesti lengyel követ visszaemlékezései" [Memoirs of Leon Orlowski, the Polish minister in Budapest], *Studia Caroliensia*, no. 2 (2001): 36.
153 "He was very pleasant, told stories and although I was there an hour, I could barely get away." In Tibor Frank, ed., *Discussing Hitler. Advisers of U.S. Diplomacy in Central Europe 1934–1941* (Budapest: CEU Press, 2003), p. 109.
154 John Flournoy Montgomery, *Hungary the Unwilling Satellite* (Morristown: Vista Books, 1993), pp. 126–127.
155 Teleki, *Magyar politikai gondolatok*, pp. 37–38.

Transylvania on scientifically based and internationally widely approved methodology. The first step of his plan was to gain the support of the international decision makers. At the beginning of 1940 Teleki bought a very large number of books and presumably used these volumes in the preparation of the extensive memorandum that he was pleased to submit to the Foreign Office on March 6, 1940.[156] The draft was probably identical with the document that Rudolf Andorka, the Hungarian minister in Madrid, handed over to Marshall Philippe Pétain, then the French ambassador in Madrid, while János Pelényi informed Washington.[157]

The memorandum was accompanied by thirty-five attachments and it was the most composed expression of Teleki's ideas about revision. He called the war an opportunity to remedy the mistakes the peacemakers had made in 1919 in upsetting the European order. The ethnographic principles they represented had backfired on them.[158] Teleki concluded that, "We have accepted the solution although we did not believe in the principle."[159] He acknowledged that in Transylvania there was a Romanian majority even without those who settled there during the past twenty years, but he called it a mockery of the ethnic principle that in addition to three million Romanians, two million Hungarians were left in the new country. He repeated a thesis he had been citing since the beginning of the 1930s, saying, "We know very well that in order to maintain peace in Europe we cannot expect that all our demands will be met or that we will receive all that is rightfully ours." For this reason he limited the Hungarian demands to the areas along the border and the to the Székely settlements. The Hungarian population living between these two large blocks should be returned, not on ethnic principles, but according to economic reasons and strategic needs. Teleki spoke of Slovakia as well and showed clearly that he did not consider the First Vienna Award and the return of Subcarpathia as the final stage in the fate of upper Hungary. He declared that after the twenty years of Czech-Slovak symbiosis, the Hungarian and Slovak people would once again find the way to live side by side in friendship.[160]

---

156 Juhász, ed., *Magyarország külpolitikája*, pp. 728–729; and Domokos Szentiványi, "Csonkamagyarország külpolitikája" [Dismembered Hungary's foreign policy], vol. 1, fols. 302–304, Szentiványi Papers, C/80, RL. Macartney recalled the memorandum from memory in *October Fifteenth*, vol. 1, pp. 387–388; see also Bán, *Hungarian-British Diplomacy*, pp. 82–83.
157 Juhász, ed., *Magyarszag külpolitikája*, pp. 706-707; and L. Balogh, *A magyar-román kapcsolatok*, p. 89.
158 Copy handed in by György Barcza in London on March 6, 1940, TNA, FO 371, vol. 24427, fols. 45–45.
159 Ibid., fol. 47.
160 For the complete text of the memorandum, see TNA, FO 371, vol. 24428, fols. 103–133.

The response of the Foreign Office was neither supportive nor hostile.[161] His proposal was not discussed on any higher level. The British reserve reduced Teleki's ability to maneuver. He decided that he would combine his Easter vacation in Italy with some foreign policy discussions and endeavor to gain Italian support for his revisionist plans.

"I am not a machine and 1 am no longer thirty-five-years old. I believe I am entitled to a few days of rest," he told journalists about the reasons for his trip to Italy.[162] Very few were misled by this claim for a vacation. Even though the prime minister did visit his relatives in Trieste, this was not his primary goal. He had already asked from Budapest whether he might meet with the American Deputy Secretary of State Sumner Welles who was visiting in Rome. He was received by the pope and tried to contact the British ambassador in Rome.[163] He did not meet the American diplomat but they exchanged notes and the American ambassador was present at the reception at the Holy See indicating that Washington was interested in the Hungarian intentions.[164] Teleki's bad temper in Rome was made worse by the fact that he could not meet with his old acquaintance, Sir Percy Loraine, the British ambassador, and had to be satisfied in talking to the charge d'affairs.[165]

One of the purposes of the discussions with Ciano was to attempt to obtain Italy's support for a Hungarian move against Romania. Mussolini, however, told the Hungarian prime minister to be patient and added only that Romania was like an artichoke and had to be dismantled one leaf at a time.[166] Teleki also raised the question whether Italy would be prepared to defend Hungarian neutrality if Germany were to use Hungary as a transit area against Romania. This was a serious concern for London and Paris and the prime minister wished to get a clear answer. He was obviously not serious about it, as he said, because Hungary and the Hungarian army would certainly not lift a finger in Romania's defense.

---

161 Comments on the Teleki memorandum, TNA, FO 371, vol. 24427, fols. 39–43.
162 Baroness Lily Doblhoff, "Nem érdekelnek a szenzációk, ugyanabban az irányban vezetem a nemzetet, mint eddig" [I am not interested in sensations, I will lead the country along the same path as before], *Magyarország*, March 26, 1940, p. 2.
163 Juhász, ed., *Magyarország külpolitikája*, pp. 736–738.
164 "XII. Pius masfélórás kihallgatáson fogadta Teleki Pál miniszterelnököt" [Pope Pius XII received Teleki for an audience of an hour and a half], *Nemzeti Újság* [National News], March 29, 1940.
165 Report from Patrick Scrivens to section head Kirkpatrick. Rome, March 28, 1940, TNA, FO 371, vol. 24887, fols. 337–339.
166 György Réti, *Hungarian-Italian Relations in the Shadow of Hitler's Germany, 1933–1940* (Boulder, CO: Social Science Monographs, 2003), pp. 224–225.

Mussolini's answer was worrisome. He told Teleki that Hungary should give up its neutrality and even hinted that Italy might enter the war at the proper time.[167] Thus the Hungarian government received no assurance that its revisionist goals would be supported or that its neutrality would be protected. This prospect embittered him and in unofficial conversations with Ciano he lambasted the Germans, stated that he feared a German victory like the plague and hoped that Berlin would be defeated, albeit not too badly.[168] It was at the breakfast with the Italian minister of foreign affairs that the celebrated exchange took place. Teleki asked Ciano if he played bridge, "for the day when we are together in the Dachau concentration camp."[169] It was a theatrical statement and it was probably occasioned by his disappointments in Rome. He realized that there was only one path that would lead to revision, the path of German support but he was very apprehensive of taking this path. He remembered the disputes about mining rights in Subcarpathia and the bitter economic debates between Germany and Hungary at the beginning of 1940 when the German delegation under the leadership of Carl von Clodius repeatedly threatened German economic sanctions if the Hungarian government refused to adjust the mark to the pengő exchange rate in Germany's favor. This was resisted not only by the Anglophil president of the national bank but also by the Germanophil Minister of Finance Lajos Remenyi-Schneller.[170]

On arriving home he was met by a big hullabaloo. Béla Imrédy overturned the political armistice that existed since the previous autumn and at Easter initiated an attack against the government on the pages of the *Uj Magyarság*. In an article entitled "A Sincere Word about the Hungarian-German Relationship," the former prime minister claimed that a closer adaptation to German foreign policy, adoption of National Socialism and the crushing of anti-German agitation were the correct political moves for the country.[171] This manifesto caused a storm in the opposition press and this was a good excuse for the Imrédy group to force the prime minister into overt action. One hundred members of the MÉP demanded that the government suppress the "Jewish press" which was agitating against the policies of the MÉP.[172]

---

167 Juhász, ed., *Magyarország külpolitikája*, pp. 763–764.
168 Muggeridge, ed., *Ciano's Diary 1939–1943*, pp. 225–228.
169 Ibid., p. 228.
170 January 12, 1940, no. 21 on the agenda, box 204, K 27, MNL OL; Telegram from Erdmannsdorff, Budapest January 6, 1940, R 28784 (microfiche 1266), PA AA; and Ránki, Pamlényi, Tilkovszky, and Juhász, eds., *A Wilhelmstrasse és Magyarország*, no. 295.
171 P. Sipos, *Imrédy Béla*, pp. 148–149.
172 Ibid., p. 152.

Teleki tried to win over several groups leaning toward Imrédy and took a strong stand to ward off fractionation. He gave the agrarian group some positions in the leadership of the party and strengthened the censorship of the press. He railed against the ones who failed to understand, "I will do my duty until I perish but I can say that I am looking forward to it. What I have said is coming from an old man who has no more expectations in this world." Somewhat later he waved a sealed envelope before a fraction and said that it contained an order from the regent to prorogue the parliament and that he was authorized to use it at any time.[173] He claimed that this desperate and theatrical move was very successful and that the audience applauded at the end of the speech.[174] These gestures temporarily calmed the tempest within his own party and as a sign of the reestablishment of peace, on April 25, 1940, in a response to a parliamentary query he defended Imrédy against an accusation of treason.

When it appeared that, with great difficulty peace had been established, he took a step toward revision that was very difficult for him. After failures in London and Rome, he was forced to turn to Berlin. On April 17, 1940, he wrote a letter to Hitler in which he emphasized Hungary's obligations toward the Axis. He raised the possibility of tripartite, German-Italian-Hungarian negotiations so that, in view of the recent events in the Balkans and along the Danube, "discussions be started in order for all three countries being ready for all eventualities… that the discussions encompass those possibilities that lay beyond the normal measures of diplomacy and also the related political, economic and transportation issues."[175] This somewhat vague terminology covered a definite purpose. With his letter to Hitler Teleki hinted that Hungary was prepared to grant transit rights to German troops in exchange for support in the revision of Transylvanian territory.[176] This trend was suggested by Teleki's striking reluctance when the British minister in Budapest tried to get a definitive answer about the troop transit. Teleki said curtly that in this matter Hungary would not tolerate any foreign interference. Whatever Hungary would decide to do under German pressure was strictly a Hungarian matter and not subject to British pressure.[177] Through an unofficial

---

173 P. Sipos, *Imrédy Béla*, pp. 145–155.
174 Report of Minister O'Malley. Budapest, April 23, 1940, TNA, FO 371, vol. 24427, fol. 176.
175 Juhász, ed., *Magyarország külpolitikája*, pp. 771–772.
176 Juhász, *A Teleki-kormány külpolitikája*, p. 107.
177 Minister O'Malleys's report, April 23, 1940, TNA, FO 371, vol. 24427, fols. 173-182. Csáky advised the German minister about the content of the above conversation. See Ránki, Pamlényi, Tilkovszky, and Juhász, eds., *A Wilhelmstrasse és Magyarország*, no. 313.

channel he sent word to London that Hungary would not open its country for an attack against Greece, but if Transylvania were promised to Hungary, the Hungarian army could not be controlled.[178]

The letter to Hitler arrived in Berlin at the worst possible moment. Germany overran Denmark and the southern part of Norway. All of Hitler's time was taken up with planning the western campaign. The Hungarian offer did suggest, however, that Hungary was open to blackmail and this came home to Hungary during the summer at the time of the Transylvania crisis. In Berlin plans were made for a delegation to go to Hungary but Hitler's letter of May 14 stated the immutability of the Balkan situation and his adherence to the German-Soviet pact. He stated that Hungarian revisionist plans could be met only in the distant future but he made no promises whatever.[179] Teleki understood the Führer's position and emphasized that he did not wish to endanger the great changes occurring in Europe with his plans for a conference. He did also emphasize, however, that Hungary could not relinquish its revisionist goals. He was convinced that with notes and information based on scientific arguments everybody could be persuaded.

Why did he turn to Berlin? It can be seen from memoirs, but not from official documents, that while Teleki was confident that the West would win the war, his confidence could be shaken and his hesitant and musing spirit was deeply distressed by the rapid German victories in the west. Even before the start of the German offensive, he postulated that the Western victory was years away.[180] It was not the collapse of France that shook him but the fall of the small countries that were similar to Hungary, namely Denmark, Norway, Belgium, and Holland. He had one of his students write an informative article for *Magyarország* in which he stated that it was possible to proceed through the Flanders Gap in both directions and not just from east to west and that this gap would allow the Allies to get into Germany.[181] The German advance troops were approaching the English Channel and crushed the French resistance.

Ever since the Norwegian invasion Teleki saw the collapse of his foreign policy ideas and his faith in the victory of the Allies crumbled.

---

178 Letter from Sir Ronald Campbell to Section Head William Strang, May 8, 1940, TNA, FO 371, vol. 24427, fols. 168–170.
179 Ránki, Pamlényi, Tilkovszky, and Juhász, eds., *A Wilhelmstrasse és Magyarország*, no. 317.
180 Judith Listowel, *This I Have Seen* (London: Faber and Faber, 1943), pp. 205–211.
181 Personal communication from Domokos Kosáry on September 18, 2002, and Kosáry, "A flandriai kapu" [The Flanders gate], *Magyarország* (evening edition), May 18, 1940, p. 5.

His gloomy presentiment was recognized by C. A. Macartney, the British historian, who knew him and liked him.[182] On the day following his response to Hitler and at the beginning of the French collapse, he directed the Hungarian minister in Washington to return to the Hungarian National Bank the five million dollars that were sent in March 1940 to assist in the establishment of a Hungarian exile government. These plans had to be postponed.[183] The political changes wore him down. Very soon he became ill and rumors of resignation were circulating.[184] In June he made a speech that offended many. On June 17 he complimented Hitler, "the great leader of the German nation," the German soldiers standing guard at the Palace of Versailles and the "New Europe" in a speech in the House and at the grave of Gyula Gömbös.[185]

The situation forced him to issue the declaration of loyalty. On June 13 he proposed in the House a motion of conflict of interest against two Arrow Cross representatives, Kálmán Hubay and Pál Vágó and initiated an investigation.[186] This demarche against the two representatives of domestic National Socialism was triggered by these two politicians submitting a legislative proposal about nationalities that, according to the campaign initiated by Teleki and the government press, "would have meant the end of the Hungarian nation as such."[187]

The House Committee on Conflict of Interest deprived the two Arrow Cross deputies of their mandate on July 22.[188] Teleki gained some domestic policy advantage and the Arrow Cross Party was in turmoil for a while even though they enjoyed the support of some segments of the German Reich. Even though their views clashed with the German National Socialism, as the sponsors of results of the "national revolution" they were entitled to some assistance from Germany. This is the domestic policy background behind Teleki's unreserved Germanophil state-

---

182 Macartney, *October Fifteenth*, vol. 1, pp. 393–394.
183 Gyula Borbándi, "A Teleki-Pelényi terv nyugati magyar ellenkormány létesítésére" [The Teleki-Pelényi plan to establish a Hungarian exile government], *Új Látóhatár*, no. 2 (1966): 155–170.
184 Teleki, "Izgalomra nincs ok! A szénánk rendben van" [No need for excitement. Our affairs are in good order] 8 Oral Ujsag [Eight O'clock News], June 1, 1940, p. 3. See also Macartney, *October Fifteenth*, vol. 1, p. 400; and Memoirs of István Bárczy, June 16, 1945, box 14084, fol. 23, Macartney Papers, Film Collection, X 5050, MNL OL.
185 Papp, *Teleki Pál országgyűlési beszédei*, vol. 2, pp. 266–267; and "A kormány és a Magyar Élet Pártja küldöttségének élén Teleki miniszterelnök megkoszorúzta Gömbös Gyula és Apponyi Albert síremléket" [At the head of the government and the MÉP delegation, Prime Minister Teleki placed wreaths on the tombs of Gyula Gömbös, and Albert Apponyi], *Függetlenség*, June 20, 1940.
186 Papp, *Teleki Pál országgyűlési beszédei*, vol. 2, pp. 250–266.
187 Loránt Tilkovszky, "A nyilasok törvényjavaslata a nemzetiségi kérdés rendezéséről" [The Arrow Crossists legislative proposal about the regulation of the nationality question], *Századok*, no. 6 (1965): 1251.
188 Ibid., pp. 1252–1255.

ments in June. In the large-scale political game that started at the end of June Teleki needed the goodwill of Berlin more than ever before. The Soviet Union engaged in the second phase of the Molotov-Ribbentrop pact scenario and handed an ultimatum to the Bucharest government on June 26, 1940. In this ultimatum the Soviet Union demanded the transfer of Bessarabia, and even Northern Bukovina, which was not included in the secret codicils of the pact. This demarche proved to Teleki that Romania's western borders had to be changed as well.

Transylvania

For the next few months all of Teleki's attention was focused on Transylvania. "Hungary will not tolerate discrimination," he told the Council of Ministers on June 27 and this became the basis of his policy during July.[189] That same evening Döme Sztójay, the Hungarian minister in Berlin, handed a memorandum from Budapest to the Ministry of Foreign Affairs in Berlin that indicated that the Teleki government wished to negotiate with Romania about territorial matters. The request was buttressed by the government with mobilization and the army massed at the eastern border. Moscow was strikingly supportive of the Hungarian demands but Teleki declined all forms of Hungarian-Soviet joint endeavors.[190] Until July the Hungarian request was not received well in Berlin or Rome. On July 2, 1940, at 2:00 a.m. the German minister visited the sleepy minister of foreign affairs at his home and transmitted a threatening verbal communication in which he cautioned against any action that would threaten the peace in the Balkans. At the same time he did not exclude German assistance in the realization of Hungary's revisionist goals—a new and surprising development.[191] The Germans advised Budapest to practice self-control and at the same time advised Bucharest to arrange for territorial adjustments.

Teleki inundated the politicians of the Axis Powers with memoranda and maps and in these indicated that the minimum Hungary would be prepared to accept was an area of forty-eight to fifty thousand square kilometers.[2] This area would have returned to Hungary approximately 2.5 million inhabitants and amounted to

---

189 June 27, 1940, box 210, fol. 81, K 27, MNL OL.
190 László Zsigmond, ed., *Diplomáciai iratok Magyarország külpolitikájához 1936–1945* [Diplomatic Papers to Hungary's Foreign Policy], vol. 5, Magyarország külpolitikája a nyugati hadjárattól a Szovjetunió megtámadásáig 1940–1941 [Hungary's Foreign Policy from the Western Campaign to the Attack on the Soviet Union], ed. Gyula Juhász (Budapest: Akadémiai Kiadó, 1982), pp. 294–295.
191 Ránki, Pamlényi, Tilkovszky, and Juhász, eds., *A Wilhelmstrasse és Magyarország*, no. 332.

about half of the area that was detached by the Trianon treaty. This was the compromise that Teleki defined as being in the interest of both Hungary and Europe.[192]

On July 10 Hitler received the Hungarian prime minister and the minister of foreign affairs in Munich, with Ciano also being present. Teleki was not as mute this time as he had been at previous meetings. By talking about the historical and ethnographic roots of the Transylvania situation and by praising the Hungarian self-control he even outtalked the German chancellor.[193] Hitler expressed his doubts about the Hungarian army's ability to fight and also stated that the Germans in Romania did not want a change in government but was generally supportive of the Hungarian demands and recommended direct negotiations. The Hungarians obviously had hoped for a rapid settlement and that in Munich they would get started on the right road. That this did not happen made "The Magyars left dissatisfied." noted Ciano in his diary.[194]

The fact that Hitler recognized the legitimacy of the Hungarian demands was a step forward and he also promised to exert pressure on Bucharest. Thus the Transylvania question became a part of the Axis Powers' policy. Hitler tried to convince the Romanian political leaders, first in writing and then personally, that they had to give up some territory. At the end of July he received the Romanian prime minister and the minister of foreign affairs in Berchtesgaden and stated that although there was no question about the reestablishment of St. Stephen's realm, some of the Hungarian demands were legitimate.[195] The Romanian Prime Minister Ion Gigurtu, indicated that the transfer of fourteen thousand square kilometers was possible. The Hungarian demands, mentioned by Ribbentrop, were laughingly called a ludicrous hallucination by Mihail Manoilescu.[196] The good humor of the Romanian minister of foreign affairs did not last long, however. The Hungarians maneuvered very well, as shown by the linking of the Bessarabia and Transylvania matters, by working vigorously with Berlin and Rome and by a delicate combination of political and military activities.

At the ongoing Hungarian-German economic negotiations the Hungarian delegation, personally instructed by Teleki, was forced to make serious concessions

---

192 July 9, 1940, box 211, K 27, MNL OL.
193 For the report, see Juhász, ed., *Magyarország külpolitikája a nyugati hadjárattól*, p. 186; and György Ránki, ed., *Hitler hatvannyolc tárgyalása 1939–1944* [Hitler's Sixty-Eight Negotiations] (Budapest: Magvető, 1983), pp. 113–119.
194 "The Hungarians left dissatisfied," in Muggeridge, ed., *Ciano's Diary 1939–1943*, p. 275; and Juhász, A Teleki-kormány külpolitikája, p. 150.
195 L. Balogh, *A magyar-román kapcsolatok*, pp. 184–185.
196 Ibid., p. 187.

to the Germans. In the framework of the economic agreement, extended to July 31, 1941, the Hungarians gave the Germans everything they possibly could: everything that Teleki and his associates had firmly resisted until that time. The German companies were given oil exploration concessions in southern Hungary, the amount of agricultural products to be sent to Germany was increased, the mark was increased in value vis-a-vis the pengő, the market in foreign currencies was adjusted according to German demands and the requests of the Germans about customs duties were agreed to. The only thing they received in return was an increase in the price of wheat by three pengős per ton.[197]

The Hungarian government continued to send memoranda to Berlin that were received with increasing irritation by the secretary of state for foreign affairs. "Don't try to make propaganda by flooding the German government with paper," he admonished Minister Sztójay.[198] Teleki did not limit his activities to a "flood of paper" but caused his underlings and some invited historians to prepare a representative album entitled *Transylvania* that was dispatched by courier to Berlin and Rome in German and Italian translation. The prime minister supervised the preparation of the volume and made several corrections in the historical parts. He also had a young historian, a contract employee of the ministry, prepare a book on the Jewish question in Hungary in order to convince German public opinion that the Hungarian government was doing everything to resolve the problem, but that because of the magnitude of Jewish presence, the methods could not be the same as in Germany.[199] A message was received from the Göring circle that social conditions in Hungary were unsatisfactory. In response to this message Teleki explained his government's position on the Jewish question. We are not familiar with the contents of Teleki's letter and only know that it had been delivered. In view of the future developments it seems likely that Teleki promised a third anti-Jewish legislation.[200]

By the beginning of August the Hungarian-Romanian antagonisms again became more acute. Romania was willing to consider only a minimal territorial adjustment and even that only if it proved inevitable. Instead it kept emphasizing the minority problems and population exchange. A strong German move forced

---

197 Ránki, Pamlényi, Tilkovszky, and Juhász, eds., A Wilhelmstrasse és Magyarország, no. 338.
198 Ibid., no. 342.
199 Stefan Barta, *Die Judenfrage in Ungarn* (Budapest: Verlag Stadium, [194?]); and verbal communication from Domokos Kosáry, September 18, 2002.
200 Letter from Weizsäcker to Minister Sztójay, Berlin August 6, 1940, R 29785 (microfiche 1272), PA AA; and V/80, Szentiványi, "Csonkamagyarország," fols. 496-497, Szentiványi Papers, C/80, RL.

the parties into direct negotiations.[201] The Hungarian and Romanian delegations met on August 16 in Turnu Severin. The leader of the Hungarian delegation, András Hóry, the former Hungarian minister in Warsaw, was instructed personally by Teleki prior to his departure. The prime minister explained that the delegation could not ask for the return of the entire area and that the Hungarians had to exercise moderation. According to the diplomat's recollection, Teleki had no illusions about the results that could be expected from the negotiations. They would serve only to discover the weaknesses of the Romanian position and to demonstrate to Hungarian public opinion the diplomatic activities of their government. In agreement with his minister of foreign affairs, Teleki also indicated that during the negotiations the delegation had to insist on the Székely Counties, because this would bring other areas with it. Population exchange had to be resisted and autonomy by itself was not acceptable.[202] Knowing the position of the Romanian delegation, namely that delays were an important part of their program, that they emphasized territorial autonomy and population exchange, combined with minimal territorial concessions, it was evident that the chances for an agreement were negligible.

On the basis of Teleki's position, the Hungarian negotiators demanded sixty-nine thousand square kilometers from Romania. The proposed line was to go from the Trianon border to Aiud [Nagyenyed] along the Mureș River [Maros] and then north of the river Tîrnava Mare [Nagy-Küküllő] in an arc toward the Székely Counties. Between Tîrgu Mureș [Marosvásárhely] and Sighișoara [Segesvár] the line would proceed due south and reach the historical border along the Carpathians to the west of Brașov [Brassó]. The Romanian plan envisioned a minimal territorial adjustment and a population exchange. It was only at the last moment that they presented their territorial proposal to the Hungarian delegation and this was completely unacceptable to Budapest.[203]

When it became apparent that the positions would not change, Hóry returned to Budapest to report personally to the Council of Ministers. Hearing his report, Teleki declared that he knew what the final conclusion of the negotiations would mean. It was the German government that asked him to negotiate. This did not lead to any results. "Transylvania was a matter of life and death for Hungary, the *ultima ratio*. No concessions could be made," he added. "The Hungarian nation

---

201 L. Balogh, *A magyar-román kapcsolatok*, p. 223.
202 András Hóry, *Bukaresttől Varsóig* [From Bucharest to Warsaw] (Budapest: Gondolat, 1987), pp. 312–315.
203 L. Balogh, *A magyar-román kapcsolatok*, pp. 229–234.

has shouted 'no, no, never' for twenty-one years. We cannot tell the nation to shout 'yes, yes for ever.' The die is cast." The ministers accepted this position.[204] Hóry returned to Turnu Severin but further negotiations were not productive and the discussions came to an end one day later on August 24. It appeared that war was the only solution.

During these weeks and months Teleki was gambling. He did not wish to cooperate with the Soviet Union and although he did everything to obtain German support, including economic agreements, declarations to take care of the Jewish question and a flood of memoranda and maps, his purpose was not to force a German-Italian arbitration panel. He thought that only an armed conflict could extricate him and his cabinet from an irreversible and complete unilateral commitment. In case of a military solution he hoped that Germany would not help Romania or, if after a few days it would become involved, it would support Hungary. He was not getting ready for an extended armed conflict and therefore, in spite of the urging of the chief of the General Staff, he did not order the organization of air defenses for Budapest and the larger cities around the country.[205] He wanted a bloodletting. He was convinced that the nation had to bring sacrifices which it had not done with previous territorial acquisitions.

He was disappointed in the administration distorting the principles of nationality policies, in the revision, in public opinion that recognized no restrictions and no perspectives. He was also disappointed in the middle class cursed with foreign policy blindness and in the political elite. He had already commented bitterly in August 1939 about the contradictory administrative actions in the regained territories and he was very concerned about the Transylvania revision. He said that he had no hesitation to tell the Council of Ministers that unless there were some fundamental changes made, he would take the opportunity to speak before the public and tell them that under such conditions the country should not endeavor to acquire new territories for itself.[206] He was pessimistic at the end of August as well and did not believe that an armed conflict could be avoided. In a deep depression he blamed himself and considered the situation a crime. Not because of the probability of armed conflict, but because he was concerned that the Germans would take action against Hungary to stop the armed conflict.[207]

---

204 Committee, August 22, 1940, no. 1 on the agenda, box 212, K 27, MNL OL.
205 Committe, July 12, 1940, no. 30 on the agenda, box 211, K 27, MNL OL.
206 Minutes of the Council of Ministers, August 17, 1940, no. 54 on the agenda, box 202, K 27, MNL OL.
207 Juhász, *A Teleki-kormány külpolitikája*, pp. 183–184; and Macartney, *October Fifteenth*, vol. 1, pp. 417–418.

Soldiers on furlough were called back and additional units were mobilized. Oddly enough, it was a soldier, Henrik Werth, the chief of the General Staff, who indicated to Cuno Fütterer, the air attache at the German legation in Budapest, that Hungary was willing to go to arbitration. Minister of Foreign Affairs Csáky made similar statements.[208] The Axis took action and Hitler, after consultations with Ciano, wished to settle the matter by arbitration. In reaching such a decision he was not trying to inflame the two countries against each other in a Machiavellian fashion, but just the opposite. He wished, at all costs, to have peace in southeast Europe and undisturbed productivity in the Romanian oil fields. He did not view this solution as a temporary one albeit later he profited from the opportunity to raise the question of Southern Transylvania.

Representatives of the two countries were invited by Berlin to come to Vienna on August 29. The delegation was formally under the leadership of Csáky with Teleki attending as a regular member. The arbitrators demanded that the delegations come with previous firm and unconditional authorization from their government that regardless of where the final border would be set, they would accept it. The Hungarians immediately accepted this condition and the Romanians, after some hesitation and bargaining, did as well.[209]

The Second Vienna Award is well known. The arbitration results announced on August 30, 1940, at the Belvedere Palace returned more than forty-three thousand square kilometers from the area taken away from Hungary in 1920, with two and a half million inhabitants. Of this group 52 percent were Hungarian, according to Hungarian statistics, and 38 percent according to the Romanian ones. In Southern Transylvania, remaining with Romania, there were about four hundred thousand Hungarians while one million Romanians came to Hungary with Northern Transylvania. The Hungarian delegation viewed with satisfaction that Manoilescu, who earlier had laughed at the Hungarian demands, fainted at the table when the new border was proclaimed.[210] In Vienna the Germans made Hungary sign a German-Hungarian minority agreement that recognized the *Volksbund* as the only and exclusive representative of the ethnic German minority in Hungary and which also gave the Germans minority rights which the Teleki government had steadfastly

---

208 Lóránd Dombrády, *Hadsereg és politika Magyarországon 1938–1944* [The Army and Politics in Hungary] (Budapest: Kossuth, 1986), pp. 140–142. There are no references to this statement in Dombrady's otherwise very richly documented work.
209 August 29, 1940, no. 1 on the agenda, box 213, K 27, MNL OL; and L Balogh, *A magyar-román kapcsolatok*, pp. 294–297.
210 Muggeridge, ed., *Ciano's Diary 1939–1943*, p. 287.

refused.[211] No wonder that on the way back from Vienna Teleki went into a profound depression so that the train had to stop in Komárom to get some medication for the prime minister.[212]

At the Eastern Railway Station [Keleti pályaudvar] a huge crowd welcomed the returning delegation. Teleki allowed his minister of foreign affairs to take the lead and only gave a short address in which he spoke of self- examination, the mistakes of parents and forefathers, responsibility, work and conscience. He also stated emphatically that nobody should bluster about and abuse the trust and values of the nation.[213] One day later he handed in his resignation to Horthy. In this he prominently mentioned to excessive power of the military, naming Werth the chief of the General Staff as an example. He cautioned the regent against the soldiers and against the "old liberal politicians" like Bethlen.[214] He asked that he be made the commissioner for Transylvania.[215] Horthy and his associates convinced him to stay on and on September 3 he formally announced the return of Northern Transylvania in the House.[216] He emphasized that Hungary had sought an agreement with Romania but that Romania was unwilling to make any compromise. He asked the Hungarian politicians to be more peaceful and to follow the St. Stephen ideals on national politics. He also announced that nationality representatives would be hired into the administration.[217]

The Great Powers which were independent of Germany received the news in various ways. Churchill declared in the House of Commons that even though he never approved of the way Hungary was treated after the previous war, this type of dictate was not regarded as permanent by Great Britain. Foreign Secretary Halifax spoke similarly in the House of Lords. The speech of Anthony Eden, the future foreign secretary, was not well received in Hungary. He said that after the war London wished to see a "proper and just" border arrangement in central and eastern Europe. The Foreign Office staff saw the Second Vienna Award as an unmistakable sign of Hungary having become even more of a German satellite.[218] In Moscow officials

211 Spannenberger, *Der Volksbundder Deutschen*, p. 214.
212 Gyula Dessewffy, "Emlékeim Teleki Pálról" [My recollections about Pál Teleki], in *Teleki Pál és kora*, ed. Csicsery-Rónay and Vígh, pp. 34–35.
213 "Ünnepélyes fogadtatás a Keleti-pályaudvaron" [Festive reception at the Eastern Railway Station], *Esti Újság* [Evening News], August 31, 1940, p. 4.
214 Szinai and Szűcs, eds., *Horthy Miklós titkos iratai*, pp. 234–238.
215 Ránki, Pamlényi, Tilkovszky, and Juhász, eds., *A Wilhelmstrasse és Magyarország*, no. 348.
216 Report of Béla Kovrig, Budapest, September 6, 1940, cs. 1, dossier c, fols. 194-197, K. 29, MNL OL.
217 Teleki, *Válogatott politikai írások*, ed. Ablonczy, pp. 415–424.
218 Bán, *Hungarian-British Diplomacy*, pp. 99–100.

were ambiguous about the Hungarian territorial acquisition. When the Turnu Severin discussions broke up, Molotov was supportive of Hungary but, in consideration of Germany, he did not encourage a Hungarian armed invasion. The United States Department of State showed understanding.[219]

Teleki devoted all his energies, as he said, to reorganize the regained territory.[220] Even before marching in on September 4, he promised ten million pengős to Transylvania to be managed by the newly established Transylvania Social Organization.[221] He assigned government representatives, picked by him personally, to the army entering Transylvania.[222] The lower military commands permitted all sorts of excesses, wished to do everything themselves and frequently confronted the civilian authorities, getting installed at the end of November, with faits accomplish.[223] It is also true that the prime minister, illogically, provided the soldiers arguments and means that they could use against his policies. The relationship between the nationalities was seriously damaged by the atrocities that occurred during the occupation even though there were only a few of them. In some places the Hungarian troops massacred armed and unarmed Romanian civilians or stood by when the Hungarian civil population "revenged" old injuries. The worst incident occurred in Szilagyipp [Ip] where 157 people, including women and children, were killed. In Ördögkút [Trezna] there were eighty dead and in Márkaszék [Marca] nine.[224] Teleki was aware of the gravity of the events but in the House he made light of it.[225] He told the British minister, "You can't have a marriage without some broken crowns" which was about as cynical as it could be.[226] He was fully aware of the damage these actions caused to his nationality policies. Covering up the tragic

---

[219] Montgomery, *Hungary the Unwilling Satellite*, pp. 119–120; and L. Balogh, *A magyar-román kapcsolatok*, p. 308.

[220] "Teleki Pál Szegeden: 'Bele kell feküdnünk a visszatért országrészek talpraállításába'" [Pál Teleki in Szeged: "We must do everything to assist the returned areas"], *Esti Újság*, November 11, 1940, p. 3.

[221] Minutes of the Council of Ministers, September 4, 1940, no. 1 on the agenda, box 213, K 27, MNL OL.

[222] Minutes of the Council of Ministers, September 4, 1940, no. 42 on the agenda, box 213, K 27, MNL OL.

[223] Zsuzsanna Simon, "Észak-Erdély köz- és szakigazgatása a második bécsi döntés után" [Northern Transylvania's civil and special administration after the Second Vienna Award], *REGIO*, no. 4 (1995): 60–82. . See recently: Tamás Sárándi (ed.): *Levezényelt visszacsatolás. A magyar katonai közigazgatás Észak-Erdélyben, 1940.* [Ordered reannexation. The Hungarian Military Administration in Northern Transylvania, 1940] Miercurea Ciuc/Csíkszereda: 2017, Pro-Print.

[224] Péter Illésfalvi, "'Édes Erdély itt vagyunk'— Az 1940-es erdélyi bevonulás során történt atrocitásokról" ["Sweet Transylvania, here we are." The atrocities committed during the reoccupation of Transylvania in 1940], *Pro Minoritate*, no. 1 (Spring 2004): 58–77.

[225] *Képviselőházi napló, 1939–1944*, vol. 7, pp. 26–27.

[226] Report from Minister O'Malley to Foreign Secretary Anthony Eden, Budapest, April 4, 1941, TNA, FO 371, vol. 26628, fols. 15–21.

events could be explained by the fact that there were equal atrocities committed against the Hungarians who remained in Southern Transylvania and Hungarian public opinion would not have been willing to ask for an accounting or show of any remorse.

In Romania there was practically a revolution after the Second Vienna Award. The hitherto banned Iron Guardists were now admitted to the government of General Ion Antonescu who personally organized the antiminority demonstrations. There soon began a flood of refugees. Teleki reacted in a very myopic way. He made a statement on September 18 and sent the message to the people beyond the borders that the twelve to fifteen thousand refugees could not be provided with jobs even temporarily. The ones already present should not be forced out but should be encouraged to return home as soon as possible.[227] From a national perspective it would have been desirable for the Hungarians to remain at home and thus serve as an argument later on for the return of Southern Transylvania. Soon, however, the number of refugees from Romania increased to the point where the prime minister had to yield.

In October 1940 the Council of Ministers set up the National Refugee Commission that attempted to channel the flood of refugees, take care of the needy, and deflect those who should have stayed at home. In October Teleki tried to reciprocate and a number of Romanian intellectuals and officials were expelled from Kolozsvár [Cluj] and put across the border. This only made the situation worse. In this most awkward situation it was practically impossible to make the correct decisions. Discouraging the refugees suggested that the government did not regard the Vienna Award as the final word on the borders. All this, however, did not alter the fact that almost 200,000 Hungarians fled from Southern Transylvania between 1940 and 1944. Their exodus completely disrupted the Hungarian groups in Turda [Torda], Petroșani [Petrozsény], Arad [Arad], and Brașov [Brassó] with consequences that are evident even today.[228]

Teleki might have foreseen the consequences but did not look that far ahead. He devoted his suddenly revived activities to the organization of the political and economic life of Transylvania. He sent Boy Scout officers to Transylvania to perform certain social and organizational duties and used newspaper articles to out-

---

227 Minutes of the Council of Ministers, September 18, 1940, no. 22 on the agenda, box 214, K 27, MNL OL.
228 Béni L. Balogh, "Az erdélyi magyar menekültkérdés 1939 és 1944 között" [The question of Hungarian refugees from Transylvania between 1939 and 1944], *Régió*, nos. 3–4 (1999): 250–257.

line the tasks to be performed under the new conditions.²²⁹ In his bubbling enthusiasm he declared at the beginning of October that, "the appointed Romanian representatives will be seated in the House within two weeks."²³⁰ The Romanian representatives actually never sat in the Hungarian parliament. He was concerned even with such trivia as the facade of certain buildings being too ornate and needing to be rebuilt.²³¹ In the middle of October he had eighty-three new university professors, who had had been working in Szeged, appointed to the Kolozsvár [Cluj] University. These appointees included young and hitherto unknown experts including a number of his proteges, Zoltán Takáts Felvinczi, András Rónai, and his own son, Géza Teleki.²³²

The central events of the organized reintegration of Transylvania were the two conferences held in Kolozsvár. On September 23 Teleki attempted to lay down the operational guidelines of the Transylvania Social Organization. He stated that he, himself, was the leader of the organization. "I am a Transylvanian first and prime minister only second" and that the most urgent task was the preparation of the Székely Counties for the coming winter. He urged all the attendees to come up with individual solutions and to organize social assistance on an individual basis.²³³

Four weeks later he presented his views in a similar staccato fashion at the two-day monster meeting in Kolozsvár to which everybody was invited who had any role in Transylvania politics. The purpose of the meeting, from which the press was excluded, was to find solutions for Transylvania's social, cultural, and educational problems. He assured the participants that the military administration would come to an end soon.²³⁴ At the conference Teleki started his speech with cultural concerns and indicated that he wished to support denominational schools in Transylvania. He commented on every issue that was in any way linked to his earlier studies, investigations or experiences. He spoke of agricultural education, after all he did go to Magyaróvár; he spoke of economic geography, he spoke of education,

---

229 Count Pál Teleki, "Erdélyi feladatok" [Transylvanian tasks], *Keleti Újság* [Southern News], September 22, 1940, pp. 1–3.
230 "Teleki miniszterelnök érdekes beszámolóbeszéde a MÉP értekezletén" [Prime Minister Teleki's interesting report at the MÉP meeting], *Népszava*, October 2, 1940, p. 3.
231 Letter from Bálint Hóman to Lajos Reményi-Schneller, Budapest October 9, 1940, cs. 3, dossier i, K 37, MNL OL.
232 October 17, 1940, no. 34 on the agenda, box 215, K 27, MNL OL.
233 Record of the Kolozsvár [Cluj] social conference, Kolozsvár, September 23, 1940 (fragment), cs. 267, no. 83/1940, K 53, MNL OL. About the whole event, see: Attila Szavári: Teleki Pál Erdély-politikájáról: értekezletek Erdélyben. [About the Transylvania-politics of Pál Teleki: conferences in Transylvania]. *Magyar Kisebbség* [Hungarian Minority] 16, (2011), pp. 191-282.
234 Minutes on Transylvania, fols. 6-8, K 28, MNL OL.

was he not the chairman of the Public Education Council; of the Transylvania Technical University, after all he was a professor at the Budapest one; diaspo- ras, because he was an expert on nationality geography; language instruction, he had been a minister of education; administration, he did work for a few months as a honorary district administrator. He also had some comments on Hungarian in Moldavia, the Csangós. He could not say enough about his own competencies and frequently shouted down the attendees with loud references to his experiences.

On a comment by István Bethlen, he reinforced what the former prime minister asked for and indicated that teaching Romanian in Hungarian secondary schools would be required and he also wished to preserve the Romanian language in university education so that the graduates would be able to administer their areas and communicate with their people.[235] On the afternoon of the first day economic issues were discussed, principally working hours, tax breaks and other social issues and the provision of railways and hard-surface roads to the entire area.[236] It was on the second day that he used the sentence that illustrated his entire perspective, "I am neither a radical nor a conservative. I try to think logically." An hour later he added, "I have always considered myself to be apolitical and it is my endeavor to remain that way and to disembarrass myself of everything that smacks of politics."[237] This platitude reflects Teleki's constant endeavor to indicate that his policies were scientific and rational.

He also participated in the sessions of the Transylvania Economic Council where the agenda included tourism, cooperatives, changes in the tax system and the Jewish question.[238] In the two-hundred-page record of the meeting the comments of the prime minister are the most frequent entries. When reading his comments it is difficult to avoid the feeling that he was not really interested in what problems would be discussed. His comments were a two-day long press statement, the presentation of his views and a report to the Transylvanian elite about the activities of their former colleague during the past twenty years, after he had fled to Hungary. During the reattachment of Northern Transylvania he acted on his own. There was no sum too large to be assigned unhesitatingly to the development of Northern Transylvania's social infrastructure. The construction of the Déda-Szeretfalva [Deda-Sârăţel] railroad and the improvements of the Beszterce-Dés segment were

---

235 Ibid., fols. 37–38.
236 Ibid., fols. 63-72.
237 Ibid., fols. 132, and 153.
238 Records of the Economic Council of Transylvania [Erdelyrészi Gazdasági Tanács], including the record of the Kolozsvár meeting, cs. 267, fols. 2–29, K 28, MNL OL.

estimated to cost fifty-six million pengős by 1942. This corresponded to the annual budget of the Ministry of Foreign Affairs. This was only one of several similar investments.

Examining the activities of the government, it is clear that the number one goal of the Teleki government was the reintegration of Transylvania, ahead of all other concerns, including the Jewish question, land reform and social legislation. The head of the government preferred to govern by edict and of all the 558 edicts issued between September 1, 1940, and April 3, 1941, 127 (25 percent) dealt with the Transylvanian and eastern Hungaran territorial reintegration, while the number of edicts dealing in any way with the Jewish question amounted only to 30 (6 percent).

The more than forty Transylvanian representatives appointed to the House in October served the prime minister well because it was at this time that Imrédy and eighteen of his followers resigned from the government party and formed the extreme right-wing Magyar Megújulás Pártja [Party of Hungarian Renewal]. A number of Imrédy's admirers remained in the MEP. The danger of the new group was that henceforth the extreme right was not represented by the uncouth and unacceptable Arrow Crossist rabble working with terrorist techniques, but by highly educated experts, politicians and intellectuals who had many admirers in administration and in the government party. None of the twelve seats reserved for the Romanians, few though they were, was filled.

In some respects the Second Vienna Award caused significant changes in Teleki's nationality policy ideas. Autonomy as a solution was jettisoned. He did not think that it could be implemented in Transylvania, or anywhere else. In July 1940 he submitted a legislative proposal to the House on autonomy for Ruthenia, but it was never debated and the prime minister withdrew it after a short while. It was opposed by the military and by the Hungarian representatives. Some of the Ruthenian representatives, like András Bródy and his group, also opposed autonomy.[239] Teleki also wrote off Subcarpathian autonomy and appointed Miklós Kozma as governor in September 1940.[240] The strong-handed, imaginative former military officer was not in favor of autonomy and aspired to the role of governor for some time. He lived up to the expectations of the prime minister, even though he held the position for only one year. In Ungvár [Užgorod], Kozma established a Ruthe-

---

239 Géza Vasas, "A félbehagyott alkotmány. Kárpátalja autonomiájának ügye 1939–194-ben" [The abandoned constitution. The case of the Subcarpathian autonomy], in *Kárpátalja 1938–41-ben. Magyar és ukrán történeti közelítés* [Subcarpathia 1938–41. Hungarian-Ukrainian Historical Approaches], ed. Csilla Fedinec (Budapest: Teleki László Alapítvány, 2004), pp. 196–215.
240 Ormos, *Egy magyar médiavezér: Kozma Miklós*, pp. 719–725.

nian scientific association, started a periodical, stimulated the intellectual life of the region, warded off efforts to make things more Hungarian, and handled the Jewish question according to the demands of the government, i.e. with strictness.

The Second Vienna Award forced Teleki to change his ideas in another area as well, the management of the ethnic German minority.

He had objected to the activities of those people and to Berlin's meddling ever since the 1920s and he also disliked their attempts to preserve their culture and interests. Teleki looked with undisguised suspicion at Franz Basch, the leader of the Volksbund and was unwilling to even receive him for a while after the Vienna award. On their rare encounters he questioned the loyalty of the leaders of the ethnic Germans. On such occasions he hinted broadly that he considered assimilation as the only desirable outcome.[241] Initially he did not even wish to announce the nationality group agreement as a legal act, but Berlin insisted. In the end it was issued as an ordinance and not as an act, thereby further indicating the prime minister's resistance.[242] None of the Hungarian governments approved the bylaws of the Volksbund until the spring of 1944. It was the prospect of preventing the Volksbund's intentions that guided Teleki when he participated in the preparations for the census planned for 1941. In doing this he came into opposition with the president and staff of the Central Statistics Office. The experts objected to the census having a separate entry for nationality and language. Teleki insisted and in order to get his way he assigned the management and supervision of the census to experts whom he trusted.

Additional Reforms

While all of Teleki's energy was devoted to Transylvania, the clouds gathered over the Hungary with the Trianon borders. As a consequence of the amnesty announced after the return of Transylvania, Ferenc Szálasi leader of the Arrow-Cross party was released from prison in Szeged. Following his release Teleki met with him. Nothing much happened at the meeting. Teleki and the Arrow Cross leader allegedly looked at maps sitting by the fireplace. Teleki presumably had the idea of guiding the broad national socialist alliance taking place at the beginning of October and its leader into a sober and more constructive direction.[243] To prove his good inten-

---

241 Gerhard Seewann and Norbert Spannenberger, eds., *Akten des Volksgerichtprozesses gegen Franz Basch, Volksgruppenführer in Ungarn*, Budapest 1945–46 (Munich: Oldenbourg, 1999), pp. 282, and 286.
242 RT 1940. vol.4, no. 644.
243 Laczkó, *Nyilasok, nemzetiszocialisták 1935–1944*, pp. 235–236.

tion the government, on September 25, 1940, revoked ordinance 3400/1938 that was considered one of the greatest injuries to the Arrow Cross cause. Henceforth government employees could belong to political parties.[244]

The only result of the encounter was to give some measure of respectability to the Arrow Crossists who were busy organizing the largest miners' strike between the two wars. The Arrow Crossist organizing endeavors found a fruitful soil in the mining region because the mines were under military supervision, frequently operated in an arbitrary fashion and because the elections and government's anti-labor union policies kept the Social Democrats out of the area. Beginning early in September there were scattered work stoppages in some of the Nógrad area mines. Two days after the Teleki-Szálasi meeting, on October 7, the day when the Imrédy group left the government party, it became known that the government was proposing a 7 percent pay increase for industrial and mine workers. This caused the immediate outbreak of a huge strike. The movement started in the Salgótarján basin on October 8 but it was soon joined by miners from the Pécs, Dorog and Tatabánya mines and from the small mines scattered around the country. Within days 90 percent of all mine workers (40,000) were on strike. The situation was made worse by the fact that the forces ordered out to confront the miners were led by right-wing officers who sided with the miners. The situation became increasingly critical. The coal supplies of the Hungarian National Railways, of the factories, and of Budapest dwindled and the threat of a revolution, which would be followed by a German invasion, loomed. This did not happen. The government yielded to the miners, the officers siding with the miners were dismissed and then the military took forceful steps against the strikers. After cautiously supporting the strike for two weeks the Arrow Crossists backed off and the strike movement collapsed by the end of October.[245]

The wage movement confirmed Teleki in his intentions to pursue the social policy program of the government. The most spectacular step in the direction was the establishment of the National Individual and Family Assistance Fund (ONCSA). After an almost six-months-long debate the government accepted the legislative proposal during the summer of 1940. In the fall the legislators endorsed it. It would have been ONCSA's task to relieve the Treasury of some burdens and to provide social services such as home construction assistance and health care from a nation-

---

244 Minutes of the Council of Ministers, September 25, 1940, no. 39 on the agenda, box 214, K 27, MNL OL.
245 József Szekeres, "Az 1940 évi általános bányászsztrájk története" [History of the 1940 miners' general strike], *Századok*, nos. 1–2 (1967): 82–137; and Szöllősi-Janze, *Die Pfeilkreutzlerbewegung in Ungarn*, pp. 178–183.

ally based, powerful new organization. ONCSA, functioning as a Ministry of Social Services, implemented comprehensive and effective government social policies even though they could do little to ease the country's woes. Its most permanent activity was the rural home building program under which until 1944 almost 100,000 of the poorest members of society received a healthy home, a lot, and a chance to manage.[246]

Another lesson of the October miners' strike for Teleki was that he realized that it was insufficient to rely on an administrative structure and that parallel flexible organizations had to be established or the existing ones had to be modified. A characteristic of the organizations established by him were always information, propaganda, and education. In the Prime Minister's Office the Information Policy Department was set up under the leadership of his former pupil, Domokos Szentiványi. Its tasks were collecting information, publishing scientific and propaganda documents, supervision of organizations and structures having foreign contacts, such as the Revision League and the World Alliance of Hungarians (Magyarok Világszövetsége), and guiding the defensive and offensive nationality activities.[247]

The other propaganda organization that worked within the country was the Social Policy Department in the Prime Minister's Office. The section was established at the time of Imrédy. Its tasks included providing information to the residents of the villages, lectures, survey and upgrading of trashy literature, the transmission of the works of authors who were seen as being close to the people and who were constructive in their approach, broadcasting educational programs, organizing expositions, providing grants and stipends, formulating movie and broadcast policies and organizing independent women's movements.[248] Naturally ten associates were insufficient for this task and immediately turf battles started between the Ministry of Culture and Education and this new organization. The latter had an informational service available consisting mostly of members of the Catholic organizations. It was with their assistance that a leaflet war against the Arrow Crossists was

---

246 Katalin Berey, Szociálpolitikai kísérlet Magyarországon a 40-es évek elején [A social political experiment in Hungary at the beginning of the 1940s] (Budapest: A Művelődési Minisztérium Marxizmus-Leninizmus Oktatási Főosztálya, 1981), pp. 12–54, and 77.
247 Feljegyzés a Miniszterelnökség IV. Osztályának megalakulásáról, feladatköréről és első 18. havi működéséről, Budapest, 1941. majus 1. [Notes on the establishment, responsibilities and accomplishments of the Fourth Department of the Prime Minister's Office during its first 18 months], Budapest, May 1, 1941, Szentiványi Papers, box 3, t. 10, C/80, RL.
248 Péter Hámori, "Kísérlet egy 'propagandaminisztérium' létrehozására Magyarországon" [Experiment to create a propaganda ministry in Hungary], *Századok*, no. 2 (1997): 356–357.

started and in this it could count on the support of a number of veterans groups and other professional organizations, supported by the Prime Minister's Office. These organizations operated traveling libraries, published brochures and held educational conferences.[249] The system perfectly reflected Teleki's ideas, built on parallelism, rejecting the traditional and official system and susceptible to romantic dreams.

While making some changes in how various parts of his office functioned, Teleki also made some changes in his government. In December 1940 he dismissed Mihály Teleki, the minister of agriculture, and appointed Dániel Bánffy in his place. The dismissal of Mihály Teleki had been whispered about since the previous summer, presumably because he stood too close to the Imrédy fraction of the government party. Teleki appointed his university colleague, Dezső Laky, to be the minister of public food supplies and Reményi-Schneller became minister of economics in addition to his responsibilities as minister of finance. Reményi-Schneller's fight with the president of the Hungarian National Bank progressed to the point where the minister, claiming ill health, handed in his resignation at the end of March 1941. Events prevented a discussion of his letter.[250]

His government was working on two major domestic policy matters, in addition to the passing of the 1941 budget in November-December 1940. Neither of the two came to fruition but both were started on Teleki's initiative and were monitored by him. One was the corporate constitution proposal and the other one was the preparation of the third anti-Jewish law.

Reforming the constitution was an old dream of his and he also wanted to use this path to negate the radical, extreme right plans for restructuring the country.[251] Teleki's attraction to a corporative structure began in the early 1930s and was a European idea of the times. The idea was ripening in his thinking about political systems and the papal encyclical of 1931, *Quadragesimo Anno,* supported his ideas. The 1926 reconstitution of the Upper House already had corporative overtones. Many members of Hungarian public life believed that a professional government, restructured according to Italian, German, or Portuguese models, was more suitable for meeting the demands of the day. It would do away with party fights and instead of barren politicking would concentrate on the solution of problems and its

---

249 Ibid.
250 Letter from Lajos Reményi-Schneller to Pál Teleki. March 28, 1941, Budapest People's Court, Criminal Records, box 282, Nb. 628/46, Sztójay and fellow defendants, fol. 2098, XXV, 1 a, BFL.
251 "A parlamenti rendszer elfajulása miatt sürgős az országgyűlés reformja" [Because of the degeneracy of the parliamentary system a revision of the National Assembly has become urgent], *Nemzeti Újság*, November 6, 1940.

activities would be a better expression of its drive for modernity. Teleki was most deeply impressed by the example of the Portuguese head of state, Antonio de Oliveira Salazar. They were linked by a similar scientific background and by the size and marginal position of their countries as well as by their deeply felt faith. Teleki wrote the preface to a Hungarian language edition of Salazar's selected speeches.[252] According to the constitutional proposal, the Upper and Lower Houses would have been filled by representatives of the professional working groups and the administrative delegates selected and sent by the counties. The political parties would either disappear entirely or would, at least be sharply curtailed. He had no plans for the nationalities and would have discontinued the inherited right of the aristocracy to sit in the Upper House.[253]

The plan was not much to the liking of the dignitaries to whom he had sent it. The mixed reception of his plan did not initially discourage him and he called himself the "priest of the nation" when he was working on the reforms. Yet, at the beginning of 1941, he stopped talking about it. The increasingly complex foreign policy matters at the turn of 1940 and 1941 were not conducive to major legislative innovations. While Teleki was clearly anxious to strengthen the powers of the prime minister he was not an advocate of a totalitarian dictatorship. In addition to his convictions, his character traits also made him unsuitable for such a position.

Concerning the third anti-Jewish law, there is no doubt that it was Teleki who initiated the planning for it. In the electoral campaign, in May 1939, he still said, "we have passed the anti-Jewish legislation and with this the matter is closed. Let no one think about a third anti-Jewish legislation. We have more important things to do."[254] The extreme right-wing opposition started agitating within days of the election and demanded a third, more radical anti-Jewish legislation. Teleki resisted these demands for some time albeit a number of ordinances were issued during 1940 further restricting the rights of the Hungarian Jews. The Israelite (Jewish) denomination lost its right to be represented in the Upper House and in the reattached territories the citizens who were considered Jews could no longer serve on municipal-and/or local boards.[255] Other lesser ordinances also made the life of the Hungarian Jews more difficult. In March the minister of industry announced the steps taken to disenfranchise the Jewish companies that controlled 80 percent of

---

252 Oliveira Salazar, *Békés forradalom* [Peaceful Revolution] (Budapest: Atheneaum, 1941).
253 Teleki, *Válogatott politikai írások*, ed. Ablonczy, pp. 443–463.
254 Teleki, *Beszédek 1939*, p. 74; and "Beszél a miniszterelnök" [The prime minister speaks], *Új Magyarság*, May 12, 1939, pp. 2–3.
255 Gyurgyák, *A zsidókérdés Magyarországon*, pp. 152–153, and n. 167.

the sugar trade.²⁵⁶ There were regulations about the Jewish labor battalion service and in May 1940 a separate chamber of film producers was set up ²⁵⁷ and certain Jewish businesses were forced to be open on Saturdays.²⁵⁸ The compensation of those who lost their jobs as the consequence of the anti-Jewish legislation was reduced, and in March 1941, Act IV of 1939 was extended to Northern Transylvania.²⁵⁹ The land reform also affected the Jewish land owners and renters more than others. It is also true, however, that in the Highland more Jewish attorneys were admitted to the Lawyers' Guild than was permitted under the law.²⁶⁰

In an answer to an interpellation in the House in June 1940, Teleki indicated a willingness to introduce new and more restrictive legislation.²⁶¹ At the Prime Minister's Office a collection of material on Jewish history was begun.²⁶² The prime minister's thoughts were reflected in some of the passages in a volume referred to earlier. They included complete segregation, dealing with Jewish capital and assets, and a rapid resettlement in association with actions initiated by the Axis Powers.²⁶³ The first draft was considered too lenient by Teleki and therefore the drafters made it more stringent.²⁶⁴ In response to a parliamentary question Teleki stated in October that, "a simple, clear, radically simple anti-Jewish legislative proposal was being drafted."²⁶⁵ At the end of the year he announced that a new law was being readied.²⁶⁶ At that time Jews were excluded from the Boy Scout movement. At the end of the year Teleki wrote an article in an MÉP bulletin in which he justified the need for the new legislation by saying that the intellectuals of the capital were corrupted by being permeated with the Jewish spirit. He mitigated the rigidity of his position by agreeing not to deprive all livelihood of "800,000 people and another 200,000 mixed ones." According to the plans of the prime minister this would mean a grace period in the economy lasting from one to five years.²⁶⁷

---

256 Minutes of the Council of Ministers, March 4, 1940, no. 11 on the agenda, box 205, K 27, MNL OL.
257 Minutes of the Council of Ministers, May 31,1940, no. 9 on the agenda, box 209, K 27, MNL OL
258 Ibid., no. 21 on the agenda.
259 1941, vol. 4, no. 92, RT.
260 Minutes of the Council of Ministers, April 12, 1940, no. 14 on the agenda, box 206, K 27, MNL OL.
261 Papp, *Teleki Pál országgyűlési beszédei*, vol. 2, p. 305.
262 File labeled "Jewish matters," cs. 2, dossier h, K 29, MNL OL.
263 Barta, *Die Judenfrage in Ungarn*, pp. 193–196.
264 Report to the Ministry of Foreign Affairs, Berlin, November 19, 1940, R 101157, (microfiche, 3004), PA AA.
265 Teleki, *Válogatott politikai írasok*, ed. Ablonczy, pp. 437–442.
266 "Gróf Teleki Pál a MÉP országos értekezletén" [Count Pál Teleki at the National Conference of MEP], *Magyar Nemzet* [Hungarian Nation], December 17, 1940, p. 4.
267 "Teleki Pál gróf miniszterelnök a társadalom feladatairól" [Prime Minister Count Pál Teleki on the tasks of society], *Függetlenség*, December 25, 1940.

Work on the third anti-Jewish law was initiated by Teleki and the available documents indicate that his solution, as far as Jewish fortunes were concerned, was more severe than the legislative proposal submitted by his successor that dealt primarily with a ban on intermarriage between Christian and Jew. On March 21, 1941, Teleki announced to the government party that five meetings had taken place discussing the final forms of the anti-Jewish legislation and that the proposal would be submitted shortly.[268] It seems as though the sinful and tragic consequences of his ideology never entered into Teleki's conscience. In August 1940, for instance, he wrote a letter to Bálint Hóman, the minister of education in which he asked as a favor that an employee of the Sociographic Institute, who was of Jewish extraction, be allowed to do his practice teaching in one of the Budapest high schools. According to the existing anti-Jewish legislation this was not permissible and, in fact Hóman refused to comply.[269] Teleki believed firmly that there were great principles but that these had little to do with everyday life, at least in his proximity, and that he was familiar with all possible exceptions to the rule.

The Yugoslav Crisis

Even though the country was not at war, it increasingly felt the effects of the war. The country increasingly depended on Germany and this significantly reduced the ability of Hungarian foreign policy to maneuver.

The first major signal was that in October 1940 Hungary was obliged to agree to the transit of German "military instructors," i.e., forces sent to protect the Romanian oil fields. These forces traveled in sealed carriages and along a predetermined route. It could also be considered a *quid pro quo* for the Vienna Award that on November 20, 1940, Hungary joined the Tripartite Pact in Vienna. This pact had replaced the Anti-Comintern Pact. This was the last time that Teleki saw Hitler and he enveloped himself in a depressive cloak of silence. He broke his silence only once, when he urged Hitler to expel the Jews from Hungary and Europe. Joining the Tripartite Pact signified another step, albeit a coerced one, on Hungary's path toward full cooperation with the Axis Powers. In London it was accepted calmly that Hungary was increasingly abandoning its armed neutrality and was lining up

---

268 "Teleki Pál gróf miniszterelnök beszéde az aktuális bel- és külpolitikai kérdésekről" [Prime Minister Count Pál Teleki's speech on current foreign and domestic policy matters], *Újság* [News], March 21, 1941.
269 Letter from Bálint Hóman to Pál Teleki (draft), Budapest, August 22, 1940, cs. 2, dossier B/l 1, K 30, MNL OL.

more and more closely with the enemy. They were pleased to acknowledge that Hungary insisted on keeping the British Legation in Budapest open.[270] The real meaning of the Tripartite Pact was not evident at the time. The only concrete stipulation of the agreement was that the "the contracting parties will come to each other's aid if one of them is attacked by a party not involved in the ongoing war in Europe or the Sino-Japanese conflict."[271] This could have meant an attack by the United States or the Soviet Union and in the autumn of 1940 this was not an immediate danger. Teleki hoped to acquire merit for Hungary's further revisionist goals, precede the Romanians in signing and disarm its own right-wing opposition that always demanded that he "adjust to the demands of the day."

In response to the country's increasing foreign policy isolation and in order to keep a window open, Hungary signed the Eternal Friendship Pact with Yugoslavia on December 12, 1940. Hungarian diplomacy was left with very few options. Slovakia did not have an independent foreign policy and Romania had not yet recovered from the shock of August 1940. This left Yugoslavia. The agreement did not mean that Hungary had relinquished all its revisionist goals vis-a-vis Yugoslavia, it simply meant that these goals were put on the back burner for the time being.

Hungarian diplomats in London tried, more or less successfully, to describe the Belgrade agreement as having been signed as gesture of friendship toward Great Britain. With less honesty, but with equal enthusiasm, the pact was described in Berlin as an attempt to draw Yugoslavia closer to the Tripartite Pact. In the House, the vote in favor of the friendship pact and of the Tripartite Pact was taken at the same session. The right-wing deputies abstained from voting on the former and the left-wing deputies abstained from voting on the latter.[272] About the same time Hungary signed a friendship agreement with Iraq and with Afghanistan, but neither of these was an "eternal" pact. The Hungarian-Yugoslav agreement had another result. At the hunt, following the signing of the pact in Belgrade, Minister of Foreign Affairs Csáky caught a cold, became very ill and died at the end of January.

Teleki had known him for twenty years and even though many members of Teleki's entourage urged him to dismiss the arrogant, frequently inconsiderate, haughty minister of foreign affairs who seemed to be a devoted Germanophile, Teleki always kept him on. Csáky started out as a firm royalist and then became an uncritical admirer of Nazi dynamism. He occasionally spoke tastelessly in Berlin about Hun-

---

270 Telegram from Halifax to O'Malley. London, December 2, 1940, TNA, FO 417, vol. 42, fol. 85.
271 Halmosy, *Nemzetközi szerződések*, pp. 502–503.
272 *Képviselőházi napló*, 1939–1944, vol. 9, pp. 131–134.

gary's foreign policy and was often rude to the ministers of both large and small countries. In 1940 his relationship to his chief also deteriorated. Teleki complained to his entourage, "Look at this Csáky. In 1920 he was my secretary as a youngster and look, how he dares to talk to me now. I hesitate to send him away."[273] It is also true, however, that at the end of 1940, when the British minister had to use a side door to visit the regent, for fear of German spies, Csáky leaked confidential and secret information to the British minister.[274] Macartney, who was a keen observer of the relationship between Teleki and Csáky, was probably right when he opined that there was a tacit division of labor between the two men with Csáky proving his loyalty to Germany while Teleki strengthened the ties with Great Britain.[275] László Bárdossy, the Hungarian minister in Bucharest was appointed Csáky's successor. He was not headstrong and led the ministry on the Dísz Square reliably.

When Yugoslavia joined the Tripartite Pact on March 26, 1941, a coup, organized with British assistance, erupted on March 27 in Belgrade and caused the Cvetković government to fall. The news reached Teleki in Szatmár. This was the second visit since the area had returned to Hungary. He had offered his estate to the Hungarian nation but he still had to watch locally that his best political intentions had failed. In Pribékfalva, between 1940 and 1944, the only elementary school was Hungarian even though the population was 100 percent Romanian.[276] He stated in Szatmár, "I never wanted this position where I stand and many of you here know it. I do not care if they are angry with me because if you hold this position for long you lose friends and your popularity diminishes. This does not matter. The important thing is for one to do his duty. If he is worn out he can be replaced but the replacement should be telling the truth as well."[277]

He came back to Budapest in a very bad frame of mind. Döme Sztójay, the minister in Berlin, was waiting for him with a message from Hitler in which the Führer offered the return of all the territories lost to Yugoslavia in 1918, provided the Hungarian army cooperated with the German one in an action against Yugosla-

---

273 Recollections of István Bárczy, June 16, 1945, Macartney Papers, box 14084, fol. 21-22, X 5050, MNL OL.
274 Letter from O'Malley to Knatchbull-Hugessen, British ambassador in Ankara. Budapest November 19, 1940, TNA, FO 371, vol. 26609.
275 Macartney, *October Fifteenth*, vol. 1, p. 331.
276 "A felajánlásról: elpirult a miniszterelnök" [The prime minister is blushing], *Nemzeti Újság* [National News], October 13, 1940, p. 6.
277 "A megbékülés, az összeforrás és a szabadság politikáját folytatjuk" [We continue the policy of pacification, union and freedom], *Magyarország*, March 27, 1941, p. 5.

via.²⁷⁸ The dilemma reflected the stations on the road followed by Hungarian policies since 1939 and also the increasingly shrinking room to maneuver. In September 1939 Budapest could refuse to grant transit to German troops; one year later it had to agree but still with certain stipulations; in April 1941 it could no longer avoid armed intervention in conjunction with the German forces. Horthy was enthusiastic about the prospect of further revisions and authorized the beginning of discussions between the German and Hungarian military leaderships. Teleki bitterly realized that the regent preferred the soldiers intriguing against him, particularly Henrik Werth, the chief of General Staff. At the Council of Ministers meeting, on March 28 he announced his resignation and withdrew it only upon the pleas of the council.²⁷⁹ On April 1, the Supreme Defense Council (LHT), consisting of the Council of Ministers, the regent and the chief of the General Staff, met and, after some discussion, accepted Teleki's recommendations. We know from the recollection of the participants that the prime minister did not take a stand against the acquisition of parts of Serbia but about the means to achieve it.²⁸⁰ On the basis of the conclusions reached at the March 28 council meeting, the Hungarian leadership agreed to the military action on the following conditions:

1. Hungarian troops could cross the border only after Croatian independence had been proclaimed since this would mean that Yugoslavia no longer existed.
2. Hungarian troops could not fight beyond the historic Hungarian borders.
3. The General Staff and the minister of defense could make preparations for action and could negotiate with the German General Staff but the final decision for action could be made only by Horthy.
4. Hungarian troops could not be commanded by Germans.²⁸¹

At the same time Teleki instructed the Hungarian minister in London to advise the Foreign Office about the decisions made by the Supreme Defense Council and to inquire tactfully about the British position. The prime minister increasingly felt that he was in a trap. He desperately tried to reduce the number of troops promised by the General Staff even though he knew that a large part of the government party supported the action against Yugoslavia. In the morning of April 2 he wrote a let-

---

278 Czettler, *Teleki Pál és a magyar külpolitika*, p. 272.
279 Juhász, *A Teleki-kormány külpolitikája*, pp. 299–300.
280 Sándor Szakály, ed., *Náray Antal visszaemlékezése* (Budapest: Zrínyi, 1988), pp. 44–53.
281 Juhász, *Teleki-kormány külpolitikája*, p. 306; and Czettler, *Teleki Pál és a magyar külpolitika*, p. 294.

ter to Gábor Apor, the Hungarian minister at the Holy See, in which he outlined the dilemma,

> This Yugo affair drew us into the most terrible situation. H|itler| sent a message through that Nazi Sztójay to the K[ormányzó] [Regent]....The K[ormányzó] was very enthusiastic at once, and not less but more so after he slept on it. He wanted to write that he was body and soul with them and would go along. It cost Bárdossy and me immense efforts to delete the dangerous passages from his letter and to leave doors open. Finally after two days the situation improved somewhat because he came to realize that we would lose our honor before the world if we attacked the Yugos....But my situation is extremely difficult—because K[ormányzó], the army, half the government, and the parliamentary majority are against me. I am trying to find a way out and save face.[282]

That evening the Hungarian minister in London, György Barcza's telegram arrived from London in which he stated that His Majesty's government would not condone Hungary's armed participation in an action against Yugoslavia and that this would mean a declaration of war.[283] At almost the same time, the evening of April 2, allegedly Horthy told Teleki, over the telephone, that some of the conditions set at the Supreme Defense Council meeting the previous day, would be ignored on German request. That same day Teleki was informed about the true content of the Hungarian-German military agreement and he was shocked by the magnitude of the operation.[284] These items overwhelmingly affected the prime minister's state of mind.

Suicide

Teleki must have felt that he was walking down an increasingly narrow corridor with fewer and fewer exits. Around Christmas Countess Teleki contracted pneumonia and at the beginning of the year developed severe liver insufficiency (perhaps heart trouble) and had to be referred to a sanatorium. The physicians believed that

---

282 Letter from Pál Teleki to Gábor Apor, Budapest, April 2, 1941, Macartney Papers, box 14085, X 5050, MNL OL.
283 Barcza, Diplomataemle'keim 1911-1945, pp. 493-494; and Juhász, ed., Magyarország külpolitikája a nyugati hadjarattol, pp. 991-992.
284 Loránt Tilkovszky, *Teleki Pál titokzatos halala* [Pál Teleki's Mysterious Death] (Budapest: Helikon, 1989), pp. 116-117.

the illness was terminal and only gave her a few months to live. Teleki was given this information on March 29. Countess Teleki actually died in July 1942. Teleki was also worried about his mother whose health was deteriorating rapidly. The death or severe illness of a family member is a very stressful situation that can easily lead to depression. The Teleki children no longer lived at home and so Teleki was by himself in the Sándor Palace during these fateful days. His social isolation aggravated his depression. His diary for 1941 records numerous visits to physicians. While he probably argued about politics with some of the professors, there is no question that he did need medical attention.[285] Six weeks before his death he was walking on the Bástya Promenade when he fell into a ditch and suffered painful bruises.[286] During his last few weeks he also suffered from insomnia.[287] Even on April 2, he received his last caller of the day around midnight. His old depressive symptoms also returned and during his last days both his public appearances and his private meetings were characterized by glumness. He felt that his twenty years of arduous work on behalf of revision had failed.

The reconstruction of Teleki's last day, April 2, 1941, raises serious problems. There are so many who claim that they saw him that day and, in fact, that they were the last one to see him and there are so many who came forth with theories and explanations about the causes and circumstances of his death that it is very difficult, if not impossible, to be certain. It is certain, however, that about 11:00 a.m., Antal Naray, the secretary of the Supreme Defense Council, saw the prime minister, who gave him his own notes about the Supreme Defense Council meeting. At noon the prime minister went to the House but did not enter the chamber. He chatted with the deputies in the corridor and about forty-five minutes later returned to his office for lunch. In the afternoon he visited his wife at the Park Sanatorium.[288] It may have been here that he was reached on the telephone and learned, perhaps from the regent himself, that Horthy had yielded to the German demands. Sometime during the afternoon Teleki received Zoltán Tildy the leader of the Smallholder Party and then, or perhaps early in the evening, he went over to the Ministry of Foreign Affairs to see Minister Bárdossy. Presumably it was here that he read the Barcza telegram mentioned above.[289] In the evening he participated at the pre-Easter retreat of the

---

285 The 1941 appointment calendar, passim, Papers of Pál Teleki, cs. 3, dossier p, K 37, MNL OL.
286 "Bakay Lajos emlékezásei" [Lajos Bakay's Recollections!, Historia, no. 4(1983): 28.
287 Fodor, *Teleki Pál*, p. 240.
288 The name of the sanatorium is given differently by several sources. Some say it was the János Sanatorium.
289 Elemér Újpétery, *Végállomás Lisszabon* [Last Stop Lisbon] (Budapest: Magvető, 1987), pp. 160-163; Tilkovszky, Teleki Pál titokzatos halála, pp. 114-121.

Boy Scout officers in St. Stephen's Basilica and got ready for communion the next day. He went to confession and afterward had a long talk with Father Béla Witz.[290] He then returned to the prime minister's residence, the Sándor Palace on Castle Hill, and retired to his apartment. He tried to reach his secretary but she was not at home and he then called the Ministry of Foreign Affairs. He asked his former pupil, Elemér Újpétery, to come to his office. The young diplomat did so just before midnight and brought a copy of the Barcza telegram with him. Presumably he was the last one who saw Teleki alive.

The prime minister shot himself in the head sometime between 2:00 and 2:30 a.m. At the autopsy a brain embolus was found that must have occurred fourteen to sixteen hours before his death so that during his last hours Teleki must have suffered from a severe headache.[291]

When the valet came to open the curtains he noted that something had happened to the prime minister who was lying in bed. After some confusion the physicians were summoned and Teleki's family was notified. The members of the cabinet were informed and gathered in the Sándor Palace during the morning. For about thirty minutes the Regent was left alone with the body of Pál Teleki. This must have given Horthy occasion for some thoughts particularly because he was the addressee of Teleki's last two letters. One of the letters contains the lines that have become legendary,

> Excellency,
> We have become word-breakers—out of cowardice—and broke our promise of the eternal friendship agreement based on your Mohács speech. The nation senses that we have cast away its honor.
> We have sided with the villains because the atrocities they reported are a pack of lies. There were none against Hungarians and none even against Germans! We will be robbing a corpse! We will be the most miserable of nations. I did not hold you back. I am guilty.
> Pál Teleki April 3, 1941.[292]

---

290 Bela Witz, *Teleki Pál vallásossága* [The Religiosity of Pál Teleki] (Budapest: Középponti Katolikus Kör, 1943), p. 8.
291 Macartney, *October Fifteenth*, vol. 1, pp. 474-490. For the reconstruction of the last day, see História, no. 4 (1983): 26-29, and 35; and the series of articles by István György, "Teleki Pál dosszié 1-8" [Pál Teleki dossier 1-8], Népszabadság [People's Freedom], July 6-14, 1968.
292 Ádám Juhász, and Kerekes, eds., *Magyarország és a második világháború*, pp. 63-70; and Szinai and Szucs, eds., *Horthy Miklós titkos iratai*, pp. 291-292.

In the second letter Teleki told Horthy that should he survive, he was resigning from his position as head of government. Horthy appointed László Bárdossy that same day to be prime minister. A third letter has been discovered in 2019: it was adressed to Péter Incze, his private secretary and reinforced the thesis of the suicide.[293]

Teleki's associates and family members never doubted that the prime minister had committed suicide. His son, daughter-in-law, son-in-law, and other family members, his closest associates, political acquaintances and friends were in agreement. They included Bálint Hóman, István Bethlen, András Rónai, Péter Incze, Miklós Kozma, and others.[294] Those contemporary opinions that suggested murder came generally from people who knew Teleki but did not belong to the inner circle. Such an outrage is not inconceivable, but to date there is no logical, understandable and historically probable evidence whatever to suggest such an act. The expert medical opinion, signed by the police surgeon and by the eminent Professor Lajos Bakay, who knew Teleki well, diagnosed suicide without any possible question. It is worthwhile to quote their opinion,

> On the right side, by his neck, in contact with his right index finger, there was a large caliber Browning automatic. The pillow was covered with blood clots and blood dripped over both sides. On the right side, at the temple, just below the hairline we found the entry wound surrounded by scorched hair. Fragments of brain had seeped out through the opening. The exit wound is in the area of the left temporal bone. It is about the size of a two-pengő coin. It is patent and filled with dots and fragments of brain. Corresponding to the position of the head there is a filler-size hole in the wall that is surrounded by fragments of brain adhering to the wall. Examination of the body revealed that death must have occurred early in the morning. The fact of suicide has been established beyond any doubt.[295]

---

293 Pál Teleki's letter to Péter Incze, s. d. [1941], XIV.307, Incze Péter Papers, BFL (downloadable: https://bparchiv.hu/sites/default/files/atoms/files/hu_bfl_teleki_levelek_1-2.pdf, last visite: October 3, 2022)
294 János Kubassek, "Gróf Teleki Pál utolsó napjai—ahogyan veje, Gróf Zichy Nándor látta" [The last days of Count Pál Teleki—as seen by his son-in-law Count Nandor Zichy], *Napi Magyarország* [Daily Hungary], March 4, 2000, p. 31; and Margit Földesi, "A név mindig kötelez. Washingtoni találkozás Teleki Pál menyével, gróf Mikes Hannával" [The name always obliges. Meeting Pál Teleki's daughter-in-law, Countess Hanna Mikes in Washington], *Magyar Nemzet* [Hungarian Nation], November 11,2000, p. 23.
295 Report of Károly Leviczky and Lajos Bakay. Budapest, March (sic!) 3, 1941, cs. 1382, t. 3, no. 2700, K 26, MNL OL.

None of the sources and documents available today speak credibly against suicide.[296]

The Hungarian news media hesitated for a while and spoke only of the death which had occurred "with tragic suddenness." It was only in the afternoon that the Hungarian News Agency (MTI), officially announced the cause of death. The Germans were troubled by Teleki's death and the British press saw him as the victim of the Germans. A few days later Great Britain broke diplomatic relations with Hungary and the minister left Budapest. Declaration of war, however, did not take place until December. Teleki's death caused the British to take a more understanding view of the Hungarian actions. Certain other diplomats also left Hungary. The head of the Soviet mission departed and was followed by the ministers of Holland and Belgium.

Hungarian public opinion was shaken by the prime minister's death. The published obituaries unanimously praised the politician's self-sacrifice, his services to the Hungarian nation and his political activities. Not only the government papers wrote about him in the most complimentary way but so did the publications politically opposed to him. It was the Arrow Crossist *Magyarság* that was the most reticent when it emphasized that Teleki was an "adversary" but one who used "clean weapons and fought hard but honestly."[297] The Social Democrat *Népszava* also suggested an adversary situation but was not nearly as emphatic as the extreme right wing.[298] The opposition liberal Civic Freedom Party held a special memorial session in honor of the late prime minister where it recognized in party leader Teleki a great Hungarian statesman, the wise leader with a mission whose greatness and whose services to the country would be perpetuated by history.[299] Even the paper of the Jewish community, condemned by Teleki to expulsion from society and even from the country, mentioned him in glowing colors, calling him a great statesman and conveying their deepest sympathy to the family and to the nation. The writer of the obituary added, "It is not our task, and particularly not at this awful moment of mourning, to pass judgment on the politician and antagonist. We feel it is our duty to remember him as one of the outstanding, great sons of the country and with a feeling of deep grief and profound sympathy."[300] A number of poems were

---

296 About the last events concerning the debate on his death see: Balázs Ablonczy: *Búcsúlevelek és dilemmák: Teleki Pál halála*. [Suicide letters and dilemmas: Pál Teleki's Death]. In: Róbert Hermann (ed.): Összeesküvési teóriák a magyar történelemben. [Conspiracy Theories in Hungarian History] Budapest: 2022, Magyar Történelmi Társulat, pp. 165-179.
297 "Teleki Pál halála" [The Death of Pál Teleki], *Magyarság*, April 4,1941.
298 "Pál Teleki," *Népszava*, April 4, 1941.
299 *Esti Kurír*, April 3, and April 4, 1941.
300 *Magyar Zsidók Lapja*, April 3, 1941, p. 5.

written about his death, both then and also later. Regardless of party affiliation or political perspective, the authors uniformly sang of "sacrifice," "example," "humanity," and "martyrdom."

The funeral took place on April 7. Even though Teleki, in a brief note written in 1929, asked the Boy Scout Association that at his funeral "all evidence of grief" be omitted and that nobody should accompany him to the grave, a large-scale state funeral was organized.[301] According to a certificate by professor Lajos Bakay, the prime minister was not accountable at the time he committed his deed and therefore a church funeral was authorized, provided it was kept simple.[302] After the solemnities a long parade left the Parliament Square and followed the prime minister's coffin to the Kerepesi Road cemetery. There were Boy Scouts stationed all along the way. The grave was blessed by Teleki's confessor, Béla Witz, the parish priest of St. Stephen's Basilica and not by the prince primate/ archbishop of Esztergom. The ceremony was interrupted briefly by an air raid alarm. The hostilities had begun the previous day and there were Yugoslav warplanes in Hungarian airspace.

According to Teleki's recommendation, Hungarian troops did not enter Yugoslavia until April 11 when the independent Croatia was proclaimed in Zagreb. By April 13 and after only sporadic fighting, the Hungarian troops occupied the Prekmurje (Muravidék), Međimurje [Muraköz], the Baranya Triangle and Bačka [Bácska]. Yet, Hungarian troops did go beyond the historic borders. In contradiction of the March 28 stipulations, the Rapid Deployment Force [gyorshadtest] advanced deep into Serbia under German command.

---

301 About Teleki's note, see Papp Papers., n.d. (presumably 1929). His 1929 instructions about his funeral arrangements was published in Nepszava, April 4, 1941, under the headline: "Teleki 12 év előtti intézkedése saját temetéséről" [Teleki's instructions about his own funeral, which had been made twelve years before].
302 *Pesti Hírlap*, April 5, 1941, p. 3.

Afterword

There is no complete scholarly study of the life of Pál Teleki, this strange twentieth century central European conservative politician, although assessment of his life began immediately after his death. In the eulogy at his graveside, his successor, Prime Minister Laszló Bárdossy, referred to him as the "schoolmaster of the nation."

During the years after his death, even during World War II, a large number of brochures and articles were published to illustrate various aspects of his life, such as the religious Teleki, the Boy Scout Teleki, the educator Teleki, and the ethnic politician Teleki. During the war only one lasting and scholarly publication appeared. Antal Papp, a former state secretary and a close collaborator for twenty years, published Teleki's collected parliamentary speeches in 1944. It can be seen in the newspapers of the time that on the anniversary of his death and in holiday issues, e.g., Christmas, articles were published that emphasized his anti-German stance and his desire to maintain the independence of the country. The articles had a "back to Teleki" attitude that was complimentary to his memory. This was true especially for those papers which opposed him when he was prime minister. To the extent possible during the war years, a personal cult developed that focused on his activities in the Boy Scout movement.

Teleki's evaluation was modified between 1945 and 1947. His politics did not conform to the value system of the evolving Soviet bloc. Because of the way he died, he appeared to much of Hungarian public opinion in the role of a victim although the Soviet leaders, including Foreign Minister Vyacheslav Mikhailovich Molotov, advised their Hungarian contacts that showing Teleki in a positive way was not acceptable to them. His death and his policies while he was prime minister made him a martyr in the eyes of the public. When the Communists came to power in 1947, they wished to make a radical change in this assessment.

During the period of high Stalinism of the Communist regime, in the first half of the 1950s, the perceptions of the government were reflected in a brochure by Erzsébet Andics, the leading Communist historian, according to whom, "Hungary had an essentially fascist system for twenty-five years."[1] Andics created a historiographic tradition in modern Hungarian historical literature that dominated the assessment of the years between the two World Wars well into the 1960's. The interpretations inspired by Andics, according to which the Horthy regime in its rise to power and in its methods reflected the first fascist structure in Europe, are reflected in the work of Aladár Kis, discussing the activities of Teleki.[2] His small book became obsolete the year after publication.

Gyula Juhász used a number of sources in his work analyzing the foreign policy of the Teleki government between 1939 and 1941.[3] In this volume the prime minister is depicted as "an educated, but strongly right-wing, reactionary aristocrat," who as a politician emerged "from the counterrevolution, the system that was based in domestic policies on the oppression of the working masses and in foreign policies on anti-Sovietism and on territorial revision."[4] Juhász did not depart from the Marxist canon but represented a different approach to the study of the Horthy era which negated the fascist label applied to the entirety of the Horthy era or to some of its time periods. In this Juhász was ahead of the academic debate which first covertly but after the mid-1960s openly reexamined the historiography of the previous years.[5] After the 1960s Teleki was assigned a certain, albeit not prominent, role in the antifascist pantheon of the Kádár era.[6] It was due to this new status that the principal newspaper of the MSZMP [Hungarian Socialist Workers Party], *Népszabadság,* published a series of articles about the circumstances surrounding the death of the prime minister. The writings published after the 1970s gave an increasingly nuanced picture of Teleki.

---

[1] Erzsébet Andics, *Fasizmus es reakció Magyarországon* [Fascism and Reaction in Hungary] (Budapest: Szikra, 1945), p. 3.
[2] Aladár Kis, *Magyarország külpolitikája a máodik világháború előestéjén* [Hungary's Foreign Policy on the Eve of the Second World War] (Budapest: Kossuth, 1963).
[3] Juhász, *A Teleki-kormány külpolitikája.*
[4] Ibid., pp. 18-20.
[5] Levente Püski, "Demokrácia és diktatúra között. A Horthy-rendszer jellegéről" [Between democracy and dictatorship. On the nature of the Horthy regime], in *Mítoszok. legendák, tévhitek,* ed. Romsics, pp. 207-212.
[6] Andráás Mink, 'Teleki jövője" [Teleki's future], *Beszélő* no. 4 (2004): 58-68.

The fundamental work of the British historian, C.A. Macartney, published in 1956, is a very useful study which presents Hungarian governmental policies with friendly criticism and Teleki with unmistakable sympathy.[7] Macartney based his work on personal contacts and on sources no longer available and the sixty years elapsed since the second edition, in 1961, have left their mark on the work. In order to protect his sources he had to keep some of them anonymous and he also had only limited access to archival material. He could not include the results of subsequent research in Hungary.

The first work, devoted entirely to Teleki, was written by Loránt Tilkovszky. He published a volume in 1969 which was focused primarily on the suicide of the prime minister.[8] The English edition, complete with footnotes, was published seven years later.[9] The author revised and extended his work and it was republished by Helikon Press in a series of publications focused on Hungarian historical mysteries.[10] In his work, Tilkovszky took a Marxist position when he said that the reminiscences and contemporary opinions used in his work "demonstrated a social philosophy different from ours." Yet, his description of Teleki's life was many-sided and delicate.[11] The author took a definite stand in the historiographic debate mentioned above. He saw Teleki's antiliberalism after 1919 very clearly and also his tendency toward solutions that could be harmonized with the prevailing ideas and which went well beyond parliamentary solutions. Yet he did not consider that Teleki was a fascist but, on the basis of his analysis, described him as an antidemocratic conservative whose total confidence in his own ideas and wider then usual European perspective soon turned against supporting Germany.

In the revised 1989 edition of his book Tilkovszky deals in depth with the theory of Teleki having been murdered which was increasingly raised in the 1980s. In the popular history journal, *História* and in other media opinions were presented which claimed that the prime minister was the victim of murder in April 1941.

After the democratic transition in 1990, the number of publications dealing with Teleki increased significantly. In 1991, fifty years after his death, his admirers declared it to be a "Memorial Year." The patrons of the Memorial Year were the president of the republic and the speaker of the Parliament. Prime Minister József Antall became the chairman of the committee. The work of the scholar-politician

---

7 Macartney, *October Fifteenth*, vols. 1 and 2.
8 Tilkovszky, *Teleki Pál*.
9 Lóránt Tilkovszky, *Pál Teleki—A Biographical Sketch* (Budapest: Akadémiai Kiadó, 1976).
10 Tilkovszky, *Teleki Pál titokzatos halála*.
11 Ibid., p. 42.

Teleki were discussed at two general meetings and the proceedings were subsequently published.¹²

The researches into Pál Teleki's life were continued in Switzerland by Antal Czettler. In his book, published in German in 1996 and in Hungarian in 1997, he concentrated on the foreign policy of the Teleki government.¹³ Czettler presented it in a balanced and emphatically sympathetic way. The drawback of his work is that other than a rich bibliography and a few archival data, he used no newly discovered sources although he did include some information gathered from Teleki's family and friends.

The author of the present book published two volumes on Teleki in 2000. One was a biography describing in popular form Teleki's career, the other a stout volume containing Teleki's political writings and speeches. A critical assessment of these volumes would be inappropriate in this epilogue.¹⁴

The biography, written by his former adjunct, assistant and confidant, published after a delay of fifty years, was a significant step in the Pál Teleki literature.¹⁵ About half of the five hundred page work deals with Teleki's life while the second half presents his activities and his world of ideas in a *Book of Hours* format. Fodor's work is not primarily a scholarly biography but is more of a memoir, the personal notes of one of Teleki's closest collaborators. This is shown both by the author's basic stance and also by the lack of any source material. There is practically no discussion of foreign and domestic policy matters and thus the work cannot be called a scholarly biography even though it contains useful information for those interested in the subject. In the recent years, beside the usual brochures a few historical and geographical account has been written about the differents aspects of his life: Róbert Keményfi revealed the dark sides of Teleki's geographical activity, Steven Seegel inserted his life in a larger, transnational perspective.¹⁶ Further books led to a rebirth of the assassination thesis, without new convincing arguments.¹⁷

---

12   Csicsery-Rónay and Vígh, eds., *Teleki Pál és kora*.
13   Antal Czettler, *Pál Graf Teleki and die Aussenpolitk Ungarns 1939–1941* (Munich: Studia Hungarica 43, 1996); and Czettler, *Teleki Pál és a magyar külpolitika*.
14   Ablonczy, *Teleki Pál* and Teleki, *Válogatott politikai írások és beszédek*, ed. Ablonczy.
15   Fodor, *Teleki Pál*.
16   Róbert Keményfi: Teleki Pál tudományos alapú „fajpolitikája". [The science based „racial politics" of Pál Teleki] In: Tamás Valastyán - Gergely Angyalosi (eds.): *Fakultások közt. Tudomány, tudás, alkalmazás*. [Between faculties: Science, knowledge, application]. Budapest: 2022, L'Harmattan. pp. 241-308. And Seegel: *Map men*.
17   Gábor Nyári: *A Sándor-palotától a ravatalig. Teleki Pál második miniszterelnöksége, 1939-1941*. [From the Sándor Palace to the Catafalque. The Second Premiership of Pál Teleki], 1939-1941 Budapest: 2015, Kairosz.

Having reached the end of my work I wonder what conclusions can be drawn of a Central-Eastern-European life I consider characteristic of the twentieth century. Pál Teleki's fate was unique in Hungary as a prime minister between the two World Wars and his career spans the era of the Horthy regime, this peculiar albeit not unique central European authoritarian regime. Teleki may well be the only leader of the Hungarian political elite who drew the fundamental conclusion from 1918–1919. Following the revolutions he knew that there had to be reforms and endeavored to carry them out. He was among the most important personalities of the regime and he was unique among them insofar that he used the important contacts he made as prime minister for furthering social rather than political goals.

After his 1923 illness he largely lost interest in parliamentary matters and fully rejected them after the franc scandal. His vanity was wounded by having been maligned and slandered in the press. He was active in politics only to the extent of responding to confidential mission requests from the prime minister or the minister of foreign affairs. These activities were always performed behind the scenes and consequently appealed to him. "I am in favor of secret diplomacy," he commented,[18] mainly because he disliked the press and also felt that the pettiness and superficiality of publicity and volatility of public opinion were barriers to successful diplomacy.[19] On the other hand, when he participated in such secret or confidential missions as the one in Mosul, for example, his doctrinaire views, inflexibility and obstinacy either condemned the mission to failure or compromised him personally. His suspicions of public opinion were not due simply to his aristocratic background, although that did play a role. In his person a new type of conservatism appeared in Hungary between the two World Wars.

Pál Teleki's life could be divided into four lengthy periods. Until 1918 we see a slowly emerging political and scientific career within the framework of the Dual Monarchy. Teleki experimented with political ideas, such as Turanism and eugenics, which he saw as having the potential of modifying the traditional trends of Hungarian politics. For a few years he entered politics during the critical eras of 1904–1910 and 1916–1918. At the same time he endeavored to give geography a new direction in Hungary by introducing economic geography. This duality persisted and even though Teleki was continuously tortured by feelings of inadequacy, his career is highly respected. He was the president or leading member of a number of organizations and he even became a member of the prestigious Hun-

---

18   Papp, ed., *Teleki Pál országgyűlési beszédei*, vol. 1, p. 338.
19   Ibid.

garian Academy of Science. At the end of this period, the young parliamentary representative was already viewed as a potential minister. His career can be considered fairly typical in that the initial, somewhat radical, reform-liberal views were modified by integration into the establishment to which his talents and abilities fully qualified him.

The three years between 1918 and 1921 were rich in events and present us with a vastly different political personality. The liberal democratic revolution and the Hungarian Soviet Republic changed Teleki's views of the world, impelled him into political activity and meant a turning point in his intellectual world. He was no longer a liberal and turned against his youthful ideas about biological determinism and away from his comments on the relative significance of religion. His faith in the socially constructive force of Christianity became very strong and his views about the nation being an organic unit came to the fore. His anti-Communist nationalism was stained with anti-Semitism. He believed that Hungarian Jewry, by virtue of its perceived economic, intellectual, and post-revolutionary political power was a threat to the so-called Christian middle class and therefore he stepped forth to curb its influence and favored discrimination. His fundamental experience was the revolution and his career between the two World Wars was shaped principally by the counterrevolution. His political career rose increasingly sharply. He was first active in counter-governments and then became one of the leaders of the Hungarian peace delegation. He then became minister of foreign affairs and, barely eighteen months after the collapse of the Dual Monarchy, he became prime minister. He might have had a similar career under Dualism, if he had persisted in his political activities, although advancement would have been slower. He was barely forty-one years old when he had already fallen as prime minister. The start of consolidation after the revolutions is linked closely to his name. Other major activities included the ratification of the Peace Treaty of Trianon, land reform, the control of the paramilitary organizations, the attempts at fiscal consolidation, the restriction of university admission for Jews, and the reintroduction of corporal punishment. It was not the consolidation that led to his fall but the stormy domestic policy debate concerning the rights of the Habsburg dynasty to the throne.

As he abandoned the principles of liberalism he concluded that every society had to have an organizational force that came from above and that went beyond human understanding. He denied that the community, whether a nation or a society, was simply the sum of its individual members. His attachment to traditions, his organic and elitist image of society and his deep skepticism vis-a-vis state and institutional structures aligned him with conservative circles. He represented a peculiar trend in Hungarian political life because he not only questioned the legitimacy of bureaucracy but also the utility of law as an organizational force in society and a mechanism to deliver justice. One of his favorite sayings was that each case depended, "Not on papers and regulations but on people." He believed in a strategy that activated people and networks, moved rapidly and was motivated by duty and faith and not by money, governmental will or personal profit. Duty and faith represented for him the national consciousness that he equated with nationalism He saw this ideology as the strongest organizational force and it was this that could motivate those who wished to act. It was the historicity and the traditional base of this nationalism, and indeed of Teleki's entire way of thinking, which could guarantee that the reforms essential for Hungarian society would not come about according to some foreign model. The reforms were needed in thought processes and in culture and only secondarily in social improvements or expansion. In Teleki's person a conservative, antiliberal worldview received a voice in Hungary with its nationalism linked to strong cultural aspirations. His goals in educating the nation to become a better people contained a series of positive, dynamic elements and offered the hope for the remedy of the stressful social problems of the country. This "reactionary" conservatism, buttressed with openly modernizing trends, was receptive after the end of the 1920s and the beginning of the 1930s toward the right-wing dictatorships. Because of the neo-paganism and aggressive ethnic group policies of Nazi Germany Teleki sympathized much more with Portugal and Austria, which were clerical-corporative states.

Teleki's other basic conclusion came from the collapse and Trianon. It was unpreparedness, complacency and foreign policy inexperience of Hungarian society which was punished by the peace treaty. According to Teleki, the leading elements compromised by liberalism were unsuited to protect the country from its ills. After the war he used all his efforts to raise a new elite for the country, a Christian middle class filled with a national feeling, having a—what he considered—European outlook and steeped in knowledge of many types. Its offsprings were to be groomed to take over the spiritual and practical leadership of the country. His policies were directed to the creation of this new middle class and aristocracy no longer played any part. He saw his ideas about social policies threatened by the Jewish middle class and he therefore urged that it be excluded from education, industry, and commerce.

Revision was possible only under the leadership of this new middle class which was strengthened in its values and in its contents. In order to achieve a rectification of the borders, he offered the former nationalities a relatively tolerant nationality policy and rights for territorial autonomy within the future country. The revision did not envisage a complete restoration of the pre-Trianon borders even though in Teleki's innermost thoughts this would have been the ultimate goal. He expected the Great Powers to offer assistance and the correction of the territorial arrangements of the manifestly unjust peace treaty. In order to accomplish this, there was a need for a convincing and high level of propaganda dressed up in a scientific or cultural garb. This was his principal drive in the third segment of his life between the two World Wars.

The fourth segment was short, just like the second one. It lasted a scant three years, even if we include the time when he served as minister of education. During this period, the politician endeavored to lift the networks, consisting of his people, into the government and, with their help, implement the conservative reforms for which he had established the base during the preceding period. This reform endeavor consisted of further land reform, a tolerant nationality policy, the expansion of the social services, e.g., pensions and health insurance, and new and more stringent and severe legislative anti-Semitic discrimination. In parallel with these, Teleki wished to preserve Hungary's neutrality (or at least non-belligerent status) in war-torn Europe so that the territorial revisions for which he had worked for two decades may take place. Some of these ideas were compatible over the short haul but even after a moderate amount of time it became evident that there were irreconcilable differences between them. Demanding revision meant an increasing dependence on Germany and consequently the impossibility of maintaining the country's neutrality. Depriving Hungarian Jewry of its civil rights and increasing expropriation of its assets undermined social reforms and the moral basis of Teleki's policies. It was this insoluble conflict, in addition to his poor health and unstable emotional state that led to his death.

These were not the only dichotomies in his life. He considered contemporary Hungarian society to be immature and impatient and in this he was probably correct. He himself was impatient, however, vis-a-vis Hungarian Jews when he urged their exclusion from Hungarian society and he was immature when he endorsed a number of adventurous political enterprises. He was in perpetual doubt about his own political and scientific abilities yet he tried to defeat his political opponents with scientific arguments. He fought against favoritism but invariably and strongly supported his own proteges. He had a poor opinion of the governmental organizations and of public administration but believed in the government's ability to solve problems. There were too many such contradictions in his life, too many conflicts that he engaged in and felt deeply about. He was profoundly dissatisfied with the system itself and yet had too many links to it. These conflicts and contradictions eventually destroyed Teleki and it is precisely because of these conflicts and contradictions that Teleki is still the center of debates in Hungary today. His life and times provide important perspectives to the understanding of the history of the authoritarian systems in east central Europe. Perhaps his personal failure demonstrates something about small country existence, about suffering from a lack of political alternatives due to being forcefully constrained by the Great Powers.

Bibliography

In the following list of bibliographic entries I am including only those sources which I used regularly in preparing the manuscript. I do not include newspaper articles and works used only for occasional references. I did lists works, however, which are not in the endnotes, but which I consulted regularly.

ARCHIVAL SOURCES

ARCHIVES OF BUDAPEST CORVINUS UNIVERSITY [Budapesti Corvinus Egyetem Levéltára]
    5. a. Minutes of Faculty Meetings 1920–1934
    5.b. Papers of the Dean's Office 1920–1934
    6.a. Minutes of Faculty Meetings 1934–1938
    6. b. Personnel Files in the Dean's Office

ARCHIVES OF THE FERENC HOPP EAST-ASIAN ART MUSEUM
[Hopp Ferenc Kelet-Ázsiai Művészeti Múzeum Adattára]
    Zoltán Takáts Felvinczi Papers

ARCHIVES OF THE HUNGARIAN AGRICULTURAL MUSEUM
[Magyar Mezőgazdasági Múzeum, Adattára]
    Alajos Paikert Papers

ARCHIVES OF THE HUNGARIAN GEOGRAPHICAL MUSEUM (ÉRD)
[Magyar Földrajzi Múzeum Archívuma]
    Jenő Cholnoky Papers

ARCHIVES OF THE HUNGARIAN GEOGRAPHICAL SOCIETY
[Magyar Földrajzi Társaság Irat- és Levéltára]
    Papers of the Hungarian Geographical Society

Pál Teleki

ARCHIVES AND MANUSCRIPT COLLECTION OF THE LIBRARY
OF THE HUNGARIAN ACADEMY OF SCIENCE
[Magyar Tudományos Akadémia Könyvtára, Kézirattár]
  Letters to and from Pál Teleki
  Ms.10907 Klára Tüdős, "Rongyok" [Rags]
  Ms 10455 Ferenc Fodor, "A magyar földrajztudomány története" [The history of Hungarian geography]
  Ms 10740/77 Recollections of Mrs. Ferenc Fodor

BUDAPEST MUNICIPAL ARCHIVES [Budapest Fővárosi Levéltár]
  VII. 179 Papers of Notary Ferenc Lázár
  X. 248 Papers of the Hunnia Boat Club
  XXV Trial Transcripts of the Budapest People's Court

CENTRAL ARCHIVES OF THE PIARIST PROVINCE OF HUNGARY
[Piarista Rend Magyar Tartománya Központi Levéltára]
  Papers of the Budapest Piarist Gymnasium
  Archives of the Hungarian Provincial Head Office. Personal Papers
  Géza Czirbusz Papers
  Antal Papp Papers

DÉNES MEDNYÁNSZKY LIBRARY AND ARCHIVES OF THE COLLEGE EÖTVÖS
[Mednyánszky Dénes Könyvtár és Levéltár]
  Papers about Pál Teleki's Administrative Activities
  FERENC FODOR PAPERS (PRIVATE COLLECTION)

HUMBOLDT UNIVERSITÄT—SEMINAR FÜR HUNGAROLOGIE (BERLIN)
  Gyula Farkas Papers
  Papers of the Berlin Hungarian Institute

HUNGARIAN MUSEUM OF NATURAL HISTORY,
HISTORY OF SCIENCE COLLECTION
[Magyar Természettudományi Múzeum, Tudománytörténeti Gyűjtemény]
  Lajos Lóczy Papers

HUNGARIAN NATIONAL ARCHIVES [Magyar Nemzeti Levéltár Országos Levéltára]
  K 27 Minutes of the Council of Ministers (Copies)
  K 28 Prime Ministry—Department on Minorities and Nationalities
  K 37 Semiofficial Correspondence of the Prime Minister. Pál Teleki Papers
  K 53 Papers of the Supreme Command's Governmental Commisioner on Northern Transylvanian Affairs
  K 429 Miklós Kozma Papers
  K 437 TESZK Papers
  K 608 Press Archives. Articles Relative to Pál Teleki
  K 636 Universities and Colleges
    Personal Documents of Individual Professors
    Eötvös College Papers
  P 4 Gyula Andrássy, Jr. Papers

P 545 Béla Procopius Papers
P1384 Turanian Society Papers
P2026 Teleki-Dégenfeld Papers
X 5050 Macartney Papers (on Microfilm)
X 10379 Papers of the Hungarian Boy Scout Association (on Microfilm)
Z 23 Papers of the Pesti Hazai Első Takarékpénztár [First National Savings Bank of Budapest] —Directorate
Z 100 Papers of the Pesti Hazai Első Takarékpénztár—Secretariat
Z 931 Papers of the Pesti Hazai Első Takarékpénztár—Board of Directors

LIBRARY OF THE CENTRAL STATISTICAL INSTITUTE, MANUSCRIPTS
[Központi Statisztikai Hivatal Könyvtára, Kéziratok]
Alajos Kovács Papers

MINING AND GEOLOGICAL SURVEY OF HUNGARY,
HISTORY OF SCIENCE COLLECTION
Magyar Bányászati és Földtani Szolgálat, Tudománytörténeti Gyűjtemény]
Lajos Lóczy, Sr. Papers

MINISTÈRE DES AFFAIRES ETRANGÈRES—ARCHIVES DIPLOMATIQUES (PARIS)
Série Europe 1918–1940
Sous-série Hongrie
Série Société des Nations

NATIONAL SZÉCHÉNYI LIBRARY, MANUSCRIPT COLLECTION
[Országos Széchényi Könyvtár, Kézirattár]
Letter Collecion Letters Written by Pál Teleki
Fol. Hung 1911 Gyula Schönherr Papers and Letters
Fond 1 József Balogh Papers. Papers of the Nouvelle *Revue de Hongrie* and the *Hungarian Quarterly*
Fond 7 Magyar Szemle Társaság Papers
Fond 15 Bálint Hóman Papers
Quart. Hung. 2453 István Apáthy Papers
Quart. Hung. 2454 Hungarian Social Sciences Association Papers
Quart. Hung. 2597 Géza Szüllő Notes

ORAL HISTORY ARCHIVES OF THE VERITAS INSTITUTE
[Veritas Intézet Oral History Archívuma]
Sándor Barcs Interview (No. 81)
András Rónai Interview (No. 53)
Artur Sibelka-Perlberg Interview (No. 87)

PARLIAMENT LIBRARY, UNITED NATIONS COLLECTION
[Országgyűlési Könyvtár, ENSZ Letéti Gyűjtemény]
C. 400. M. 147. 1925, VII. Question de la frontière entre la Turquie et l'Irak

POLITICAL HISTORY AND LABOR UNION ARCHIVES
[Politikatörténeti és Szakszervezeti Levéltár]
Fond 721 Révész Collection (Units 2209, 2210, and 2219)

Pál Teleki

POLITISCHES ARCHIV DES AUSWÄRTIGEN AMTES (BERLIN)
Papers Concerning Hungary 1921–1938*
Papers Transferred from the Bundesarchiv (Gesandschaft Budapest)
Clodius Papers
Nachlass Erdmannsdorff
*After 1991 the documents were renumbered and coded. The papers of the following departments were examined: Inland, Politische Abteilung, Handelspolitische Abteilung, Büro des Reichsministers, Büro des Staatssekretärs.

RÁDAY ARCHIVES [Ráday Levéltár]
C/39 Sándor II. Imre Papers
C/80 Domokos Szentiványi Papers
C/143 Andor Semsey Papers

THE NATIONAL ARCHIVES, FOREIGN OFFICE (LONDON)
FO 371 Political Departments: General Correspondence 1906–1966

THE SCOUTS HERITAGE COLLECTION (LONDON-CHINGFORD, GILWELL PARK)
TC/50 General Hungary 1924–1938

PUBLISHED DOCUMENTS

Ádám, Magda, and Győző Cholnoky, eds. *Trianon—A magyar béketüldöttség tevékenysége 1920-ban* [Trianon—Activities of the Hungarian Peace Delegation in 1920]. Budapest: Lucidus, 2000.
Ádám, Magda, György Litván, and Mária Ormos, eds. *Documents diplomatiques français sur l'histoire du bassin des Carpathes 1918–1931*. 3 vols. Budapest: Akadémiai, 1993–1999.
Ádám, Magda, Gyula Juhász, and Lajos Kerekes, eds. *Magyarország és a második világháború* [Hungary and the Second World War]. Budapest: Kossuth, 1959.
Gáspár, Ferenc, and Béla Sarusi-Kiss, eds. "Teleki Pál közjegyzői letétbe helyezett feljegyzései a frankhamisításról" [The notarized annotations of Pál Teleki about the franc forgery case], *Századok*, no. 4 (1999): 727–764.
Documents on British Foreign Policy, 1919–1939. London: H.M. Stationary Office, 1946–1985.
Halmosy, Dénes, ed. *Nemzetközi szerződések 1918–1945* [International Treaties 1918–1945]. Budapest: Gondolat Közigazgatási és Jogi Kiadó, 1983.
Képviselőházi naplók, 1920–1921, and *1939–1941* [House of Representatives Records, 1920–1921, 1939–1941].
Magyar Királyi Belügyminisztérium, Magyarországi rendeletek tára 1911–1944 [Collection of Hungarian Statutes 1911–1944], Budapest: M. Kir. Belügymin., 1911–1944.
Nemes, Dezső, and Elek Karsai, eds. *Iratok az ellenforradalom történetéhez* [Papers to the History of the Counterrevolution], Vols. 2–4. Budapest: Szikra-Kossuth, 1956–1959.
Nemes, Dezső, and László Szűcs, eds. *Horthy Miklós titkos iratai* [Miklós Horthy's Secret Papers]. Budapest: Kossuth, 1972.
Ránki, György, ed. *Hitler hatvannyolc tárgyalása 1939–1944* [Hitler's Sixty-Eight Negotiations 1939–1944]. 2 vols. Budapest: Magvető, 1983.

Ránki, György, Ervin Pamlényi, Loránt Tilkovszky, and Gyula Juhász, eds. *A Wilhelmstrasse és Magyarország* [The Wilhelmstrasse and Hungary], Budapest: Kossuth, 1968.
Seewann, Gerhard, and Norbert Spannenberger, eds. *Akten des Volksgericht prozesses gegen Franz A. Basch, Volksgruppenführer der Deutschen in Ungarn. Budapest 1945–46.* Munich: Oldenbourg, 1999.
Sipos, Péter, and András Sipos, eds. *Imrédy Béla a vádlottak padján* [Béla Imrédy in the Dock]. Budapest: Osiris-BFL, 1999.
Szinai, Miklós, and László Szűcs, eds. *Bethlen István titkos iratai* [István Bethlen's Secret Papers], Budapest: Kossuth, 1972.
Újváry, Dezső, and Francis Deak, eds. *Papers and Documents Relating to the Foreign Relations of Hungary.* 2 vols. Budapest: Ministry for Foreign Affairs, 1939, and 1946.
Vértes, Robert, ed. *Magyarországi zsidótörvények és rendeletek 1938–1945* [Anti-Jewish Laws and Regulations in Hungary 1938–1945]. Budapest: Polgár, 1997.
Zsidi, Vilmos, ed. *Dokumentumok a Budapesti Közgazdaságtudományi Egyetem történetéből 1934–1938* [Documents from the History of the Budapest Economic Science University 1934–1938]. Budapest: BKÁE, 2001.
Zsigmond, László. *Diplomáciai iratok Magyarország külpolitikájához 1936–1945* [Diplomatic Papers on Hungary's Foreign Policy 1936–1945], Vols. 3-5. Budapest: Akadémiai, 1970–1983.

MEMOIRS

Andorka, Rudolf. *A madridi követségtől Mauthausenig* [From the Madrid Legation to Mauthausen], Budapest: Kossuth, 1978.
Ashmead-Bartlett, Ellis. *The Tragedy of Central Europe.* London: Thornton Butterworth, 1923.
Barcza, György. *Diplomataemlékeim* [My Diplomat Memories]. 2 vols. Budapest: Európa, 1994.
Bassola, Zoltán. *Ki voltarn... Egy kultuszminisztériumi államtitkár vallomásai* [Who was I... Confessions of an Education Ministry State Secretary]. Budapest: Országos Pedagógiai Könyvtár és Múzeum, 1998.
Boroviczeny, Aladár. *A király és kormányzója* [The King and His Regent], Budapest: Európa, 1993.
Cholnoky, Jenő. *Utazásom Amerikába Teleki Pál Gróffal* [My Travel to America with Count Pál Teleki]. Budapest: Vajda Wichman, [194?].
Cholnoky, Jenő. *Vár ucca tizenhét* [17 Var Street], Veszprém: Veszprém Önkormányzata, 1998.
Fodor, Ferenc. *Teleki Pál.* Budapest: Mike és Társa Antikvárium, 2001.
Gecsényi, Lajos, and Péter Sipos, eds. "Grátz Gusztáv emlékiratai" [The memoirs of Gusztáv Grátz], *Történelmi Szemle*, nos. 3–4 (2000): 309–369.
Horthy, Miklós. *Emlékirataim* [My Memoirs]. Budapest: Európa-História, 1990.
Huszár, Tibor. *Beszélgetések* [Conversations]. Budapest: Magvető, 1983.
Károlyi, Michael. *Memoirs of Michael Károlyi. Faith Without Illusion.* New York: E. P. Dutton, 1957.
Kelemen, Béla. *Adatok a szegedi ellenforradalom és a szegedi kormány történetéhez* [Data to the History of the Szeged Counterrevolution and the Szeged Government], Szeged: Kelemen Béla, 1923.

Marosi, Ildikó. *Örökbe hagyott beszélgetés gróf Teleki Mihállyal* [A Bequeathed Conversation with Count Mihály Teleki]. Budapest: Argumentum, 1999.
Milotay, István. *Egy élet Magyarországért—Ami Horthy emlékirataiból kimaradt* [A Life for Hungary—What Was Omitted from Horthy's Memoirs]. Budapest: Gede Testvérek, 2001.
Montgomery, John Flournoy. *Hungary, the Unwilling Satellite*. Morristown: Vista Books, 1993.
Muggeridge, Malcolm, ed. *Ciano's Diary 1939–1943*. London: William Heinemann, 1947.
Oláh, György, *Egy kilepő naplója* [Diary of a Dissident], Budapest: Stádium, 1941.
Padányi-Gulyás, Béla. *Vallomás egy elsüllyedt világrol* [Confessions about a Sunken World]. Munich: Auróra Könyvek, 1975.
Perneki, Mihály, ed. *Shvoy Kálmán titkos naplója és emlékiratai* [The Secret Diary and Memoirs of Kálmán Shvoy], Budapest: Kossuth, 1983.
Rónai, András. *Térképezett történelem* [Mapped History], Budapest: Püski, 1993.
Szabó, Ágnes, and Ervin Pamlényi, eds. *A határban a halál kaszál. Fejezetek Prónay Pál feljegyzéseiből* [Death is Mowing on the Verges— Chapters from Pál Prónay's Notes]. Budapest: Kossuth, 1963.
Szakály, Sándor, ed. *Náray Antal visszaemlékezése* [Memoirs of Antal Náray], Budapest: Zrínyi, 1988.
Szabolcsi, Lajos. *Két emberöltő. Az Egyenlőseg évtizedei* [Two Generations. The Decades of Equality]. Budapest: MTA Judaisztikai Kutatócsoport, 1993.
Szegedy-Maszák, Aladár. *Az ember ősszel visszanéz* [One Looks Back in the Autumn]. 2 vols. Budapest: Európa, 1996.
Újpétery, Elemér. *Végállomás Lisszabon* [Last Stop Lisbon]. Budapest: Magvető, 1987.
Varga, E. László, ed. "Orlowski Leó budapesti lengyel követ visszaemlékezései" [Memoirs of the Polish minister in Budapest, Leo Orlowski], *Studia Caroliensia*, no. 2 (2001): 17–65.
Zsitvay, Tibor. *Magyarország 1921–1941*. Edited by Péter Sipos and Tamás Csiffary. Budapest: Palatinus, 1999.

PERIODICALS

Fiatal Magyarság [Young Hungary], 1931–1938.
Kővárvidék. 1905–1918.
Nemzetvédelem [National Defense], 1918.
Magyar Cserkész [Hungarian Scout]. 1922–1938.
Az Országos Kaszinó Évkönyvei [Yearbooks of the Countrywide Casino], 1921–1938.
Turán. 1913–1914, and 1916–1918.
Vezetők Lapja [Journal of Leaders], 1922–1938.

WORKS OF PÁL TELEKI

Papp, Antal, ed. *Teleki Pál országgyűlési beszédei* [Pál Teleki's Parliamentary Speeches], 2 vols. Budapest: Stúdium, [1944].
Teleki, Pál. *A földrajzi gondolat története* [The History of Geographic Thought], Budapest: Kossuth, 1996.
Teleki, Pál. "A földrajztanár továbbképzése (és a legfontosabb földrajzi irodalom)" [Continuing education for the geography teacher and the most important geographical literature].

In *Modern földrajz és oktatása* [Modern Geography and Its Teaching], edited by Pál Teleki and György Vargha, pp. 156–163. Budapest: Stúdium, 1923.

Teleki, Pál. *A gazdasági élet földrajz alapjai* [The Geographical Foundations of Economic Life]. 2 vols. Budapest: Stúdium, 1936.

Teleki, Pál, "A moszuli vitás terület természetes tájai és határai" [The natural region and boundaries of the disputed Mosul area]. In *Magyar földrajzi évkönyv az 1926. évre* [Hungarian Geographical Yearbook for 1926], edited by Pál Teleki, János Karl, and Andor Kéz, pp. 54–57. Budapest: Magyar Földrajzi Intézet, 1926.

Teleki, Pál. "A tájfogalom jelentőségéről" [On the significance of the concept of region]. *Budapesti Szemle* (November 1937): 129–141.

Teleki, Pál. "A IV. Világ Jamboree" [The Fourth World Jamboree]. Special reprint from *Testnevelés*, nos. 1–2 (1932).

Teleki, Pál. *Amerika gazdasági földrajza, különös tekintettel az Észak-amerika Egyesült Államokra* [Economic Geography of America with Special Reference to the United States]. Budapest: Centrum, 1922.

Teleki, Pál. *Az elsődleges államkeletkezés kérdéséhez. Államtudori értekezés* [To the Problem of the Original Evolution of the State. Political Science Dissertation]. Budapest: Kilián Frigyes Utóda 1904.

Teleki, Pál. "Az európai probléma" [The European problem]. *Magyar Szemle*, no. 3 (1931): 209–220.

Teleki, Pál. "Az Imatra" (The Imatra]. In *Magyar földrajzi évkönyv az 1928. évre* [Hungarian Geographical Yearbook for 1928], edited by Pál Teleki, János Karl, and Andor Kéz, pp. 193–196. Budapest: Magyar Földrajzi Intézet, 1928.

Teleki, Pál. *Beszédek 1939* [Speeches 1939l. Budapest: Stúdium, n.d.

Teleki, Pál. "Dr. gróf Teleki Pál előadása a 'Magyar társadalmi politikáról'" [Dr. Count Pál Teleki's lecture on Hungarian social policies]. In *Az Országos Kaszinó évkönyve az 1926. évről* [Yearbook of the Countrywide Casino for 1926], 131–146. Budapest: Országos Kaszinó, 1927.

Teleki, Pál. *Európáról és Magyarországról* [On Europe and Hungary]. Budapest: Athenaeum, 1934.

Teleki, Pál. *The Evolution of Hungary and Its Place in European History*. New York: Macmillan, 1923.

Teleki, Pál. *Földrajz és néprajz* [Geography and ethnography]. Budapest: Magyar Néprajzi Társaság, 1920.

Teleki, Pál. "Gróf Teleki Pál előadása az 'angliai cserkészjamboree'- ról" [Count Pál Teleki's lecture on the Boy Scout Jamboree in England]. In *Országos Kaszinó évkönyve az 1929. évről* [Yearbook of the Countrywide Casino for 1929], pp. 263–294. Budapest: Országos Kaszinó, 1930.

Teleki, Pál. "Teleki Pál megnyitó beszéde" [Count Pál Teleki's opening speech]. *Liga Értesítő* (Nov. –Dee. 1937): 70–81.

Teleki, Pál. *Gróf Teleki Pál programmbeszéde, melyet Szeged első választokerületének Keresztény Nemzeti Egyesülés Pártja alakuló és képviselőjelölő nagygyűlésén mondott el, Szegeden, a Tisza szálló nagytermében 1919. év december havának 14. napján* [Count Pál Teleki's program speech that he delivered in Szeged in the Banquet Hall of the Tisza Hotel at the General Meeting of the Christian National Unification Party Organizing and Candidate Selection Meeting in the First Electoral District of Szeged on the 14th Day of December, 1919]. Szeged: Tevel-nyomda, n.d.

Teleki, Pál. "Hagyomány és forradalom" [Tradition and revolution]. *Katholikus Szemle* (February 1934): 115–117.
Teleki, Pál. *Magyar politikai gondolatok* [Hungarian Political Thoughts]. Budapest: Nemzeti Könyvtár, 1941.
Teleki, Pál. "Szellemi vértezettségünkről" [On our spiritual preparedness]. In *A Collegium Hungaricum Szövetség zsebkönyve* [The Collegium Hungaricum Association Handbook], Edited by János Martonyi, pp. 1–5. Budapest: Királyi Magyar Egyetemi Nyomda, 1936.
Teleki, Pál. *Szociálpolitika és hadigondozás* [Social Policy and Veteran Affairs], Budapest: Országos Hadigondozó Hivatal, 1918.
Teleki, Pál. "Teleki Pál Wekerle emlékserleg-beszéde" [Pál Teleki's Wekerle Memorial Cup speech]. In *Az Országos Kaszinó Évkönyve az 1934. évről* [Yearbook of the Countrywide Casino for 1934], pp. 168–176. Budapest: Országos Kaszinó, 1935.
Teleki, Pál. *Válogatott politikai írások és beszédek* [Selected Political Speeches and Writings]. Edited by Balázs Ablonczy. Budapest: Osiris, 2000.

BOOKS AND MONOGRAPHS

Ablonczy, Balázs. *Teleki Pál*. Budapest: Osiris, 2005.
Ablonczy, Balázs. *Teleki Pál*. Budapest: Elektra, 2000.
Arday, Lajos. *Térkép, csata után. Magyarország a brit külpolitikában 1918–1919* [Map after the Battle. Hungary in British Foreign Policy 1918–19191. Budapest: Magvető, 1990.
Bán, András D. *Illúziók és csalódások* [Illusions and disappointments], Budapest: Osiris, 1998.
Barta, Stefan. *Die Judenfrage in Ungarn*. Budapest: Verlag Stadium [194?].
Berey, Katalin. *Szociálpolitikai kísérlet Magyarországon a 40-es évek elején. Az Országos Nép- és Családvédelmi Alap munkássága* [Social Political Experiments in Hungary at the Beginning of the 1940s. Activities of the National People and Family Protective Foundation]. Budapest: A Művelődési Minisztérium Marxizmus-Leninizmus Oktatási Főosztálya, 1981.
Czettler, Antal. *Teleki Pál és a magyar külpolitika* [Pál Teleki and Hungarian Foreign Policy], Budapest: Magvető, 1997.
Csicsery-Rónay, István, and Károly Vígh, eds. *Teleki Pál és kora* [Pál Teleki and his era]. Budapest: Occidental Press, 1992.
Dombrády, Lóránd. *Hadsereg és politika Magyarországon 1938–1944* [The Army and Politics in Hungary 1938–1944], Budapest: Kossuth, 1986.
Dombrády, Lóránd, and Sándor Tóth. *A magyar királyi honvédség 1919–1945* [The Royal Hungarian Army 1919–1945]. Budapest: Zrínyi, 1987.
Fierro, Alfred. *La Société de Géographie 1821–1946*. Paris: Honore Champion, 1983.
Gathorne-Hardy, G. M. *A Short History of International Affairs*. London: Oxford University Press, 1942.
Gergely, Ferenc. *A magyar cserkészet története 1910–1948* [The History of Hungarian Scouting 1910–1948]. Budapest: Göncöl, 1989.
Grátz, Gusztáv. *A dualizmus kora* [The Age of Dualism]. 2 vols. Budapest: Akadémiai, 1993.
Grátz, Gusztáv. *A forradalmak kora* [The Age of Revolutions], Budapest: Akadémiai, 1993.
Grátz, Gusztáv. *Magyarország a két háború között* [Hungary between the Two Wars]. Budapest: Osiris, 2001.
Gyurgyák, János. *A zsidókérdés Magyarországon* [The Jewish Question in Hungary]. Budapest: Osiris, 2001.

Halász, Lajos, ed. *Az Országos Kaszinó ötvenéves története 1883–1932* [The Fifty-Year History of the Countrywide Casino 1882–1932]. Budapest: Országos Kaszinó, 1932.
Holopcev, Péter, ed. *"Egyszer volt..."—Előadások a Teleki és Vay családok történetéből.* ["Once upon a Time"—Lectures on the Teleki and Vay Family Histories]. Miskolc: Teleki Tehetséggondozó Kollégium, 1998.
Hoós, Ferenc. *Teleki Ferenc gróf mint költő és ember* [Count Ferenc Teleki as man and poet]. Veszprém: Pósa Endre, 1908.
Juhász, Gyula. *A Teleki-kormány külpolitikája* [The Foreign Policy of the Teleki Government]. Budapest: Akadémiai, 1964.
Juhász, Gyula. *Hungarian Foreign Policy 1919–1945.* Budapest: Akadémiai, 1979.
Julier, Ferenc. *1914–1918—A világháború magyar szemmel* [1914–1918. The World War through Hungarian Eyes]. Budapest: Magyar Szemle Társaság, 1933.
Karsai, László. *Holokauszt.* Budapest: Pannonica, 2001.
Kis, Aladár. *Magyarország külpolitikája a második világháború előestéjén* [Hungary's Foreign Policy on the Eve of the Second World War]. Budapest: Kossuth, 1963.
Kósa, László, ed. *Szabadon szolgál a szellem—Tanulmányok és dokumentumok a száz esztendeje alapított Eötvös József Collegium történetéből* [The spirit serves free. Essays and documents of the history of the József Eötvös College established one hundred years ago]. Budapest: Gift, 1995.
Kovács, M. Mária. *Liberalizmus, radikalizmus, antiszemtitizmus* [Liberalism, Radicalism and Anti-Semitism]. Budapest: Helikon, 2001.
Kovács-Bertrand, Anikó. *Der Ungarische Revisionismus nach dem ersten Weltkrieg.* Munich: Oldenbourg, 1997.
Kovrig, Béla. *Hungarian Social Policies, 1920–1945.* New York: A Magyar Nemzeti Bizottmány Vallás és Közoktatási Bizottsága, 1954.
L. Balogh, Béni. *Magyar-román kapcsolatok 1939–1940-ben és a második bécsi döntés* [Hungarian-Romanian Relations in 1939–1940 and the Second Vienna Award], Csíkszereda: Pro-Print, 2002.
L. Nagy, Zsuzsa. *Bethlen liberális ellenzéke* [Bethlen's liberal opposition]. Budapest; Akadémiai, 1987.
L. Nagy, Zsuzsa. *Liberális pártmozgalmak 1931–1945* [Liberal party movements 1931–1945]. Budapest: Akadémiai, 1986.
Laczkó, Miklós. *Nyilasok, nemzetiszocialisták 1935–1944* [Arrow Crossists and National Socialist 1935–1944]. Budapest: Kossuth, 1966.
Ladányi, Andor. *A gazdasági válságtól a háborúig* [From the Economic Crisis to the War]. Budapest: Argumentum, 2002.
Ladányi, Andor. *Klebelsberg felsőoktatási politikája* [Klebelsberg's higher education policy]. Budapest: Argumentum, 2000.
Lindner, Ernő, and István Illés, eds. *A Királyi Magyar Automobil Club jubiláris aranykönyve 1900–1930* [Golden jubilee book of the Royal Hungarian Automobile Club 1900–1930], Budapest: KMAC, 1930.
Macartney, C. A. *October Fifteenth. A History of Modern Hungary, 1929–1945.* 2 vols. Edinburgh: Edinburgh University Press, 1957.
Matolay, Géza, and Rózsa Mudrinszky, eds. *Gróf Teleki Pál élete és munkássága a magyar revízió szolgálatában* [The Life and Activities of Count Pál Teleki in the Service of Hungarian Revision], Budapest: Halász Irodalmi és Könyvkiadóvállalat, 1941.

Mészáros, István. *Teleki Pál nemzetnevelő programja* [The National Educational Program of Pál Teleki]. Gödöllő: Teleki Pál Egyesület, 1993.
Monroe, Elizabeth. *Britain's Moment in the Middle East, 1914–1956.* London: Chattoo & Windus, 1964.
N. Szegvári, Katalin. *Numerus clausus rendelkezések az ellenforradalmi Magyarországon* [Numerus Clausus ordinances in counterrevolutionary Hungary]. Budapest: Akadémiai, 1988.
Nagy, József Zsigmond, and István Szíjártó, eds. *Tanulmányok az Eötvös Kollégium történetéből* [Essays on the History of the Eötvös Colleg]. Budapest: Eötvös József Kollégium, 1989.
Nemes, Dezső. *Az ellenforradalom története Magyarországon 1919–1921* [History of the Counterrevolution in Hungary 1919–1921], Budapest: Akadémiai, 1962.
Ormos, Mária. *Egy magyar médiavezér: Kozma Miklós* [Miklós Kozma, a Hungarian Media Tsar]. 2 vols. Budapest: PolgART, 2000.
Ormos, Mária. *From Padua to the Trianon.* Budapest: Akadémiai, 1990.
Ormos, Mária. *"Soha, amíg élek"* [Never, as long as I live], Pécs: Pannónia Könyvek, 1990.
Petri, Pál. *A magyar hadigondozás történetének vázlata* [A sketch of the history of Hungarian veteran affairs). Budapest: Országos Hadigondozó Intézet, 1917.
Pritz, Pál. *A magyar diplomácia a két háború között* [Hungarian diplomacy between the two wars], Budapest: Magyar Történelmi Társulat, 1995.
Püski, Levente. *A magyar felsőház története 1927–1945* [History of the Hungarian Upper House 1927–1945], Budapest: Napvilág, 2000.
Ránki, György, ed. *Magyarország története, 1918–1919, 1919–1945* [Hungary's history, 1918–1919, 1919–1945]. 2 vols. Budapest: Akadémiai, 1988.
Romsics, Ignác. *The Dismantling of Historic Hungary.* Boulder, CO: Social Science Monographs, 2002.
Romsics, Ignác. *István Bethlen: A Great Conservative Statesman of Hungary, 1874–1946.* Boulder, CO: Social Science Monographs, 1995.
Romsics, Ignác. *Hungary in the Twentieth Century.* Budapest: Osiris, 1999.
Romsics, Ignác, ed. *Mítoszok, legendák, tévhitek a 20. századi magyar történelemről* [Myths, legends and misconceptions about 20th-century Hungarian history], Budapest: Osiris, 2002.
Romsics, Ignác, and Iván Bertényi, Jr., eds. *Trianon és a magyar politikai gondolkodás 1920–1953* [Trianon and Hungarian political thought, 1920–1953]. Budapest: Osiris, 1998.
Sallai, Gergely. *Az első bécsi döntés* [The First Vienna Award]. Budapest: Osiris, 2002.
Seegel, Steven. *Map men. Transnational Lives and Deaths of Geographers in the Making of East Central Europe.* Chicago: Chicago UP, 2018.
Sipos, Péter. *Imrédy Béla és a Magyar Megújulás Pártja* [Béla Imrédy and the Party of Hungarian Renewal]. Budapest: Akadémiai, 1976.
Spannenberger, Norbert. *Der Volksbund der Deutschen in Ungarn 1938–1944 miter Horthy und Hitler.* Munich: Oldenbourg, 2002.
Stoffán, György. *Az utolsó Habsburg-kaland— "Én öltem meg Teleki Pált"* [The last Habsburg adventure—I murdered Pál Teleki], N. p., n.d.
Stivers, William. *Supremaccy and Oil. Iraq, Turkey, and the Anglo-American World Order 1918–1930.* Ithaca: Cornell University Press, 1982.
Szentgyörgyi, Mária. *Kővár vidékének társadalma* [The society of the Kővár Region]. Budapest: Akadémiai, 1972.

Szöllősi-Janze, Margit. *Die Pfeilkreutzlkerbewegung in Ungarn. Historischer Kontext, Entwicklung und Herrschaft.* Munich: Oldenbourg, 1896.
Tilkovszky, Loránt. *Ez volt a Volksbund* [This was the Volksbund], Budapest: Kossuth, 1978.
Tilkovszky, Loránt. *Pál Teleki—A Biographical Sketch.* Budapest: Akadémiai, 1976.
Tilkovszky, Loránt. *Revízió és nemzetiségpolitika Magyarországon 1938–1941* [Revision and nationality politics in Hungary 1938–1941]. Budapest: Akadémiai, 1967.
Tilkovszky, Loránt. *Teleki Pál.* Budapest: Kossuth, 1969.
Tilkovszky, Loránt. *Teleki Pál titokzatos halála* [Pál Teleki's mysterious death], Budapest: Helikon, 1989.
Trócsányi, Zsolt. *Teleki Mihály. Erdély és kurucmozgalom 1690-ig* [Mihály Teleki. Transylvania and the Kuruc movement until 1690]. Budapest: Akadémiai, 1972.
Vígh, Károly, ed. *Ismeretelen fejezetek Teleki Pál életéből* [Unknown chapters from Pál Teleki's life]. Budapest: Századvég, 2001.
Weindling, Paul. *Health, Race and German Politics between National Unification and Nazism, 1870–1945.* Cambridge: Cambridge University Press, 1989.
Weingart, Peter. Jorgen Kroll, and Kurt Bayertz. *Rasse, Blut und Gene—Geschichte der Eugenik und Rassenhygiene in Deutschland.* Frankfurt am Main: Suhrkamp, 1988.
Witz, Béla. *Teleki Pál vallásossága* [The religiosity of Pál Teleki]. Budapest: Középponti Katolikus Kör, 1943.
Zakar, András. *Gróf Teleki Pál halála* [Count Pál Teleki's death]. Vienna: EOLA, 1983.
Zeidler, Miklós. *A revíziós gondolat* [The revisionist Idea]. Budapest: Osiris, 2000.

ARTICLES AND ESSAYS

Ablonczy, Balázs. "A kegyelmes úr napjai—Kísérlet Teleki Pál miniszterelnök határidőnaplójának elemzésére" [His Excellency's days— An attempt to analyze the daily calendar of Prime Minister Pál Teleki], *Korall*, no. 17 (September 2004): 193–207.
Ablonczy, Balázs. "Un débat historique manqué. Le cas Teleki en Hongrie," *La Nouvelle Alternative* (Paris) 21, nos. 69-70 (June–September, 2006): 135–146.
Almasi, János. "Az 1938-as Táj- és Népkutató Kiállítás és politikai visszhangja" [The 1938 Region and Ethnography Exposition and its political repercussions]. *Elmélet és Politika—Információs Szemle*, no. 2(1986).
Bárdi, Nándor. "A Keleti Akció I—II" [The Eastern Action, Parts 1 and 2|. *REGIO*, no. 3 (1995): 89–134; no. 4 (1995): 3–28.
Bognár, Iván. "A Népjóléti Minisztérium és a Népjóléti Népbiztosság szervezete 1917–1919" [The structure of the Ministry of Social Welfare and the Social Welfare Commissariat 1917–1919]. *Levéltári Közlemények*, no. 2 (1966).
Borbándi, Gyula. "A Teleki-Pelényi terv nyugati magyar ellenkormány létesítésére" [The Teleki-Pelényi plan to establish a Hungarian exile government in the West]. *Látóhatár*, no. 2 (1966): 155–170.
Gergely, Ferenc. "Cserkész Világtábor Magyarországon (Gödöllő, 1933)" [Boy Scout World Jamboree in Hungary (Gödöllő, 1933)]. *Századok*, no. 6(1981): 1218–1243.
Győri, Robert. "Magyar gazdaságföldrajz a két világháború között" [Hungarian economic geography between the two World Wars], In *Geográfia az Ezredfordulón* |Geography at the turn of the millennium]. *Regionális Tudományi Tanulmányok* 6 [Regional Scientific Studies 6], edited by József Nemes Nagy, pp. 71–83. Budapest: ELTE Regionális Földrajzi Tanszék, 2001.

Hajdú, Zoltán. "Friedrich Ratzel hatása a magyar földrajztudományban" [The influence of Friedrich Ratzel on Hungarian geographical science]. *Tér és Társadalom*, no. 3 (1998): 93–104.

Hajdú, Zoltán. "Geográfus politikus vagy politikus geográfus? A tudomány és politika kölcsönhatása Teleki Pál életművében" [Geographer politician or politician geographer? The interaction of science and politics in Pál Teleki's life work]. *Földrajzi Közlemények*, nos. 1-2(1991): 1–9.

Hajdú, Zoltán. "Czirbusz Géza: a magyar társadalomföldrajz 'temetetlen' megalapítója" [Géza Czirbusz the "unforgotten" creator of Hungarian social geography]. In *A magyar társadalomföldrajzi kutatás gondolatvilága (Tanulmányok a hatvanéves Mészaros Rezső köszöntésére)* [The world of Hungarian social geographical thought (Essays in Honor of Rezső Mészáros's sixtieth birthday)], edited by Mrs. Jolán Palotás Abonyi, József Becsei, and Csaba Kovács, pp. 111–120. Szeged: SZTE Gazdaság- és Társadalomföldrajzi Tanszék, 2002.

Hajdú, Zoltán. "Teleki Pál tájelméleti munkássága" [Pál Teleki's work on the theory of region], *Földrajzi Közlemények*, nos. 1–2 (2001): 51–63.

Hajdú, Zoltán. "Területrendezési törekvések a magyar földrajztudományban a két világháború között" [Hungarian territorial adjustment efforts between the two World Wars]. *Földrajzi Közlemények*, no. 2 (1982).

Hámori, Péter. "Kísérlet egy 'propagandaminisztérium' létrehozására Magyarországon" [Attempt to create a Propaganda Ministry in Hungary], *Századok*, no. 2 (1997): 353–382.

Hámori, Péter. "Portugália mint 'bezzegország'—A magyar ifjúkatolikusok útkeresése és a portugál minta" [Portugal as the "can do" country. The Hungarian Catholic youth's search for a path and the Portuguese model]. *Valóság*, no. 6 (1994): 56–65.

Illésfalvi, Péter. "'Édes Erdély itt vagyunk...'— Az 1940-es erdélyi bevonulás során történt atrocitásokról ["Dear Transylvania, here we are..." On the atrocities committed during the Transylvanian occupation in 1940], *Pro Minoritate*, no. 1 (Spring 2004): 58–77.

Karády, Victor. "Le Collège Eötvös et l'Ecole Normale Supérieure vers 1900—Note comparatiste sur la formation d'intellectuels professionnels français." In *Intellectuels français, intellectuels hongrois Xllleme-XXeme siecles*, edited by Béla Köpeczi and Jacques Le Goff. Budapest: Akadémiai Kiadó: 1985.

Klinghammer, István, and Gábor Gercsák. "Der ungarische Geograph Pál Teleki als Mitglied der Mossul-Kommission." *Cartographica Helvetica* 19, no. 1 (Januar 1999): 17–25.

Kosáry, Domokos. "Az Eötvös Kollégium történetéből—Az első évtizedek: 1895–1927" [From the history of the Eötvös College—the first decades, 1895–1927]. In *Tanulmányok az Eötvös Kollégium történetéből* [Essays on the History of the Eötvös College), edited by József Zsigmond Nagy and István Szíjártó, pp. 9–40. Budapest: Eötvös József Kollégium, 1989.

Ladányi, Andor. "A numerus clausus törvény 1928. évi módosításáról" [On the 1928 amendments to the numerus clausus legislation], *Századok*, no. 6 (1994): 1118–1134.

Mihalik, István. "Küzdelem az önálló egyetemi szintű közgazdaszképzésért" [Fight for university level economist training]. In *Tanulmányok a magyarországi közgazdasági felsőoktatás történetéből* [Essays on the history of higher education for economists in Hungary], edited by László Szögi and Vilmos Zsidi, pp. 71–91. Budapest: A Budapesti Közgazdaságtudományi Egyetem Levéltárának Kiadványai, 1995.

Molnár, Máté. "A Nemzetközi Szakszervezeti Szövetség bojkottja Magyarország ellen (1920. június 20–Augusztus 8)" [The International Trade Union Association boycott against Hungary], *Századok*, no. 3 (1996): 639–656.

Nerpel, József, and József Wohlrab. "Írásszakértő és történettudomány" [Graphologist and historical scholarship], *História*, no. 1 (1985): 20-23.
Niklay, Péter. "A Magyar Szociográfiai Intézmény szervezete és gyűjteményei" [The organization and collections of the Hungarian Sociographic Institute]. In *A Magyar Társaság és a Falukutató Intézet Évkönyve—1935* [Yearbook of the Hungarian Society and Village Study Institute, 1935], edited by Antal Bodor. Budapest: MTFI, 1935.
Ormos, Mária "Hamis frankokkal teli bőröndök" [Suitcases full of forged francs]. In *Skandalum. Magyar közéleti botrányok 1843–1991* [Scandal. Hungarian public life scandals 1843–1991], edited by András Gerő, pp. 175–193. Budapest: T-Twins, 1993.
Pásztor, Mihály. "A százötvenéves Lipótváros" [The 150 year-old Lipótváros]. *Statisztikai Közlemények* 93, no. 4 (1940).
Petrichevich Horváth, Emil. "Honnan származtak a Garázdák és Szilágyiak?" [Where did the Garázda and the Szilágyi clan come from?]. *Magyar Családtörténeti Szemle*, nos. 6-8 (August 1938): 137–139.
Pintér, István. "A kényszerpályára szavazó ország—1939" [Voting for a path the country is forced to take—1939], In *Parlamenti választások Magyarországon 1920–1998* [Parliamentary elections in Hungary 1920–1998). Edited by György Földes and László Hubai, pp. 176–207. Budapest: Napvilág, 1999.
Ránki, György. "A Clerk-misszió története" [The history of the Clerk Mission]. *Történelmi Szemle*, no. 2 (1967): 157–187.
Richly, Gábor. "Magyar katonai segítségnyújtás az 1939–1940-es finn-szovjet háborúban" [Hungarian military assistance in the 1939–1940 Finn-Soviet war]. *Századok*, no. 2 (1996): 403–444.
Romsics, Ignác. "Franciaország, Bethlen és a frankhamisítás" [France, Bethlen and the franc forgery], *Történelmi Szemle*, no. 1 (1983): 67–86.
Romsics, Ignác. "A magyar birodalmi gondolat" [Hungarian imperial ideas]. In *Nem élhetek birodalom nélkül* [I cannot live without an empire], edited by Hedi Volosin and Csaba Gombár, pp. 41–81. Budapest: Helikon, 2002.
Sieferle, Rolf Peter. "Rassismus, Rasenhygiene, Menschenzuchtideale." In: *Handbuch zur "Volkischen Bewegung" 1971–1918*, edited by Uwe Puschner, Walter Schmitz-Justus, and H. Ulbricht. Munich: KG Saur, 1999.
Simon, Zsuzsanna. "Észak Erdély köz- és szakigazgatása a második bécsi döntés után" [Northern Transylvania's civil and technical administration after the Second Vienna Award], *REGIO*, no 4 (1995): 60–82.
Sipos, József. "A kisgazdapárt és a Teleki-kormány lemondása" [The Smallholder Party and the resignation of the Teleki government]. In *A Szegedi Móra Ferenc Múzeum Évkönyve, 1978–1979* [Yearbook of the Ferenc Móra Museum, 1978–1979], Szeged: Móra Ferenc Múzeum, 1979.
Sipos, Péter, Miklós Stier, and István Vida. "Változasok a kormánypárt parlamenti képviseletének összetételében 1931–1939 [Changes in the composition of the parliamentary government party 1931–1939], *Századok*, nos. 3–4 (1967): 602–621.
Szekeres, József. "Az 1940. évi általános bányászsztrájk története" [History of the 1940 miners' general strike]. *Századok*, nos. 1–2 (1967): 82–137.
Tóth, Endre. "Az első kétoldalú tárgyalások Csehszlovakia és Magyarország között (1921) Bruck an der Leitha II" [The first bilateral negotiations between Czechoslovakia and Hungary in 1921 in Bruck an der Leitha. Part 2], *Fórum*, no. 2 (2002): 59–75.

Tóth, Endre. "Az első kétoldalú tárgyalások Csehszlovakia és Magyarország között (1921) Márianske Lazne II" [The first bilateral negotiations between Czechoslovakia and Hungary in 1921 in Márianske Lazne. Part 2]. *Fórum*, no. 1 (2003): 49–64.

Varga, László E. "Orlowski budapesti lengyel követ visszaemlékezései II" [The recollections of Orlowski, the Polish minister in Budapest. Part 2]. *Századok*, no. 6 (2003).

Vasas, Géza. "A ruszin autonómia válaszútjain (1939. március–szeptember)" [Ruthenian autonomy at the crossroads, March–September, 1939], *Aetas*, no. 4 (2000): pp. 64–87.

MANUSCRIPTS

B. Bernát, István. "A TESZK a revíziós propaganda egységéért" [The TESZK for the unity of revisionist propaganda], Ms. 591/1987/1. László Teleki Alapítvány Papers, OSZKK, Fond 625.

Farkas, Ildikó. "A turánizmus" [Turanism]. PhD diss., ELTE BTK, 2001.

Füves, Ödön. "Görögök Pesten 1686–1931" [The Greeks in Pest. 1686–1931]. 3 vols. PhD diss., Hungarian Academy of Science, 1972.

Kessler, József A. "Turanism and Pan-Turanism in Hungary: 1890–1945." PhD. Diss., University of California, Berkeley, 1967.

Vargyai, Gyula. "Az észak-erdélyi magyar katonai közigazgatás megszervezése" [Organization of the Northern-Transylvanian Hungarian military administration]. László Teleki Alapítvány Papers, OSZKK, Fond 625.

ABBREVIATIONS

ÁBTL: Állambiztonsági Szolgálatok Történeti Levéltara [Historical Archives of State Security]
BFL: Budapest Főváros Levéltára [Budapest Municipal Archives]
HU-SH: Seminar für Hungarologie, Humboldt Universität
LONA-ASDN: League of Nations Archives—Archives des Societés des Nations
MAE AD: Ministère des Affaires Etrangères. Archives Diplomatiques
MBFSZ TtGy: Magyar Bányászati és Földtani Szolgálat - Tudománytörténeti Gyűjtemény [Mining and Geological Survey of Hungary - History of Science Collection]
MDKL: Mednyánszky Dénes Könyvtár és Levéltár - Eötvös Collegium Levéltára. [Dénes Mednyánszky Library and Archives - Eötvös College Archives] [Archives of the Eötvös College]
MFMA: Magyar Földrajzi Múzeum Archívuma [Archives of the Hungarian Geographical Museum]
MFT IL: Magyar Földrajzi Társaság Irat- és Levéltára [Archives of the Hungarian Geographical Society]
MNL OL: Magyar Nemzeti Levéltár - Országos Levéltár [Hungarian National Archives]
PRMTKL: Piarista Rend Magyar Tartománya Központi Levéltára [Central Archives of the Piarist Province in Hungary]
MTAKK: Magyar Tudományos Akadémia Könyvtára, Kézirattár [Archives and Manuscript Collection of the Library of the Hungarian Academy of Science|
MTM TtGy: Magyar Természettudományi Múzeum, Tudománytörténeti Gyűjtemény [Hungarian Museum of Natural History, History of Science Collection]
OHA: Veritas Intézet Oral History Archívuma [Oral History Archives of the Veritas Institute]

OK: Országgyűlési Könyvtár, ENSZ Letéti Gyűjtemény [Parliament Library, United Nations Collection]
OSZKK: Országos Széchényi Könyvtár, Kézirattár [National Széchényi Library, Manuscript Collection]
PA AA: Politisches Archiv des Auswärtigen Amtes
RL: Ráday Levéltár [Ráday Archives]
TLA: Teleki László Alapítvány Könyvtára [Library of the Laszló Teleki Foundation]
TNA FO: The National Archives, Foreign Office

Name Index

Ablonczy, Zsofia, 3
Ábrahám, Dezső P., 65
Albert (Albrecht), Archduke, 93
Allizé, Henri, 60, 61
Almásy, László Ede, 95
Andics, Erzsébet, 254
Andorka, Rudolf, 219
Andrássy, Count Gyula, 20, 21, 54, 59, 110
Antall, József, 255
Antonescu, Ion, 233
Apafi, Mihály, 5
Apáthy, István, 48
Apor, Baron Gábor, 247
Apponyi, Count Albert, 70, 71, 76
Apponyi, Count György, 212
Aradi, Zsolt, 152
Ashmead-Bartlett, Ellis, 60
Asquith, Herbert Henry, 103

Baden-Powell, Robert, Lord, 142, 143, 146, 147, 150, 151
Bajcsy-Zsilinszky, Endre, 205
Bakay, Lajos, 250, 252
Balbi, Adriano, 27
Balogh, Jenő, 18
Balogh, József, 120
Bánffy, Baron Dániel, 240
Bánffy, Count Miklós, 35, 42, 102, 105, 110
Barcza, György, 209, 247–49
Bárczy, István, 35
Bárdossy, László, 245, 247, 248, 250, 253
Baross, Gábor, 137
Bartha, Károly, 188, 210
Bartos, József, 13
Basch, Ferenc, 237
Beaverbrook, William, Lord, 103
Benard, Agoston,
Bencs, Zoltán, 69
Beneš, Edvard, 87, 105

Bergson, Henri, 32
Bertényi, Iván, Jr., 40n94
Berthelot, Philippe, 104
Berzeviczy, Albert, 35, 156
Bethlen, Countess Margit, 37
Bethlen, Count István, 37, 54, 58–61, 64, 66, 69, 76, 77, 92, 94, 97, 102, 110–13, 118, 119, 131–33, 135–38, 148, 165, 174, 188, 213, 215, 231, 235, 250
Bignon, Paul, 72
Bismarck-Schönhausen, Count Gottfried von, 163
Bissingen-Nippenburg, Johanna (Countess Hanna, see also Teleki, Countess Pál), 37, 110, 171, 172, 177, 178, 247, 248
Bissingen-Nippenburg, Rudolf, 37
Blache, Vidal de la, 28
Bóli (Pál Teleki), 10, 58
Boromissza, Tibor, 37
Botez, Ioan, 24n137, 175n306
Bowman, Isaiah, 31, 106, 131
Briand, Aristide, 104
Bródy, András, 236
Brunhes, Jean de, 28
Bryce, James, Lord, 103
Buchinger, Manó, 198
Buie, Vasile, 175n306

Cadogan, Alexander, 104
Cecil, Robert, 103
Chaix, Emile, 31, 131
Charles IV, King, 53, 92–94, 96, 104, 110, 151
Chisholm, George C., 56
Cholnoky, Jenő, 15, 23, 24, 26, 27, 29–34, 122, 123, 167
Chorin, Ferenc, 35
Chotek, Countess Sophie, 38
Ciano, Count Galeazzo, 202, 209, 220, 221, 226, 230
Clemenceau, Georges, 60, 70–72

279

Pál Teleki

Clerk, George, 66, 67
Clodius, Carl von, 221
Cordier, Henri, 21–22, 25
Csáky, Count Imre, 69, 85, 88
Csáky, Count István, 69, 187, 188, 192, 202, 203, 209, 210, 214, 217, 230, 244, 245
Cuninghame, Thomas, 56, 60
Curzon, George Nathaniel, Lord, 125
Cvetković, Dragiša, 245
Czettler, Antal, 256
Czirbusz, Géza, 27–29

Darányi, Ignác, 35
Darányi, Kálmán, 179, 202, 215
Davis, W. M., 31, 106
De Valera, Eamon, 217
Djewad, Pasha, 128
Dodge, H. P, 63
Drasche-Lázár, Alfréd, 76

Eckhardt, Tibor, 188, 190, 199, 212
Economo, János, 37
Eden, Anthony, 231
Engels, Friedrich, 18
Eötvös, Baron József, 140
Eötvös, Baron Loránd, 140
Erdmannsdorff, Otto von,
Esterházy, Count Móric, 10, 49, 51, 215

Fejérváry, Géza, 20–22
Felvinczi Takats, Zoltán, 10, 234
Festetits, Prince György, 203
Fodor, Ferenc, 69, 122, 123, 143, 152, 169, 185, 256
Fontenay, Louis Gabriel, 63
Fouchet, Maurice, 74, 75, 86, 87
Francis Ferdinand, Archduke, 38
Francis Joseph, King, 20, 53
Friedrich, István, 66–68, 80
Fütterer, Cuno, 230

Gabriel, Marcel, 22, 63
Galton, Francis, 47
George, David Lloyd, 71
Germanus, Gyula, 44, 45
Gerő, András, 3
Gerő, László, 133–37
Gigurtu, Ion, 226

Gobineau, Arthur de, 44
Gömbös, Gyula, 54, 132, 187, 202, 204, 224
Goode, William, 209
Göring, Herman, 227
Grant-Smith, Ulysses, 94
Gratz, Gusztav, 87, 91, 199
Győrffy, István, 180

Habsburg, József (see also Joseph, Archduke), 66, 68, 93, 157
Habsburg, Otto von, 151
Hajts, Lajos, 137
Halifax, Edward F. L. Wood, Lord, 231
Haller, István, 83
Haller, Countess Matilda, 6
Halmos, Károly, 72
Hanna, Countess (Bissingen- Nippenburg, Johanna), 37
Harding, Warren G., 110
Hashimi, Yasin Pasha, 127
Hatvany Deutsch, Baron József, 35
Hegedűs, Lóránt, 91, 92
Héjjas, Iván, 78, 86
Hekler, Antal, 44
Himmler, Heinrich, 163
Hitler, Adolf, 162, 163, 179, 182, 190, 192, 194, 202, 208–10, 222–24, 226, 230, 243, 245
Hoffmann, Géza, 48
Hohler, Thomas, 243, 250
Hóman, Bálint, 156, 157, 188
Hóry, András, 228, 229
Hotewetz, Rudolf, 87
Hubay, Kálmán, 191, 212, 224
Hughes, Charles Evans, 110
Hunfalvy, János, 14
Huszár, Károly, 67, 69
Huxley, Aldous, 160

Imrédy, Béla, 171, 179, 182, 184, 186–89, 193, 203, 204, 206, 215, 221, 222, 236, 238–40
Incze, Péter, 171, 250
Ismet (Inönü), Mustapha Pasha, 125

Jankovich, Arisztid, 132
Jaross, Andor, 187, 189, 214
Jászi, Oszkár, 54, 58
Jomard, Edme-François, 25

Name Index

Joseph, Archduke (see also Habsburg József), 66, 68, 93, 157
Juhász, Gyula, 254

Kahr, Gustav Ritter von, 87
Kánya, Kálmán, 87, 187
Károlyi, Count Imre, 133, 134, 137
Károlyi, Count Gyula, 61, 188
Károlyi, Count Mihály, 35, 53, 54, 57–59, 107, 134
Keresztes-Fisher, Ferenc, 188, 202, 204, 214
Keyser, John E., 197
Keyserling, Hermann von, 158, 163
Kis, Aladár, 254
Klebelsberg, Kuno, 123, 138, 161, 162
Korányi, Baron Frigyes, 90, 92
Korff, Baron Serge A., 106
Kósa, László, 2
Kossuth, Ferenc, 22
Kossuth, Lajos, 22
Kovács, Alajos, 69, 200
Kovács, Gáspár, 132
Kovrig, Béla, 214
Kozma, Miklós, 54, 97, 236, 250
Kramers, J. H., 127
Kristóffy, József, 20
Krisztics, Sándor, 115
Kultsár, István, 181
Kunder, Antal, 187, 189, 214
Kunfi, Zsigmond, 57

Leopold I, Emperor, 6
Listowel, Judith Hale, Lady, 209
Lobit, Paul de, 60
Lóczy, Lajos, 14–16, 22, 25–27, 29, 32, 34, 51, 56, 73
Loraine, Sir Percy, 220
Loucheur, Louis, 72
Ludendorff, Erich, 87

Macartney, C. A., 224, 245, 255
Madzsar, József, 49
Magyary, Zoltán, 185
Majcsi (Mária Teleki, daughter of Pál), 38, 176
Mankovich, György, 132
Mannheim, Karl, 158
Manoilescu, Mihail, 226, 230
Márffy-Mantuano, Judit, 209
Margerie, Emmanuel de, 31

Marsovszky, György, 132
Martin, Hubert S., 147
Martin, Lawrence, 56, 106
Martonne, Emmanuel de, 31, 55
Marty, Count Chenal, 147
Mendöl, Tibor, 52
Micaș, Ioan, 175n306
Millerand, Alexandre, 75, 78, 86, 102, 105
Mocsonyi, Georgine, 37
Mocsonyi, Lívia, 37
Molotov, Vyacheslav, 216, 225, 232, 253
Montgomery, John F., 218
Morgan, Lewis H., 18
Muller, Max, 33
Muráti, Ilona, 9n13
Muráti, Iren (see also Teleki, Countess Géza), 7, 9
Muráti, Konstantin, 7, 8
Muráti, Panajot, 8
Muráti, Szilard, 8
Mussolini, Benito, 190, 202, 209, 220, 221

Nádosy, Imre, 132, 135–37
Nagyatádi Szabó, István, 67, 78, 89, 96
Náray, Antal, 248
Newton, Thomas Wodehouse Legh, Lord, 103
Nisbet, Robert, 159
Nopcsa, Ferenc, 55
Nordau, Max, 158
Nordenskjöld, Otto, 25

O'Malley, Owen, 217
Oláh, György, 152
Orlowski, Leon, 218
Ostenburg, Gyula, 82

Pacelli, Eugenio, Cardinal (Pius XII), 181
Paikert, Alajos, 35, 36
Pakocs, Károly, 175
Paleologue, Maurice, 72, 86
Pallavicini, Marquess Edina (m. Countess Rafael Zichy), 10
Pallavicini, Marquis György, 10, 110, 134, 135
Paneretov, Stefan, 106
Papp, Antal, 113, 253
Pataky, Tibor, 214
Paulis, Albert, 126, 130
Pázmány, Péter, 121

281

Peidl, Gyula, 65, 111
Pelényi, János, 219
Pétain, Henri-Philippe, 219
Petri, Pál, 57
Picot, Francis, 124
Pikler, Gyula, 18
Pius XII (Cardinal Pacelli), 181
Ploetz, Alfred, 47
Poincaré, Raymond, 104
Potiorek, Oskar, 39
Princip, Gavrilo, 38
Prónay, Pál, 78, 82

Quast, Matthijs, 25

Rába, Dezső, 132, 135–37
Radocsay, László, 214
Rákóczi, Prince Ferenc II, 23
Rákóczi, Prince György II, 5
Rassay, Károly, 188, 191, 198, 212
Ratzel, Friedrich, 14, 15, 17, 18, 44
Ribbentrop, Joachim von, 202, 209–11, 216, 226
Ritter, Carl von, 14
Robien, Louis de, 72
Roddolo, Marcello, 127
Romsics, Ignác, 2
Rónai, András, 186, 234, 250
Roosevelt, Nicholas, 56
Rothermere, Harold Sidney, 146
Rothschild, Charles, 103
Rubido-Zichy, Baron Ivan, 128
Rubinek, Gyula, 76
Rumbold, Sir Horace, 58

Sacelláry, Mária, 8
Salazar, Antonio de Oliveira, 217, 241
Schultze, Arthur, 134
Seeckt, Hans von, 87
Semsey, Andor, 72
Seton-Watson, Robert, 67
Sigray, Count Antal, 95, 191
Simonyi-Semadan, Sándor, 73, 74, 76
Smuts, Jan, 60
Somló, Bódog, 18
Spencer, Herbert, 18
Spengler, Oswald, 158
St. Stephen, 101, 116, 117, 120, 200, 226, 231

Sykes, Sir Mark, 124
Szablya-Frischauf, Ferenc, 15
Szálasi, Ferenc, 191, 237, 238
Szász, Zoltán, 45
Széchenyi, Count Béla, 42
Széchenyi, Count István, 42
Szentiványi, Domokos, 239
Szterényi, József, 51
Sztójay, Döme, 194, 225, 227, 245, 247

Taine, Hippolyte, 44
Tasman, Abel, 25
Tasnádi Nagy, András, 187, 189, 198–200, 214
Teleki families, 5
Teleki, Count Ede, 6, 38
Teleki, Count Géza (father of Pál), 6–9, 11, 13, 15, 20, 35, 38, 154, 172
Teleki, Count Géza (son of Pál), 38, 143, 154, 176, 234
Teleki, Count János, 214
Teleki, Count Jenő, 10
Teleki, Count Mihály, 6, 187, 188, 240
Teleki, Count Mihály II, 5
Teleki, Count Mihály III, 6
Teleki, Count Sámuel, 13
Teleki, Count Sándor (son of Mihály), 6
Teleki, Count Sándor (uncle of Pál), 10
Teleki, Count Tibor, 174
Teleki, Countess Edina, 10
Teleki, Countess Mária, 38, 176
Teleki, Countess Pál (née Johanna Bissigen-Nippenburg), 37
Teleki, Countess Sándor (née Júlia Kende), 103
Tildy, Zoltán, 248
Tilkovszky, Loránt, 255
Tiso, Jozef, 183, 184, 194
Tisza, Count István, 19, 22, 35, 42, 49, 53
Tisza, Count Kálmán, 7
Tittoni, Tommaso, 106
Trautmann, Eugen, 134, 137
Troubridge, Sir Ernest Charles Thomas, 63

Uhlig, Carl, 31
Újpétery, Elemér, 249
Ullmann, Adolf, 72

Vágó, Pál, 224

Name Index

Vaida-Voevod, Alexandru, 22, 23
Valéry, Paul, 160
Vámbéry, Ármin, 34
Vanik, Miklós, 122n85
Varga, József, 213
Vázsonyi, János, 191, 199
Vienne, Louis de, 119
Vix, Fernand, 54
Vörnle, János, 193

Wekerle, Sándor, 21, 200
Welles, Sumner, 220
Wenckheim, Count Frigyes, 10
Werth, Henrik, 188, 194, 210, 230, 231, 246
Wertheimstein, Rózsika, 103
Wickham-Steed, Henry, 67
Windischgraetz, Prince Lajos, 132–37
Wirsen, Carl Einar Thure af, 126, 130
Witz, Béla, 249, 252

Zichy, Count István, 15
Zita, Queen, 94

Place Index

Abbázia (Opatija), 13
Afghanistan, 71, 244
Africa, 13, 14, 27
Aiud (Nagyenyed), 228
Albany, 30
America, 30–32, 56, 106
Amu Darya, 45
Ankara, 126, 127
Arad, 5, 39, 61, 133, 233
Argos, 176
Árpád Bridge, 208
Arrowe Park, 147
Asia, 34, 45
Aswan, 24
Athens, 9, 167, 176
Auschwitz, 201
Austria, 42, 75, 84, 85, 91, 93, 103, 175, 259

Bačka (Bacska), 252
Baden, 148
Baghdad, 125–29
Baia Mare (Nagybánya), 175
Balatonboglár, 211
Balkans, 5, 8, 33–35, 42, 43, 121, 222, 225
Ballhausplatz, 74
Baltic Sea, 163
Banat, 73, 108
Baranya County, 104, 252
Bástya Promenade, 248
Békés County, 5
Belgium, 223, 251
Belgrade, 40, 53, 62, 63, 202, 244, 245
Berchtesgaden, 226
Beregovo, 194
Berlin, 47, 48, 87, 118, 155, 162, 167, 175, 181, 184, 190, 192, 194, 202, 208, 209, 211, 221–27, 230, 237, 244, 245
Berne, 58, 59
Bessarabia, 225, 226

Bihar (Bihor) County, 5
Birkenhead, 147
Birmingham, 30
Bohemia, 39
Bois de Boulogne, 70
Bosnia, 39
Brașov (Brassó), 228, 233
Bratislava (Pozsony), 84, 184, 20
British Empire, 168
Brittany, 176
Bruck, 86, 87, 105
Brussels, 126, 130
Bucharest, 87, 126, 225, 226, 245
Budaörs, 110
Budapest, 10, 11, 14, 20, 23, 25, 27, 30, 34, 35, 37–39, 44, 53, 54, 56, 57, 59, 60, 63, 65, 66, 70, 73, 74, 77, 81–86, 91, 92, 95, 98, 102, 103, 105, 106, 110, 117–21, 129, 131, 132, 146, 147, 149, 158, 172, 173, 182–84, 191–93, 200, 202, 203, 211, 216, 217, 220, 222, 225, 228–30, 235, 238, 243–46, 251
Buffalo, 30

Cairo, 24
Carpathian Basin, 71, 106, 109, 115, 116, 127, 168, 196
Carpathians, 85, 193, 194, 228
Castle Hill, 249
Chicago, 30, 48
China, 34
Chiorana (Kővárvidék), 6, 10, 19, 20, 174
Cluj (Kolozsvár), 6, 14, 24, 48, 53, 112, 113, 233, 234
Constantinople, 39, 43
Copenhagen, 145
Crimean Tatar Republic, 43
Croatia, 39, 76, 252
Csákvár, 10
Csík County, 5
Czechoslovakia, 84, 87, 89, 95, 182–84, 186, 194

Dachau, 221

Pál Teleki

Damascus, 126
Danube River, 63, 73, 98, 208, 222
Deák Square, 10
Deda-Szeretfalva (Deda-Sărăţel), 235
Delphi, 176
Denmark, 223
Denver, 30
Dés (Dej), 6, 235
Detroit, 30
Dísz Square, 192, 245
Doboj, 39
Dohány Street, 191
Dresden, 47
Drina River, 40
Duluth, 30

East Prussia, 210
Edinburgh, 56
Egypt, 24
English Channel, 223
Europe, 24, 55, 78, 84, 98, 99, 101, 118, 120, 127, 134, 143, 144, 158, 160, 163, 176, 183, 212, 216, 219, 223, 226, 243, 244, 254, 260, 261

Fehér (Alba) County, 5
Fehérszék, 50
Ferencváros, 146
Finland, 106, 124, 216
Fiume (Rijeka), 13
Flanders Gap, 223
Florence, 167

Geneva, 24, 25, 131, 193
Gerasdorf, 175
Gödöllő, 1, 149, 150, 176, 181, 191
Grand Canyon, 30
Great Britain, 58, 103, 124, 125, 127, 131, 143, 182, 191, 210, 231, 244, 245, 251
Great Plain, 30, 35, 92, 168, 181, 193
Greece, 8, 176, 223
Gyergyó County, 5
Gyömrő, 174
Győr, 190

Hamburg, 175
Harmincad Street, 8
Herend, 149

High Tatra, 195
Hohenheim, 7
Holland, 151, 223, 251
Holy Roman Empire, 6
Holy See, 220, 247
Hungary, 1, 5, 6, 14, 18, 20, 25, 28, 29, 32, 34 35, 37, 39, 42, 43, 49, 52–56, 59–64, 67, 71–76, 78, 83–94, 98, 101, 103–119, 131, 132, 134, 137, 139, 140, 142, 144, 146, 148, 149, 151–54, 158, 163, 164, 166, 168, 179, 181–84, 186, 187, 190–96, 201–3, 209–12, 216–32, 235, 237, 243–45, 251, 254, 255, 257, 259, 261
Huszt (Chust), 194

Iglo, (Spišská Nová Ves), 195
Ipolyság (Sahy), 184
Iraq, 124–30, 244
Istanbul, 43
Italy, 41, 53, 63, 182, 192, 193, 209, 220, 221

Japan, 21, 24, 25, 34
József Nádor Square, 8, 9, 171, 178

Kandersteg, 175
Kansas City, 30
Karánsebes (Caransebeş), 69
Karulya (Coruia), 23
Kászonszék County, 5
Kenderes, 176
Kerepesi Road, 252
Keszthely, 46
Kiskun County, 6
Kispest, 214
Kolozsvár (Cluj), 6, 14, 24, 48, 53, 112, 113, 233, 234
Komárom, 183, 184, 186, 231
Komárom County, 214
Košice (Kassa), 23, 72, 184, 210
Kővár (Cetatea Chioarului), 5
Kővárvidék (Chiorana), 6, 10, 19, 20, 174
Kővárvidék County, 7, 17
Krassó-Szörény County, 37

Lausanne, 125
Leipzig, 14, 25
Leitha River, 87
Lipót Boulevard, 80
London, 13, 24, 59, 74, 102–4, 128, 175, 192, 195, 203, 209, 216, 220, 222, 223, 231, 243, 244, 246, 247

Losonc (Tatra-Lučenec), 195
Lyon, 31

Madrid, 70, 167, 219
Magyaróvár, 15, 234
Máramaros (Maramureș) 5, 17, 108
Marburg (Maribor), 41
Mariánské Lázně (Marienbad), 105
Márkaszék (Marca), 232
Marosvásárhely (Tîrgu Mureș), 7, 228
Marseilles, 9, 175
Massachusetts, 106
Medimurje (Muraköz), 252
Memphis (Egypt), (USA), 24, 30
Miskolc, 60
Mohács, 249
Moldavia, 235
Moscow, 54, 192, 216, 225, 231
Mosul, 124-30, 137, 175, 257
Munich, 48, 134, 163, 175, 182, 183, 210, 226
Munkács (Munkačevo), 184, 186
Mureș (Maros) River, 228
Mycenae, 176

Nagybánya (Baia Mare), 175
Nagyenyed (Aiud), 228
Nagysomkút (Șomcuta Mare), 7n6, 10, 19, 20, 22, 27, 36
Nagyvárad (Oradea), 103, 112
Nauplion, 176
Near East, 34, 35, 125, 127
New York, 30, 106, 131
Nile River, 24
Nitra (Nyitra), 184
Nógrád County, 6, 238
Normandy, 176
Northern Bukovina, 225
Northern Transylvania, 230, 231, 235, 242
Norway, 223

Opatija (Abbázia), 13
Ördögkút (Trezna), 232
Ostend, 13
Ottoman Empire, 34
Oxford, 119

Pannonhalma, 2

Paris, 9, 21, 22, 24, 25, 31, 54, 56, 58-60, 62, 69-76, 91, 100, 102, 104, 111, 119, 127, 133, 137, 158, 160, 162, 175, 216, 220
Parliament Square, 252
Paszmos (Pasmuș), 6
Pécs, 64, 115, 238
Pest, 6, 8, 76, 173
Petroșani (Petrozsény), 112, 233
Phoenix, 30
Pilis County, 6
Pinkafeld (Pinkafő), 94
Poland, 5, 72, 78, 85, 86, 89, 190, 192, 193, 203, 208-12
Portland, 30
Portugal, 164, 259
Pozsony (Bratislava), 53, 84, 184
Prague, 67, 85-87, 133
Prangins, 94
Pribékfalva (Pribileşti), 6, 10, 11, 24, 38, 39, 50, 124, 174, 175, 245

Quai d'Orsay, 70, 72, 76, 86, 104, 133
Rhineland, 13
Rijeka (Fiume), 13
Rockies, 30
Romania, 5, 24n37, 37, 53, 64, 72, 75, 89, 108, 174, 194, 209, 217, 218, 220, 225-31, 233, 244
Rome, 30, 93, 167, 190, 192, 202, 203, 209, 220-22, 225-27
Russia, 43, 60, 64, 70
Ruthenia, 59, 60, 73, 117, 193-95, 218, 236

Sabac, 40
Šahy (Ipolyság), 184
Sajó River, 60
Salt Lake City, 30
San Francisco, 30
Santa Fe, 30
Sarajevo, 38, 39
Sárospatak, 1
Sátoraljaújhely, 60, 184
Seattle, 30
Segesvár (Sighișoara), 228
Šemša (Semse9, 72
Serbia, 37-40, 108, 246, 252
Sic (Szék), 5
Sofia, 167
Solt County, 6

287

Pál Teleki

Southern Transylvania, 46, 230, 233
Soviet Union, 80, 192, 216, 225, 229, 244
St. Gilgen, 175
Subcarpathia, 86, 117, 187, 193–95, 207, 208, 211, 218, 219, 221, 236
Switzerland, 31, 58, 59, 93, 94, 98, 175, 256
Szamos, (Someş) River, 10
Szászföld, 108
Szatmár, 37, 245
Szatmár County, 19, 20, 23
Szczecin (Stettin), 163
Szeged, 61–68, 82, 83, 92, 107, 110–12, 131, 180, 187, 205, 234, 237
Szék (Sic), 5, 9
Székely Counties (Székelyföld), 72, 228, 234
Szent István Boulevard, 80
Szilágyipp, 232
Szombathely, 94, 95
Sèvres, 125

Tacoma, 30
Tata, 181
Tatra Mountains, 103, 195
Telek (Teleac), 5
Temes County, 37
Temesvár (Timişoara), 112
The Hague, 24, 130
Thessaloniki, 176
Tisza River, 60, 64, 69, 73, 74, 193, 209
Tirgu Mureş (Marosvásárhely), 7, 228
Tirnava Mare (Nagy-Küküllő), 228
Tokaj, 182, 205
Torda (Turda) County, 5, 233
Transdanubia, 63, 64, 66, 166
Transylvania, 5, 6, 45, 46, 54, 55, 59, 73, 114, 116, 153, 174, 179, 219, 223, 225–37, 242

Trezna (Ördögkút), 232
Trianon, 76, 80, 88, 101, 106, 111, 115, 144, 147, 155, 174, 226, 228, 237, 258–60
Tübingen, 31
Turkey, 42, 125–27, 130
Turnu Severin, 228, 229, 232

Užgorod (Ungvár), 236
Üllői Road, 146
United States of America, 30–32, 47–49, 110, 175, 232, 244

Váradolaszi (Oradea), 6
Velejte (Veľaty), 210
Venice, 13
Versailles, 76, 224
Vienna, 9, 21, 56, 59–61, 64, 85, 91, 94, 106, 110, 171, 179, 186, 193, 218, 219, 230, 231, 233, 236, 237, 243
Vogelenzang, 151

Warsaw, 86, 202, 210, 228
Washington, D.C., 30, 35, 106, 219, 220, 224
Western Europe, 33, 105, 108, 211, 217
Williamstown, 106
Wolfgangsee, 175
Württemberg, 7

Yellowstone National Park, 30
Yugoslavia, 57, 75, 95, 114, 202, 217, 244–46, 252

Zágorhíd (Zagăr), 5
Zagreb, 252
Zaránd (Zarand) County, 5
Zernyest (Zamesti), 6
Zurich, 14, 90

www.ingramcontent.com/pod-product-compliance
Lightning Source LLC
Chambersburg PA
CBHW042048280426
43673CB00090B/497/J